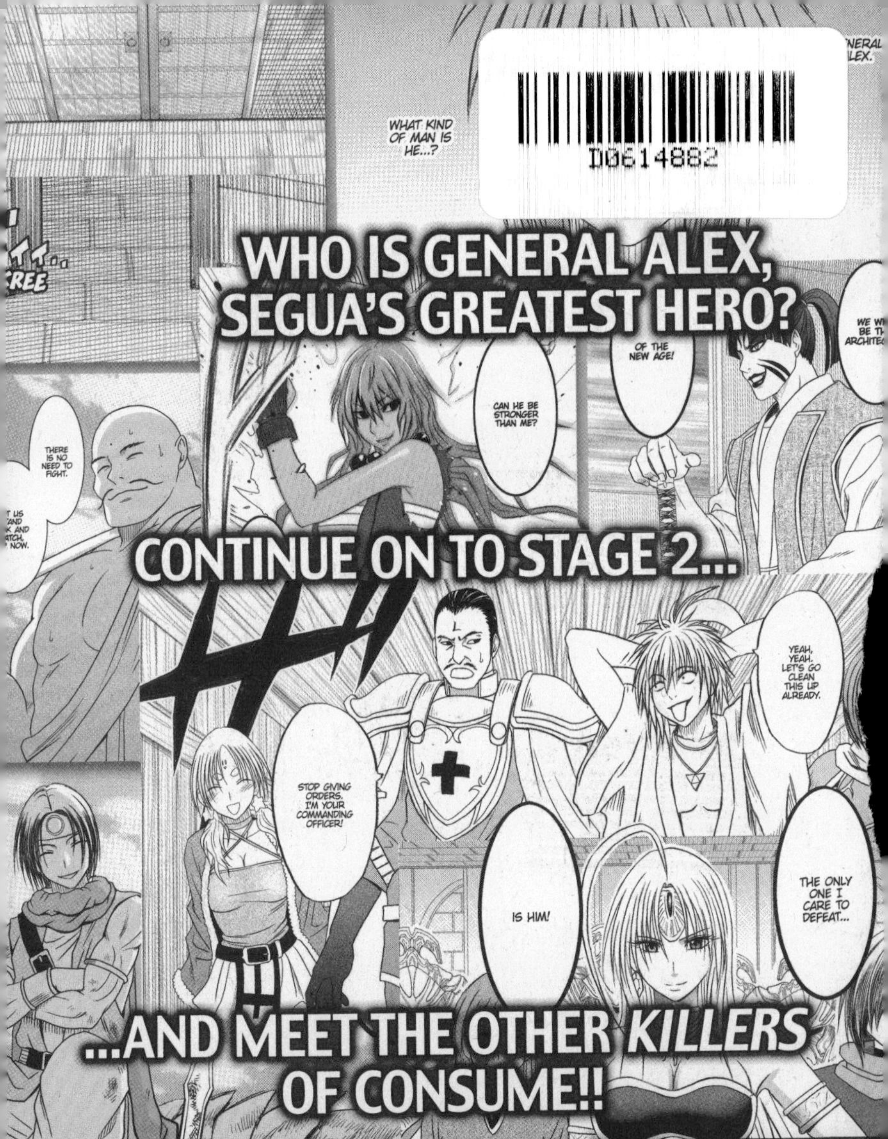
WHAT KIND OF MAN IS HE...?
OF THE NEW AGE!
CAN HE BE STRONGER THAN ME?
THERE IS NO NEED TO FIGHT.
YEAH, YEAH. LET'S GO CLEAN THIS UP ALREADY.
STOP GIVING ORDERS. I'M YOUR COMMANDING OFFICER!
THE ONLY ONE I CARE TO DEFEAT...
IS HIM!

WHO IS GENERAL ALEX, SEGUA'S GREATEST HERO?

CONTINUE ON TO STAGE 2...

...AND MEET THE OTHER *KILLERS* OF CONSUME!!

WORLD WAR BLUE VOL. 2

COMING SOON!

WORLD WAR BLUE

VOLUME 1

art by Crimson
ry by Anastasia Shestakova

STAFF CREDITS

translation **Adrienne Beck**
adaptation **Patrick King**
lettering **Laura Scoville**
logo design **Courtney Williams**
cover design **Nicky Lim**
proofreader **Janet Houck, Shanti Whitesides**
editor **Adam Arnold**

publisher **Jason DeAngelis**
Seven Seas Entertainment

AOI SEKAI NO CHUSINDE KANZENBAN VOL. 1
© 2010 ANASTASIA SHESTAKOVA / © 2010 CRIMSON
This edition originally published in Japan in 2010 by
MICROMAGAZINE PUBLISHING CO., Tokyo. English translation
rights arranged with MICROMAGAZINE PUBLISHING CO., Tokyo
through TOHAN CORPORATION, Tokyo.

ISBN: 978-1-937867-96-6
Printed in Canada
First Printing: July 2013
10 9 8 7 6 5 4 3 2 1

FOLLOW US ONLINE: *www.gomanga.com*

READING DIRECTIONS

This book reads from *right to left*, Japanese style.
If this is your first time reading manga, you start
reading from the top right panel on each page and
take it from there. If you get lost, just follow the
numbered diagram here. It may seem backwards
at first, but you'll get the hang of it! Have fun!!

REPUBLIC OF ELIEL

A country rich in
metals. Their tomes
of alchemy are
considered to be the
greatest authority on
the subject. Exports
a wide variety of
gourmet nuts.

KINGDOM OF SLOVIA

Like Eliel, a kingdom
rich in metals. Slovia
produces the most
advanced technology
on the continent.

TATRAND

Ruled by I. Vazar, the
legendary conqueror
who once ruled the
entire continent.

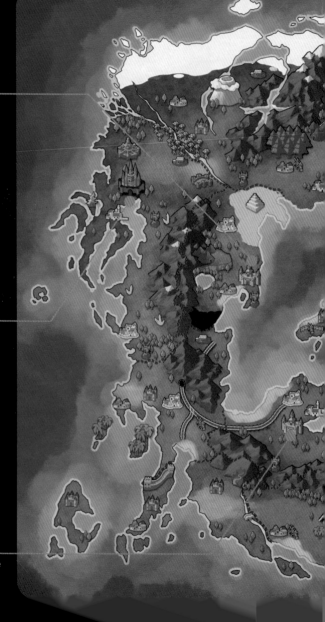

art by **Crimson**

story by **Anastasia Shestakova**

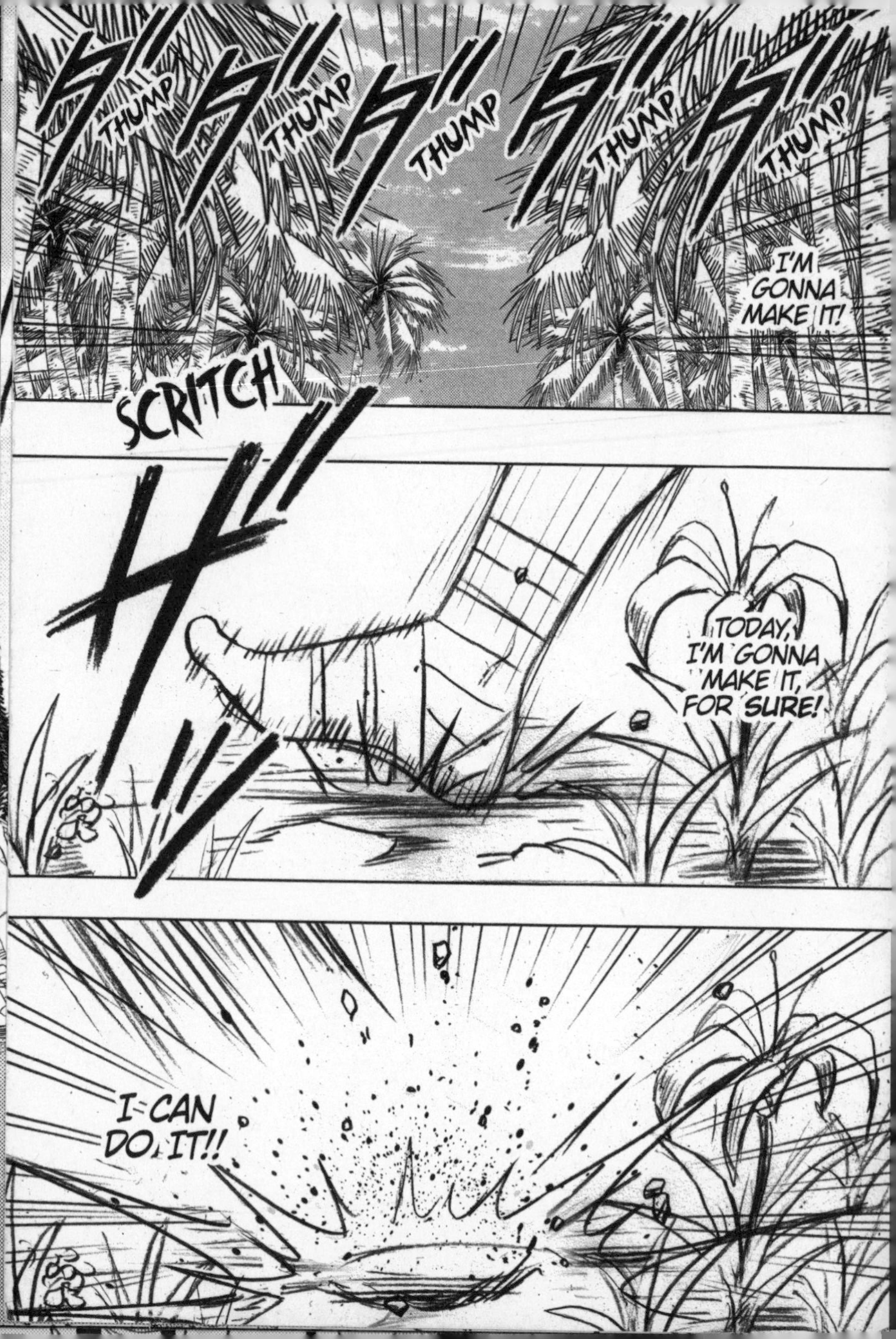
THUMP
THUMP
THUMP
THUMP
THUMP
I'M GONNA MAKE IT!
SCRITCH
TODAY, I'M GONNA MAKE IT, FOR SURE!
I CAN DO IT!!

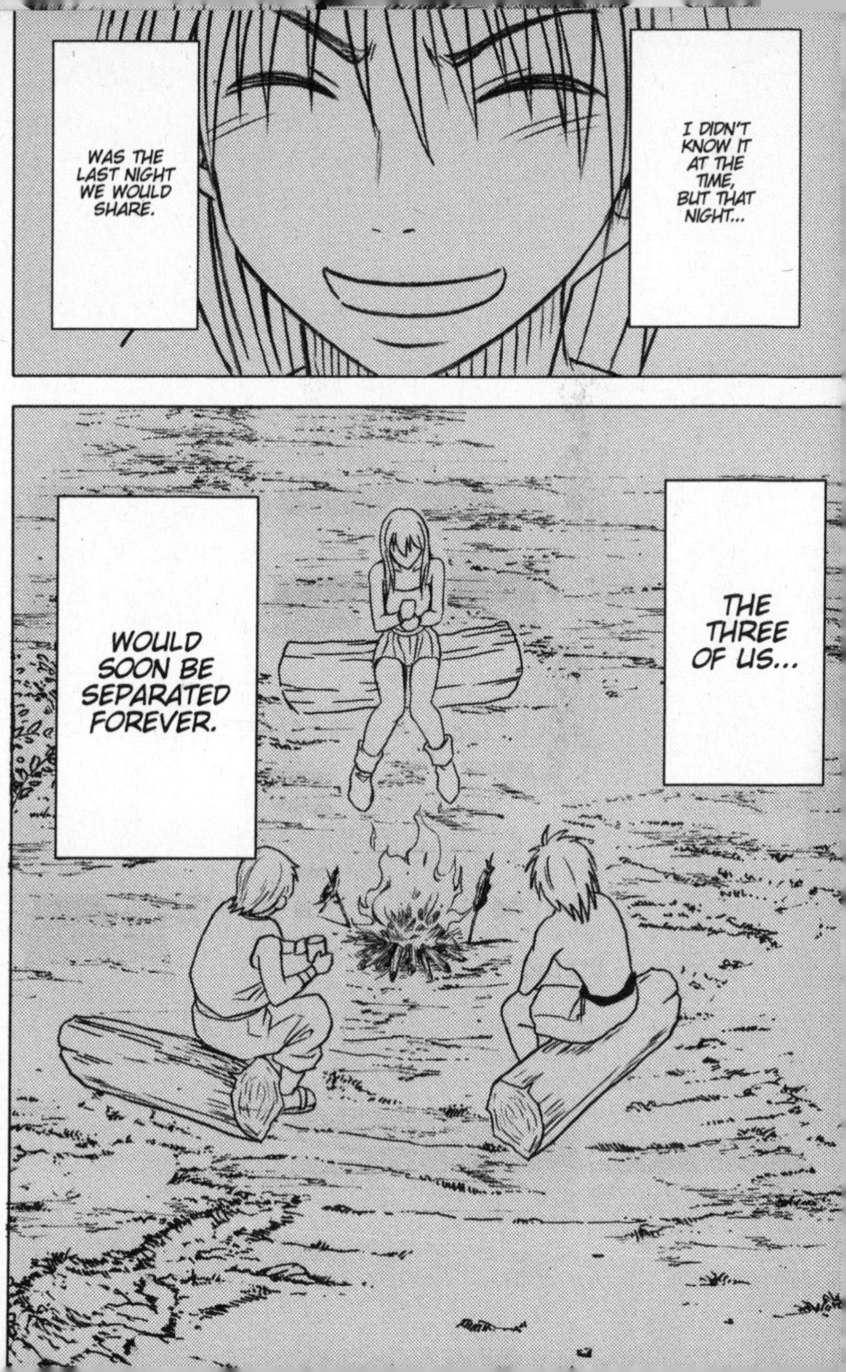
I DIDN'T KNOW IT AT THE TIME, BUT THAT NIGHT...
WAS THE LAST NIGHT WE WOULD SHARE.
THE THREE OF US...
WOULD SOON BE SEPARATED FOREVER.

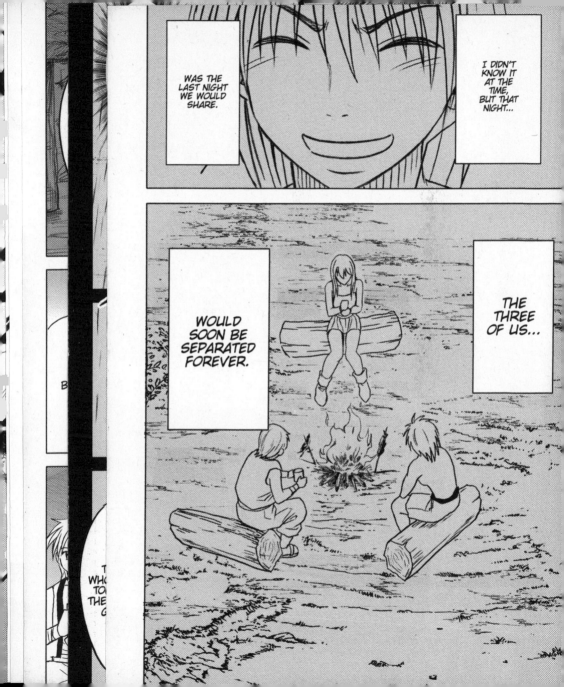

CHAPTER 1

THE SUPERSONIC RODENT

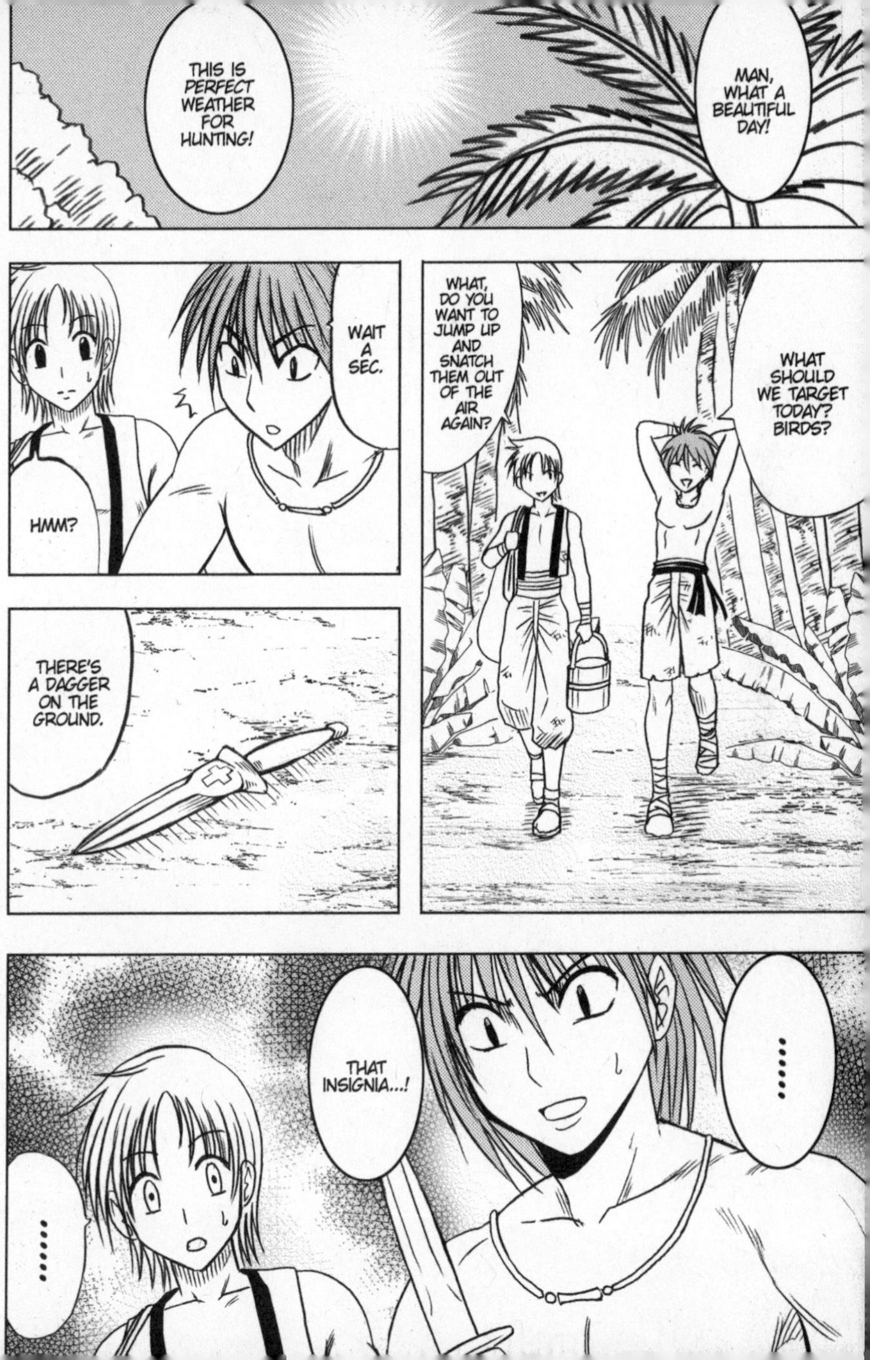
MAN, WHAT A BEAUTIFUL DAY!
THIS IS PERFECT WEATHER FOR HUNTING!
WHAT SHOULD WE TARGET TODAY? BIRDS?
WHAT, DO YOU WANT TO JUMP UP AND SNATCH THEM OUT OF THE AIR AGAIN?
WAIT A SEC.
HMM?
THERE'S A DAGGER ON THE GROUND.
......
THAT INSIGNIA...!
......

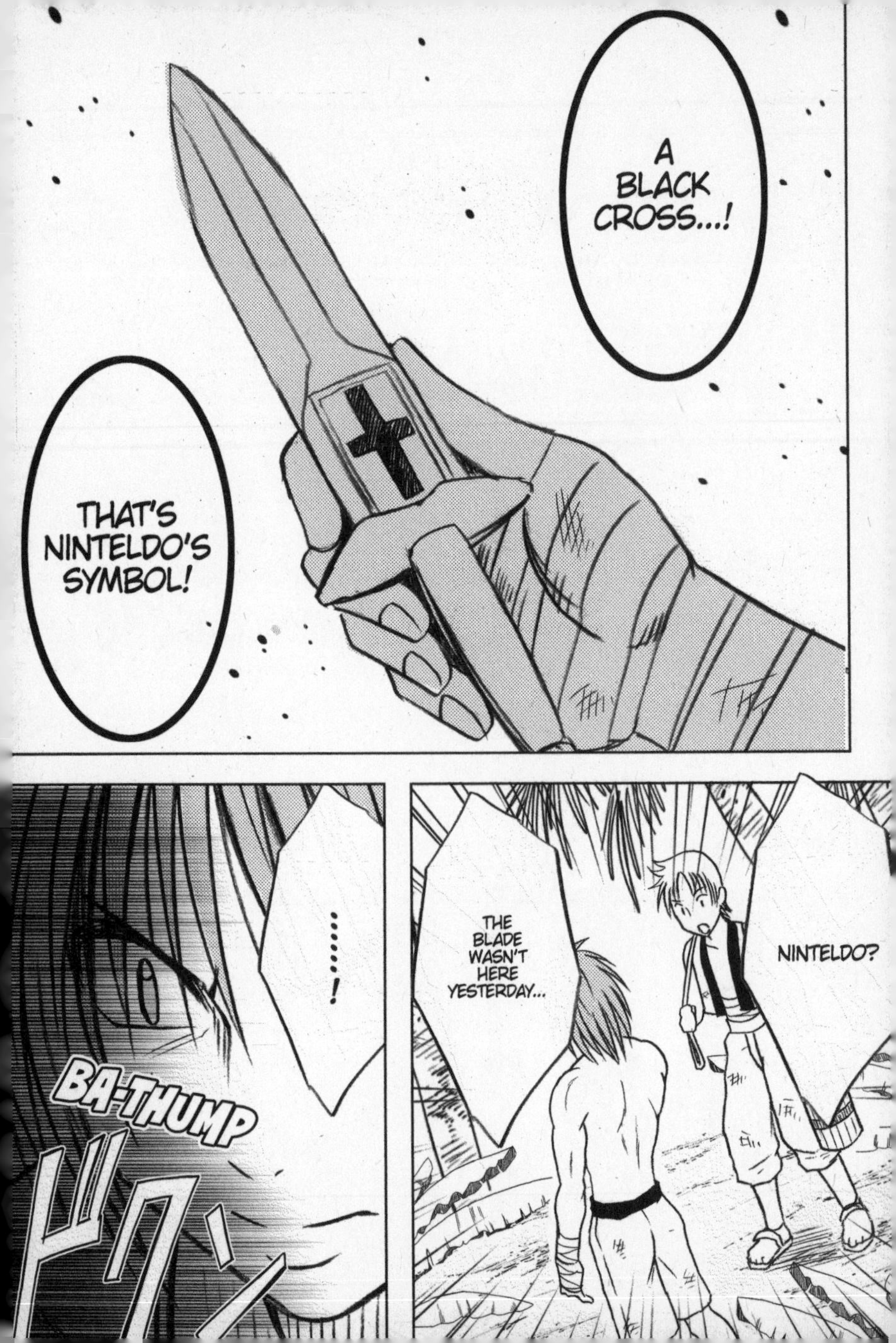
A BLACK CROSS...!
THAT'S NINTELDO'S SYMBOL!
NINTELDO?
THE BLADE WASN'T HERE YESTERDAY...
......!
BA-THUMP
ドクン

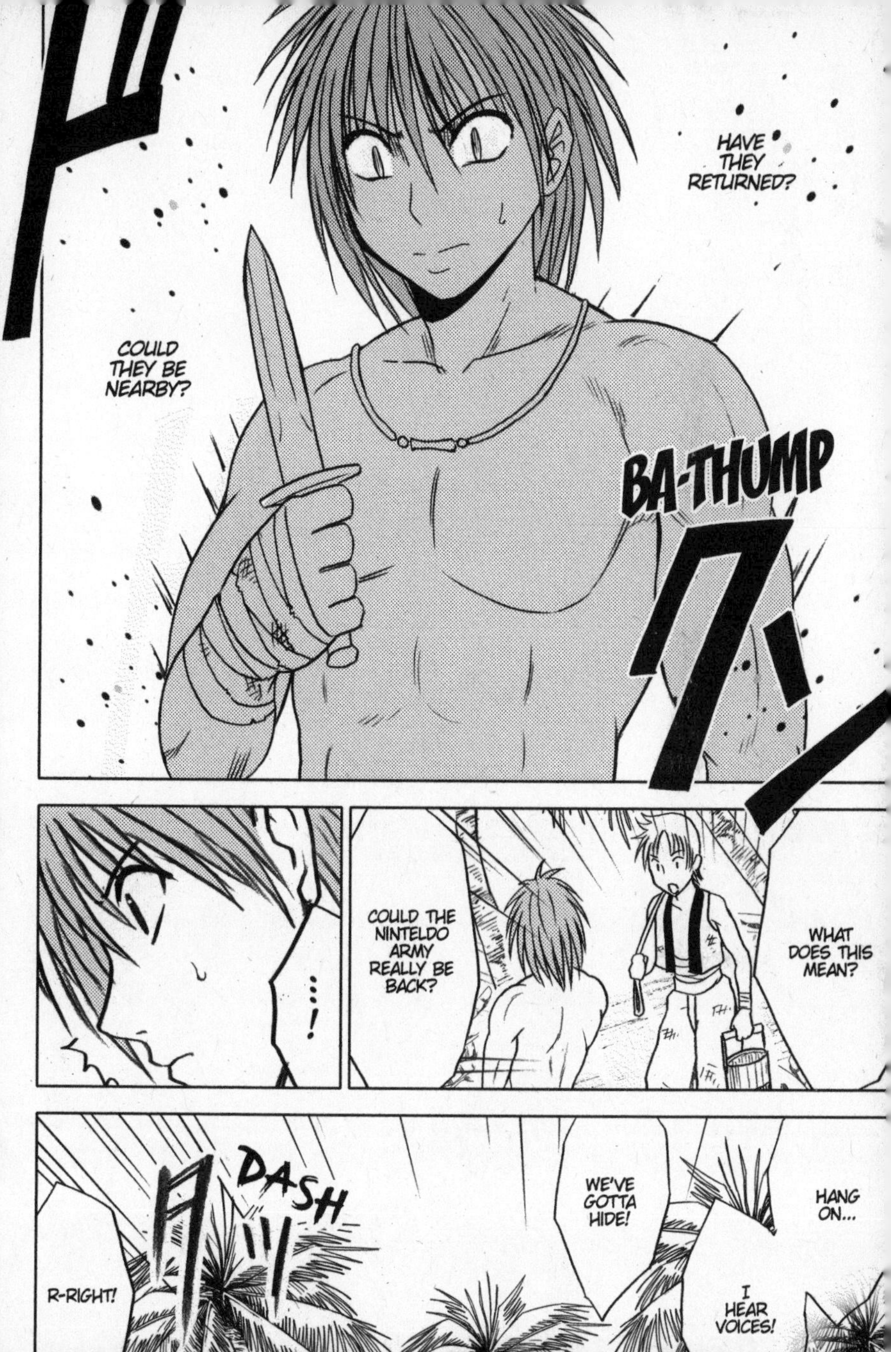
HAVE THEY RETURNED?
COULD THEY BE NEARBY?
BA-THUMP
WHAT DOES THIS MEAN?
COULD THE NINTELDO ARMY REALLY BE BACK?
...!
HANG ON...
I HEAR VOICES!
WE'VE GOTTA HIDE!
DASH
R-RIGHT!

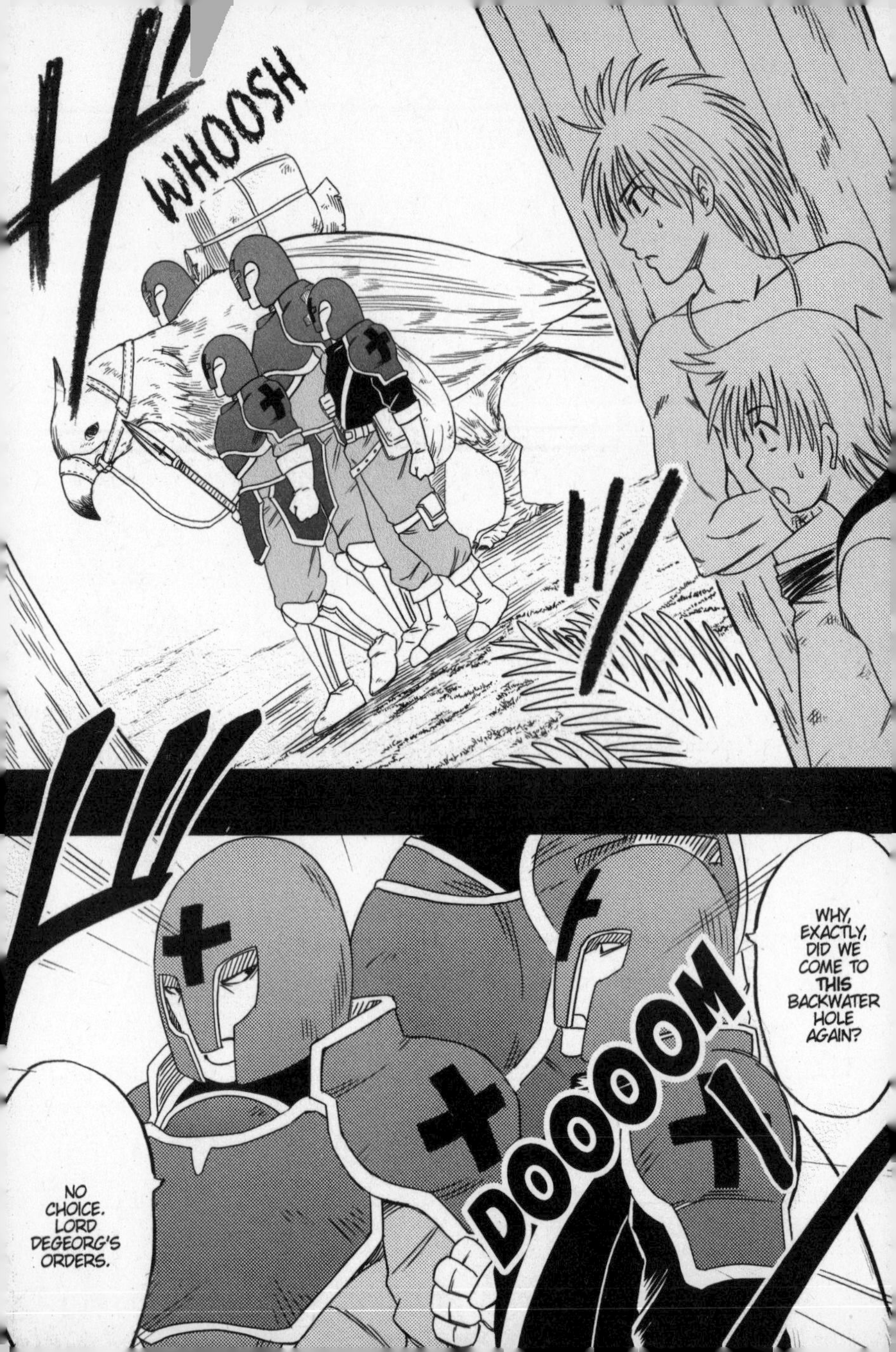
WHOOSH
WHY, EXACTLY, DID WE COME TO THIS BACKWATER HOLE AGAIN?
DOOOOOM
NO CHOICE. LORD DEGEORG'S ORDERS.

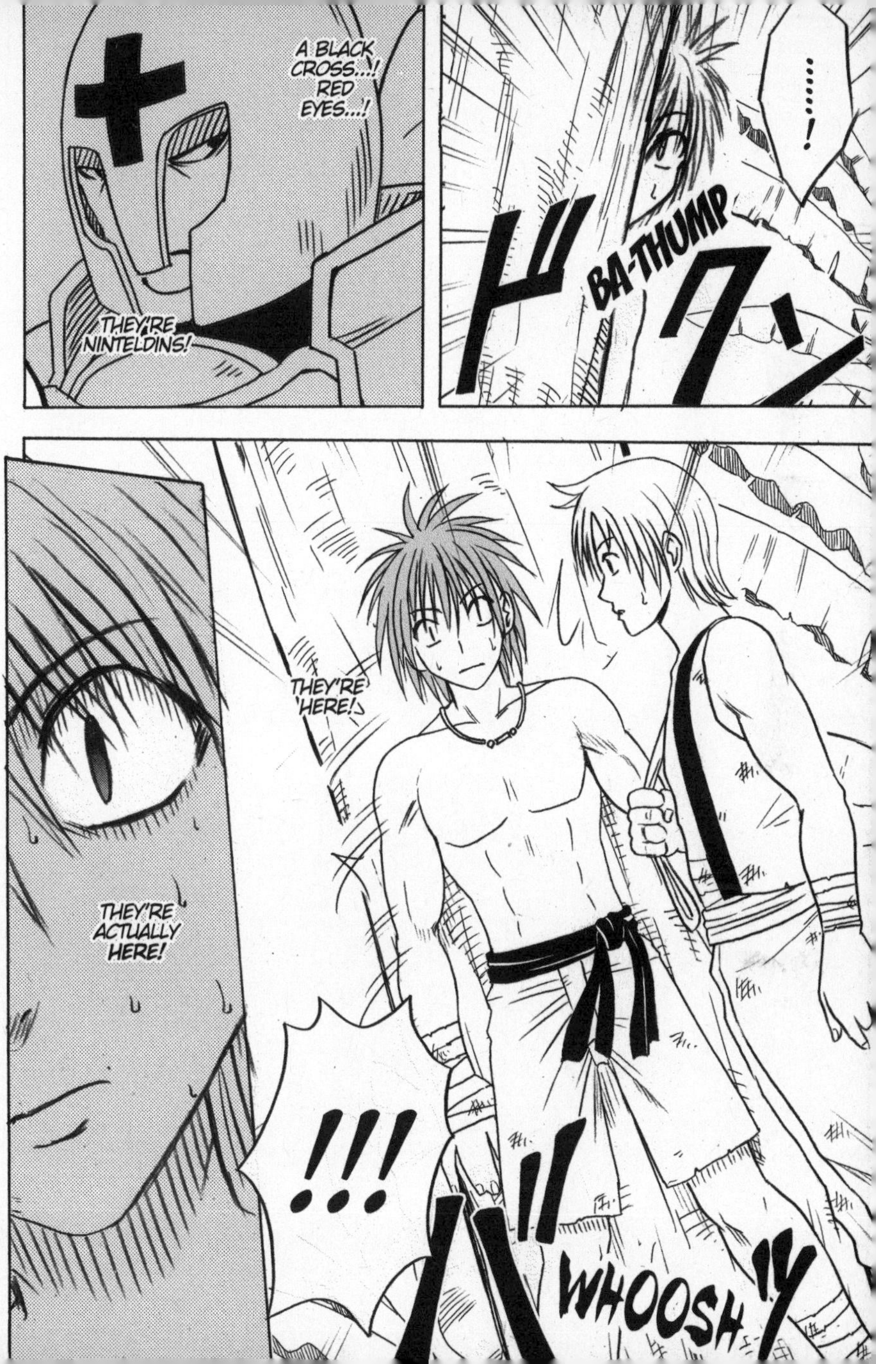
....!
BA-THUMP
A BLACK CROSS...! RED EYES...!
THEY'RE NINTELDINS!
THEY'RE HERE!
THEY'RE ACTUALLY HERE!
!!!
WHOOSH!!

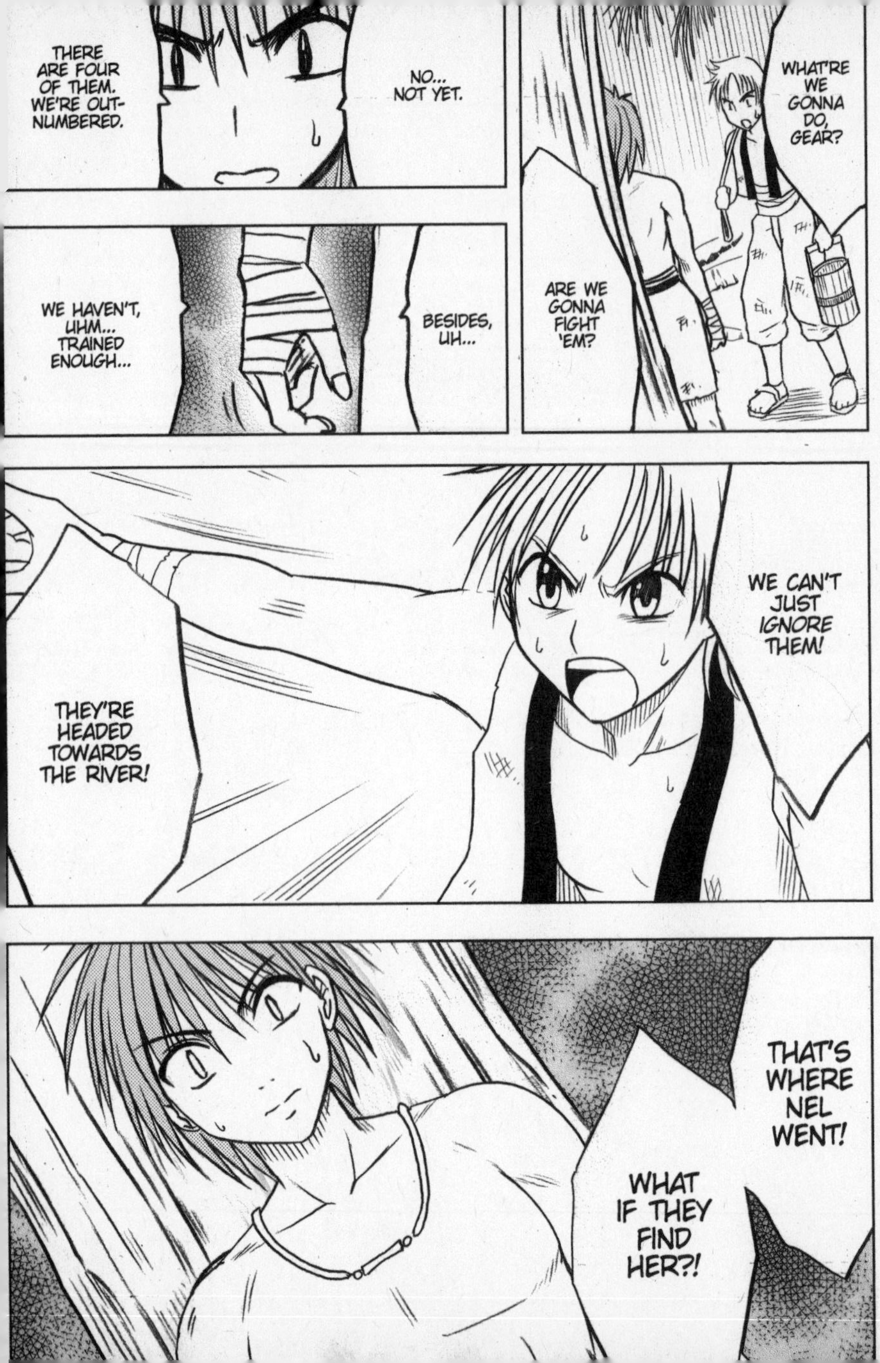
WHAT'RE WE GONNA DO, GEAR?
ARE WE GONNA FIGHT 'EM?
NO... NOT YET.
THERE ARE FOUR OF THEM. WE'RE OUT-NUMBERED.
BESIDES, UH...
WE HAVEN'T, UHM... TRAINED ENOUGH...
WE CAN'T JUST IGNORE THEM!
THEY'RE HEADED TOWARDS THE RIVER!
THAT'S WHERE NEL WENT!
WHAT IF THEY FIND HER?!

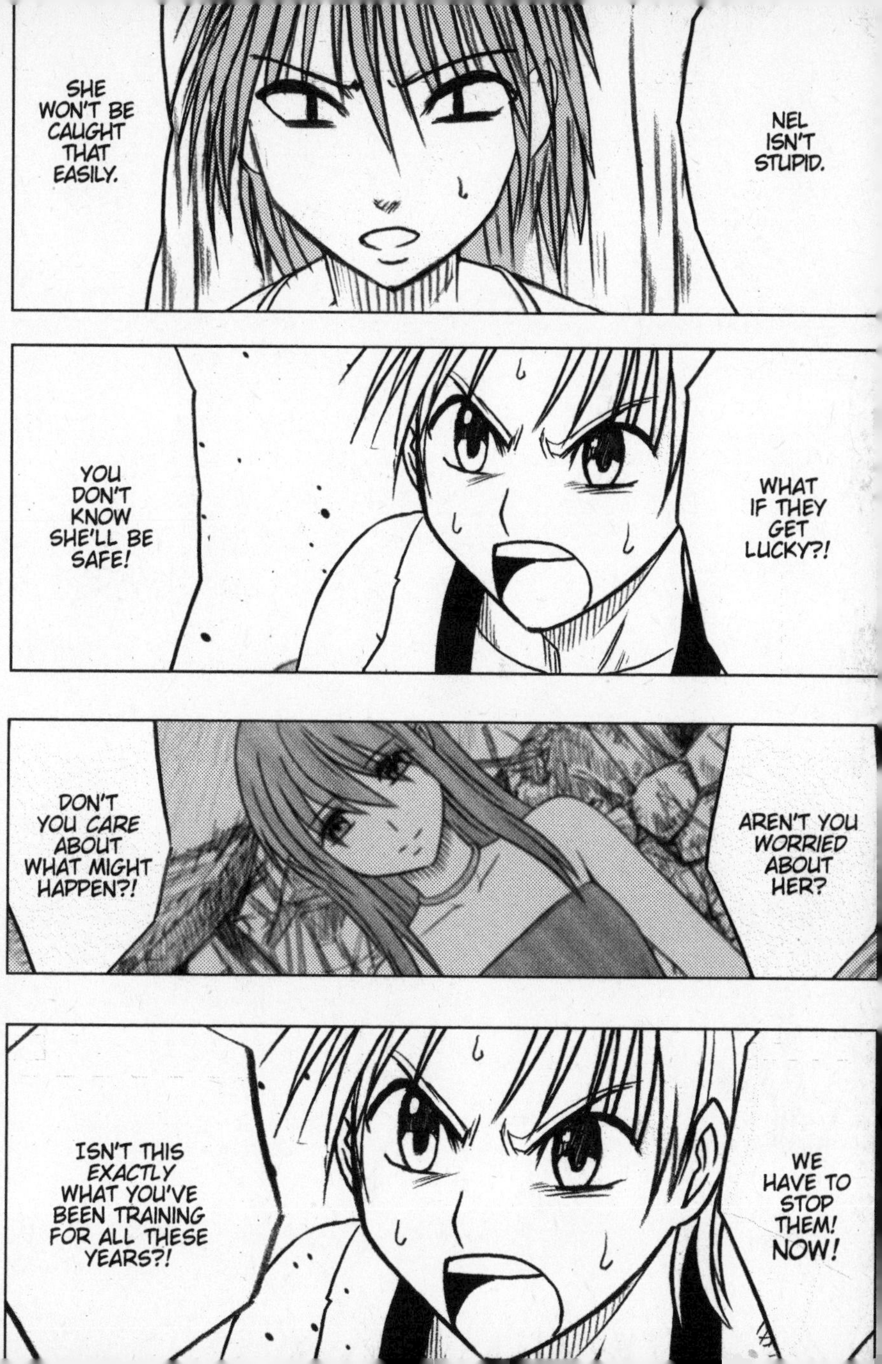
NEL ISN'T STUPID.
SHE WON'T BE CAUGHT THAT EASILY.
WHAT IF THEY GET LUCKY?!
YOU DON'T KNOW SHE'LL BE SAFE!
AREN'T YOU WORRIED ABOUT HER?
DON'T YOU CARE ABOUT WHAT MIGHT HAPPEN?!
WE HAVE TO STOP THEM! NOW!
ISN'T THIS EXACTLY WHAT YOU'VE BEEN TRAINING FOR ALL THESE YEARS?!

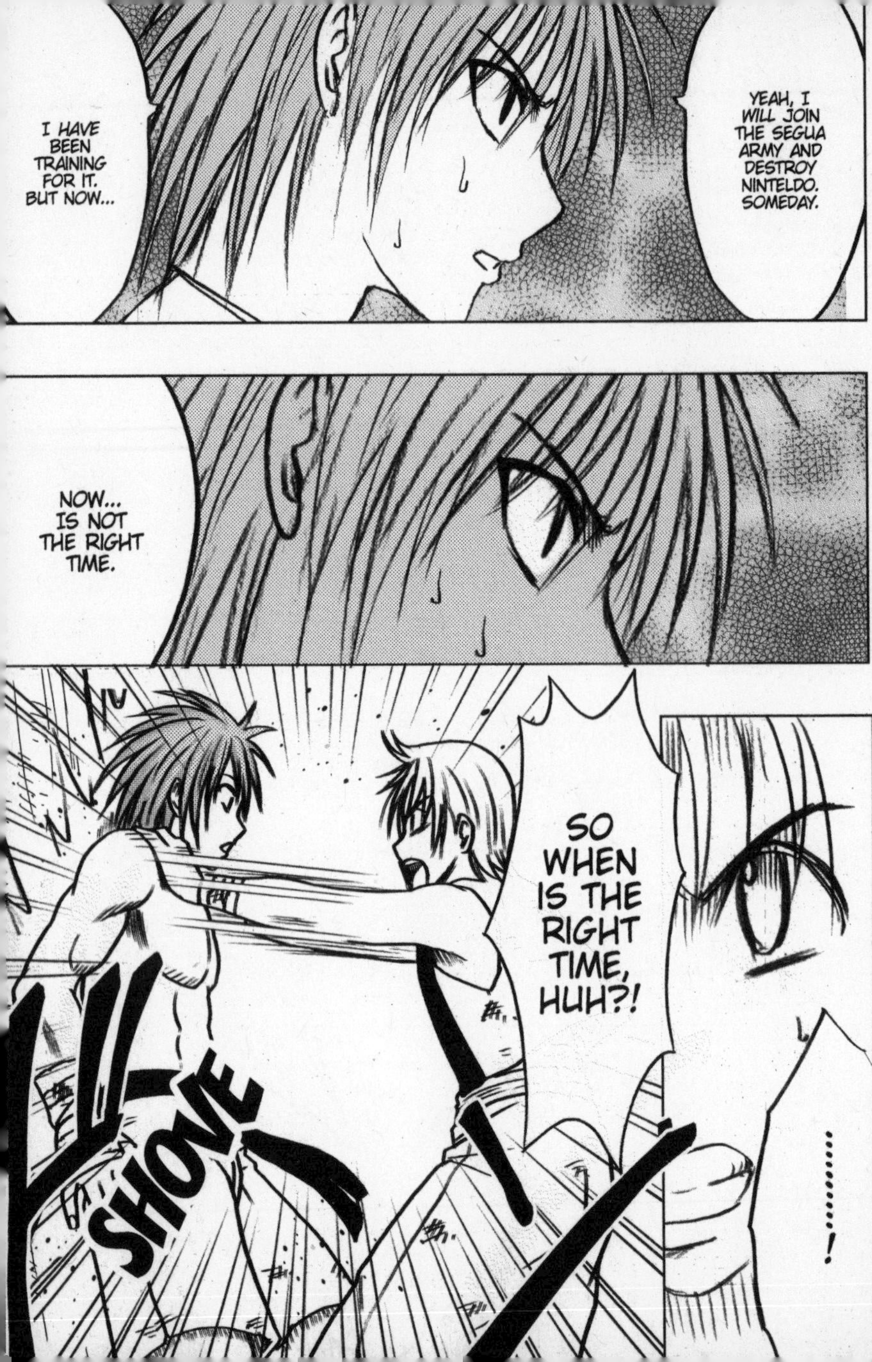
YEAH, I WILL JOIN THE SEGUA ARMY AND DESTROY NINTELDO. SOMEDAY.
I HAVE BEEN TRAINING FOR IT. BUT NOW...
NOW... IS NOT THE RIGHT TIME.
SO WHEN IS THE RIGHT TIME, HUH?!
SHOVE
......!

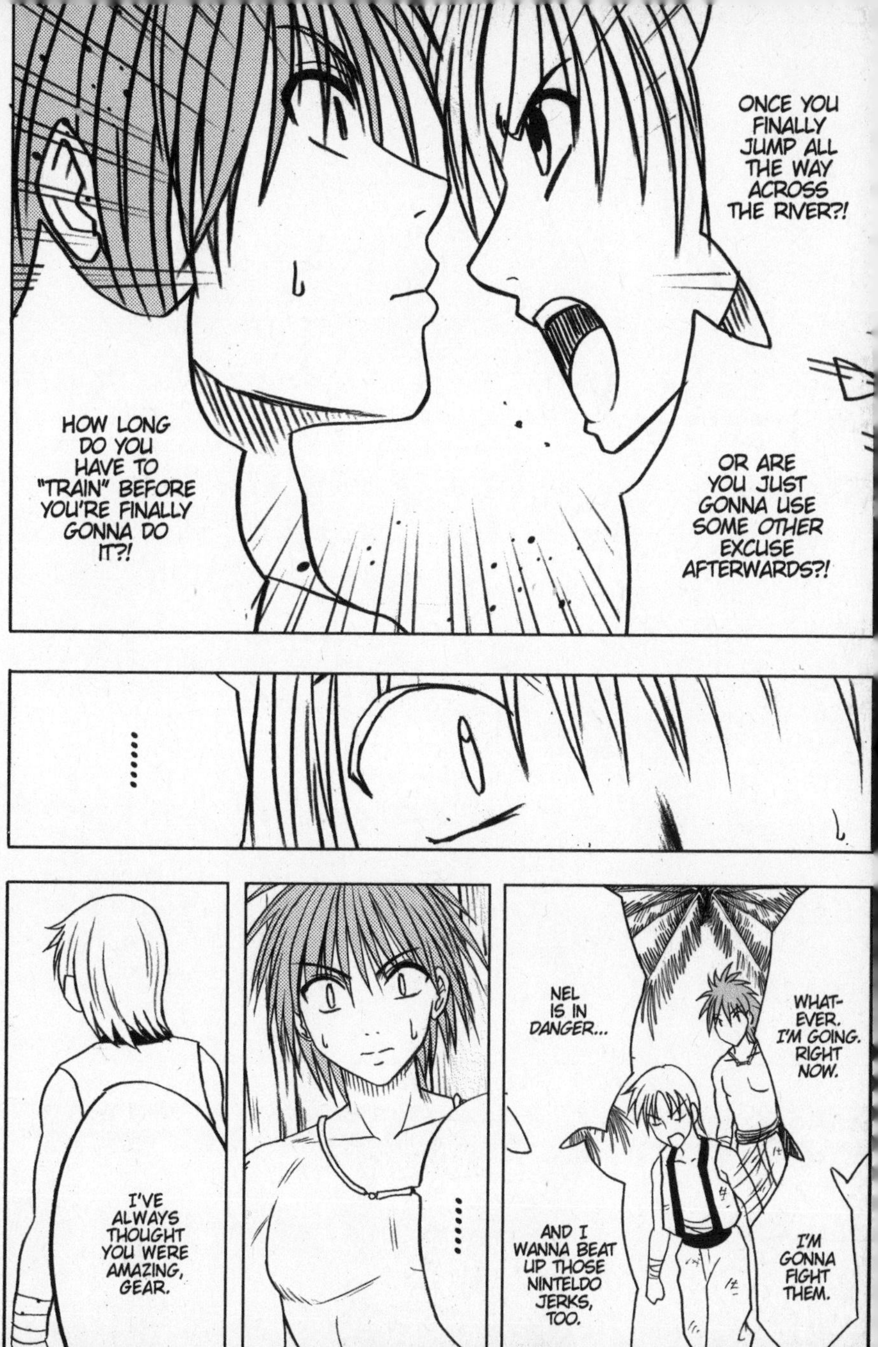
HOW LONG DO YOU HAVE TO "TRAIN" BEFORE YOU'RE FINALLY GONNA DO IT?!
ONCE YOU FINALLY JUMP ALL THE WAY ACROSS THE RIVER?!
OR ARE YOU JUST GONNA USE SOME OTHER EXCUSE AFTERWARDS?!
......
WHATEVER. I'M GOING. RIGHT NOW.
NEL IS IN DANGER...
I'M GONNA FIGHT THEM.
AND I WANNA BEAT UP THOSE NINTELDO JERKS, TOO.
......
I'VE ALWAYS THOUGHT YOU WERE AMAZING, GEAR.

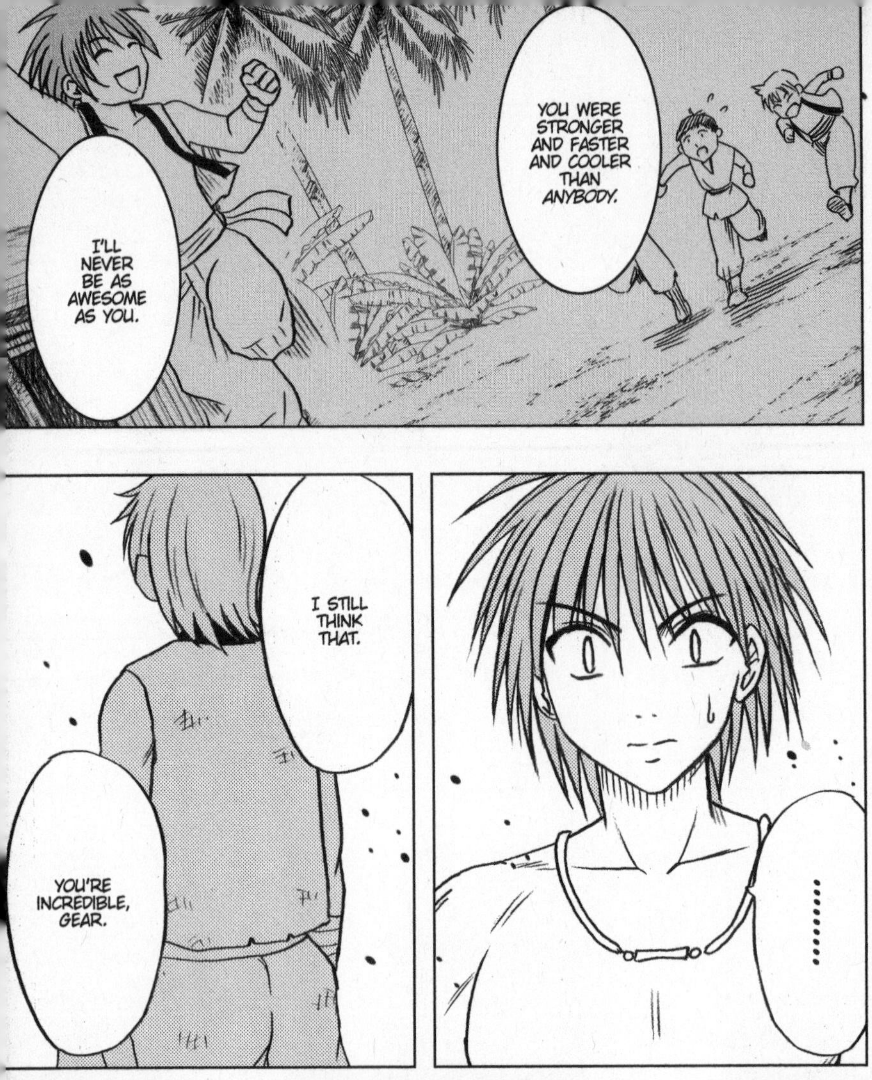
YOU WERE STRONGER AND FASTER AND COOLER THAN ANYBODY.
I'LL NEVER BE AS AWESOME AS YOU.
......
I STILL THINK THAT.
YOU'RE INCREDIBLE, GEAR.

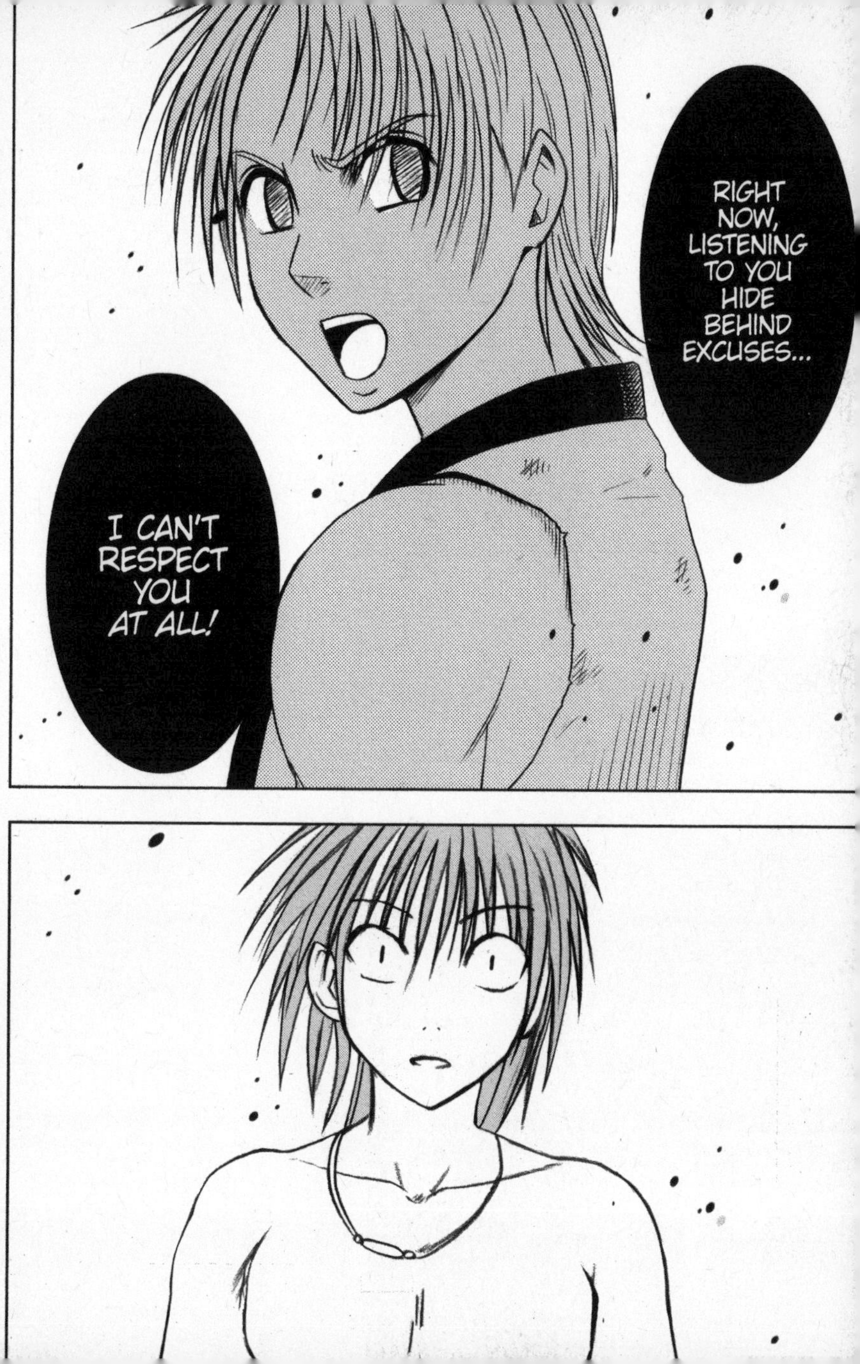
RIGHT NOW, LISTENING TO YOU HIDE BEHIND EXCUSES...
I CAN'T RESPECT YOU AT ALL!

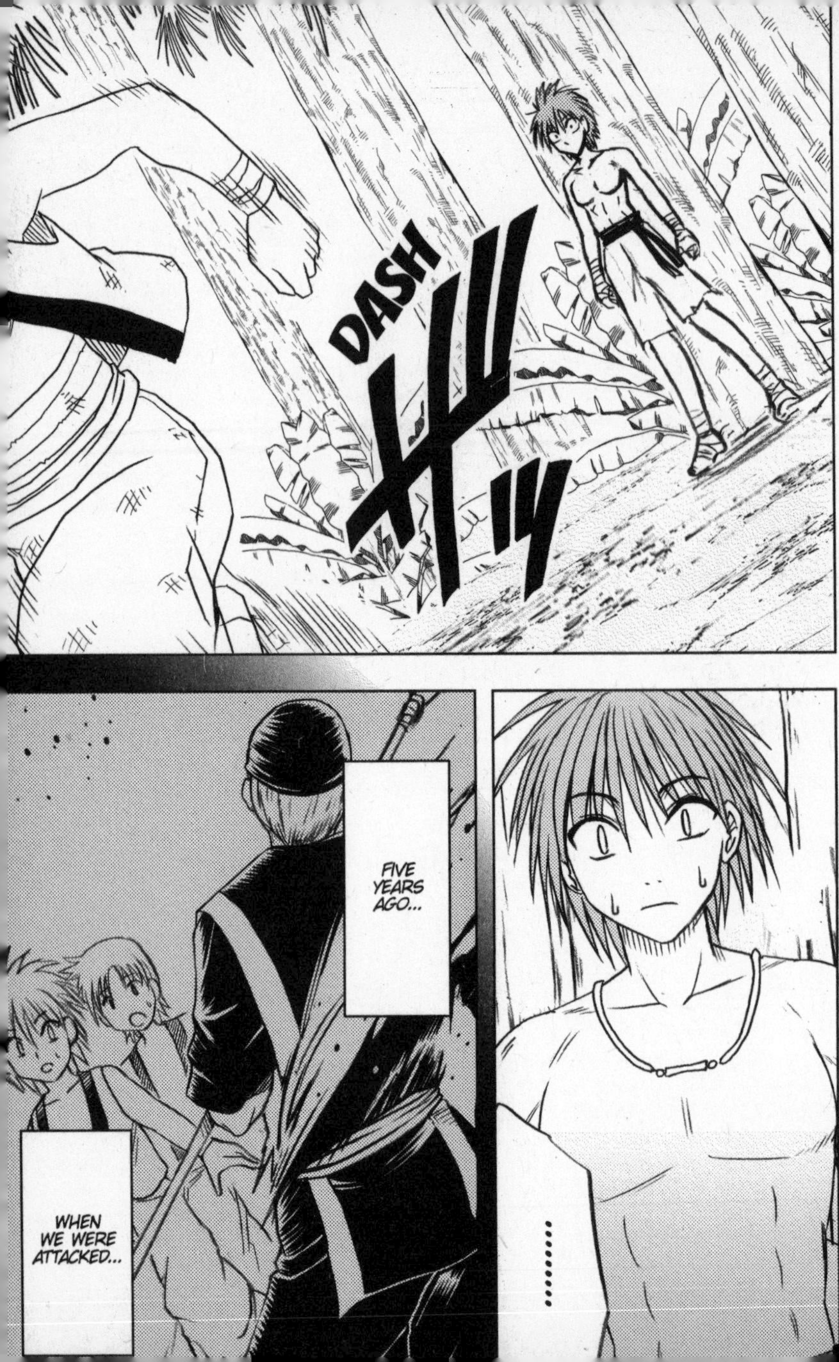
DASH
......
FIVE YEARS AGO...
WHEN WE WERE ATTACKED...

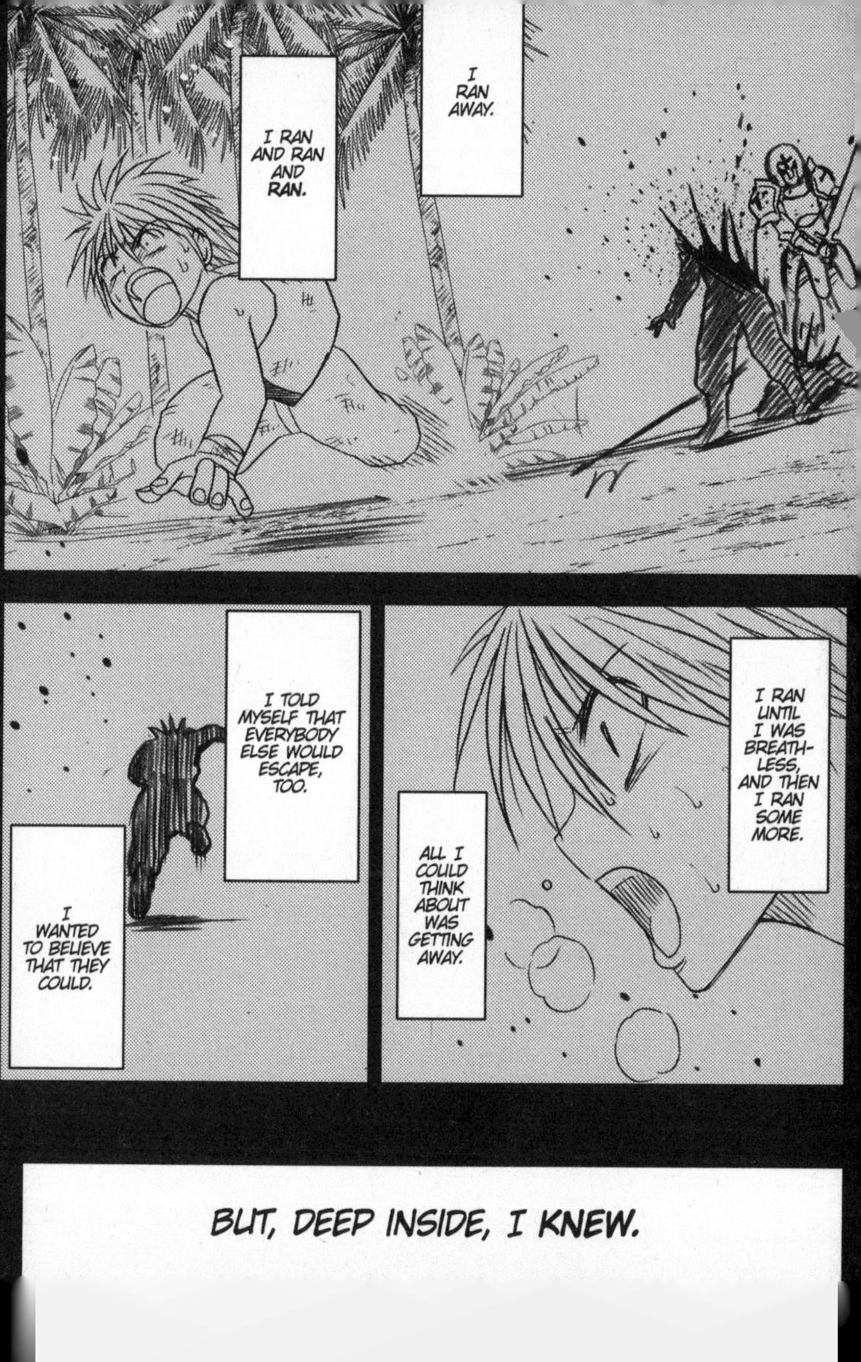
I RAN AWAY.
I RAN AND RAN AND RAN.
I RAN UNTIL I WAS BREATH-LESS, AND THEN I RAN SOME MORE.
ALL I COULD THINK ABOUT WAS GETTING AWAY.
I TOLD MYSELF THAT EVERYBODY ELSE WOULD ESCAPE, TOO.
I WANTED TO BELIEVE THAT THEY COULD.
BUT, DEEP INSIDE, I KNEW.

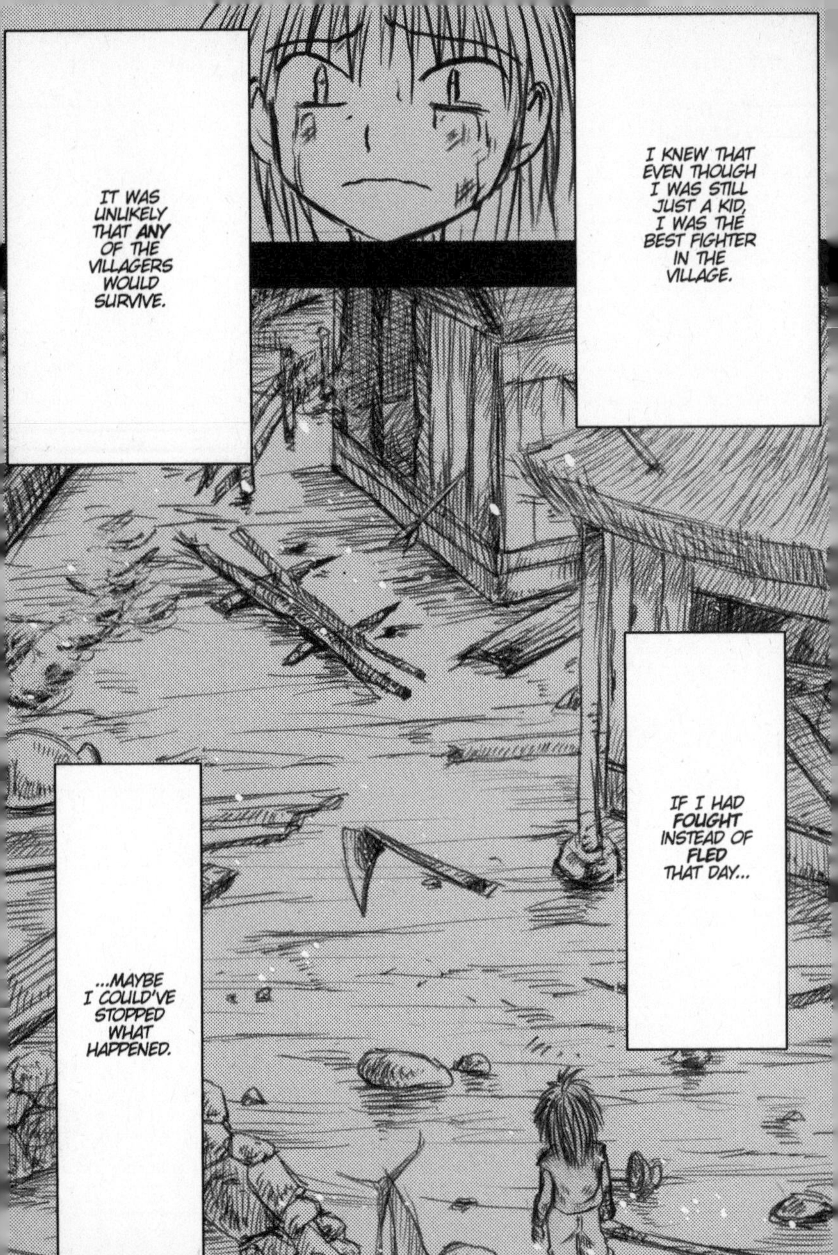
I KNEW THAT EVEN THOUGH I WAS STILL JUST A KID, I WAS THE BEST FIGHTER IN THE VILLAGE.
IT WAS UNLIKELY THAT ANY OF THE VILLAGERS WOULD SURVIVE.
IF I HAD FOUGHT INSTEAD OF FLED THAT DAY...
...MAYBE I COULD'VE STOPPED WHAT HAPPENED.

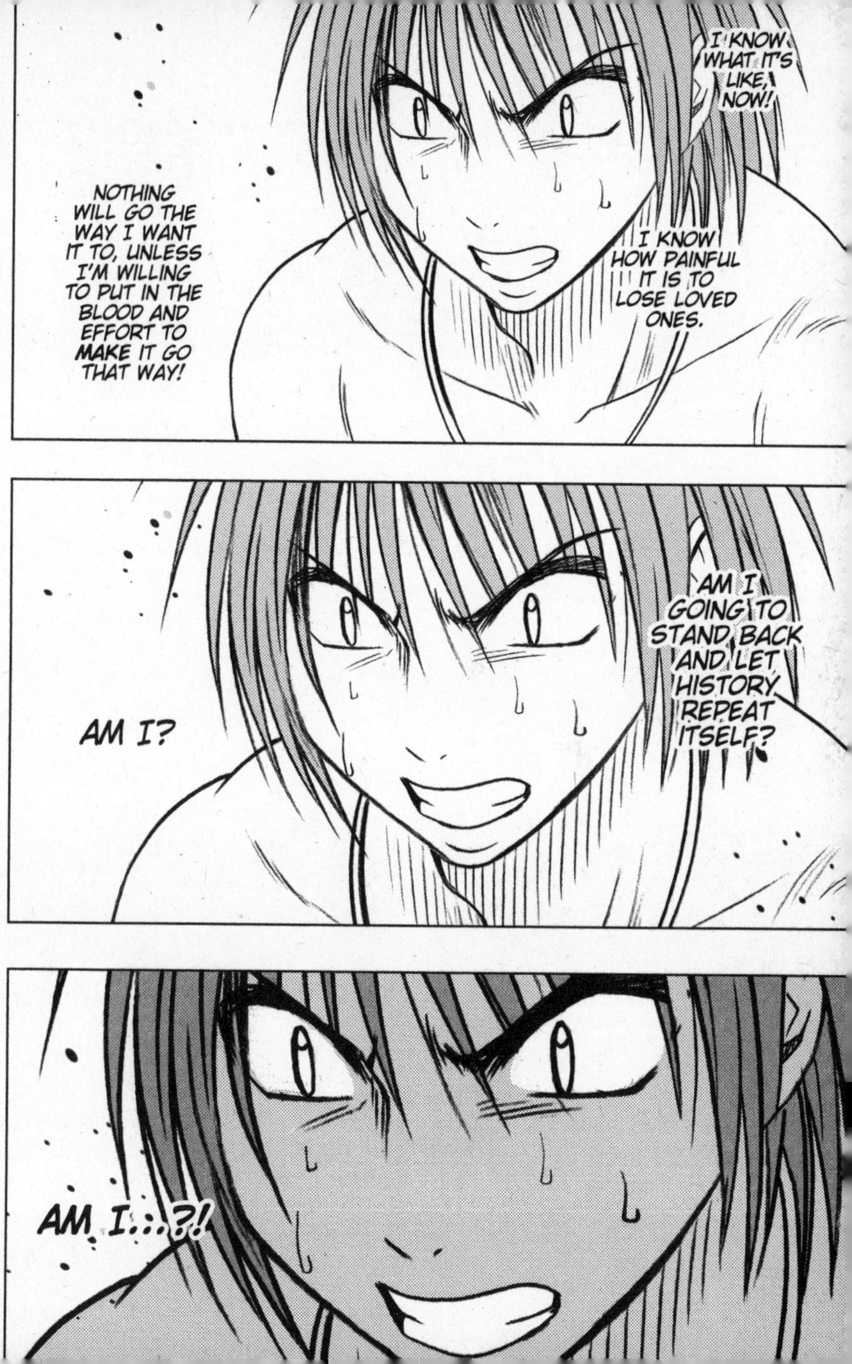
I KNOW WHAT IT'S LIKE, NOW!
I KNOW HOW PAINFUL IT IS TO LOSE LOVED ONES.
NOTHING WILL GO THE WAY I WANT IT TO, UNLESS I'M WILLING TO PUT IN THE BLOOD AND EFFORT TO MAKE IT GO THAT WAY!
AM I GOING TO STAND BACK AND LET HISTORY REPEAT ITSELF?
AM I?
AM I...?!

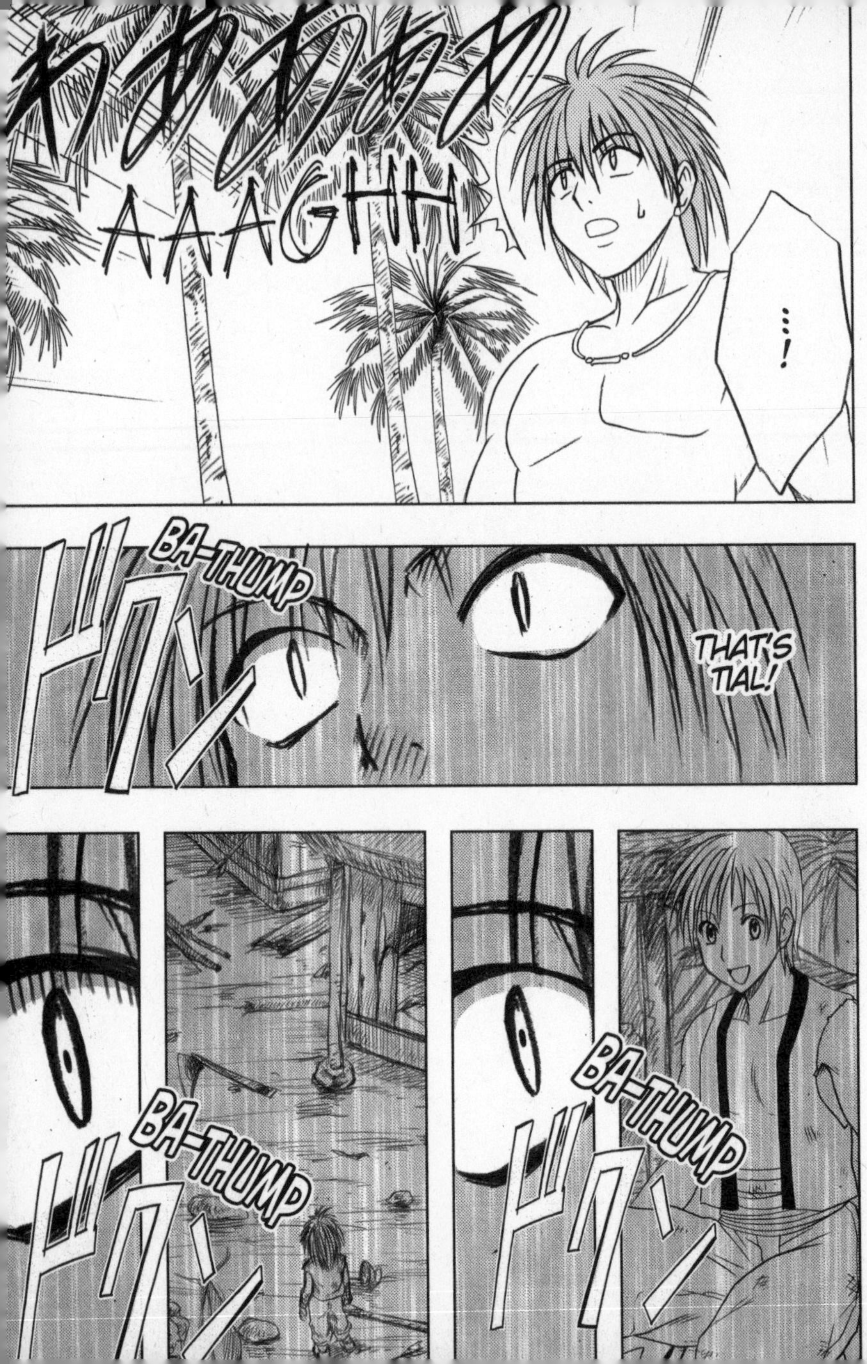

わああああ
AAAGHH
...!
THAT'S TIAL!
ドクン
BA-THUMP
ドクン
BA-THUMP
ドクン
BA-THUMP

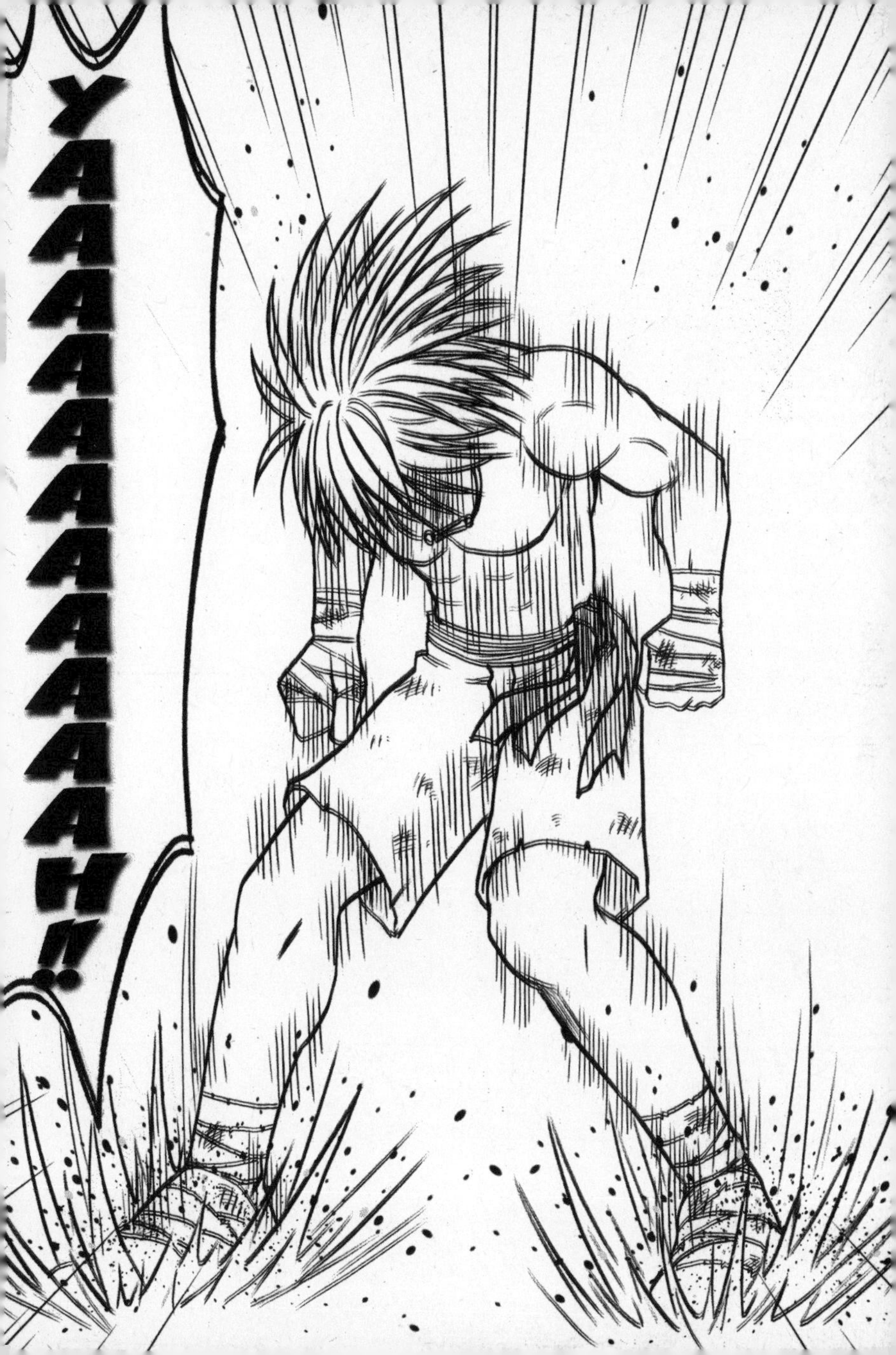
YAAAAAAAAAAAH!!

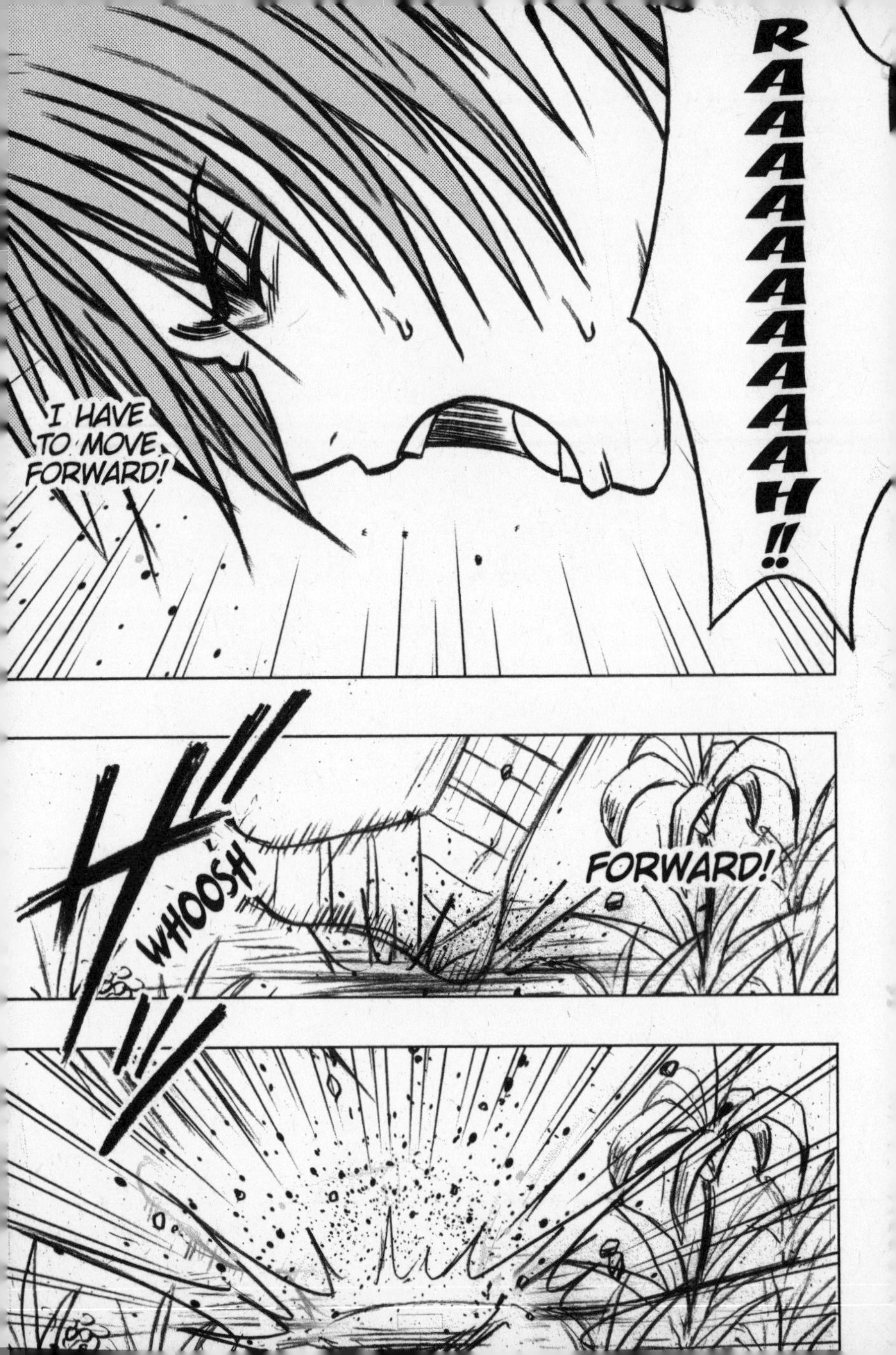

RAAAAAAAAAAH!!
I HAVE TO MOVE FORWARD!
FORWARD!
WHOOSH

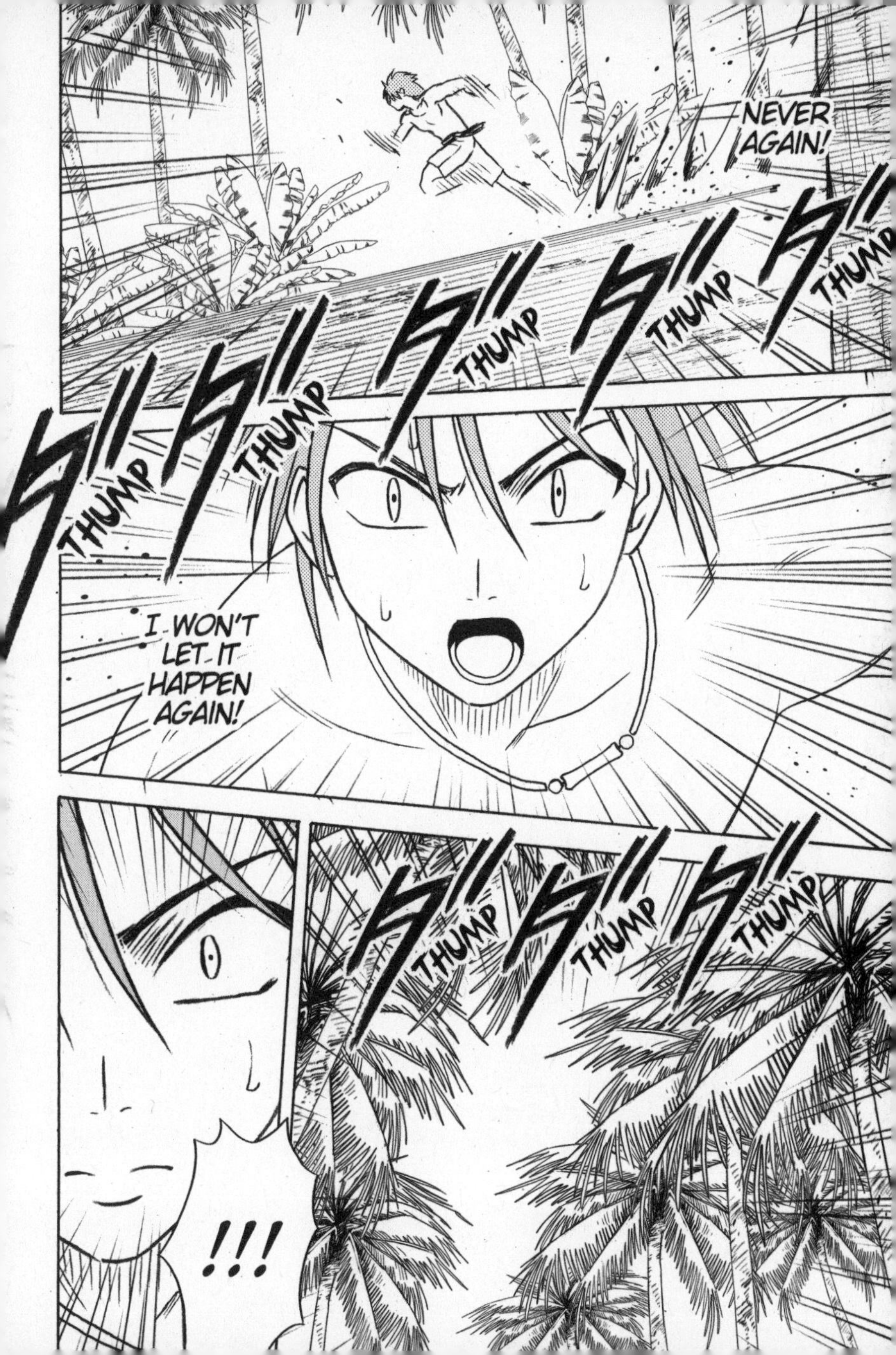
NEVER AGAIN!
THUMP THUMP THUMP THUMP THUMP THUMP
I WON'T LET IT HAPPEN AGAIN!
THUMP THUMP THUMP
!!!

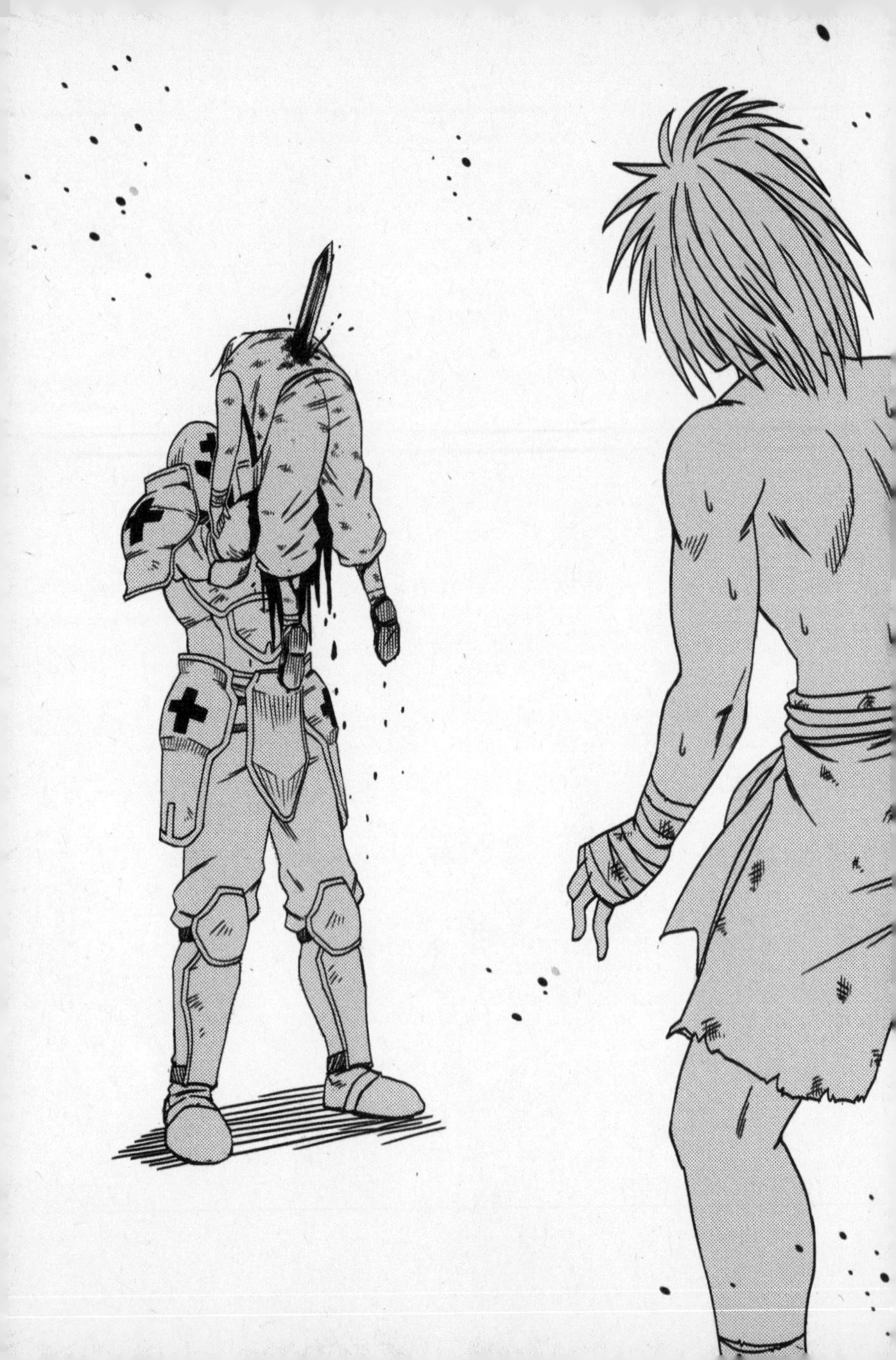

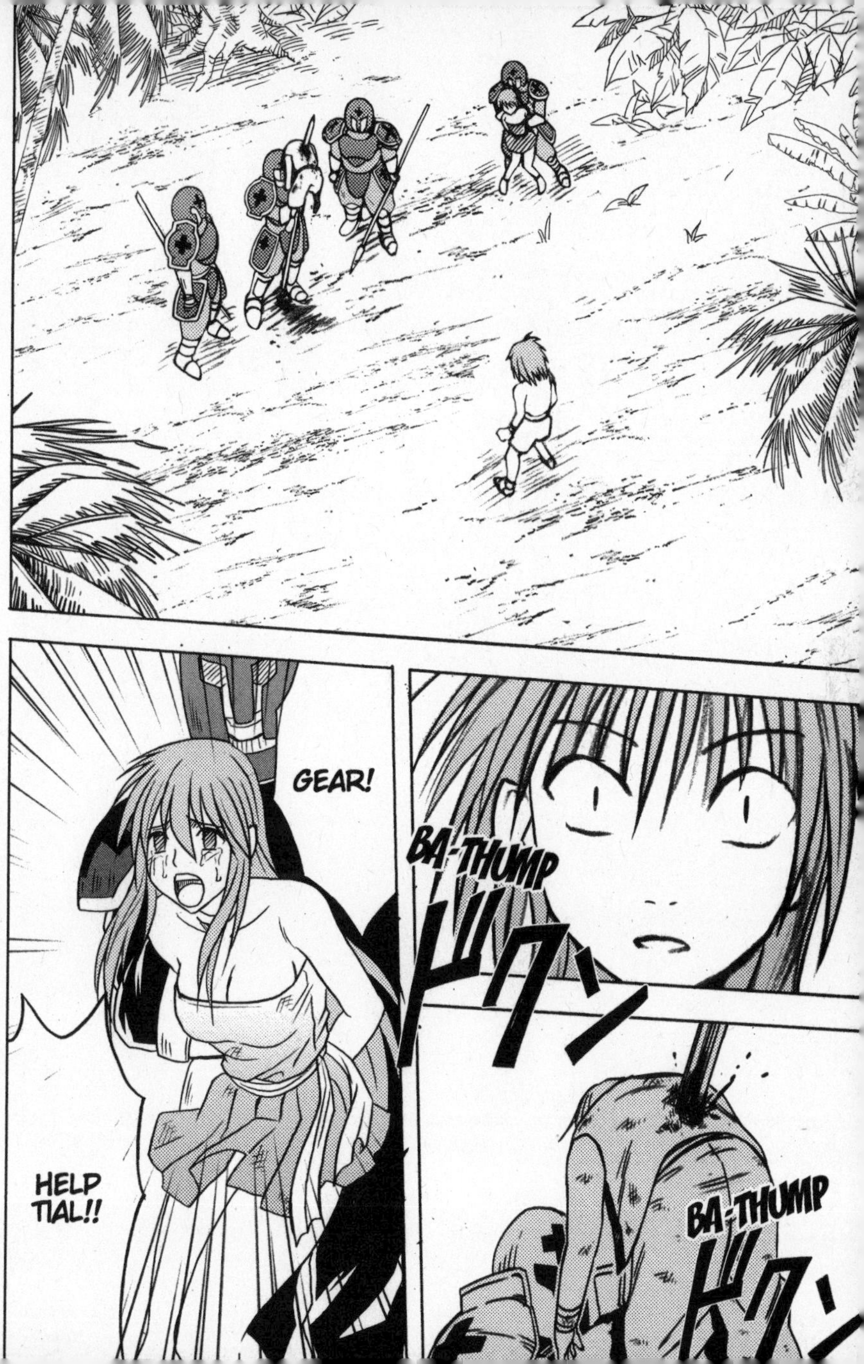
BA-THUMP
ドクン
BA-THUMP
ドクン
GEAR!
HELP
TIAL!!

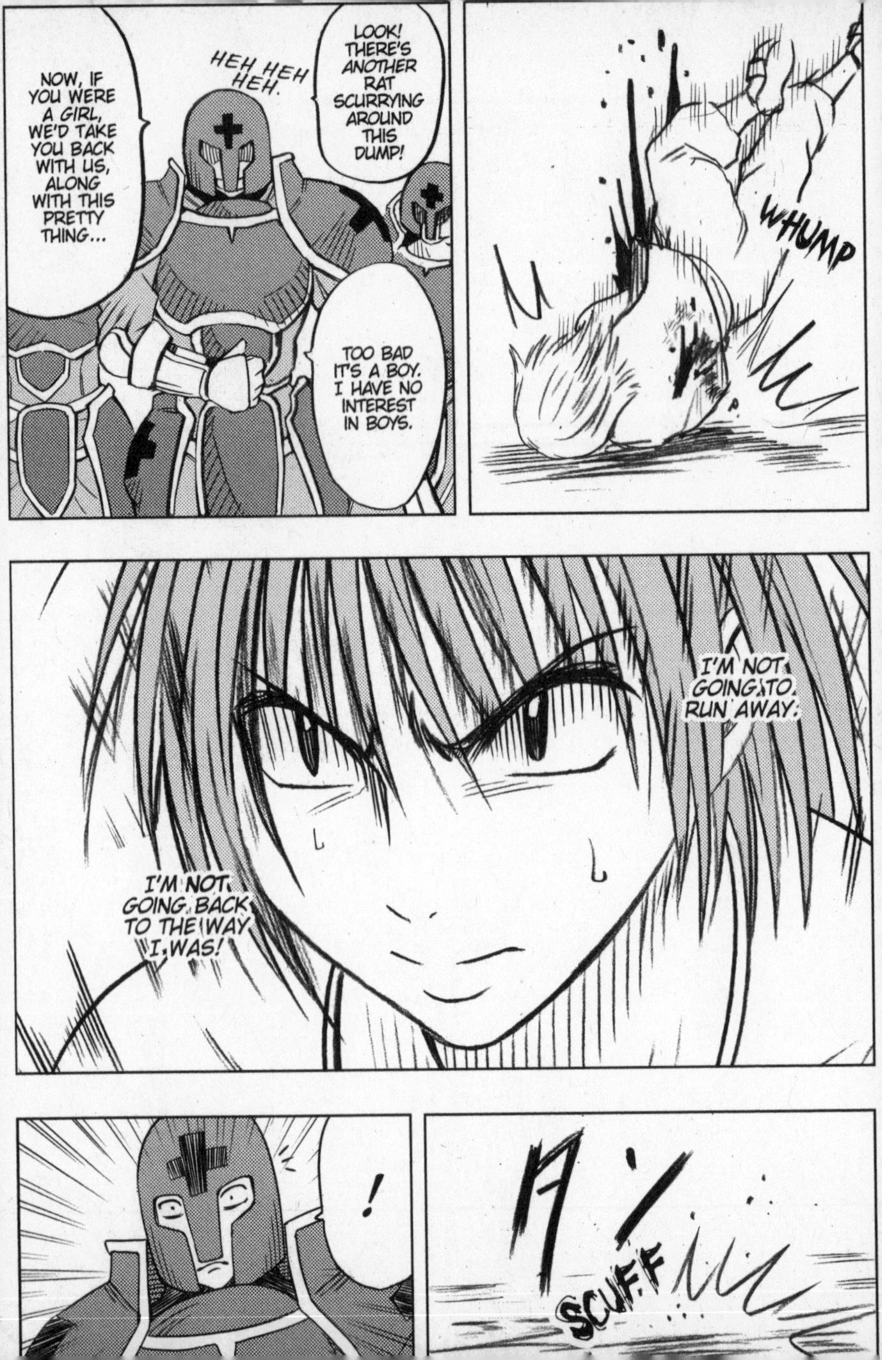
WHUMP
LOOK! THERE'S ANOTHER RAT SCURRYING AROUND THIS DUMP!
HEH HEH HEH.
NOW, IF YOU WERE A GIRL, WE'D TAKE YOU BACK WITH US, ALONG WITH THIS PRETTY THING...
TOO BAD IT'S A BOY. I HAVE NO INTEREST IN BOYS.
I'M NOT GOING TO RUN AWAY.
I'M NOT GOING BACK TO THE WAY I WAS!
SCUFF
!

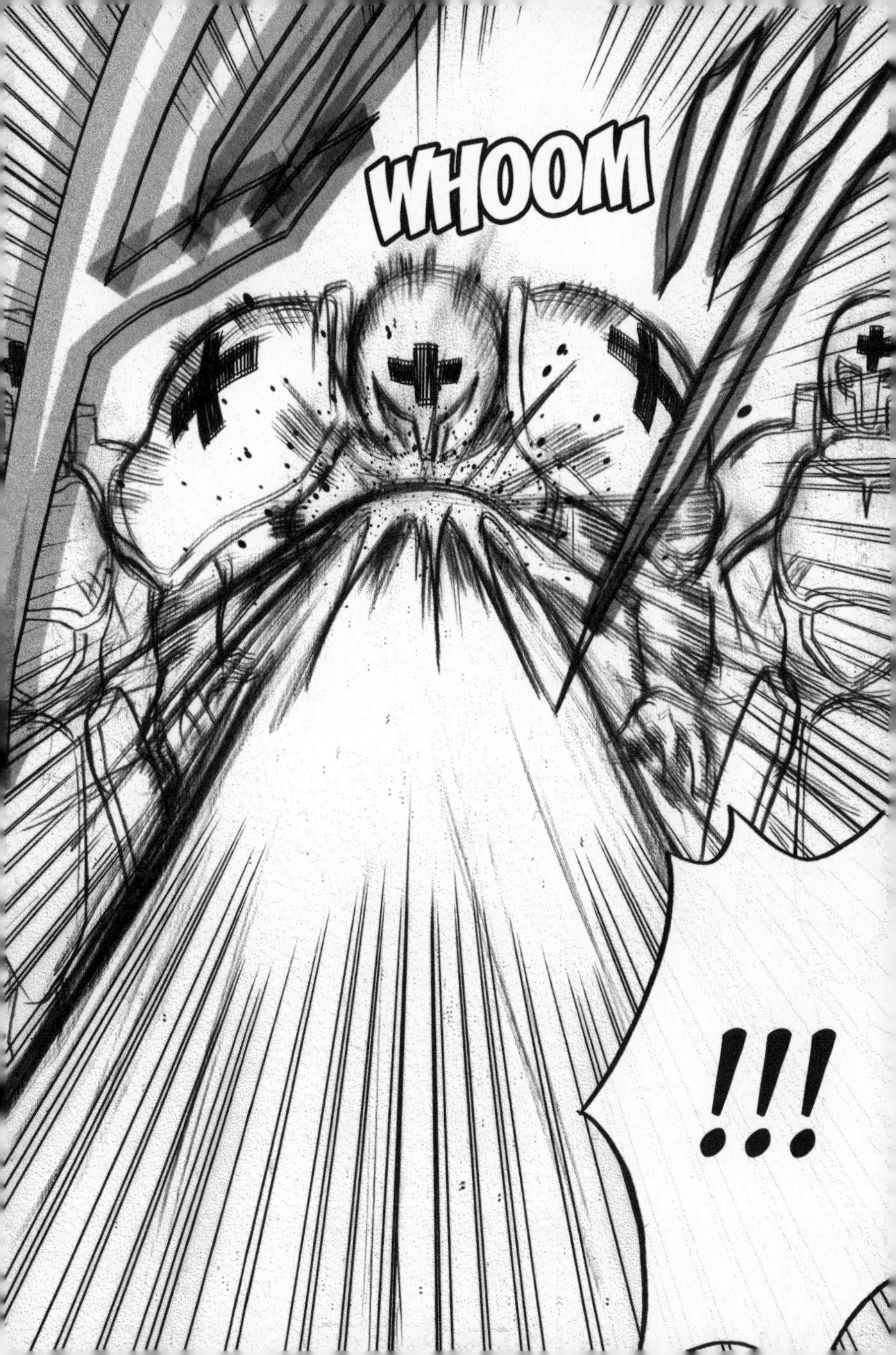
WHOOM
!!!

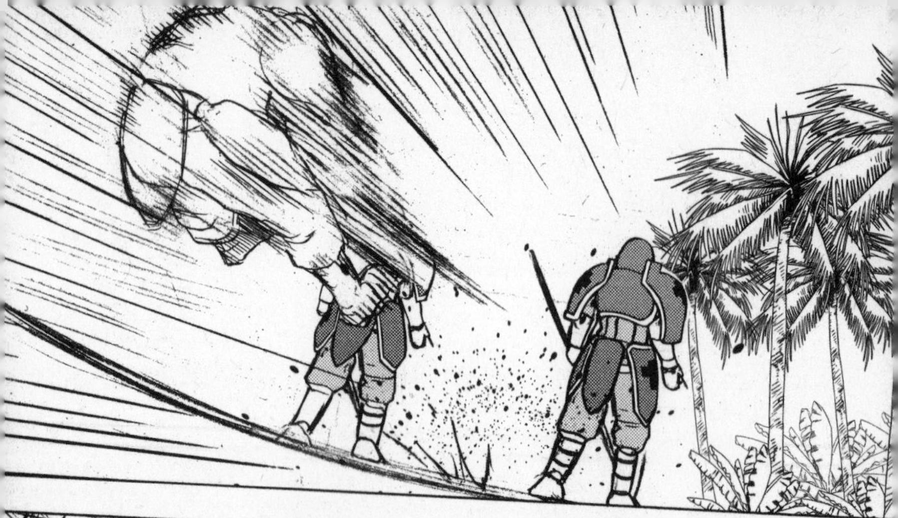
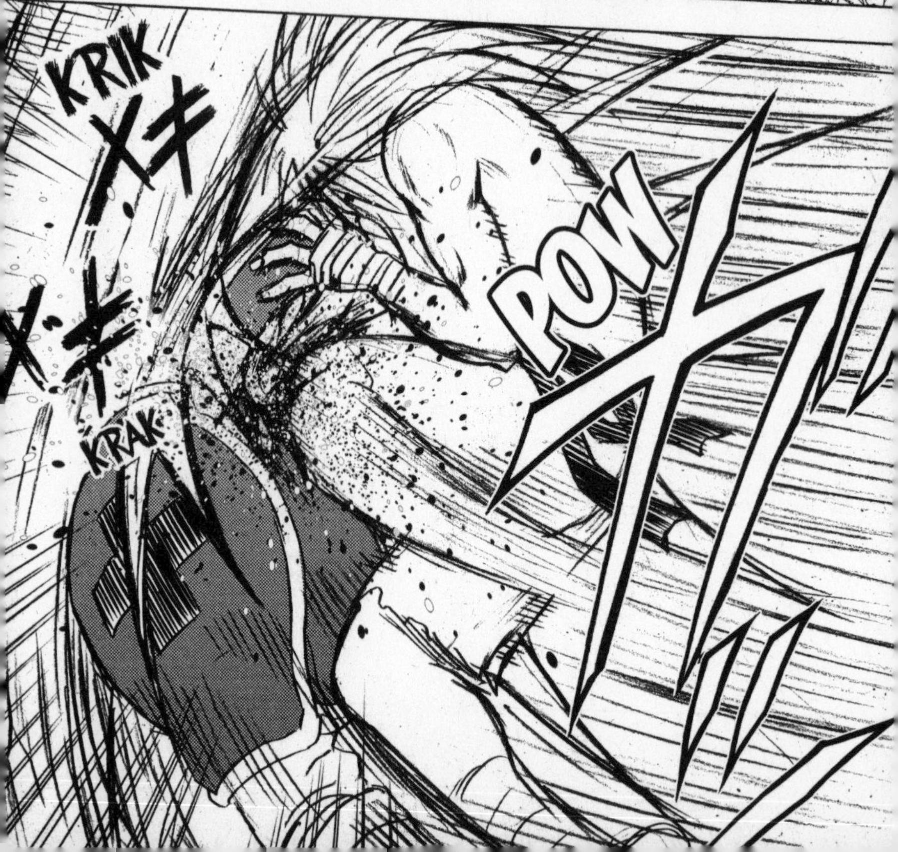
POW
KRIK
メキ
メキ
KRAK

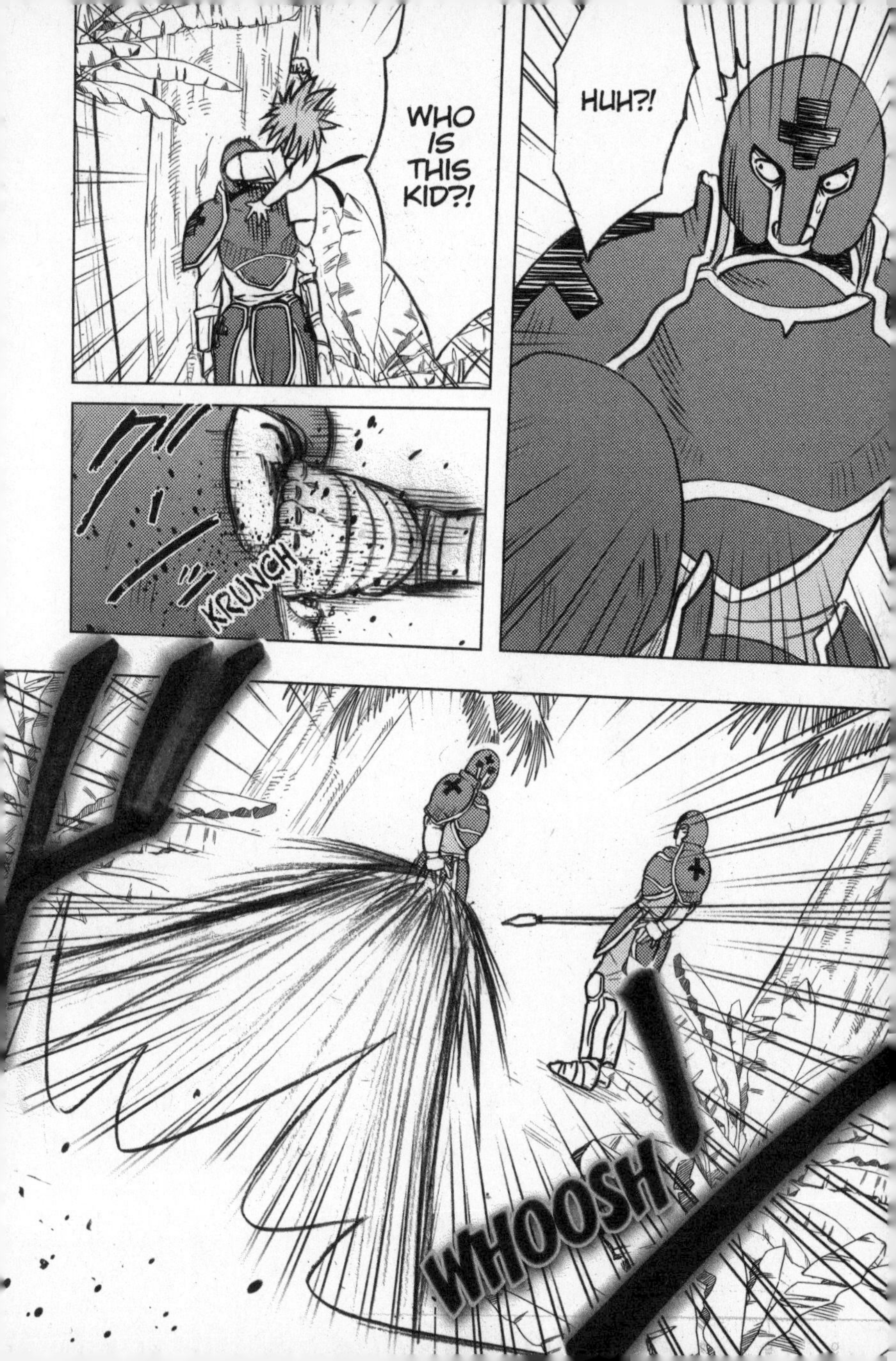
HUH?!
WHO IS THIS KID?!
KRUNCH
WHOOSH

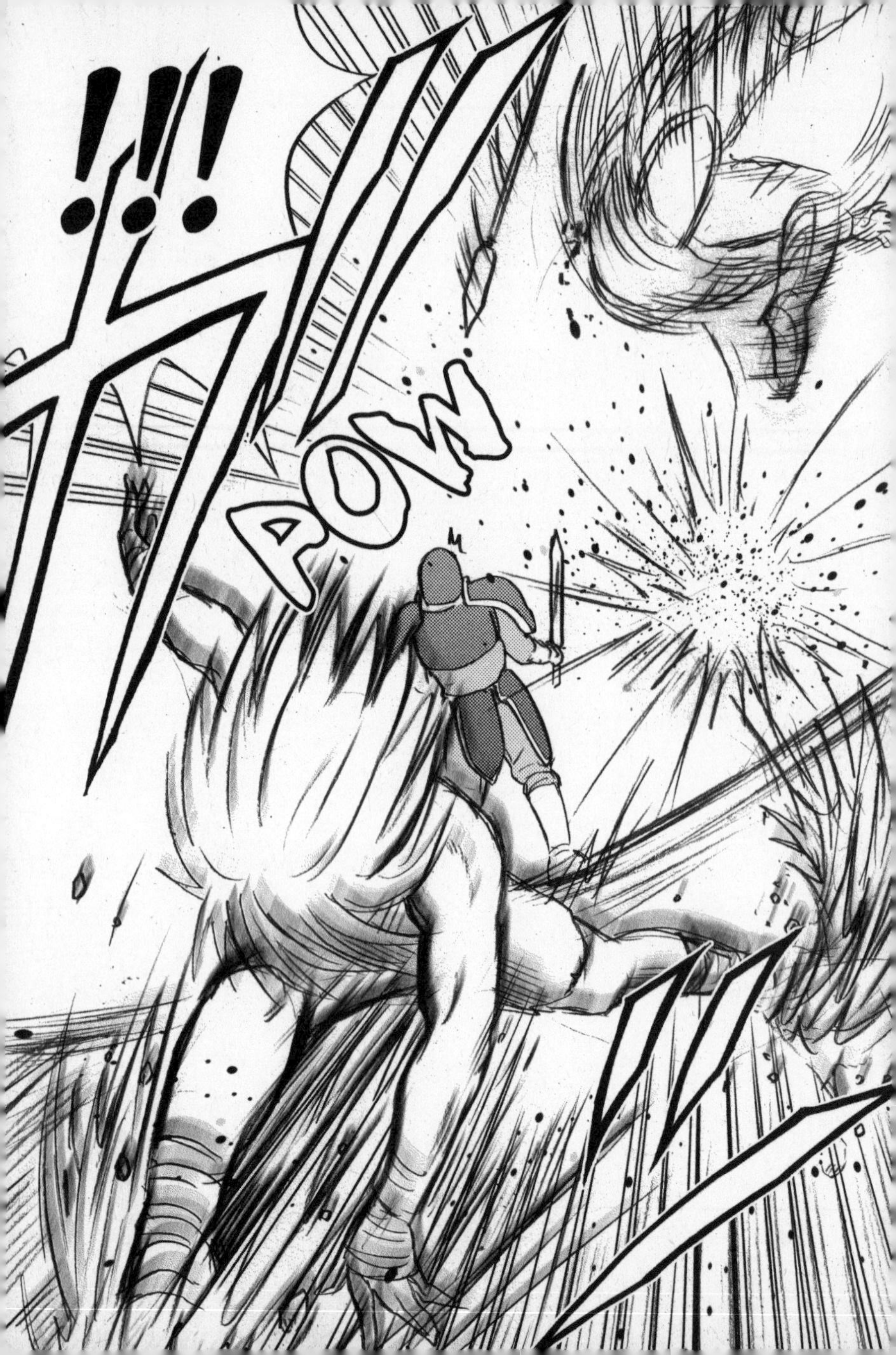
!!!
POW

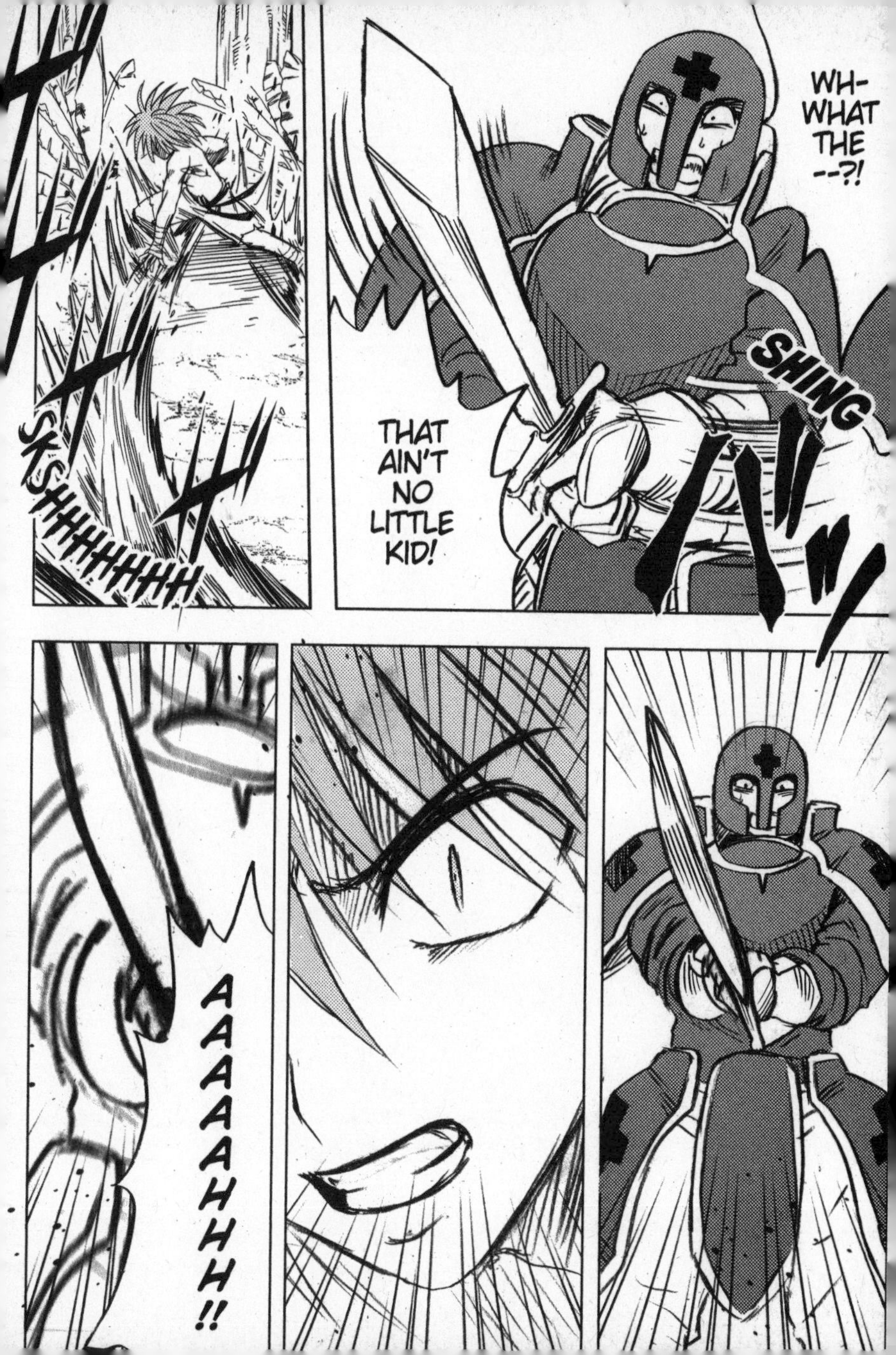
WH- WHAT THE --?!
SHING
THAT AIN'T NO LITTLE KID!
SKSHHHHHHHHH
AAAAAAHHHH!!

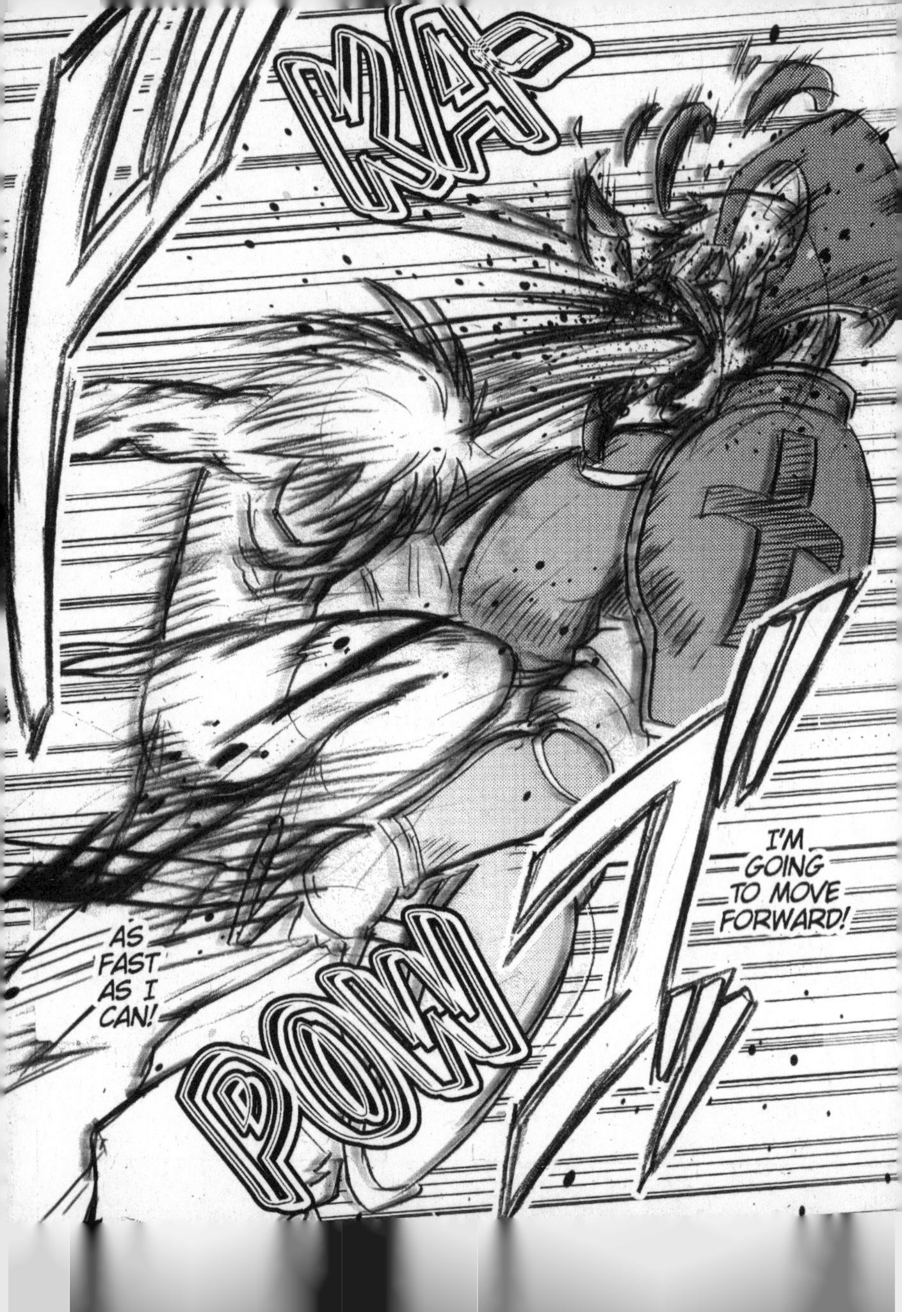
I'M GOING TO MOVE FORWARD!
POW
AS FAST AS I CAN!

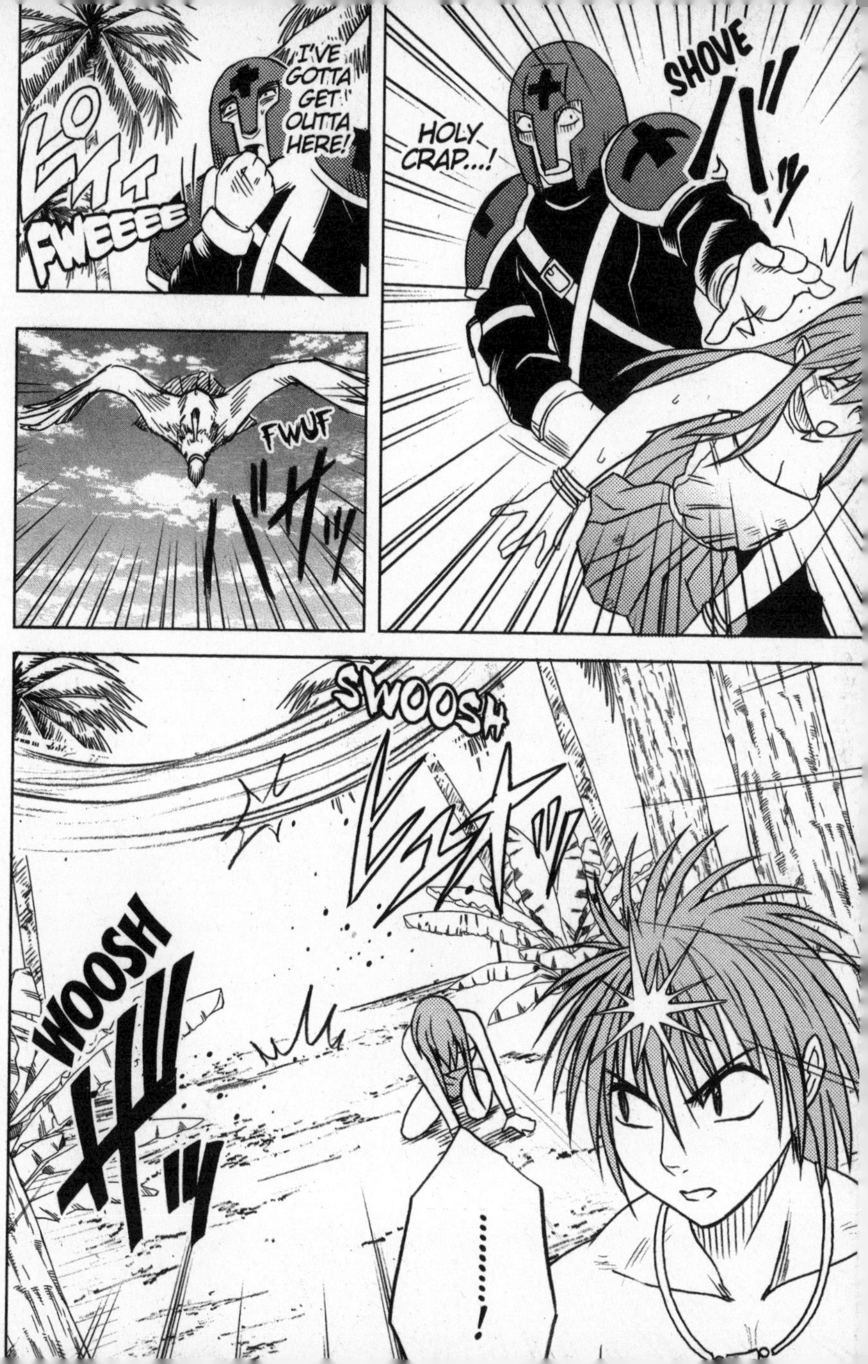
HOLY CRAP...!
SHOVE
I'VE GOTTA GET OUTTA HERE!
FWEEEEE
FWUF
SWOOSH
......!
WOOSH

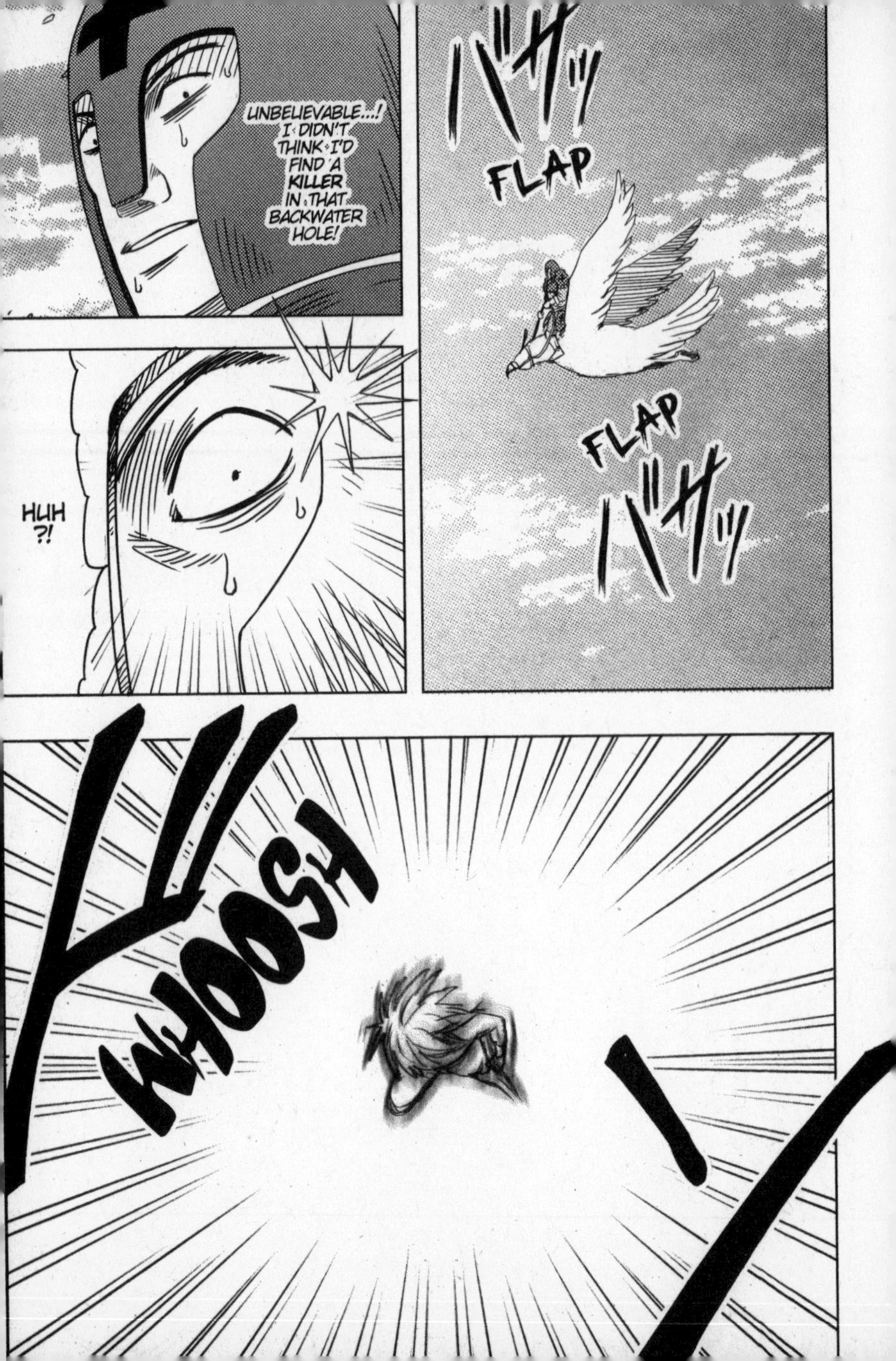
バサッ
FLAP
FLAP
バサッ
UNBELIEVABLE...! I DIDN'T THINK I'D FIND A KILLER IN THAT BACKWATER HOLE!
HUH ?!
WHOOSH

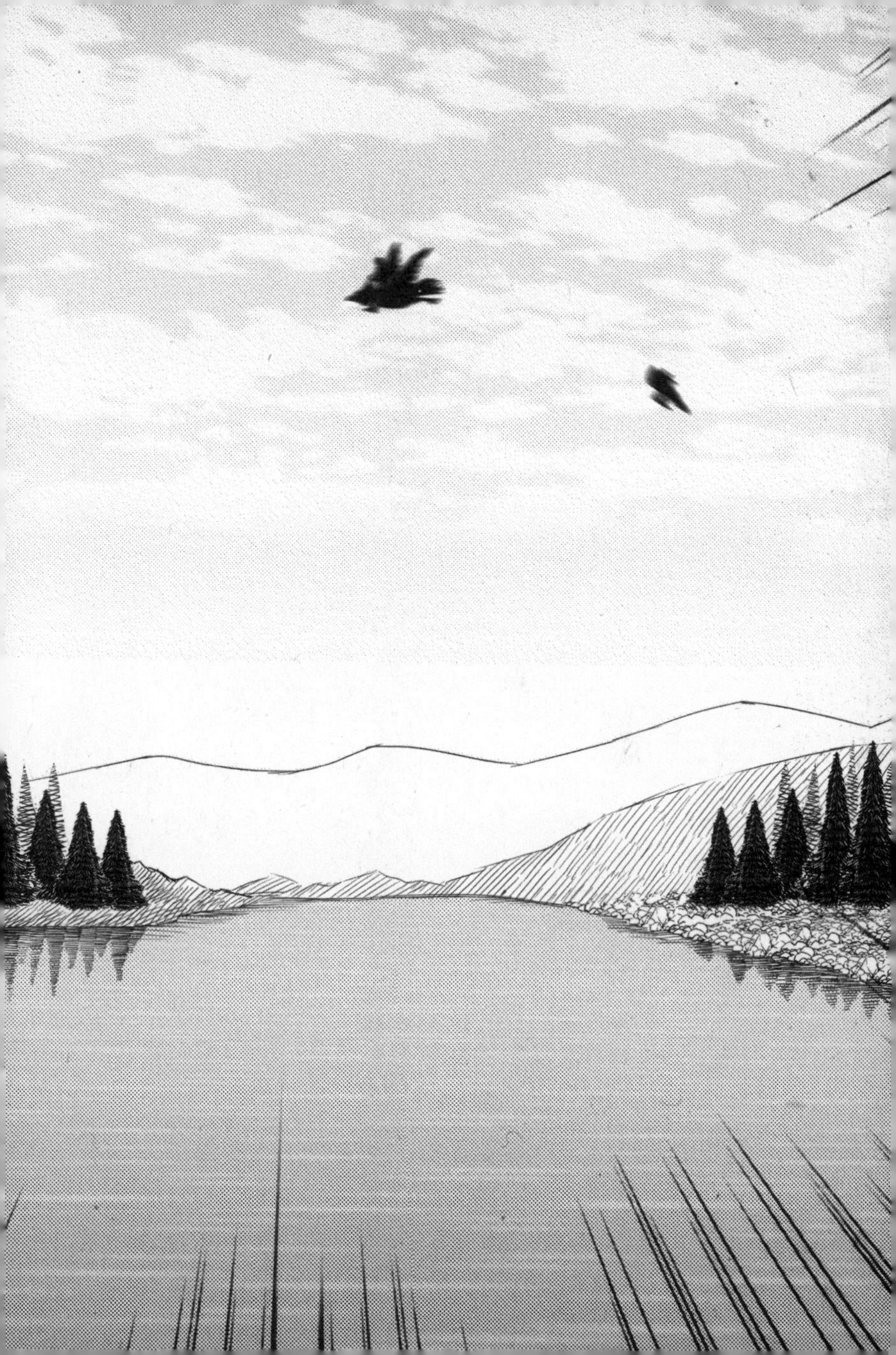

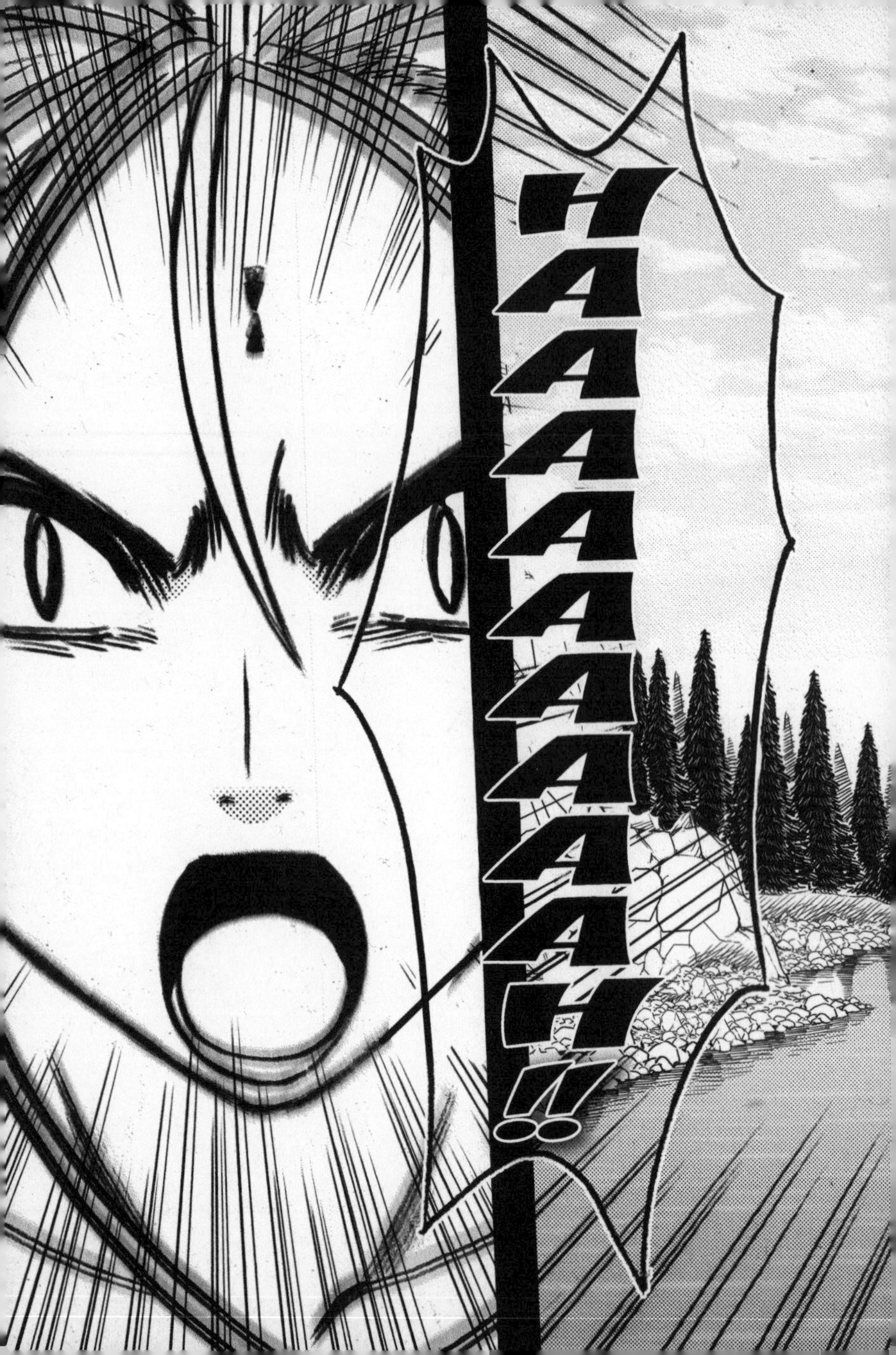
HAAAAAAAAH!!

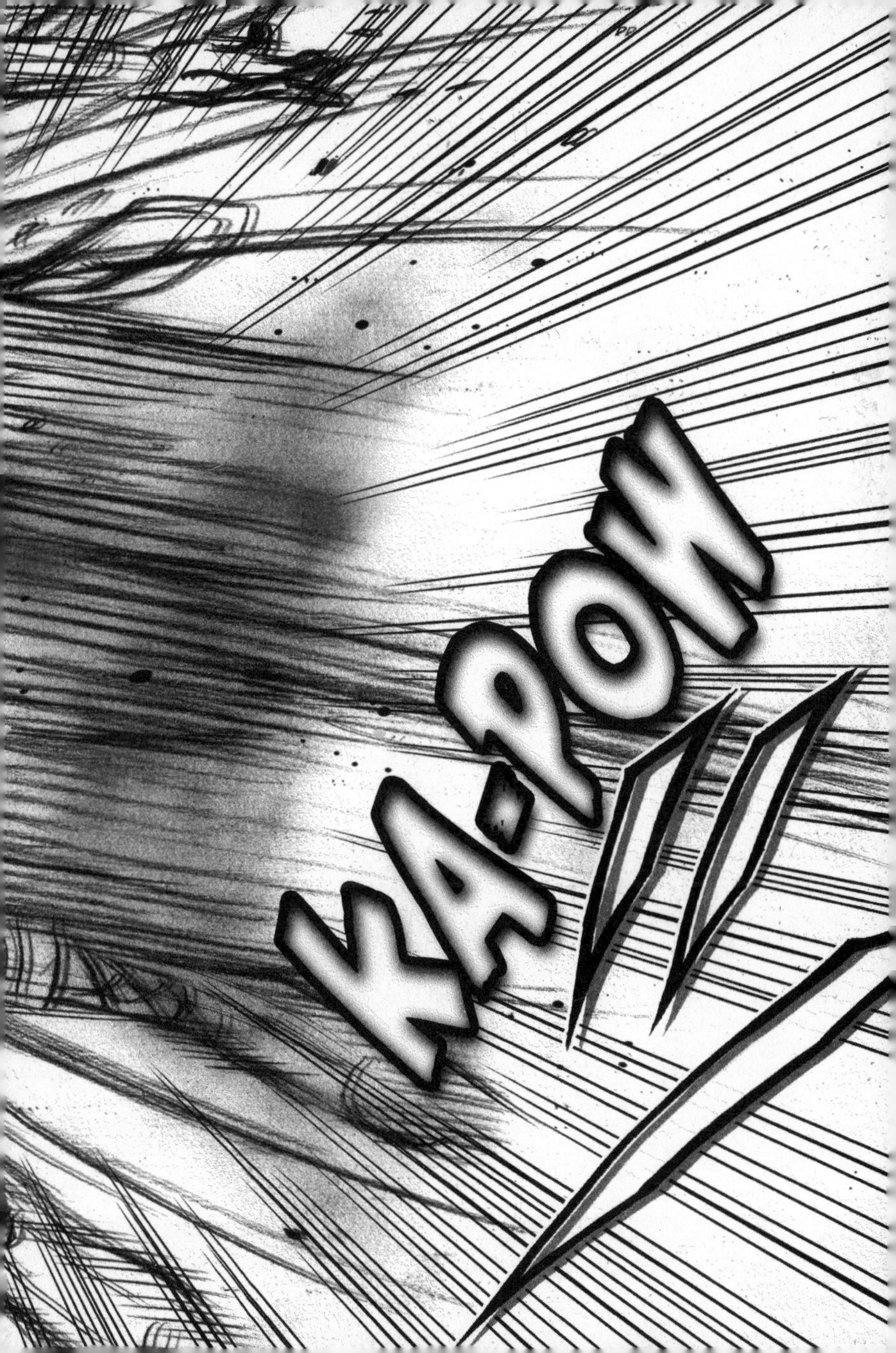
KA-POW

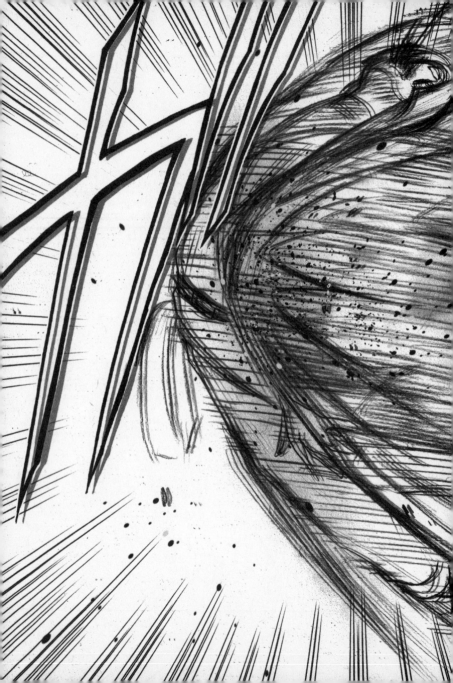

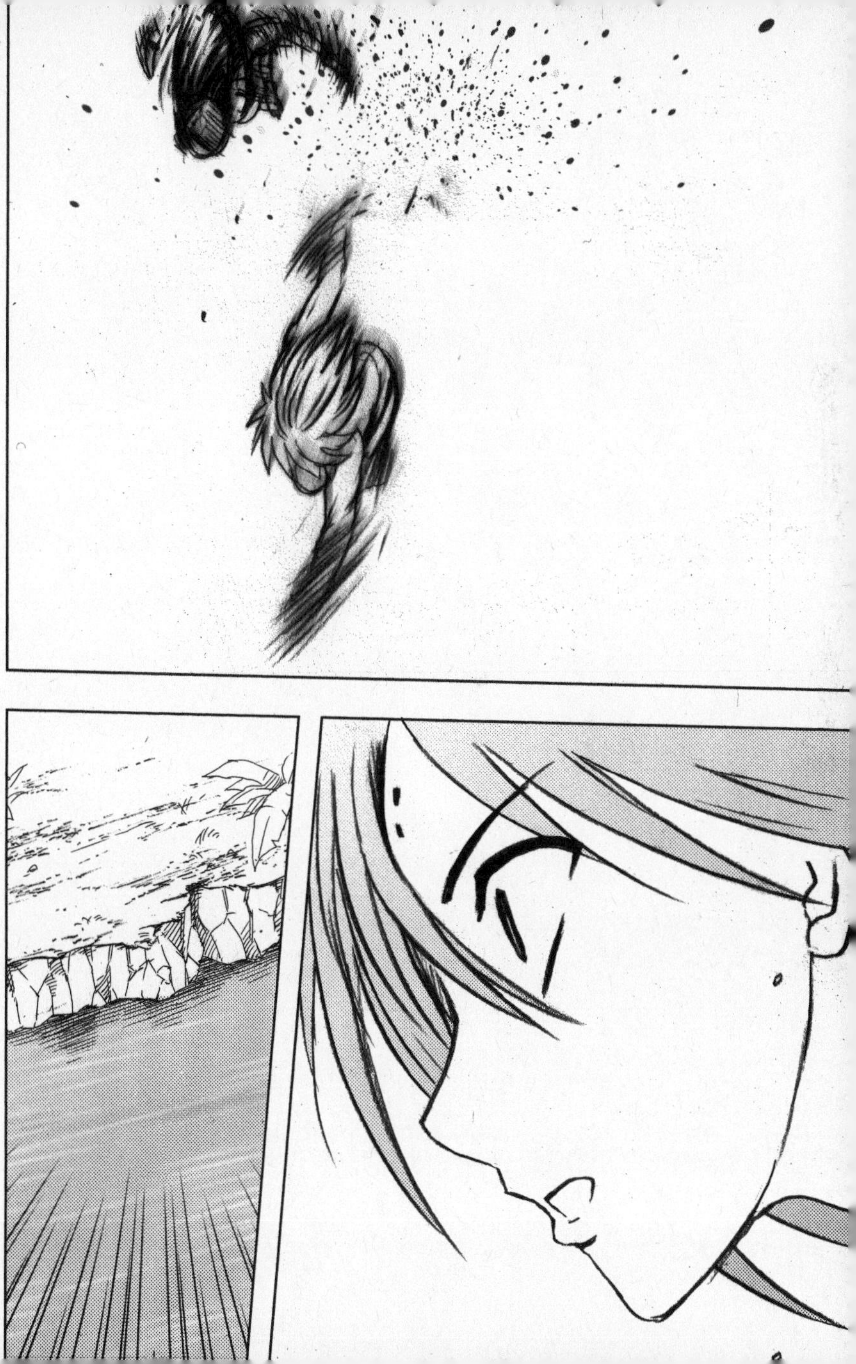

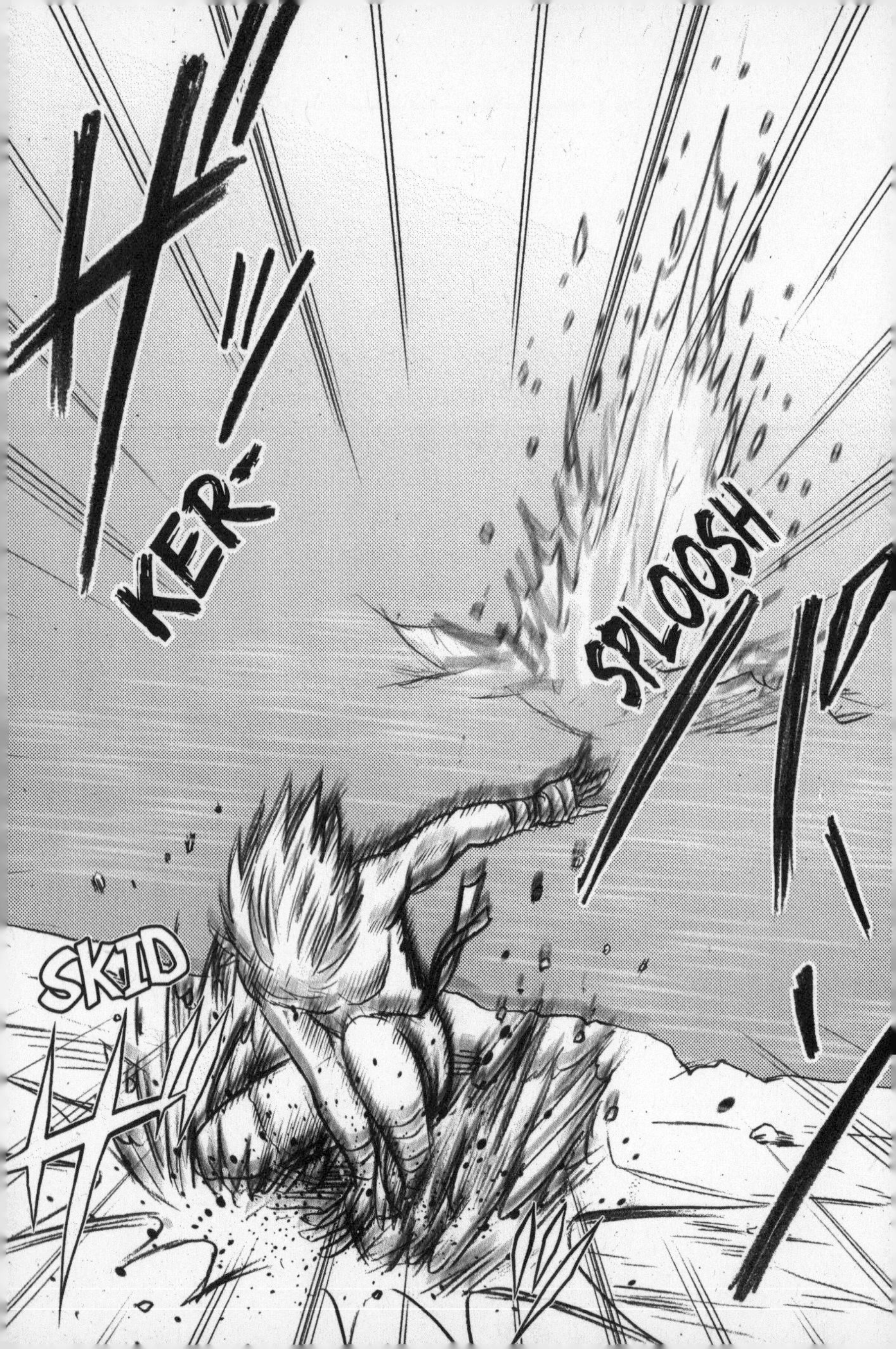
KER-
SPLOOSH
SKID

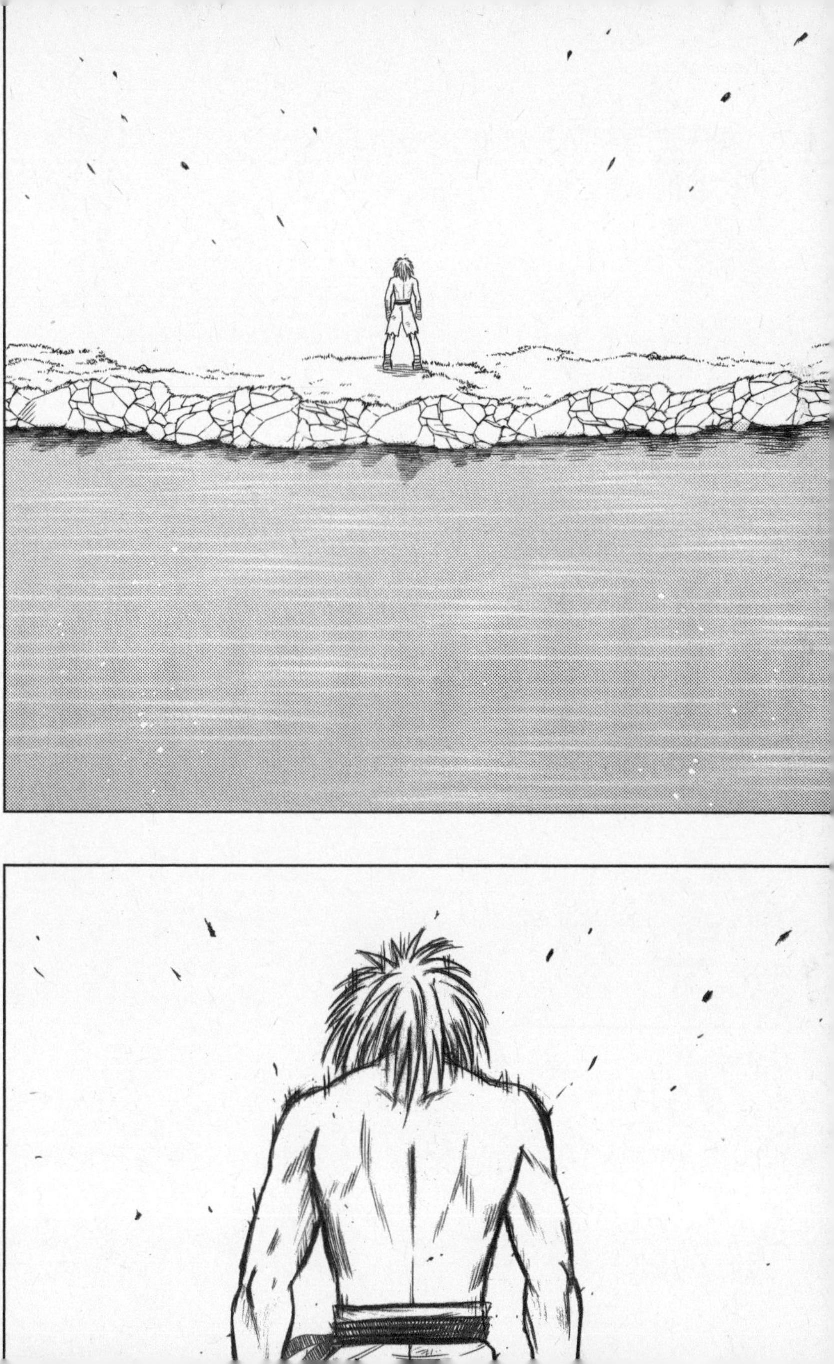

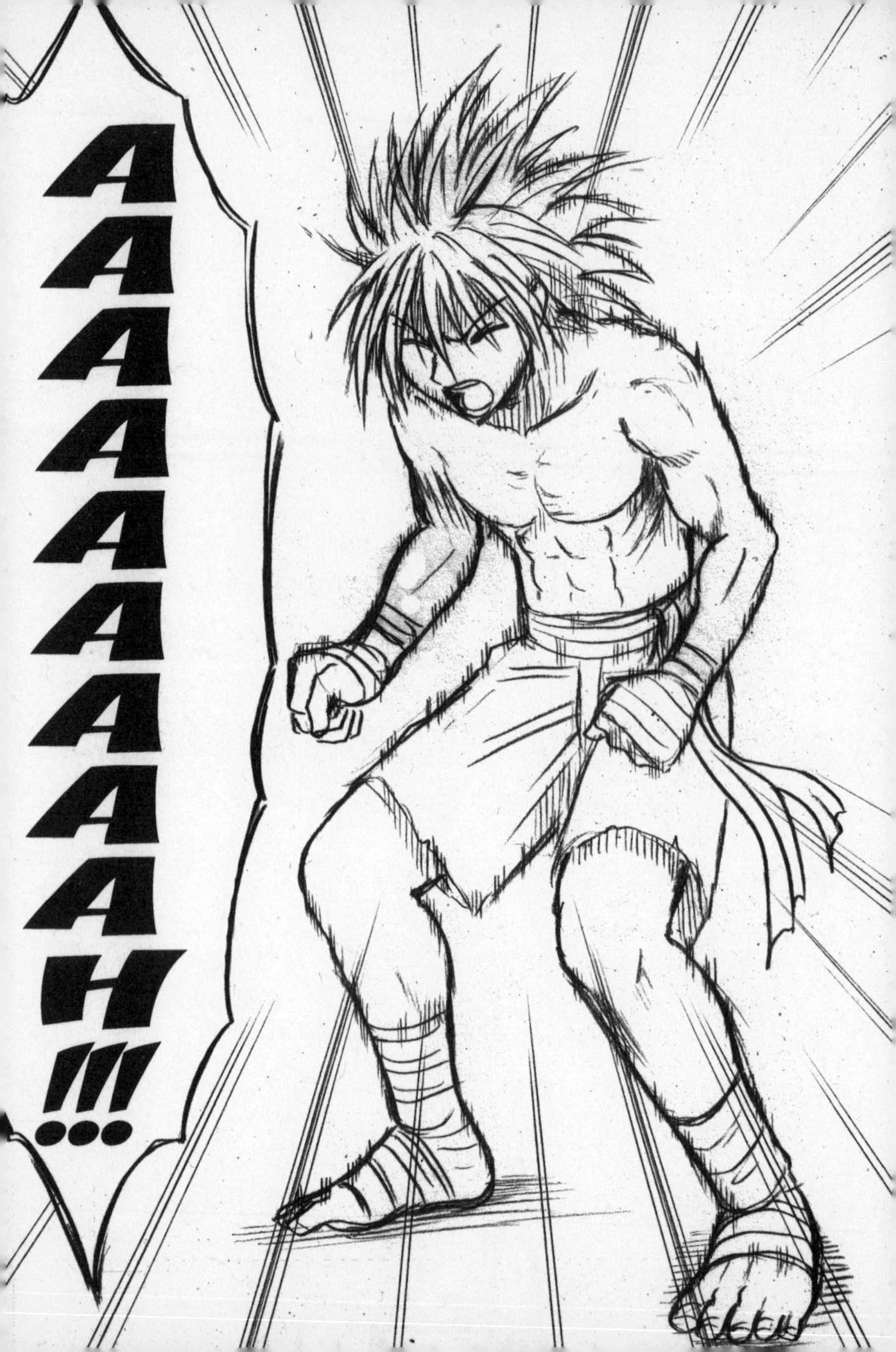
AAAAAAAAAH!!!

I...

I DID IT!

I ACTUALLY DID IT!

TIAL,
I MADE IT!!

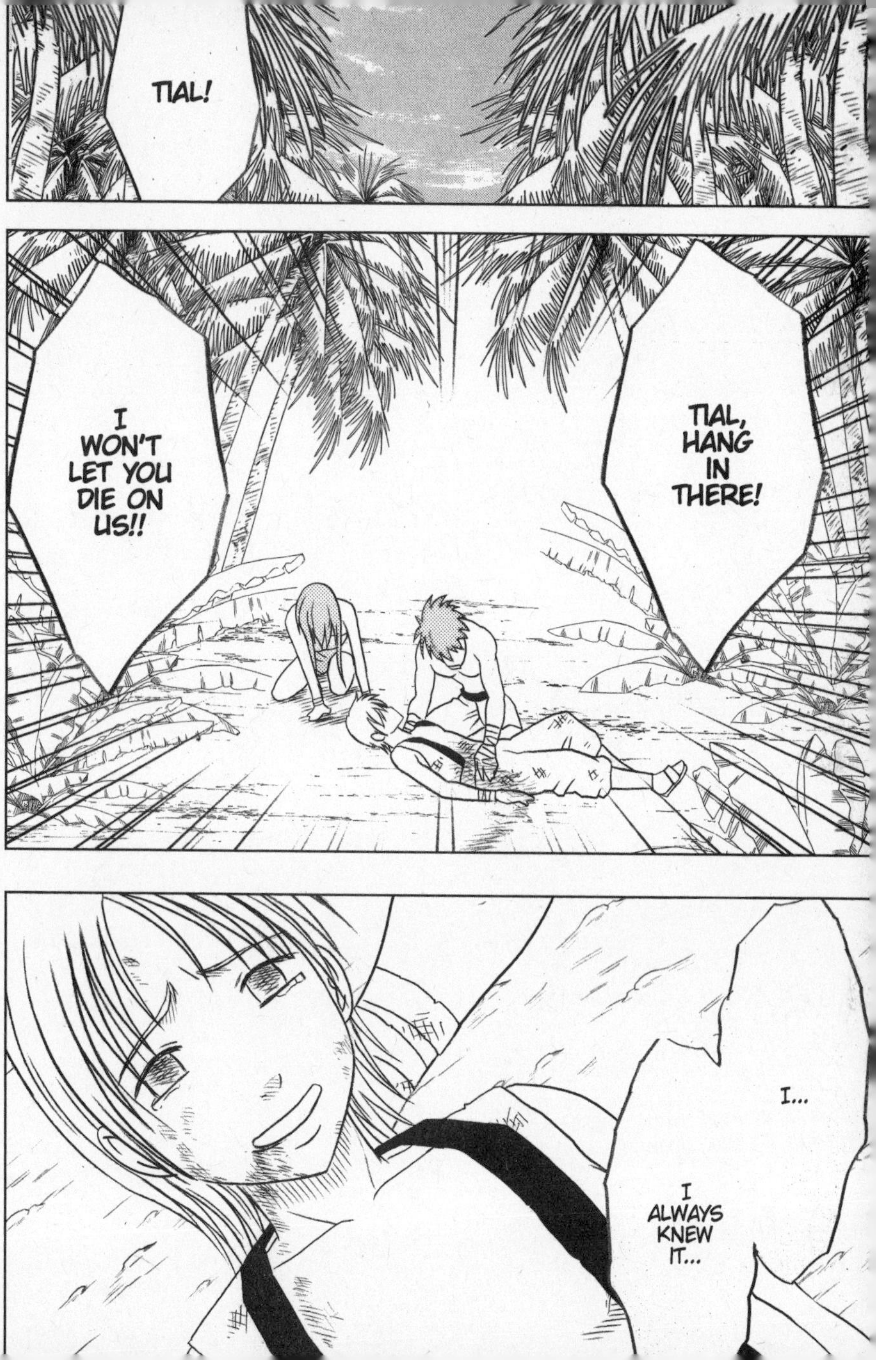
TIAL!
TIAL, HANG IN THERE!
I WON'T LET YOU DIE ON US!!
I...
I ALWAYS KNEW IT...

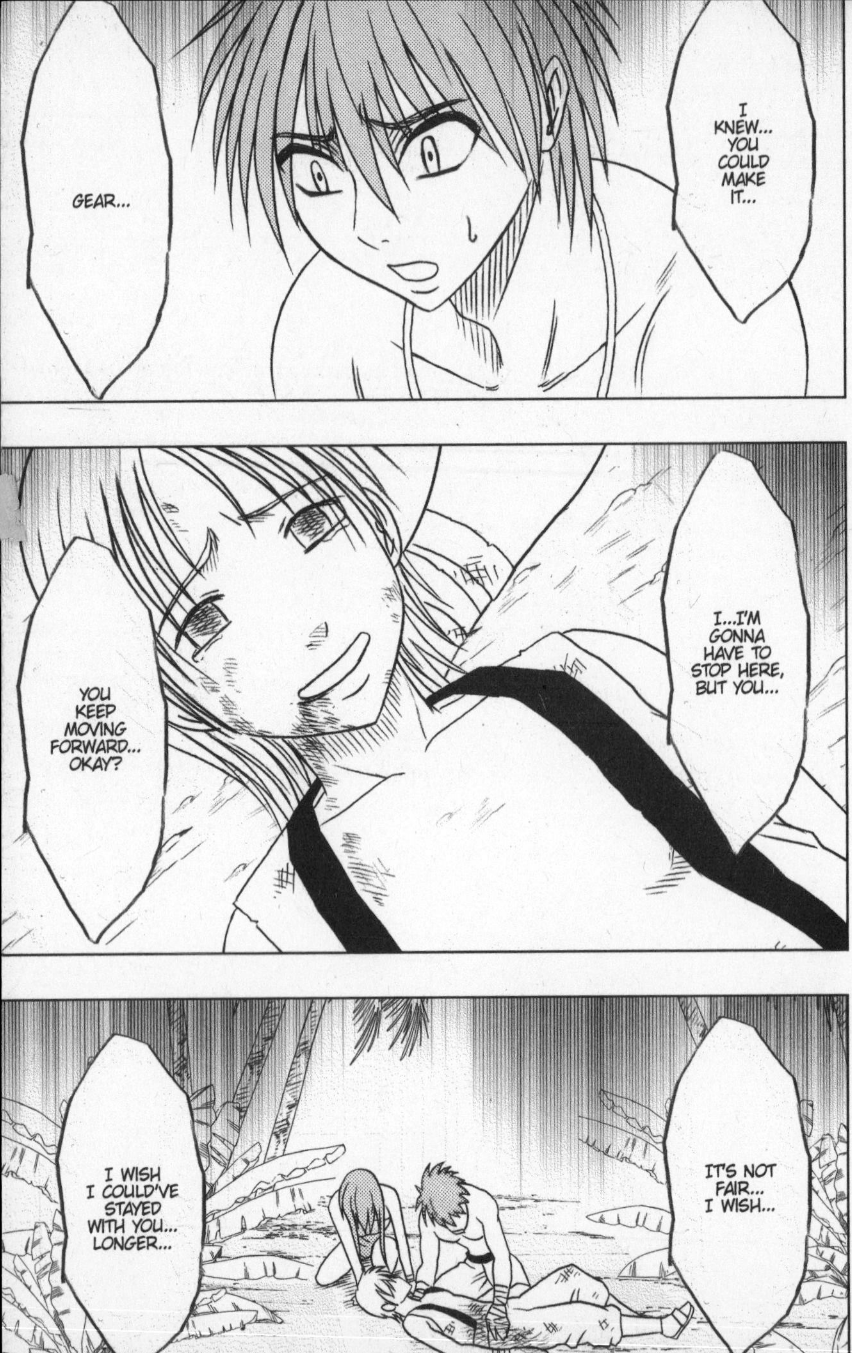
I KNEW... YOU COULD MAKE IT...
GEAR...
I...I'M GONNA HAVE TO STOP HERE, BUT YOU...
YOU KEEP MOVING FORWARD... OKAY?
IT'S NOT FAIR... I WISH...
I WISH I COULD'VE STAYED WITH YOU... LONGER...

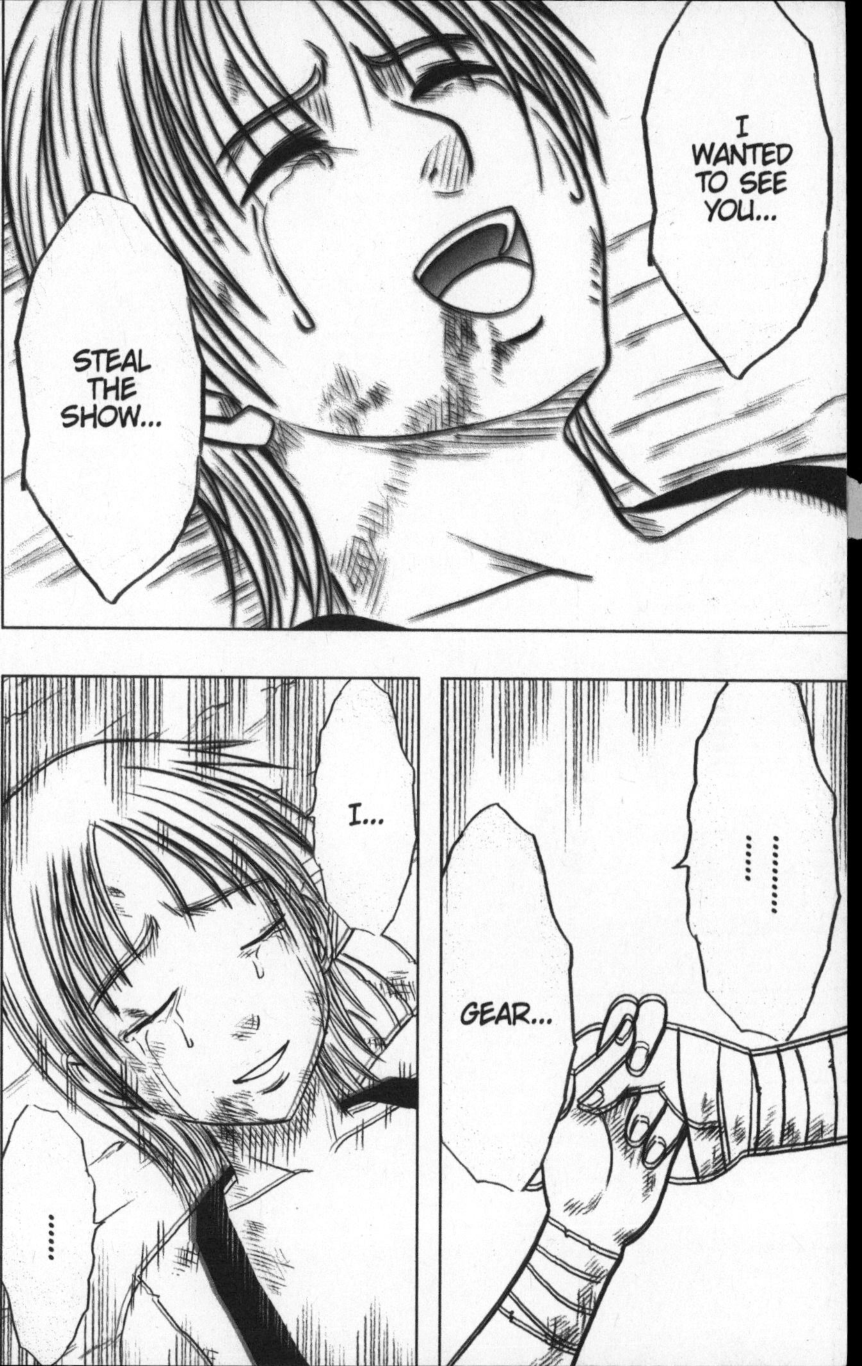
I WANTED TO SEE YOU...
STEAL THE SHOW...
......
GEAR...
I...
......

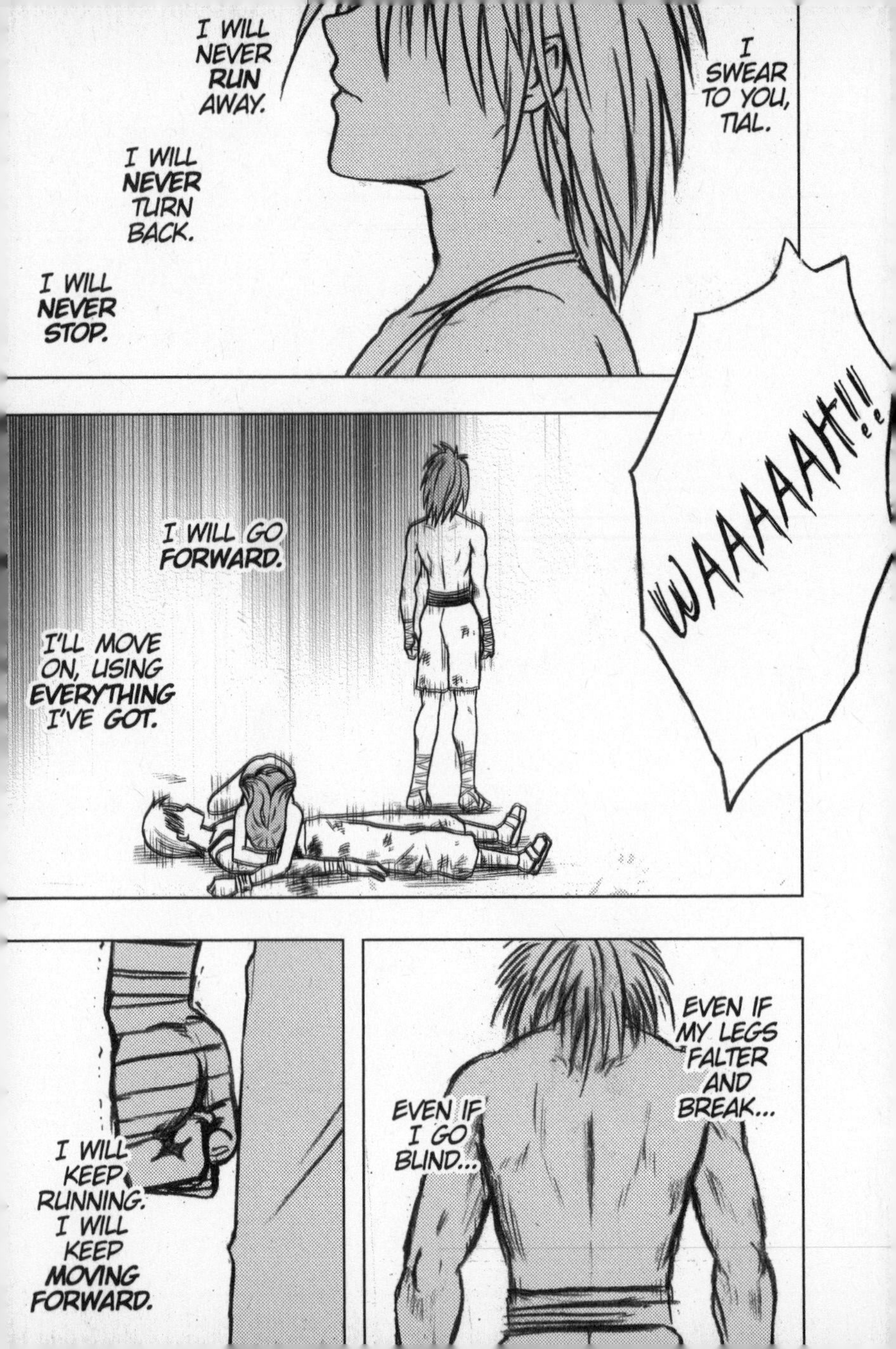
I SWEAR TO YOU, TIAL.
I WILL NEVER RUN AWAY.
I WILL NEVER TURN BACK.
I WILL NEVER STOP.
WAAAAAH!!
I WILL GO FORWARD.
I'LL MOVE ON, USING EVERYTHING I'VE GOT.
EVEN IF MY LEGS FALTER AND BREAK...
EVEN IF I GO BLIND...
I WILL KEEP RUNNING. I WILL KEEP MOVING FORWARD.

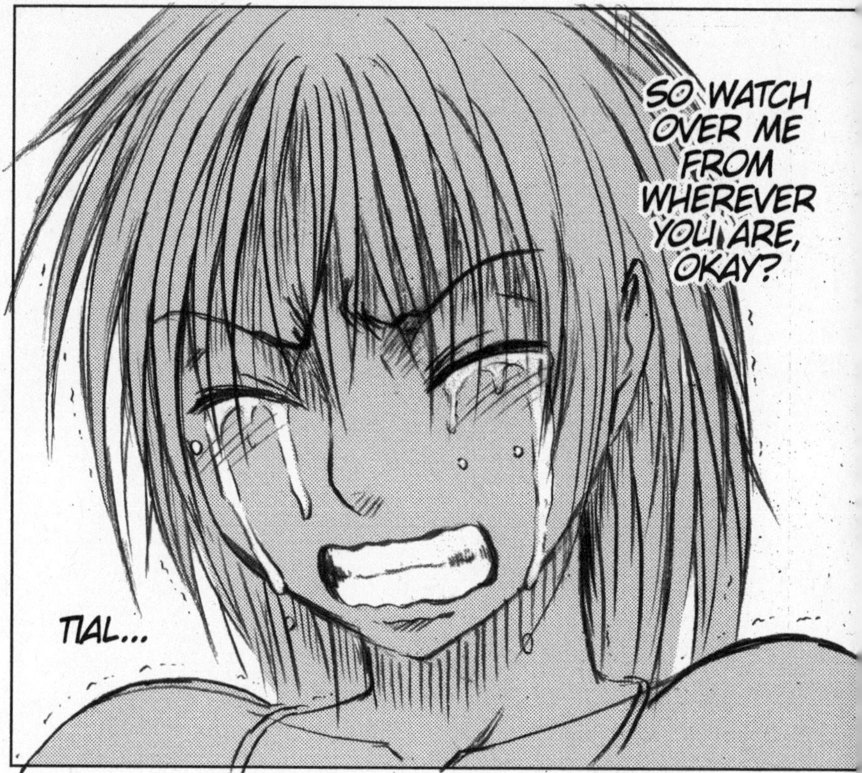
SO WATCH OVER ME FROM WHEREVER YOU ARE, OKAY?
TIAL...

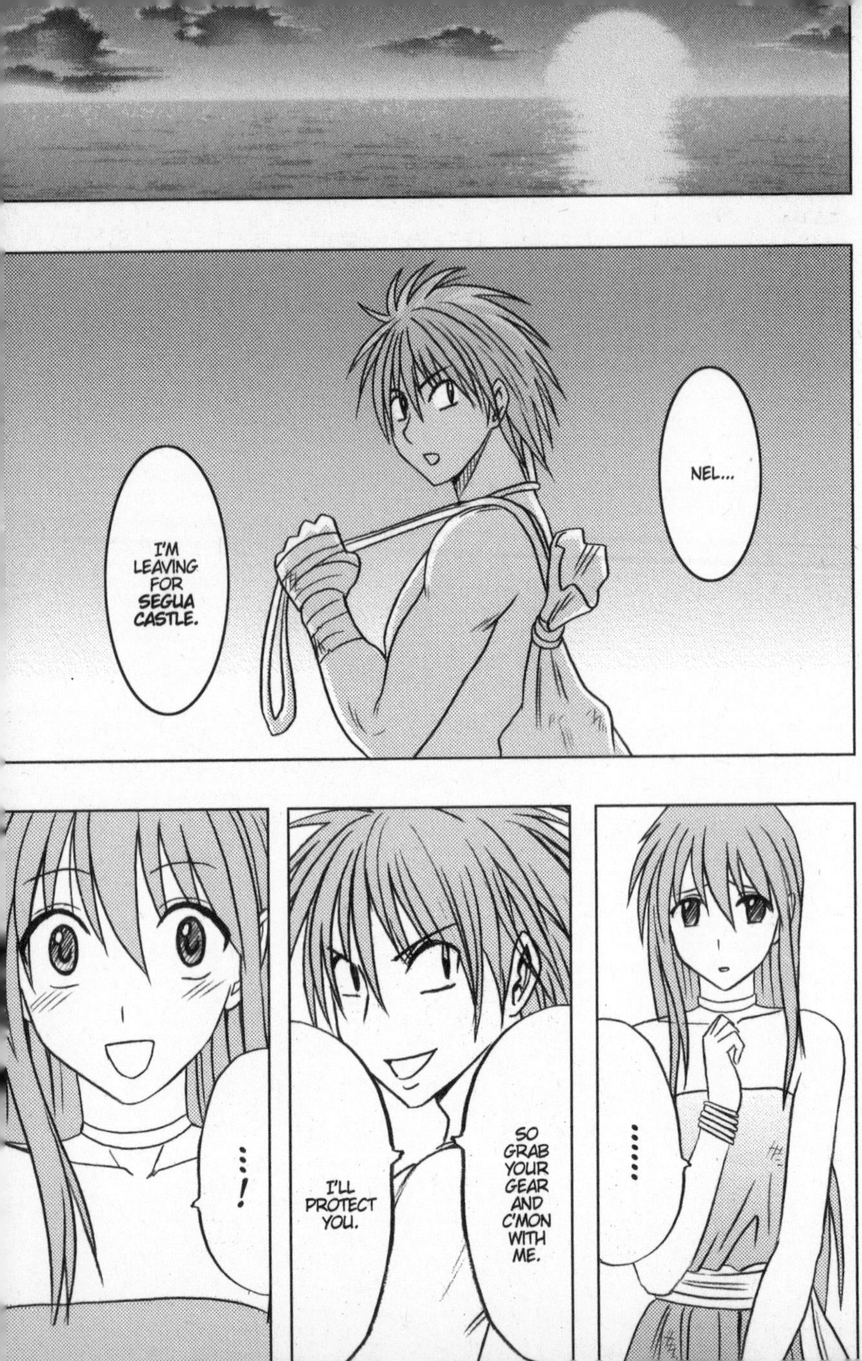
NEL...
I'M LEAVING FOR SEGUA CASTLE.
......
SO GRAB YOUR GEAR AND C'MON WITH ME.
I'LL PROTECT YOU.
...!

AND SO, I RAN...
TOWARDS THE CENTER
OF THE WORLD...

WORLD WAR BLUE
CHARACTER INTRODUCTION

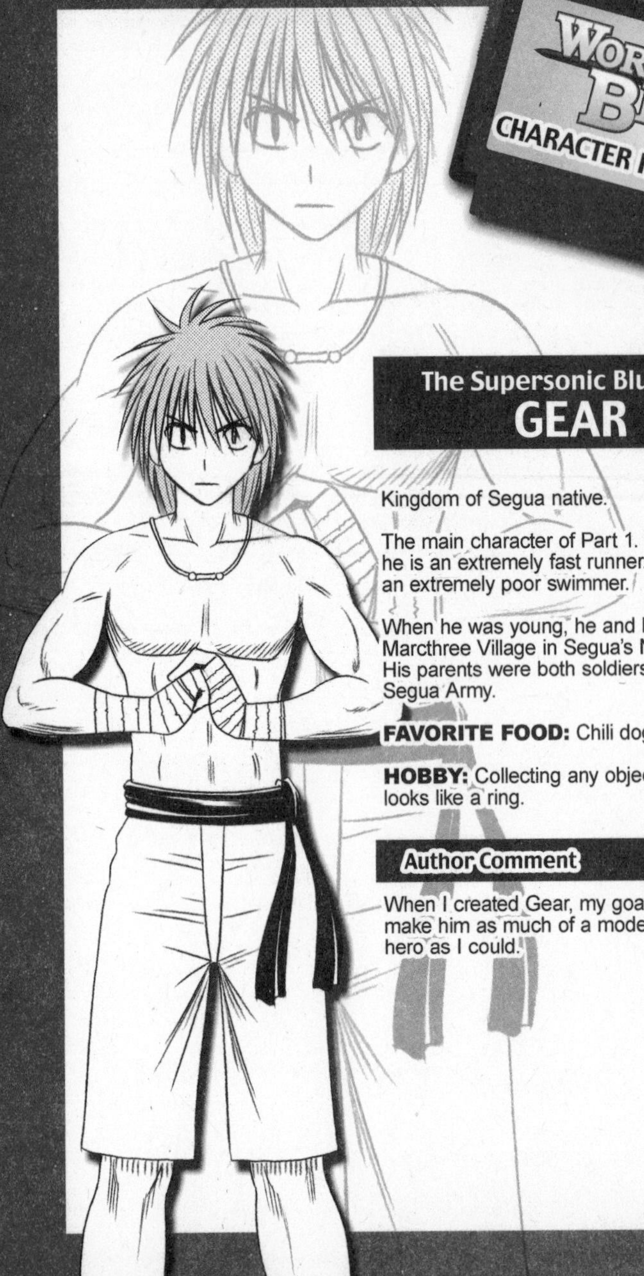

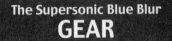

The Supersonic Blue Blur
GEAR

Kingdom of Segua native.

The main character of Part 1. Highly athletic, he is an extremely fast runner. However, he is also an extremely poor swimmer.

When he was young, he and his family escaped to Marcthree Village in Segua's Non-Combat Zone. His parents were both soldiers in the Segua Army.

FAVORITE FOOD: Chili dogs.

HOBBY: Collecting any object that looks like a ring.

Author Comment

When I created Gear, my goal was to make him as much of a model shonen-manga hero as I could.

Perusing Video Game History

ON THE EDGE OF THE BLUE WORLD

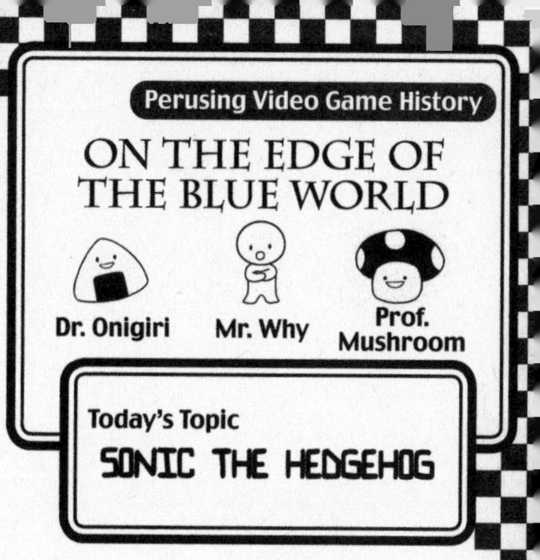

Dr. Onigiri   Mr. Why   Prof. Mushroom

Today's Topic

SONIC THE HEDGEHOG

Mr. Why: Hello, everyone! In this corner, the Doctor, the Professor, and I are going to talk a little about video games and their history. Just to give you a heads up, it's not going to have much to do with what's going on in the story.

Dr. Onigiri: Hi! I'm Doctor Onigiri. My favorite food is *osechi (New Year's bento boxes)*, and lots of it.

Prof. Mushroom: Hey there. My name's Professor Mushroom. My favorite dish is *bubuzuke (green tea and dashi, with rice)*.

Dr. Onigiri: Well then, let's dive right into today's topic. Mr. Why, how many game console makers can you name?

Mr. Why: Uh... the DS is made by Nintendo, right? Then there's Sony's PS3, and uhm... Microsoft?

Prof. Mushroom: Yep! But y'know, up until not long ago, there were tons of other console makers out there.

Dr. Onigiri: Exactly! And one of those created the blazing blue comet that streaked across gaming history—Sega!

Mr. Why: Never heard of 'em.

Dr. Onigiri: What?! Then what about Sonic?

Mr. Why: Sonic?

Dr. Onigiri: Exactly! the game's official title is *Sonic the Hedgehog*. A side-scrolling action game, it debuted on the Sega Genesis (a.k.a. Sega Mega Drive) console in 1991. The main character was a hedgehog named "Sonic." His incredible speed as he dashed across the screen won him many fans. A year later, *Sonic the Hedgehog 2* was released. It introduced Sonic's sidekick, Miles "Tails" Prower, and a new player-vs-player mode. As the star of Sega's flagship title, Sonic soon became the company's mascot.

Mr. Why: Oh yeah! Now I remember seeing pictures of him around arcades and stuff.

Dr. Onigiri: The black mouse of a certain magical kingdom, Nintendo's yellow and black mouse-thing, and Sega's blue rodent... It's amazing how many mascots out there are rodents.

Prof. Mushroom: You've gotta be kidding me...

TO BE CONTINUED...

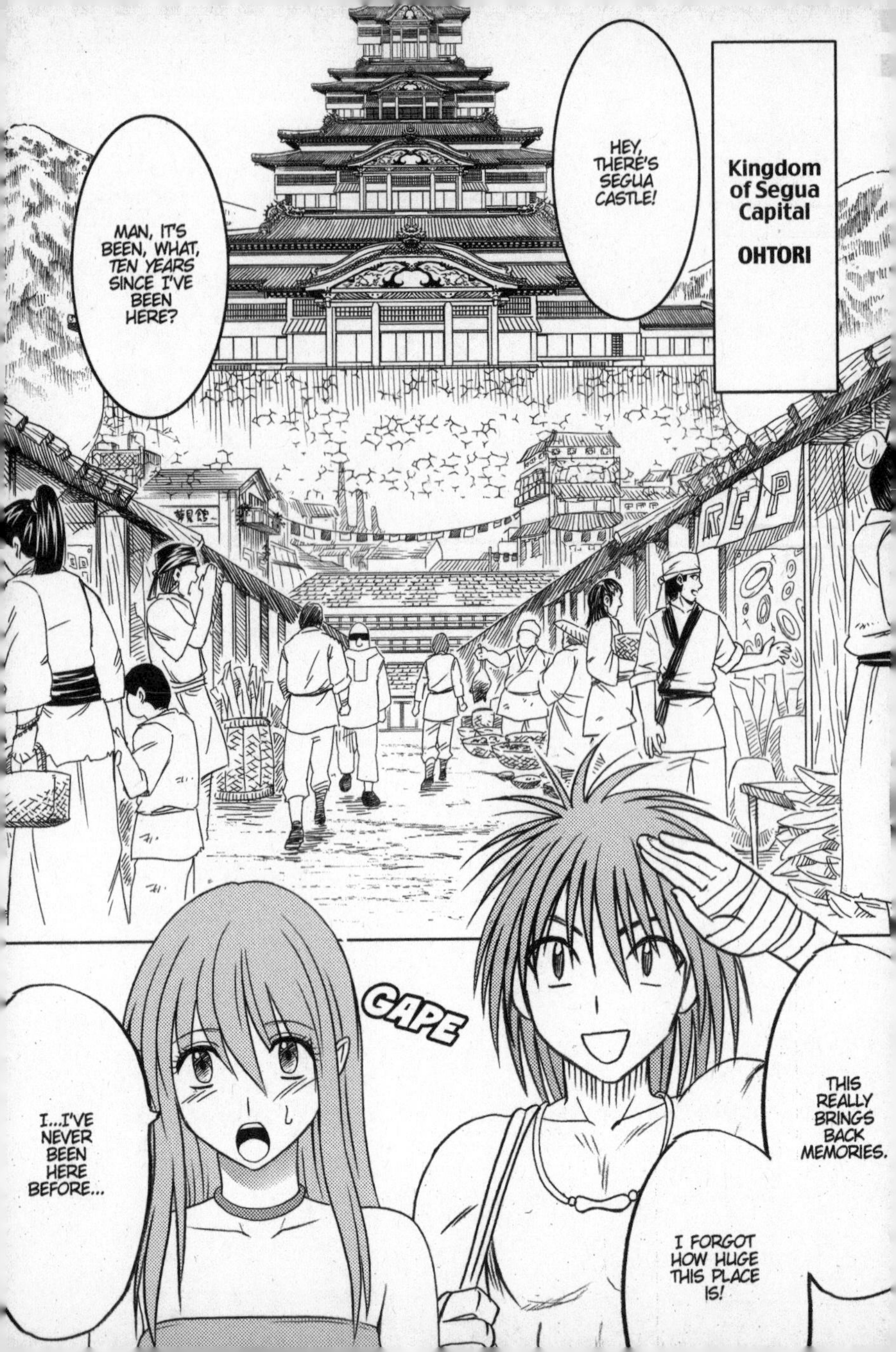
Kingdom of Segua Capital
OHTORI
HEY, THERE'S SEGUA CASTLE!
MAN, IT'S BEEN, WHAT, TEN YEARS SINCE I'VE BEEN HERE?
THIS REALLY BRINGS BACK MEMORIES.
I FORGOT HOW HUGE THIS PLACE IS!
GAPE
I...I'VE NEVER BEEN HERE BEFORE...

CHAPTER 2

HARD(WARE) BATTLE

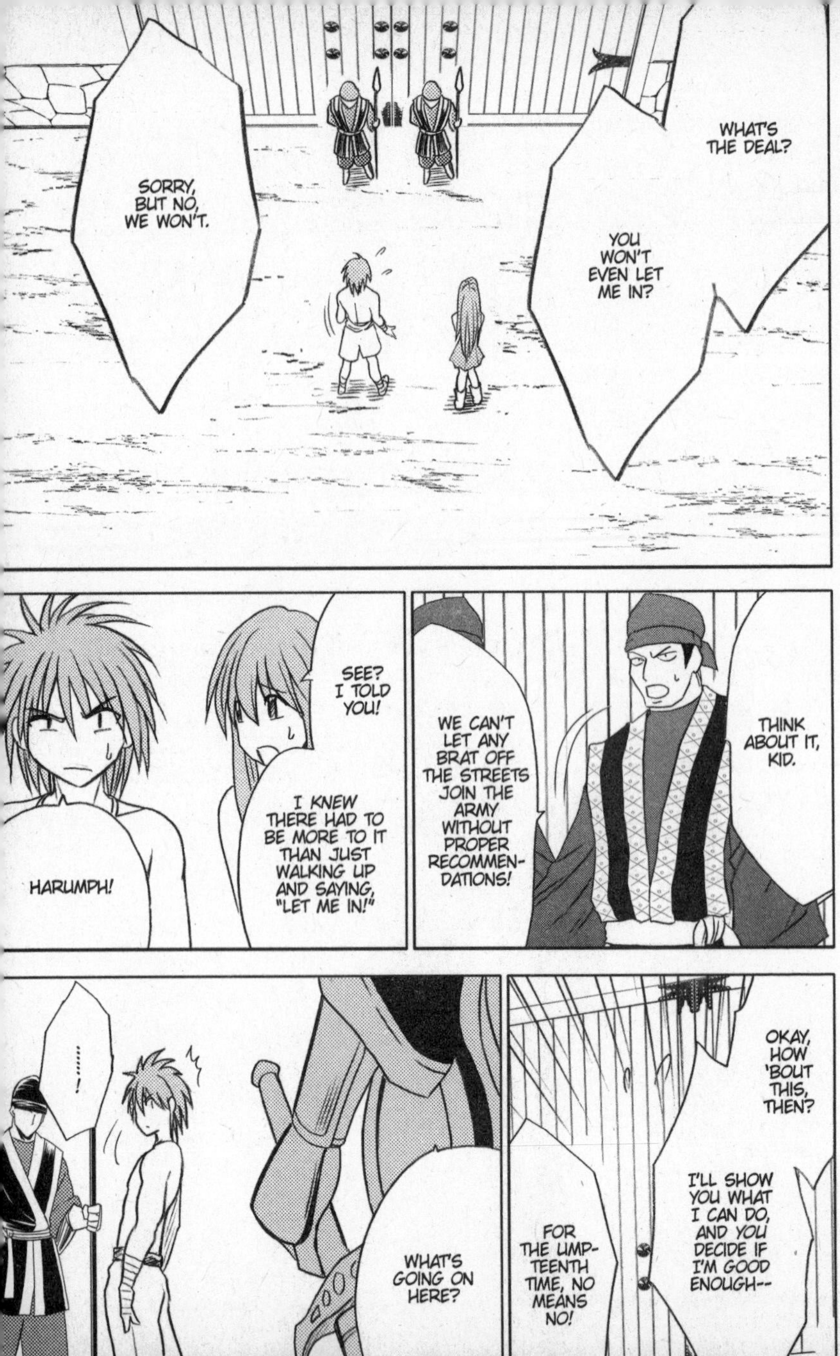
WHAT'S THE DEAL?
YOU WON'T EVEN LET ME IN?
SORRY, BUT NO, WE WON'T.
THINK ABOUT IT, KID.
WE CAN'T LET ANY BRAT OFF THE STREETS JOIN THE ARMY WITHOUT PROPER RECOMMEN-DATIONS!
SEE? I TOLD YOU!
I KNEW THERE HAD TO BE MORE TO IT THAN JUST WALKING UP AND SAYING, "LET ME IN!"
HARUMPH!
OKAY, HOW 'BOUT THIS, THEN?
I'LL SHOW YOU WHAT I CAN DO, AND YOU DECIDE IF I'M GOOD ENOUGH--
FOR THE UMP-TEENTH TIME, NO MEANS NO!
WHAT'S GOING ON HERE?
......!

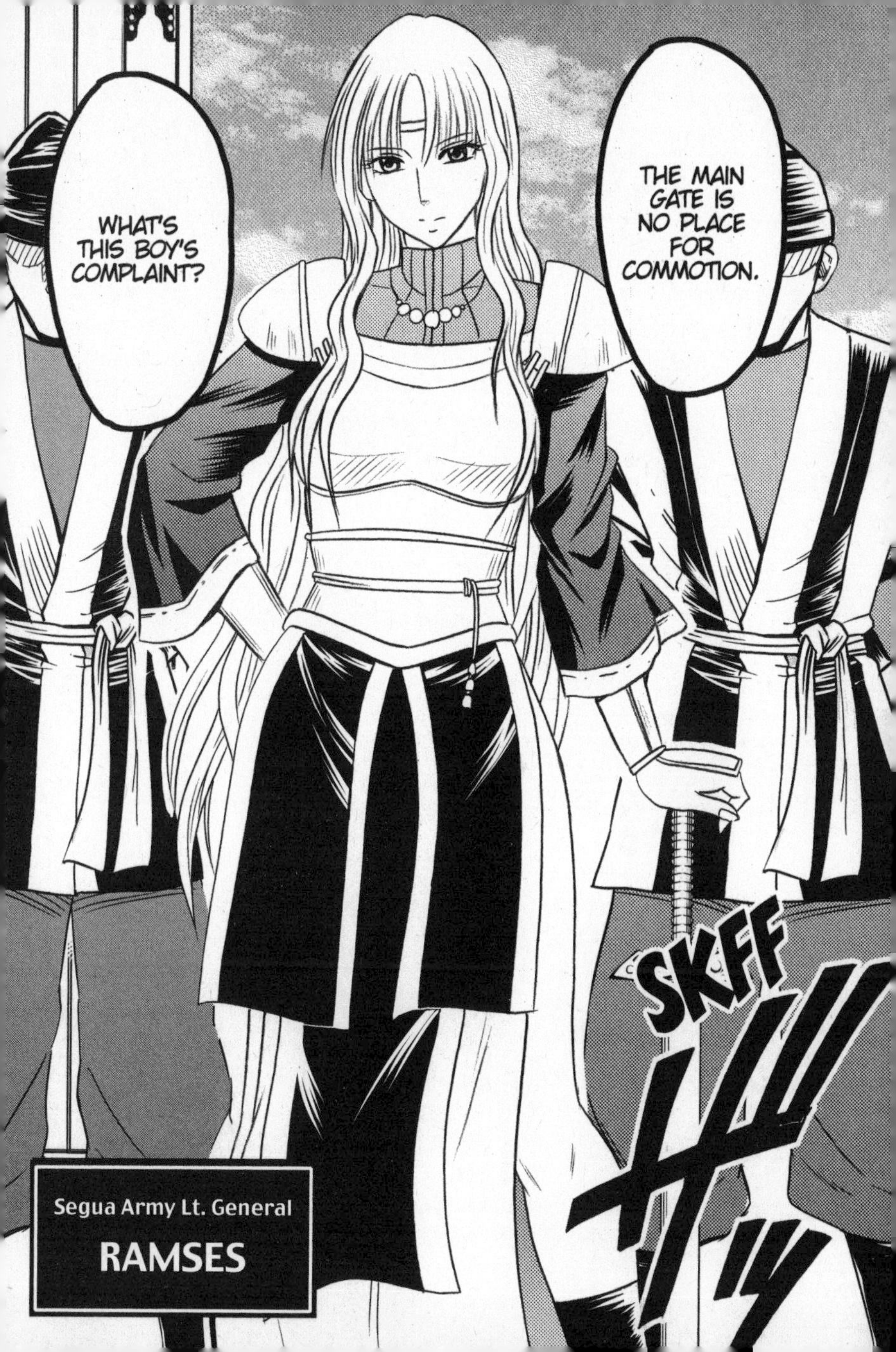
THE MAIN GATE IS NO PLACE FOR COMMOTION.
WHAT'S THIS BOY'S COMPLAINT?
SKFF
Segua Army Lt. General
RAMSES

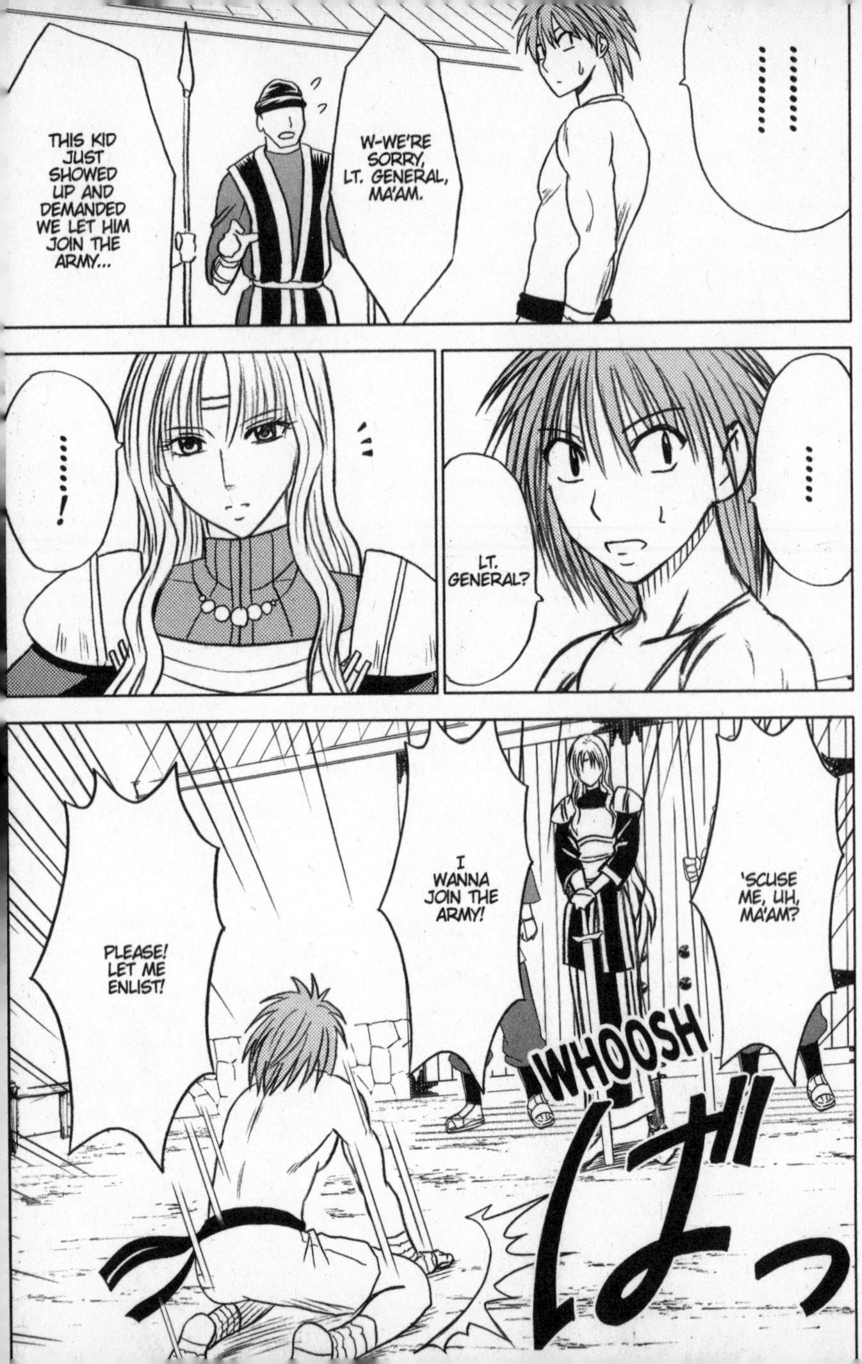
......
W-WE'RE SORRY, LT. GENERAL, MA'AM.
THIS KID JUST SHOWED UP AND DEMANDED WE LET HIM JOIN THE ARMY...
......
LT. GENERAL?
......!
'SCUSE ME, UH, MA'AM?
I WANNA JOIN THE ARMY!
PLEASE! LET ME ENLIST!
WHOOSH
ばっ

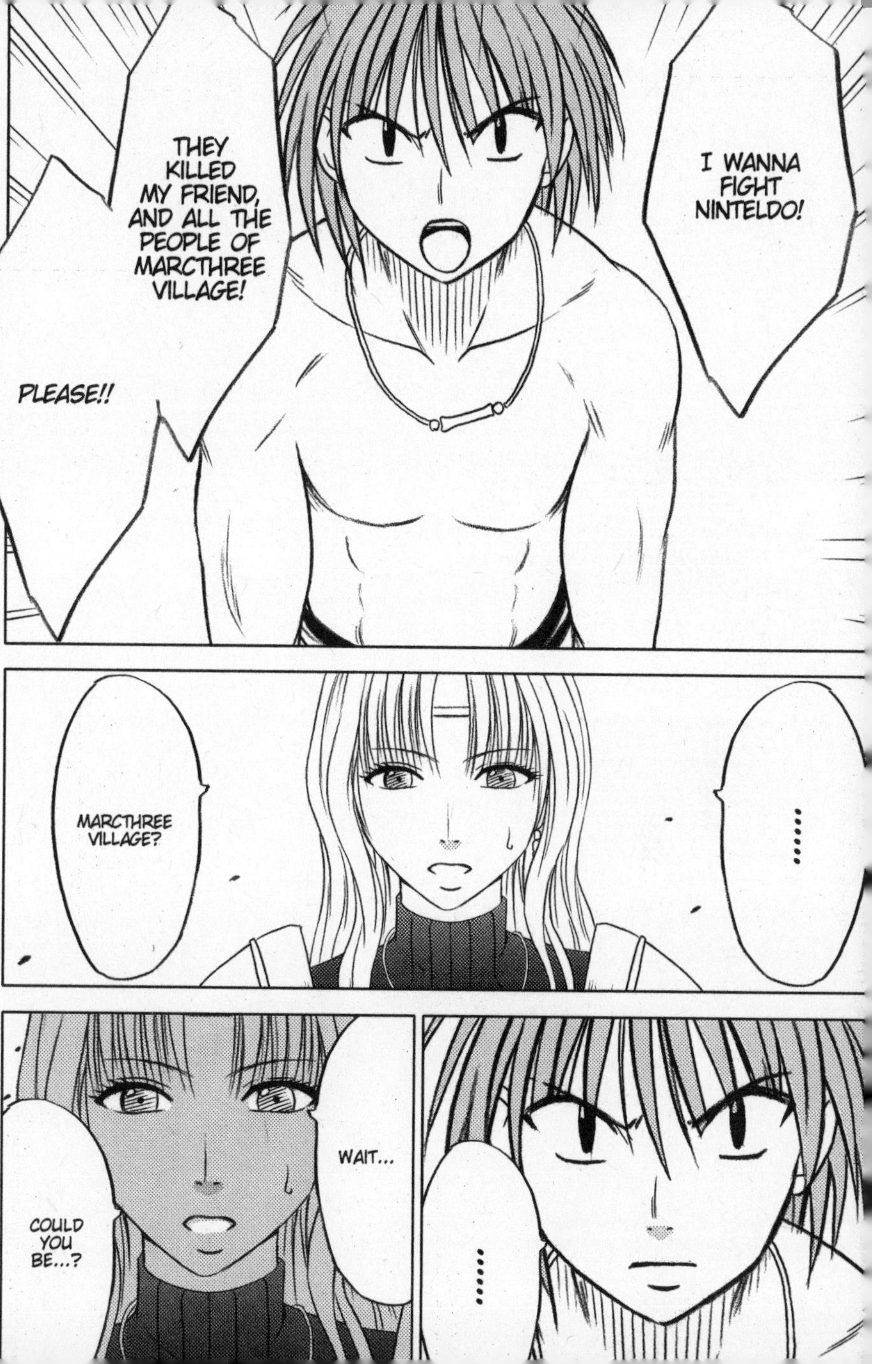
I WANNA FIGHT NINTELDO!
THEY KILLED MY FRIEND, AND ALL THE PEOPLE OF MARCHTHREE VILLAGE!
PLEASE!!
......
MARCHTHREE VILLAGE?
......
WAIT...
COULD YOU BE...?

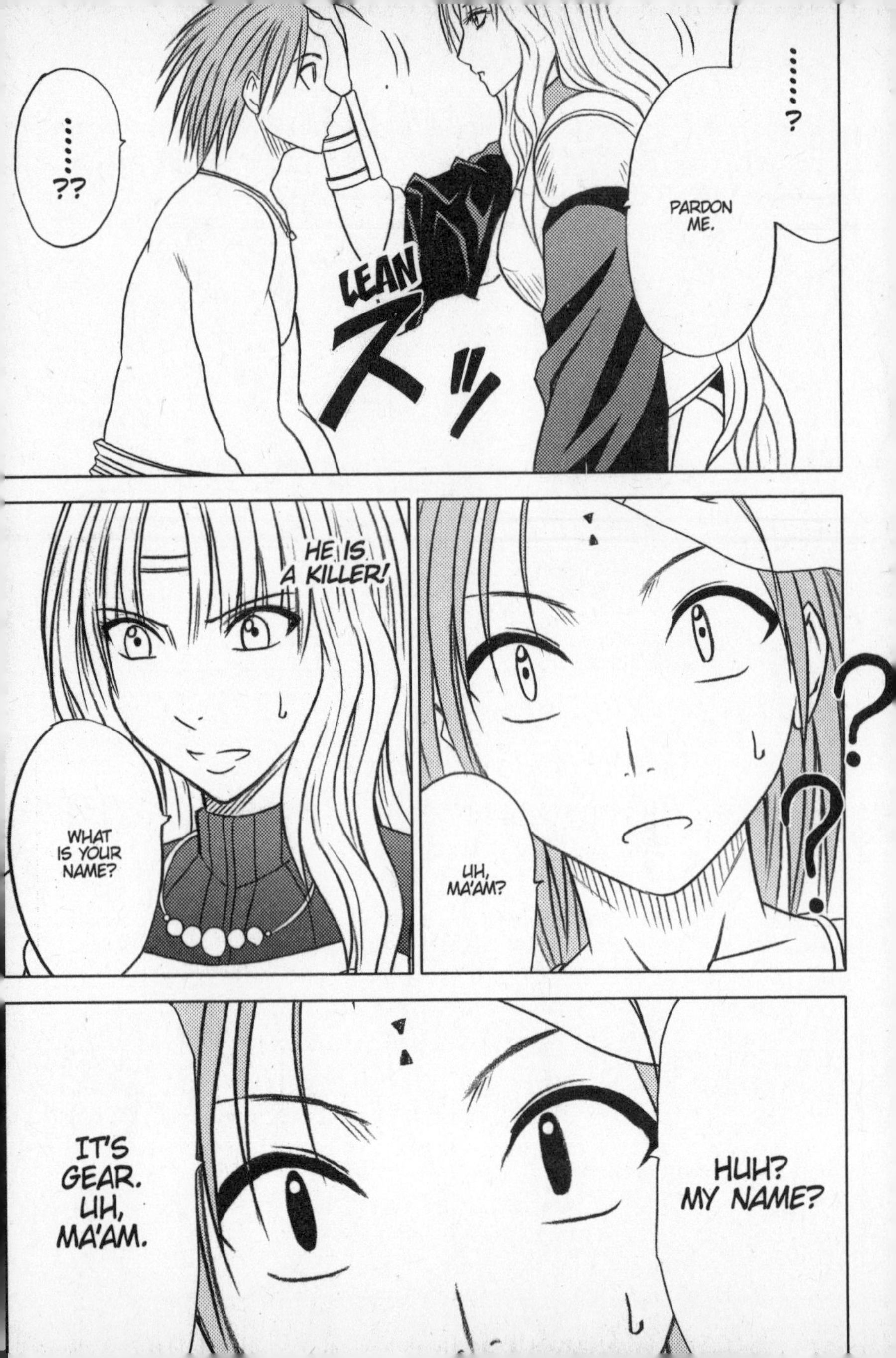

......?
PARDON ME.
LEAN
ズッ
......??
UH, MA'AM?
HE IS A KILLER!
WHAT IS YOUR NAME?
HUH? MY NAME?
IT'S GEAR. UH, MA'AM.

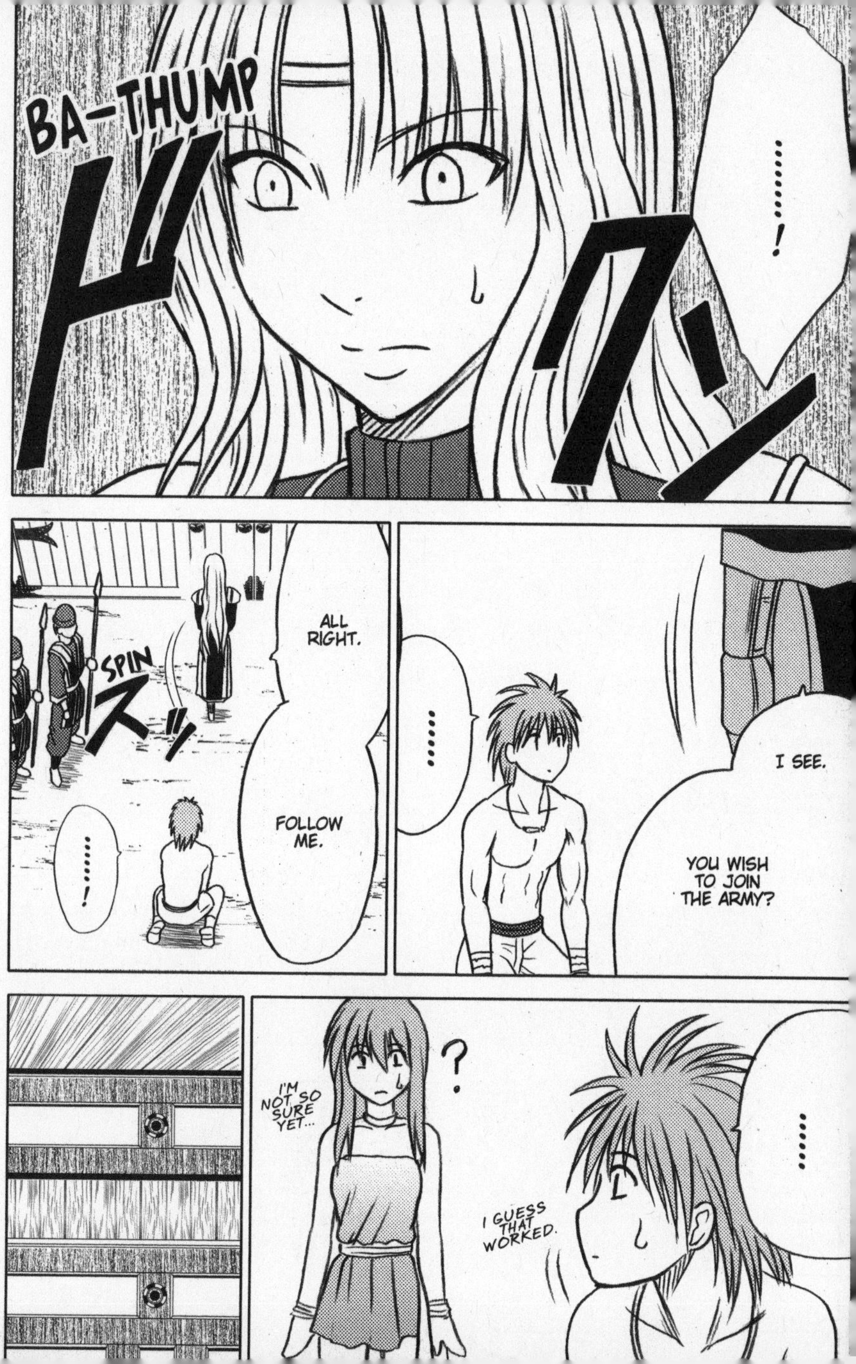
......!
BA-THUMP
I SEE.
YOU WISH TO JOIN THE ARMY?
......
ALL RIGHT.
FOLLOW ME.
SPIN
......!
......
I GUESS THAT WORKED.
?
I'M NOT SO SURE YET...

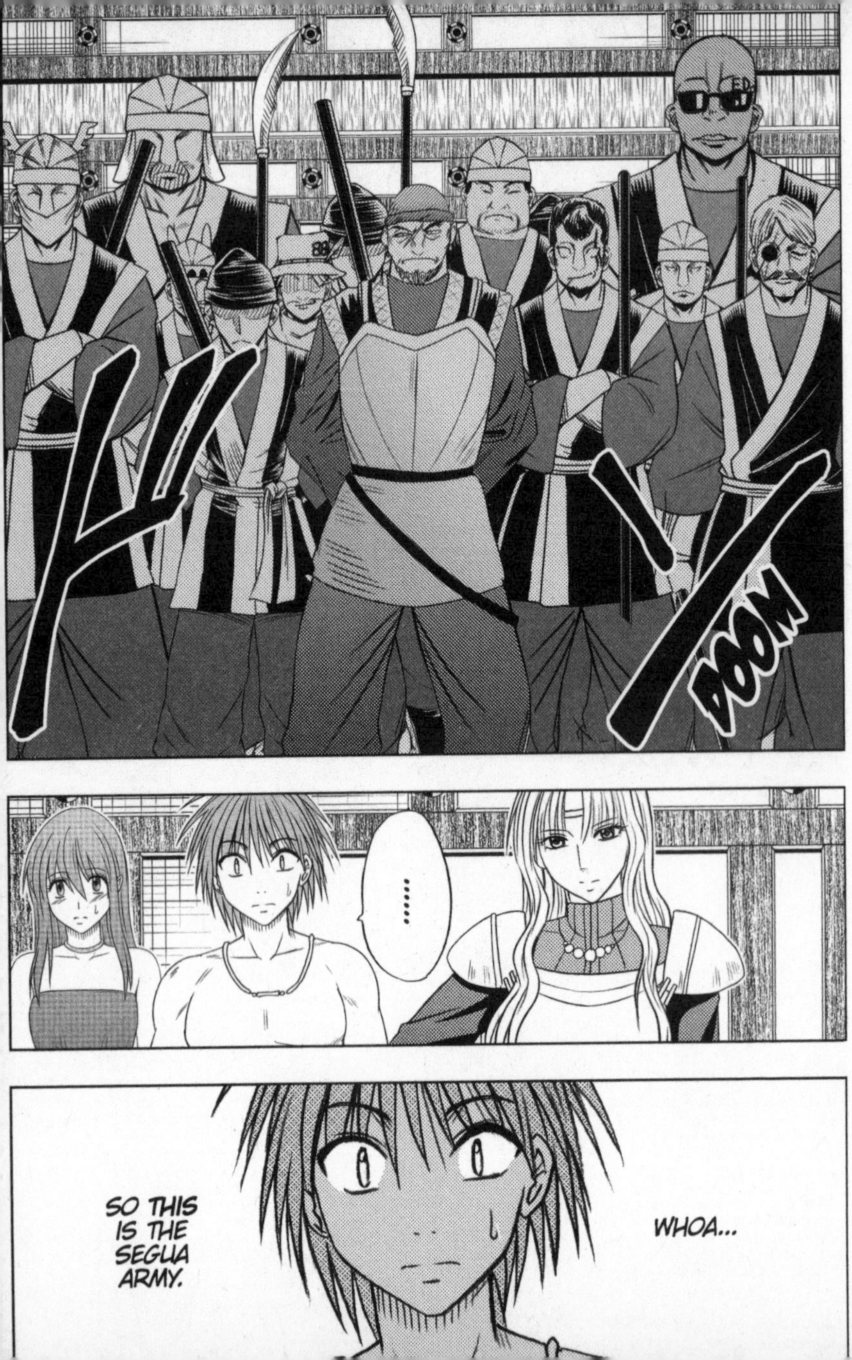
DOOM
......
WHOA...
SO THIS IS THE SEGUA ARMY.

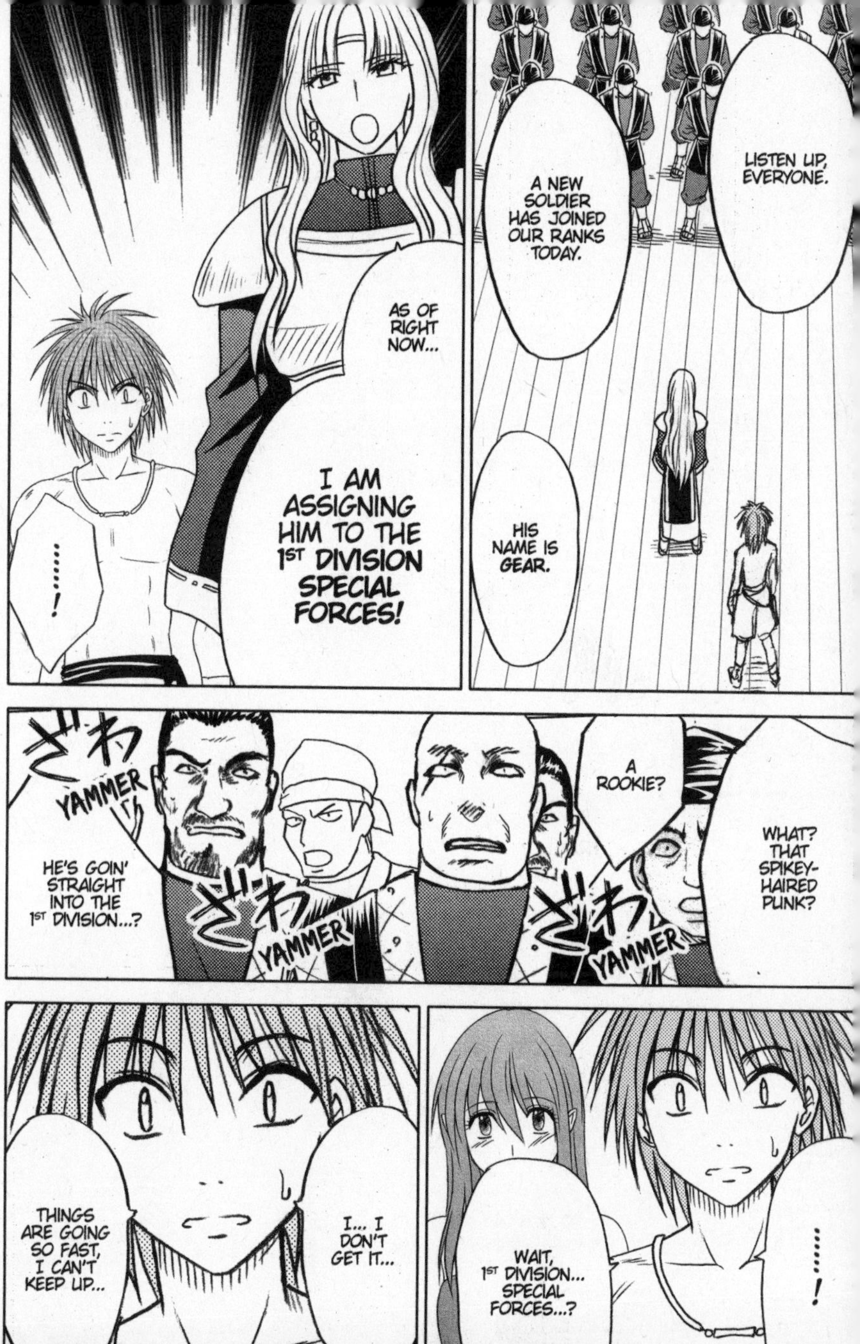
LISTEN UP, EVERYONE.
A NEW SOLDIER HAS JOINED OUR RANKS TODAY.
HIS NAME IS GEAR.
AS OF RIGHT NOW...
I AM ASSIGNING HIM TO THE 1ST DIVISION SPECIAL FORCES!
......!
A ROOKIE?
WHAT? THAT SPIKEY-HAIRED PUNK?
ざわ
YAMMER
ざわ
YAMMER
ざわ
YAMMER
HE'S GOIN' STRAIGHT INTO THE 1ST DIVISION...?
......!
WAIT, 1ST DIVISION... SPECIAL FORCES...?
I... I DON'T GET IT...
THINGS ARE GOING SO FAST, I CAN'T KEEP UP...

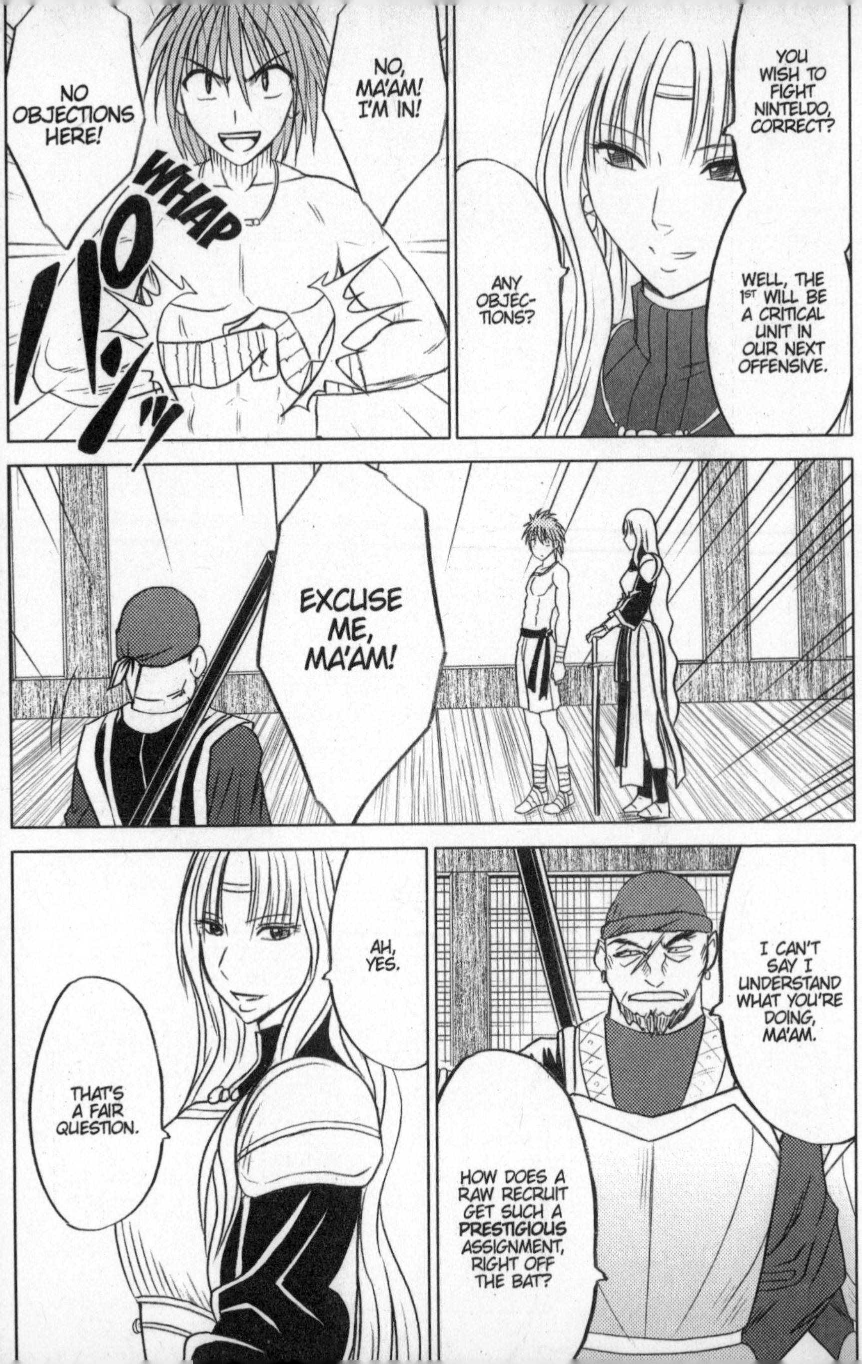
YOU WISH TO FIGHT NINTELDO, CORRECT?
WELL, THE 1ST WILL BE A CRITICAL UNIT IN OUR NEXT OFFENSIVE.
ANY OBJECTIONS?
NO, MA'AM! I'M IN!
NO OBJECTIONS HERE!
WHAP
EXCUSE ME, MA'AM!
I CAN'T SAY I UNDERSTAND WHAT YOU'RE DOING, MA'AM.
HOW DOES A RAW RECRUIT GET SUCH A PRESTIGIOUS ASSIGNMENT, RIGHT OFF THE BAT?
AH, YES.
THAT'S A FAIR QUESTION.

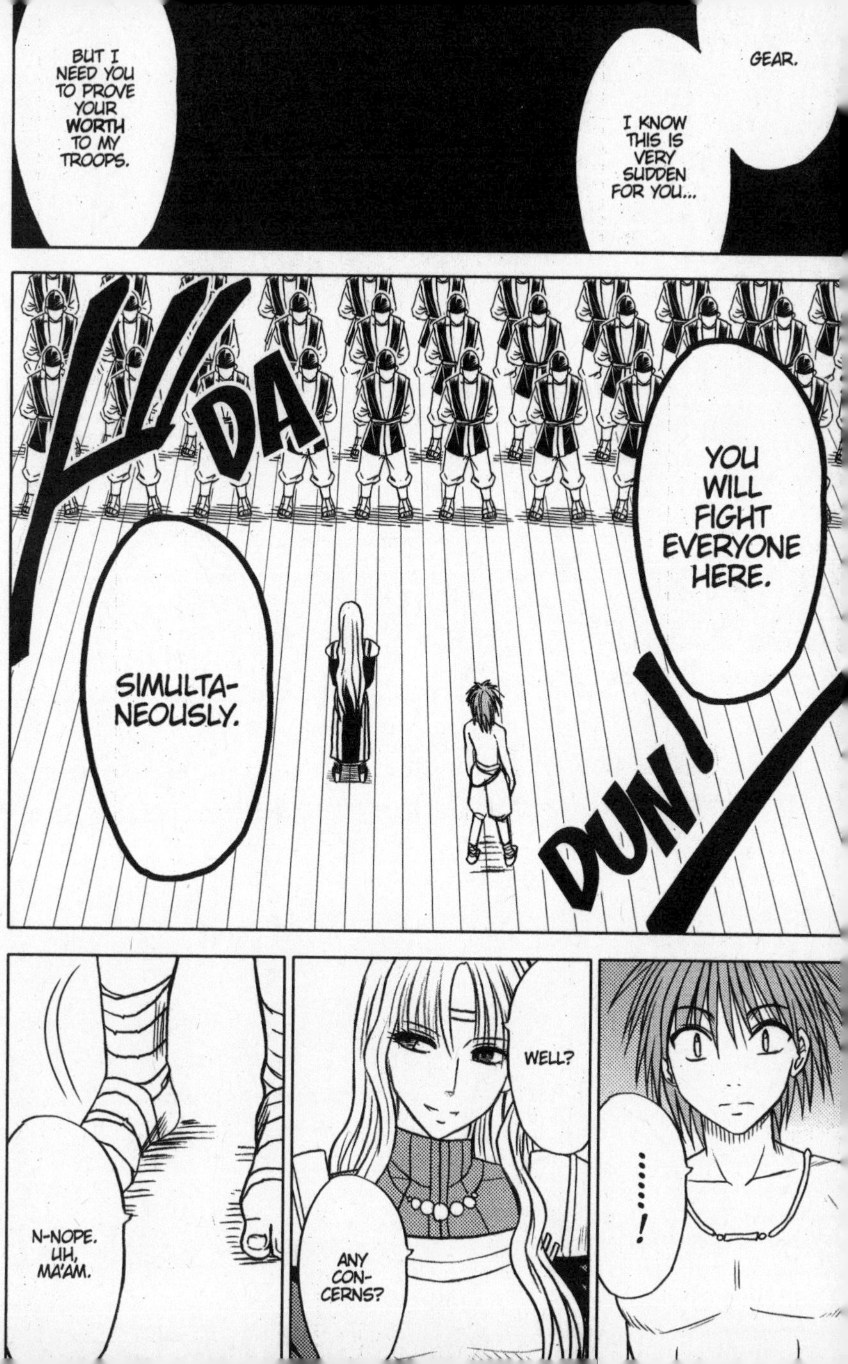
GEAR.
I KNOW THIS IS VERY SUDDEN FOR YOU...
BUT I NEED YOU TO PROVE YOUR WORTH TO MY TROOPS.
YOU WILL FIGHT EVERYONE HERE.
DUN!
SIMULTA-NEOUSLY.
DA
......!
WELL?
ANY CON-CERNS?
N-NOPE. UH, MA'AM.

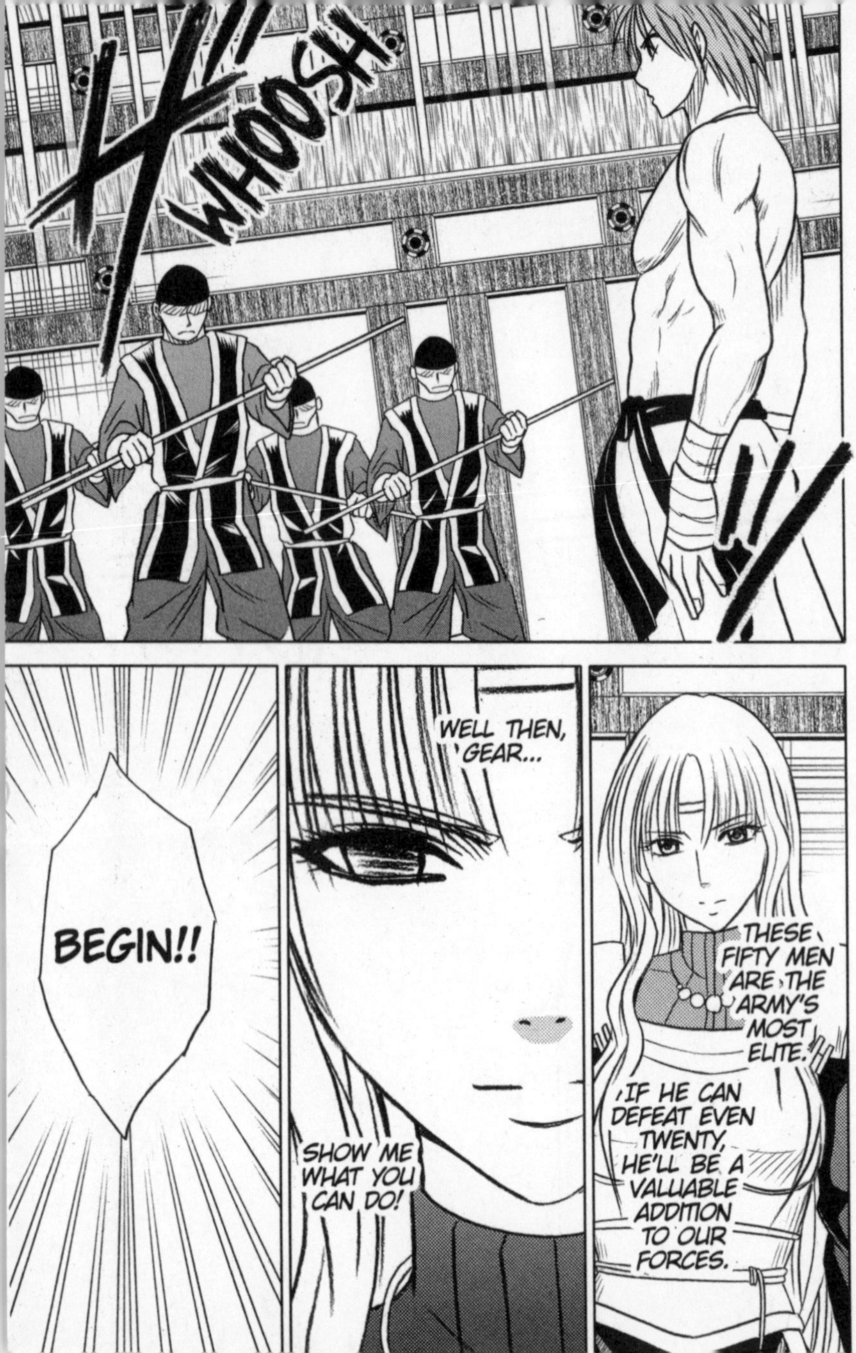
WHOOSH
THESE FIFTY MEN ARE THE ARMY'S MOST ELITE.
IF HE CAN DEFEAT EVEN TWENTY, HE'LL BE A VALUABLE ADDITION TO OUR FORCES.
WELL THEN, GEAR...
SHOW ME WHAT YOU CAN DO!
BEGIN!!

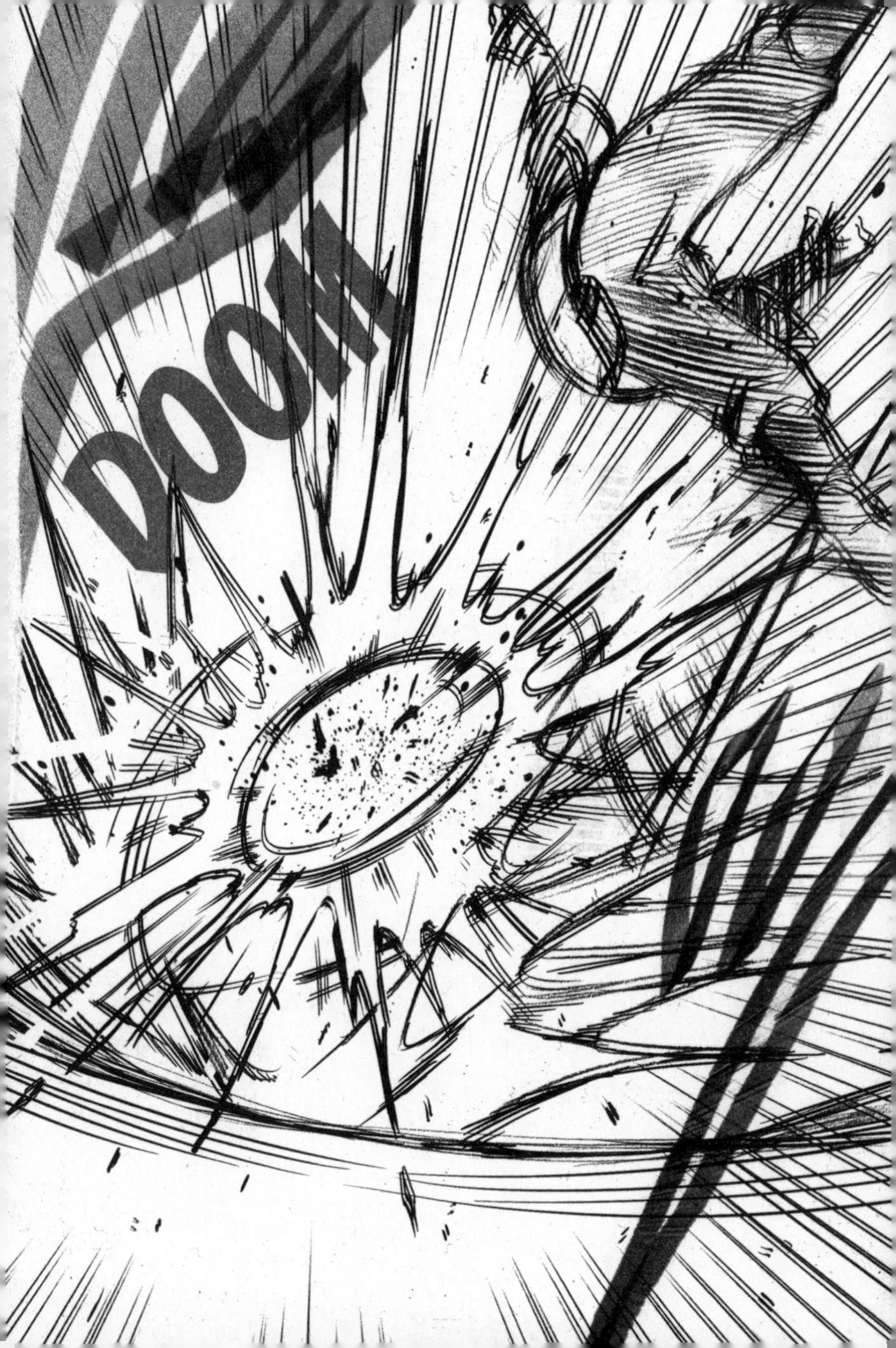
DOOM

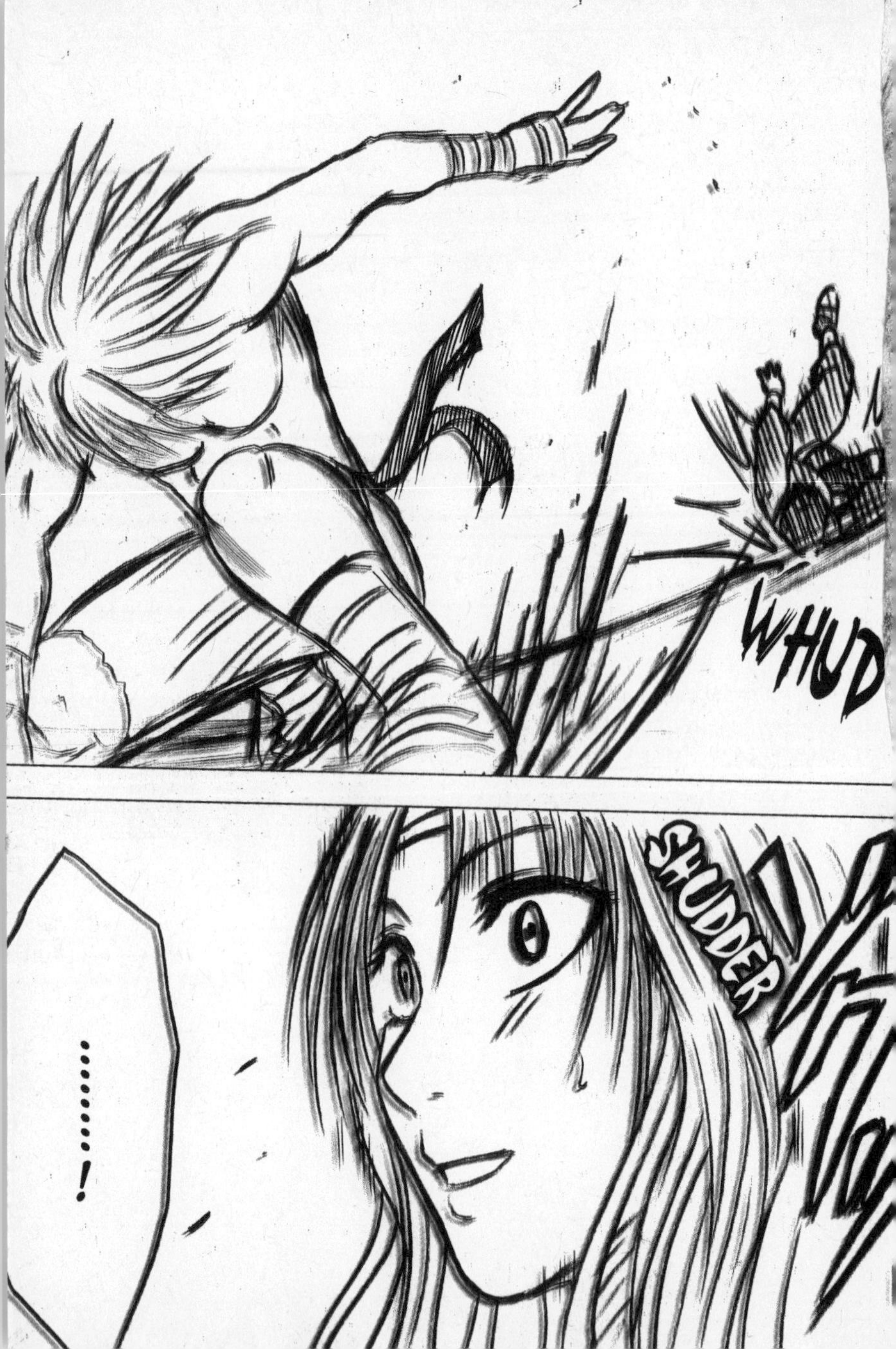
WHUD
SHUDDER
......!

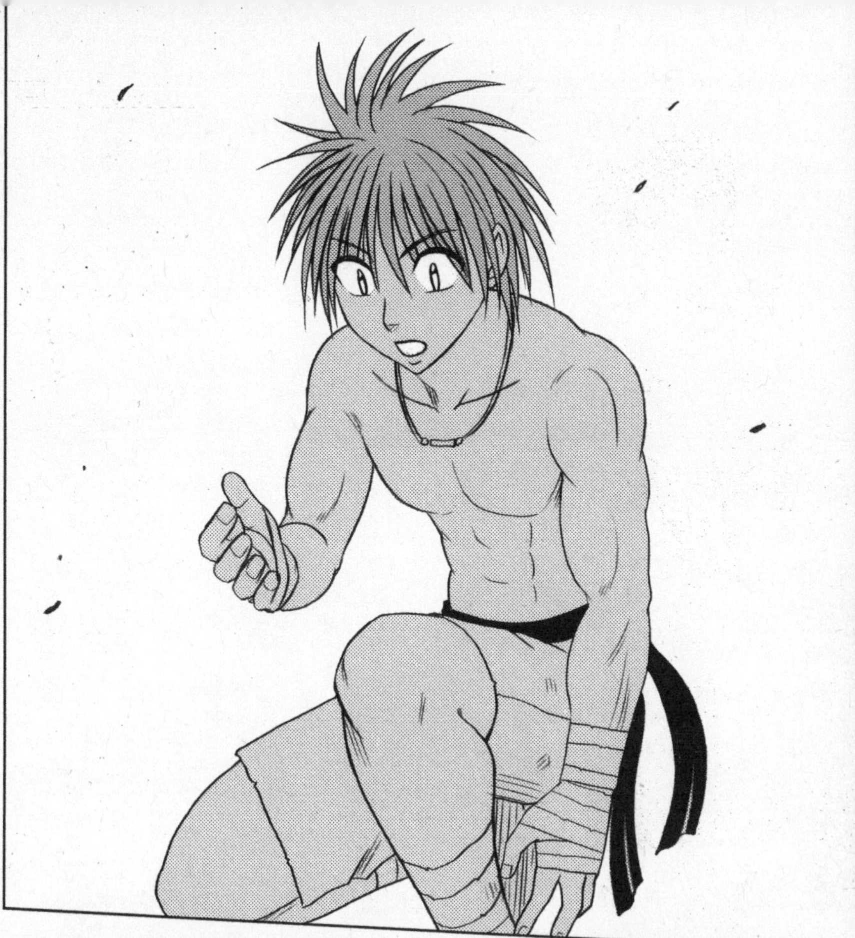

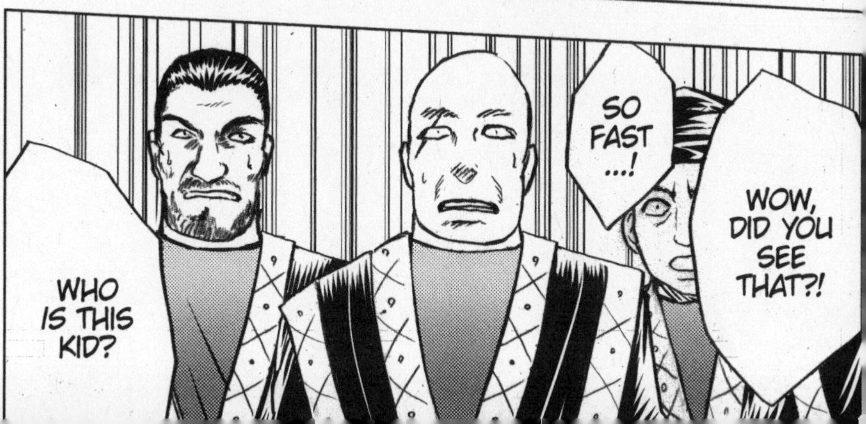
WOW, DID YOU SEE THAT?!
SO FAST ...!
WHO IS THIS KID?

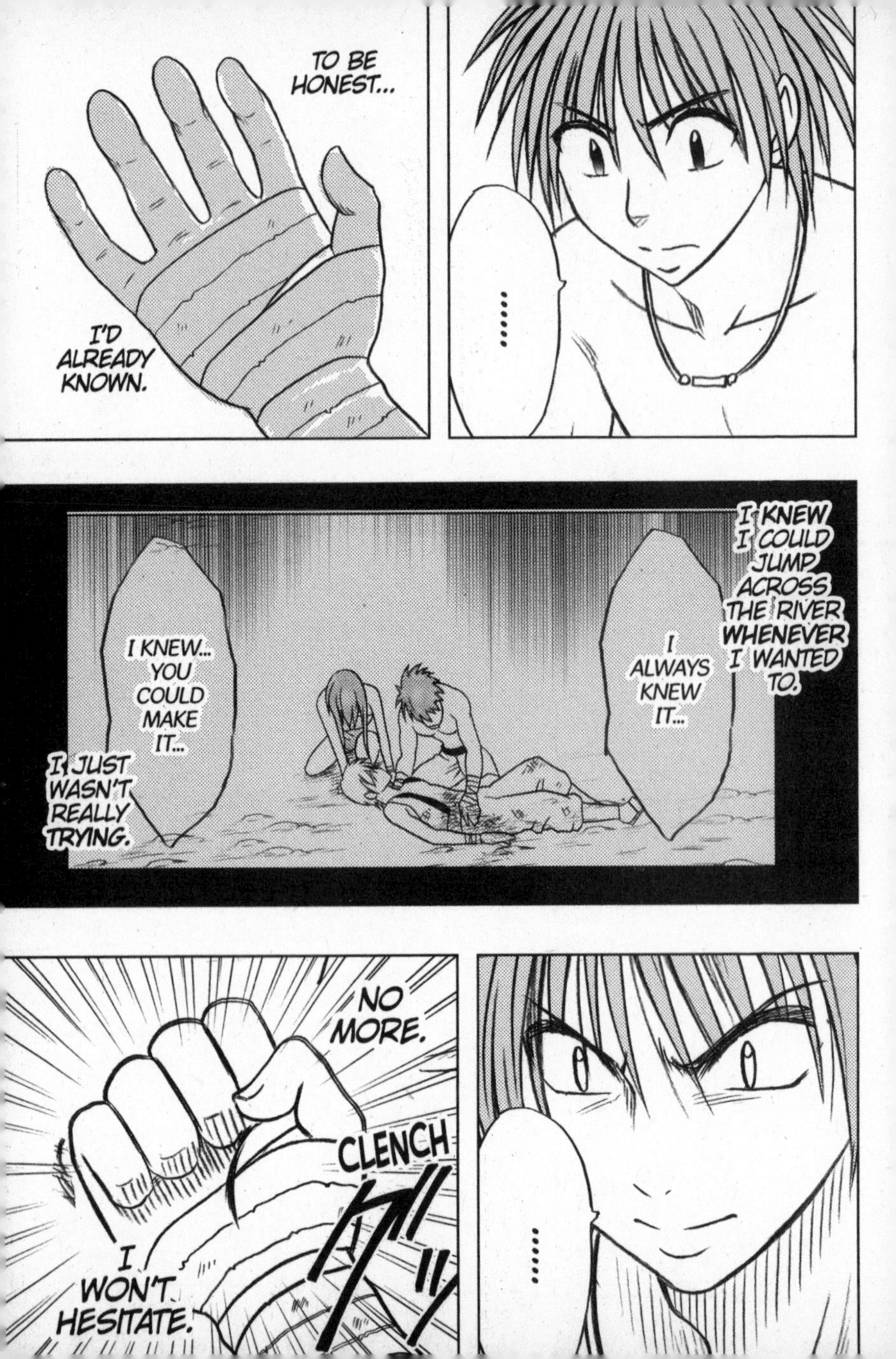
......
TO BE HONEST...
I'D ALREADY KNOWN.
I KNEW I COULD JUMP ACROSS THE RIVER WHENEVER I WANTED TO.
I ALWAYS KNEW IT...
I KNEW... YOU COULD MAKE IT...
I JUST WASN'T REALLY TRYING.
......
NO MORE.
CLENCH
I WON'T HESITATE.

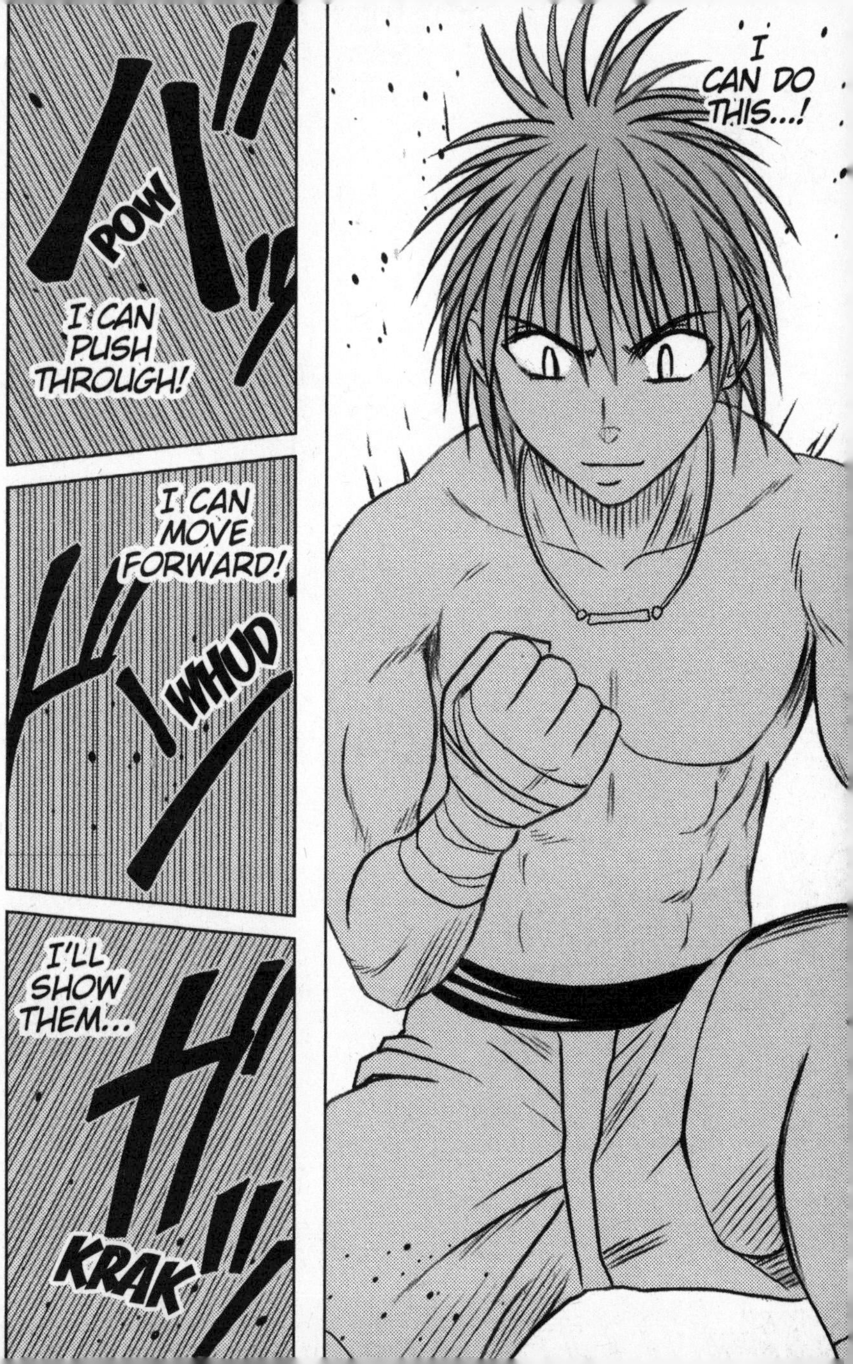
I CAN DO THIS...!
POW
I CAN PUSH THROUGH!
I CAN MOVE FORWARD!
WHUD
I'LL SHOW THEM...
KRAK

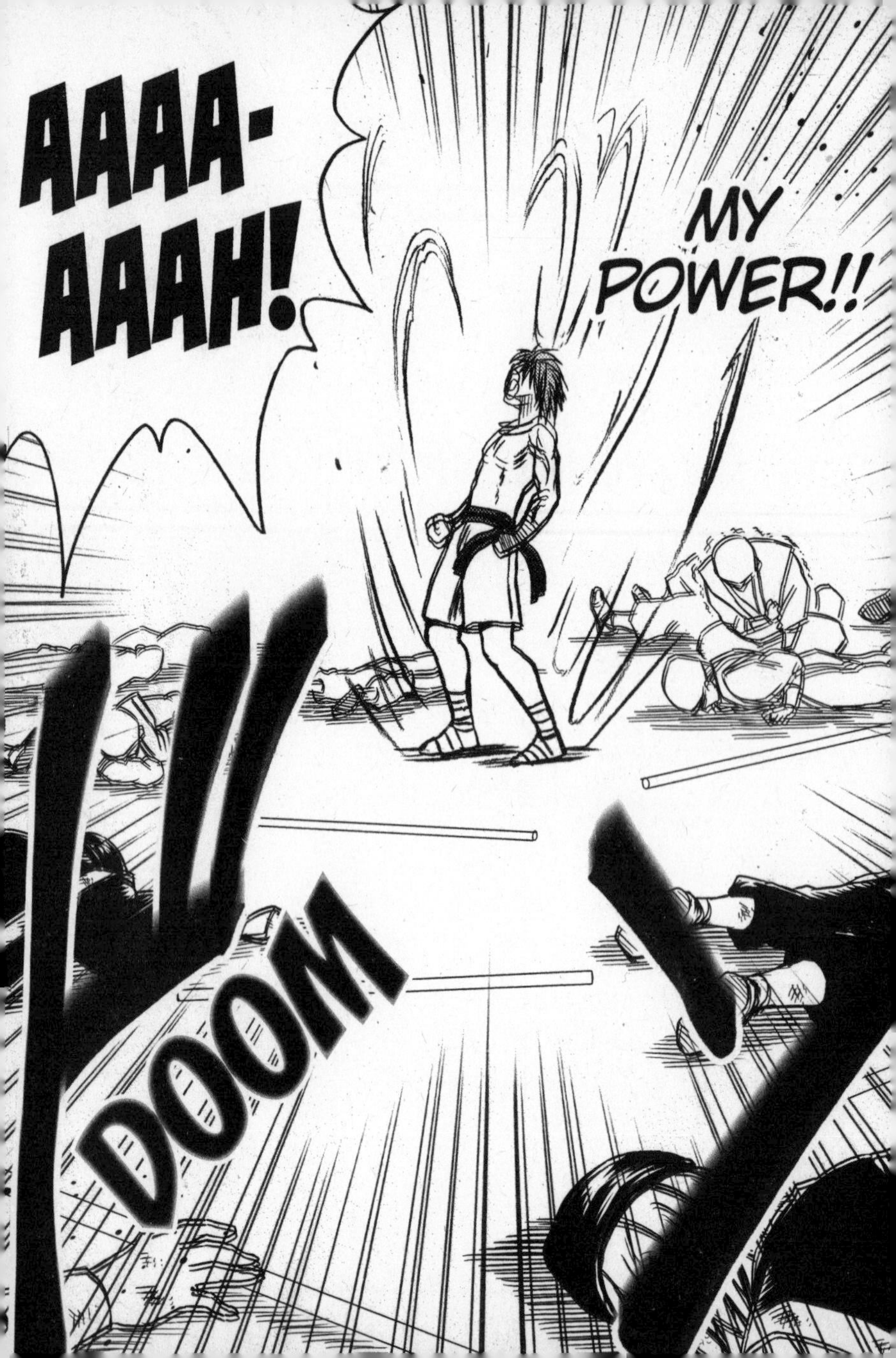
MY POWER!!
AAAA-AAAH!
DOOM

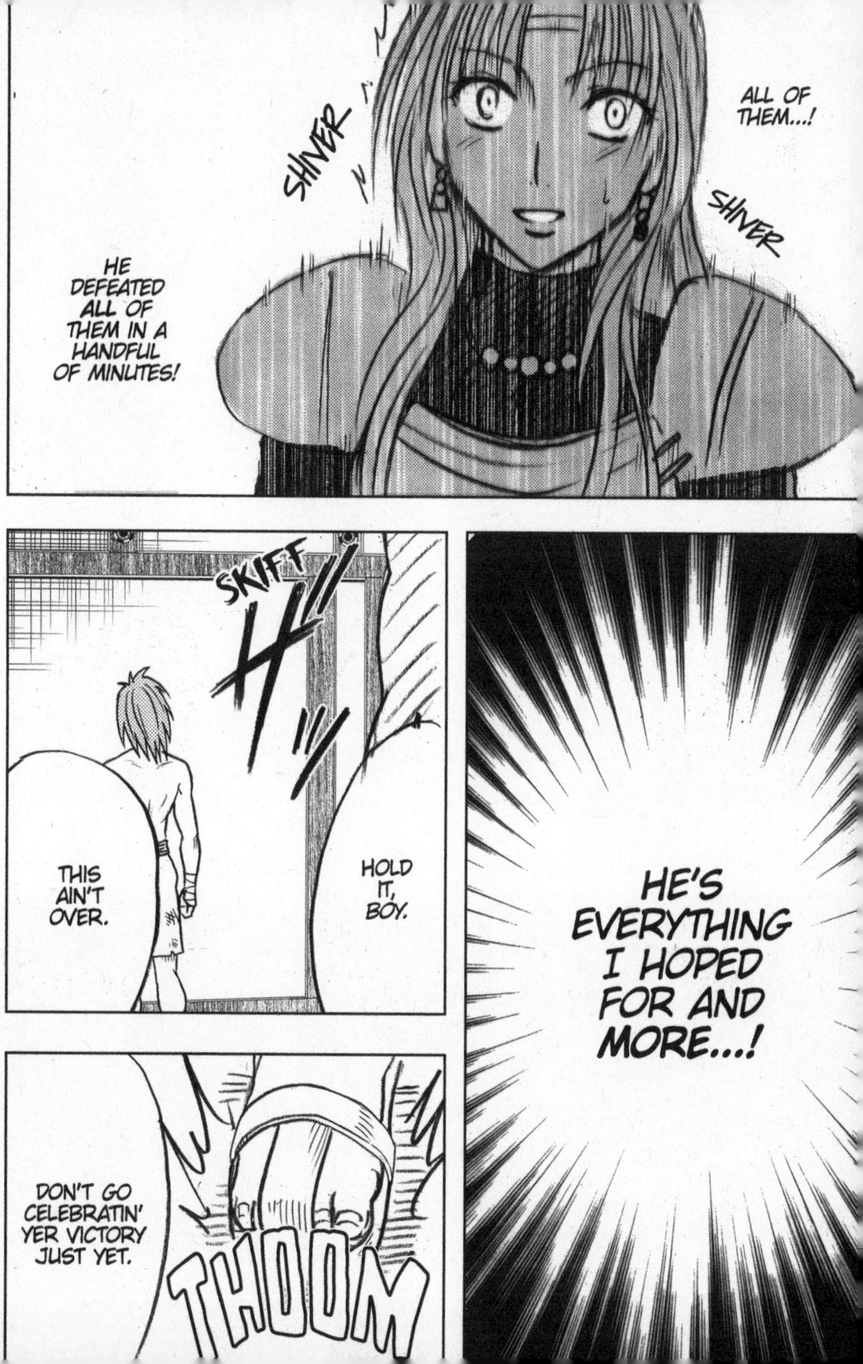
ALL OF THEM...!
SHIVER
SHIVER
HE DEFEATED ALL OF THEM IN A HANDFUL OF MINUTES!
HE'S EVERYTHING I HOPED FOR AND MORE...!
SKIFF
HOLD IT, BOY.
THIS AIN'T OVER.
DON'T GO CELEBRATIN' YER VICTORY JUST YET.
THOOM

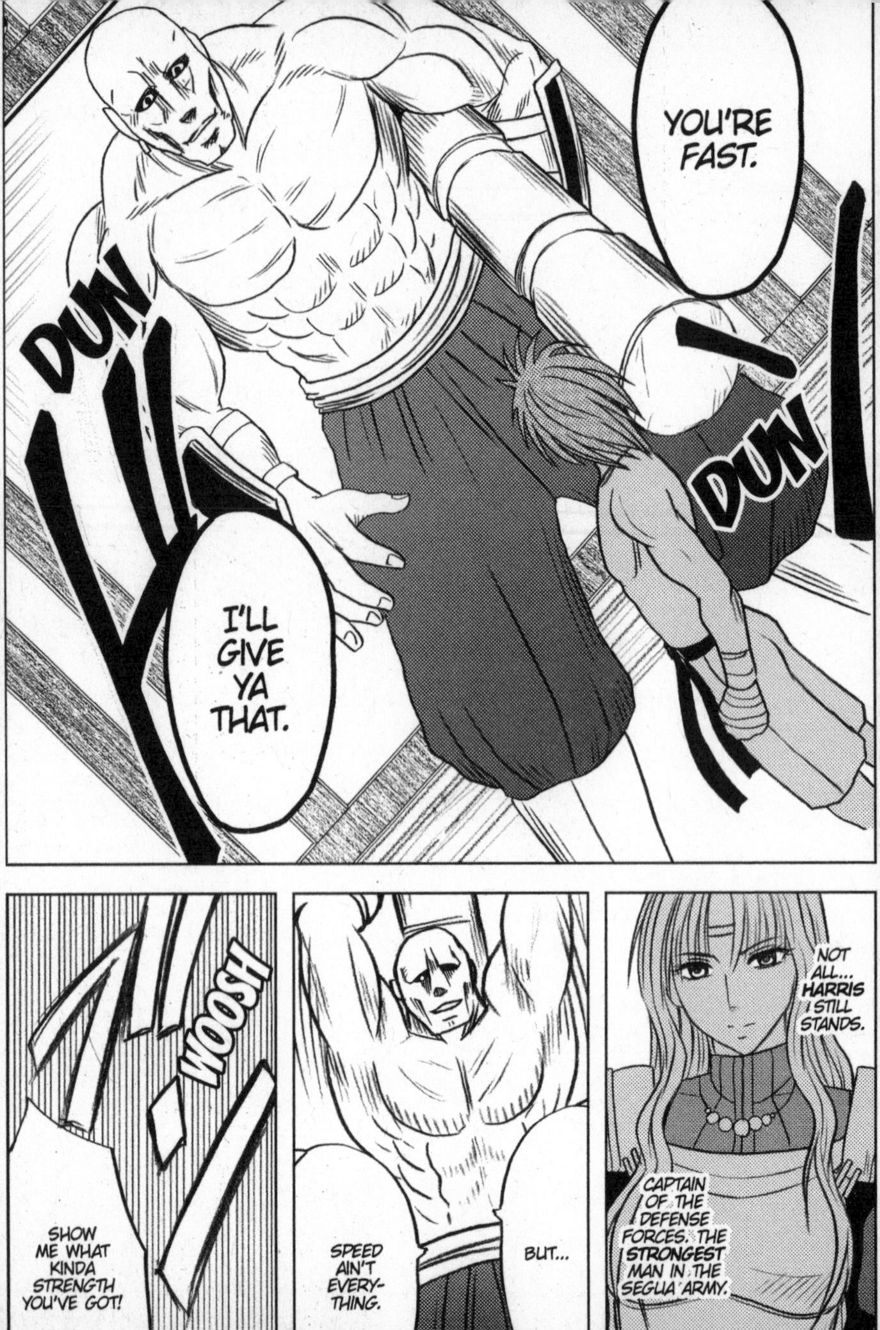
YOU'RE FAST.
DUN
DUN
I'LL GIVE YA THAT.
NOT ALL... HARRIS STILL STANDS.
CAPTAIN OF THE DEFENSE FORCES. THE STRONGEST MAN IN THE SEGUA ARMY.
BUT...
SPEED AIN'T EVERYTHING.
WOOSH
SHOW ME WHAT KINDA STRENGTH YOU'VE GOT!

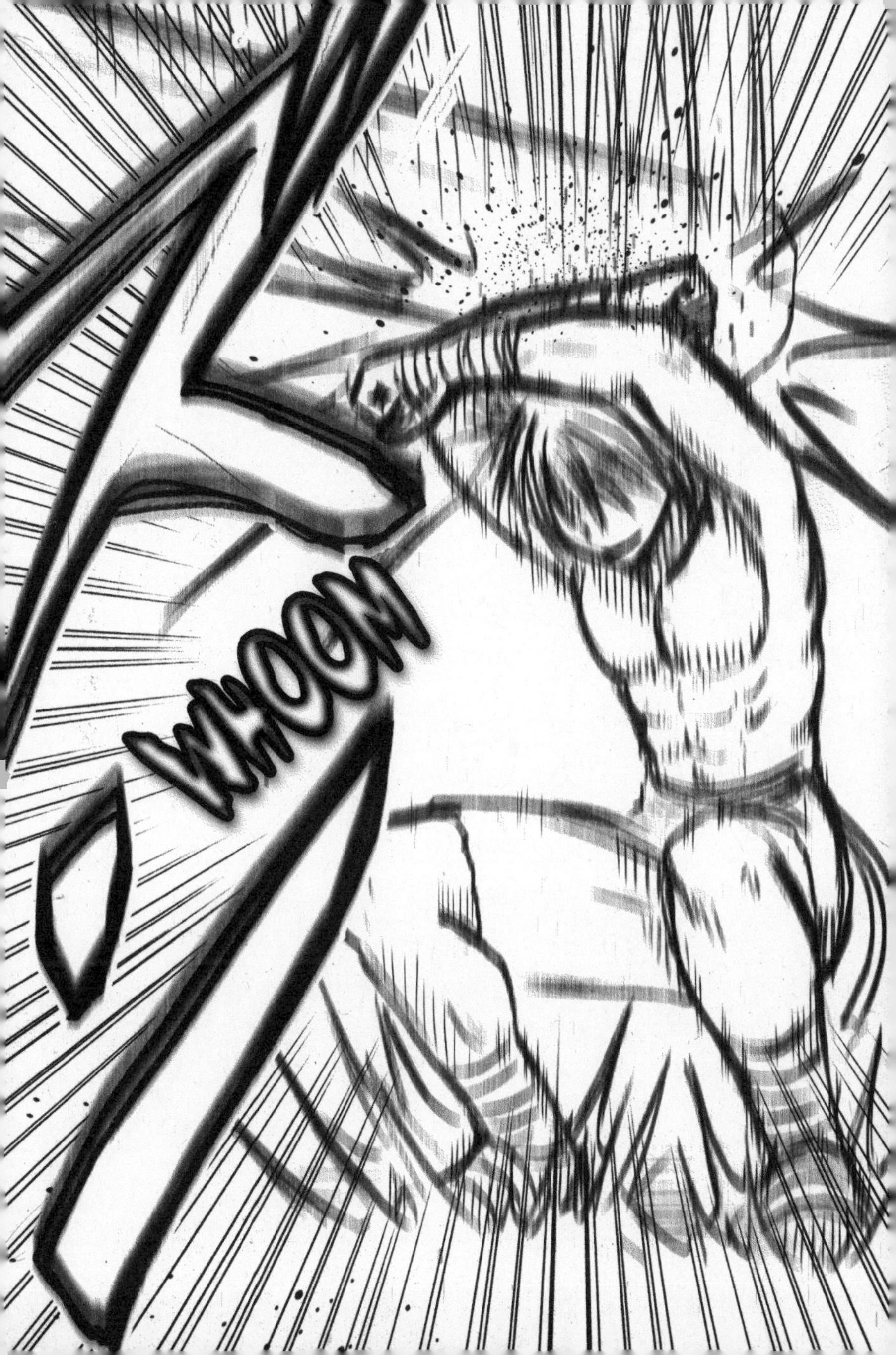
WHOOM

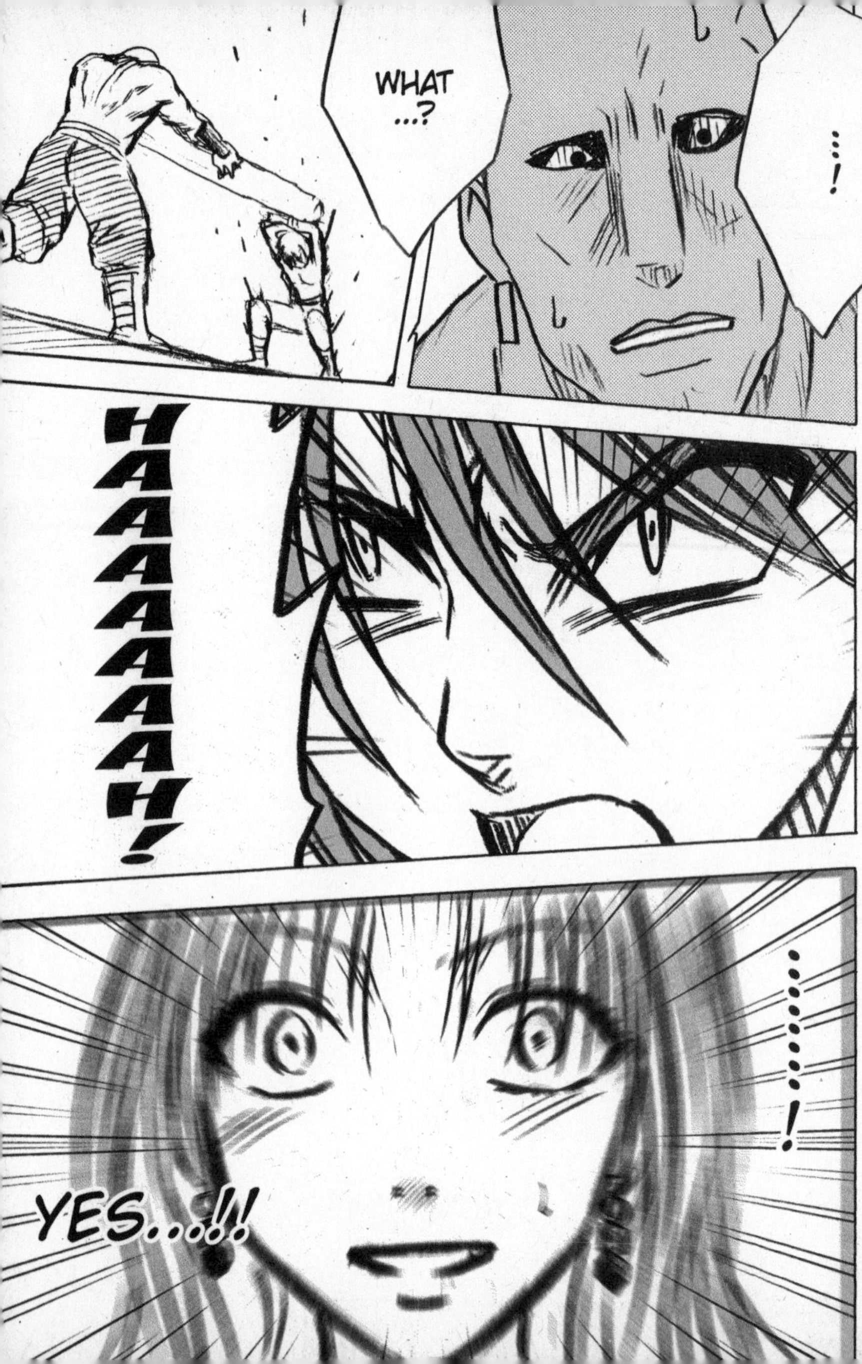
...!
WHAT ...?
HAAAAAAAH!
......!
YES...!!

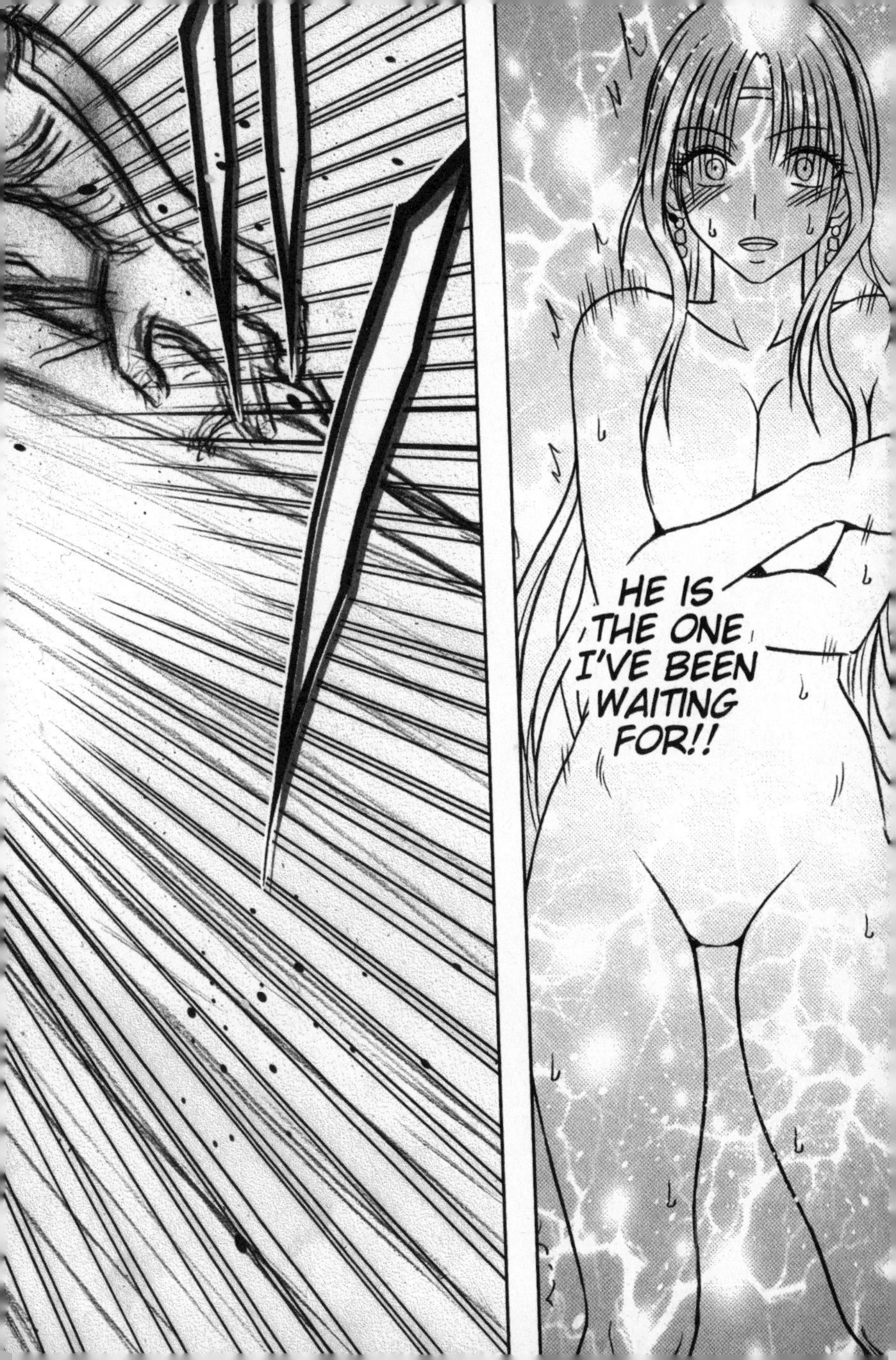
HE IS THE ONE I'VE BEEN WAITING FOR!!

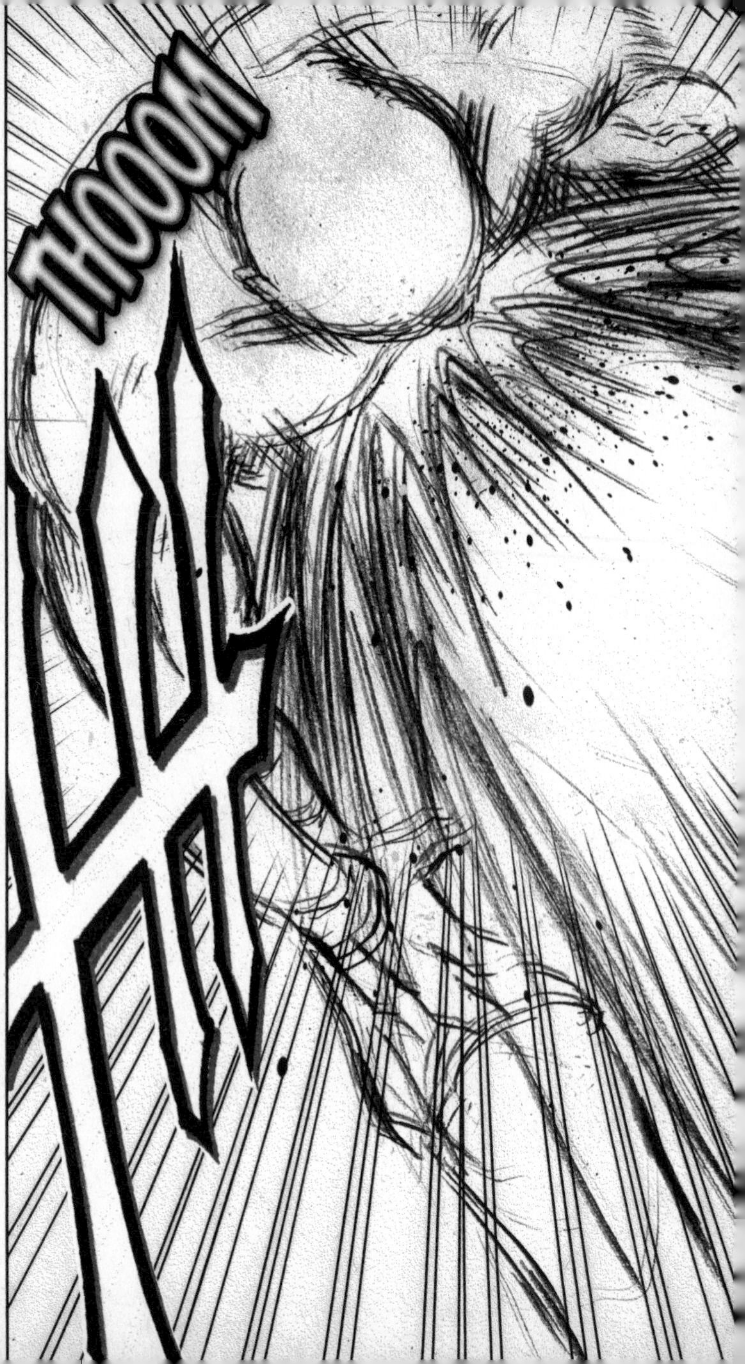
THOOOM

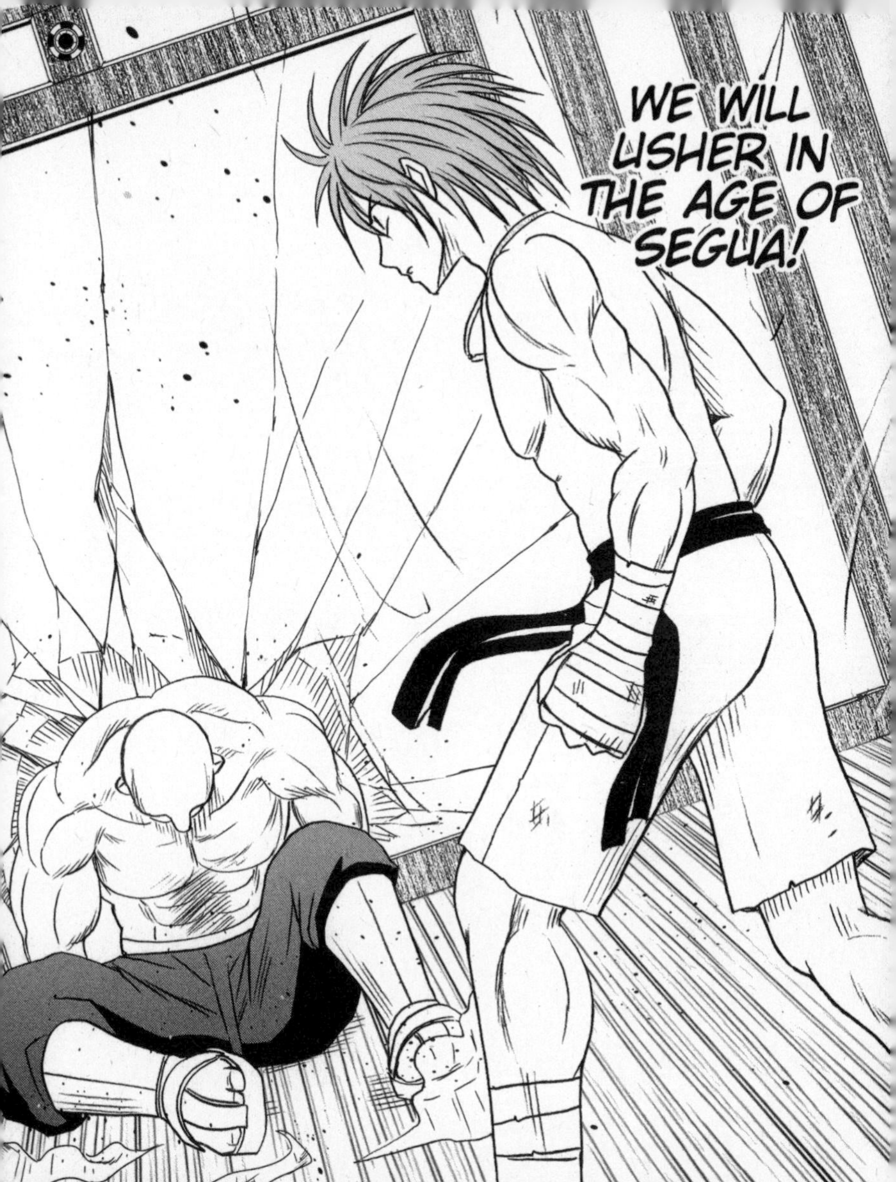
WE WILL USHER IN THE AGE OF SEGUA!

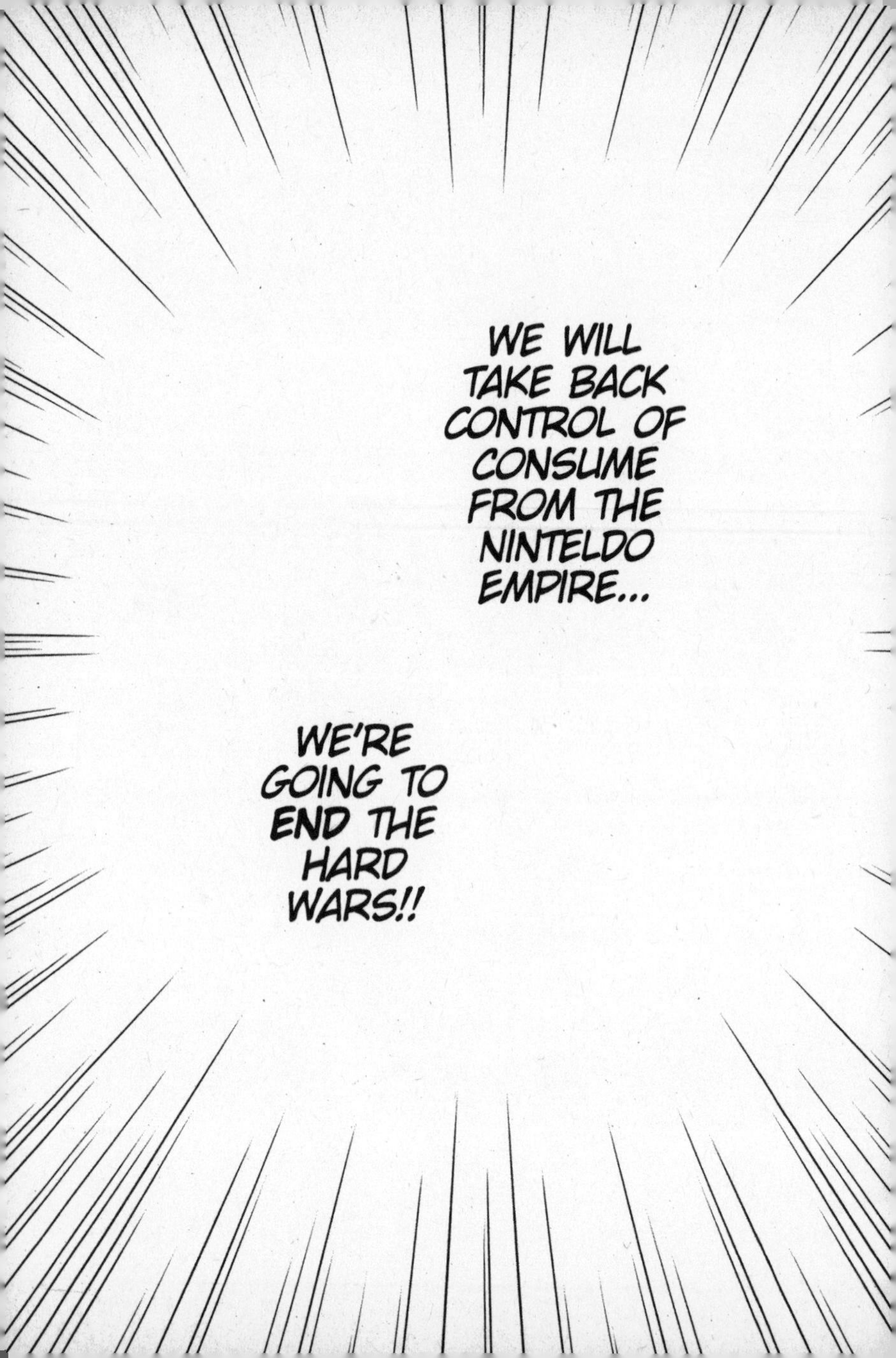
WE WILL TAKE BACK CONTROL OF CONSUME FROM THE NINTELDO EMPIRE...
WE'RE GOING TO END THE HARD WARS!!

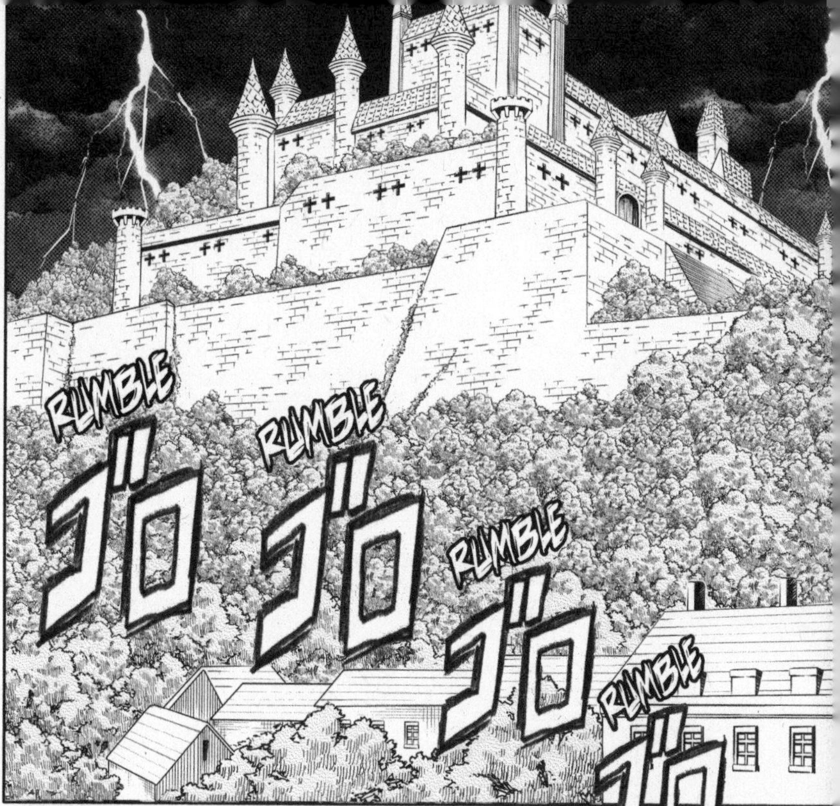
RUMBLE
ゴロ
RUMBLE
ゴロ
RUMBLE
ゴロ
RUMBLE
ゴロ

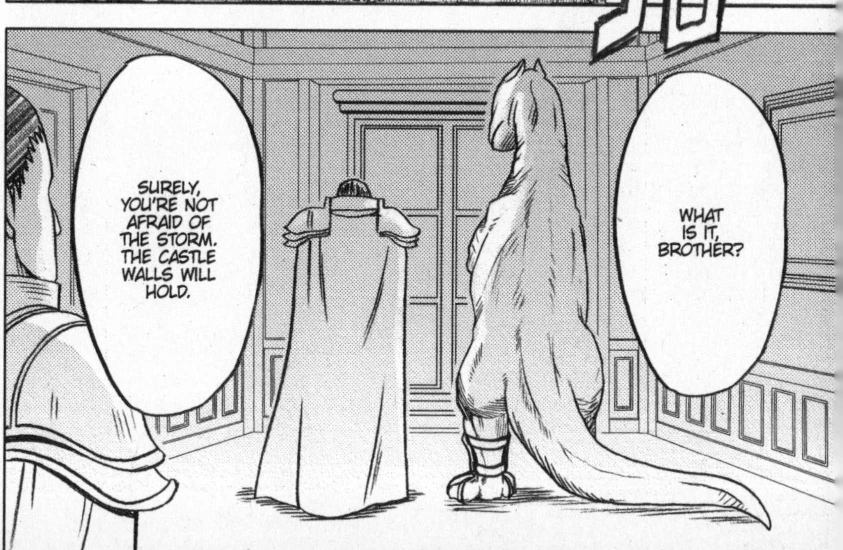
WHAT IS IT, BROTHER?
SURELY, YOU'RE NOT AFRAID OF THE STORM. THE CASTLE WALLS WILL HOLD.

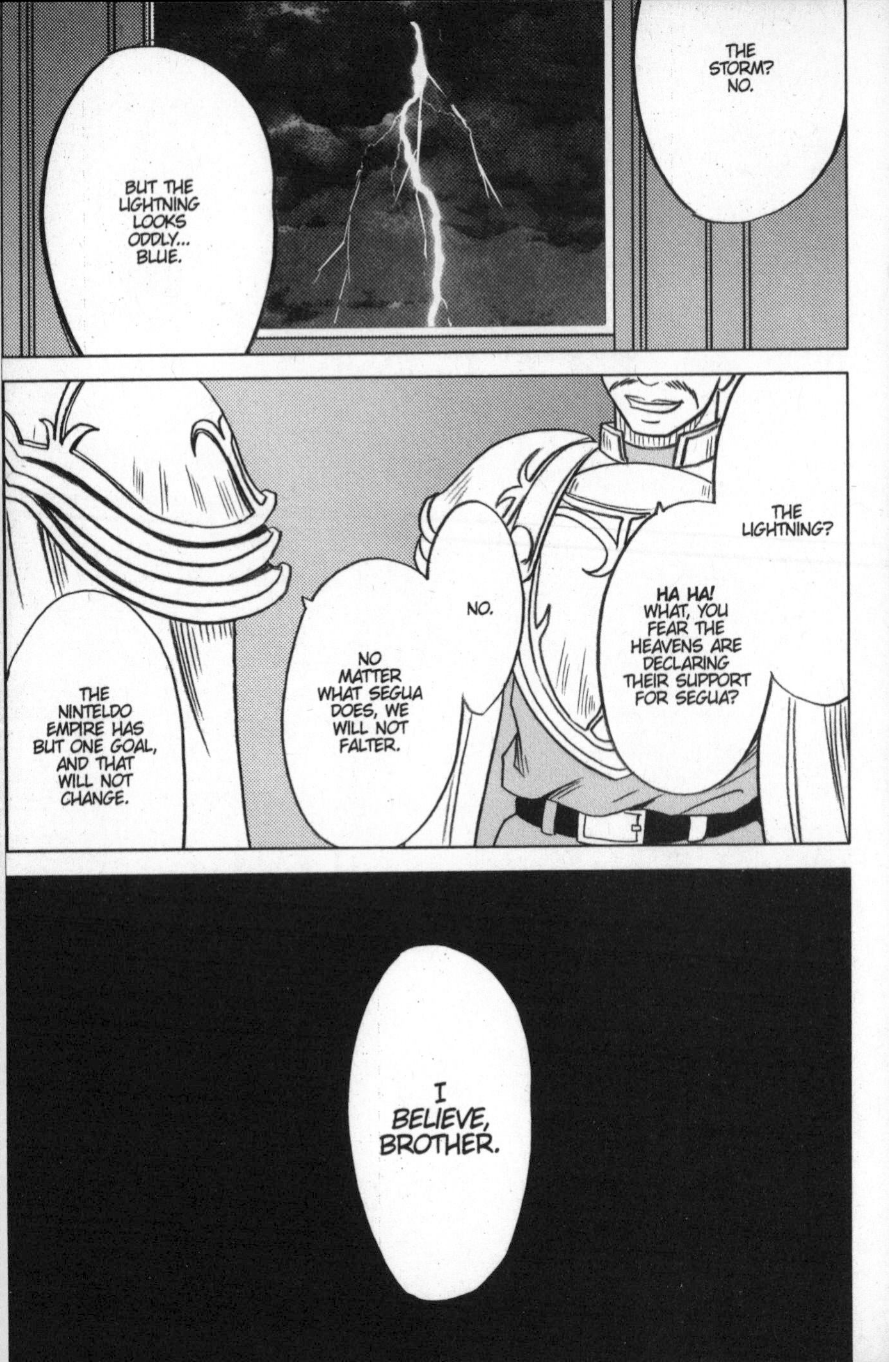
THE STORM? NO.
BUT THE LIGHTNING LOOKS ODDLY... BLUE.
THE LIGHTNING?
HA HA! WHAT, YOU FEAR THE HEAVENS ARE DECLARING THEIR SUPPORT FOR SEGUA?
NO.
NO MATTER WHAT SEGUA DOES, WE WILL NOT FALTER.
THE NINTELDO EMPIRE HAS BUT ONE GOAL, AND THAT WILL NOT CHANGE.
I BELIEVE, BROTHER.

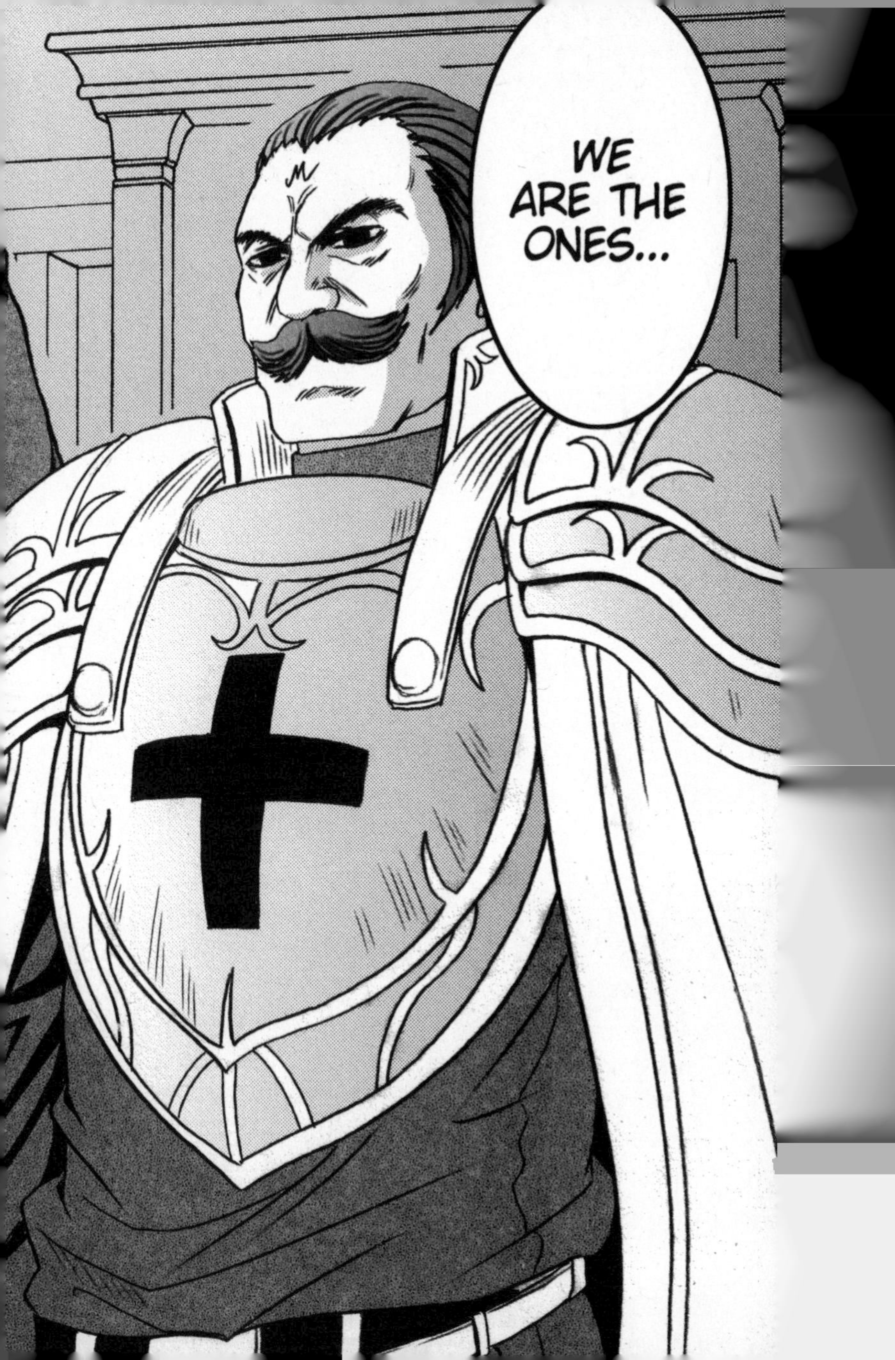
WE ARE THE ONES...

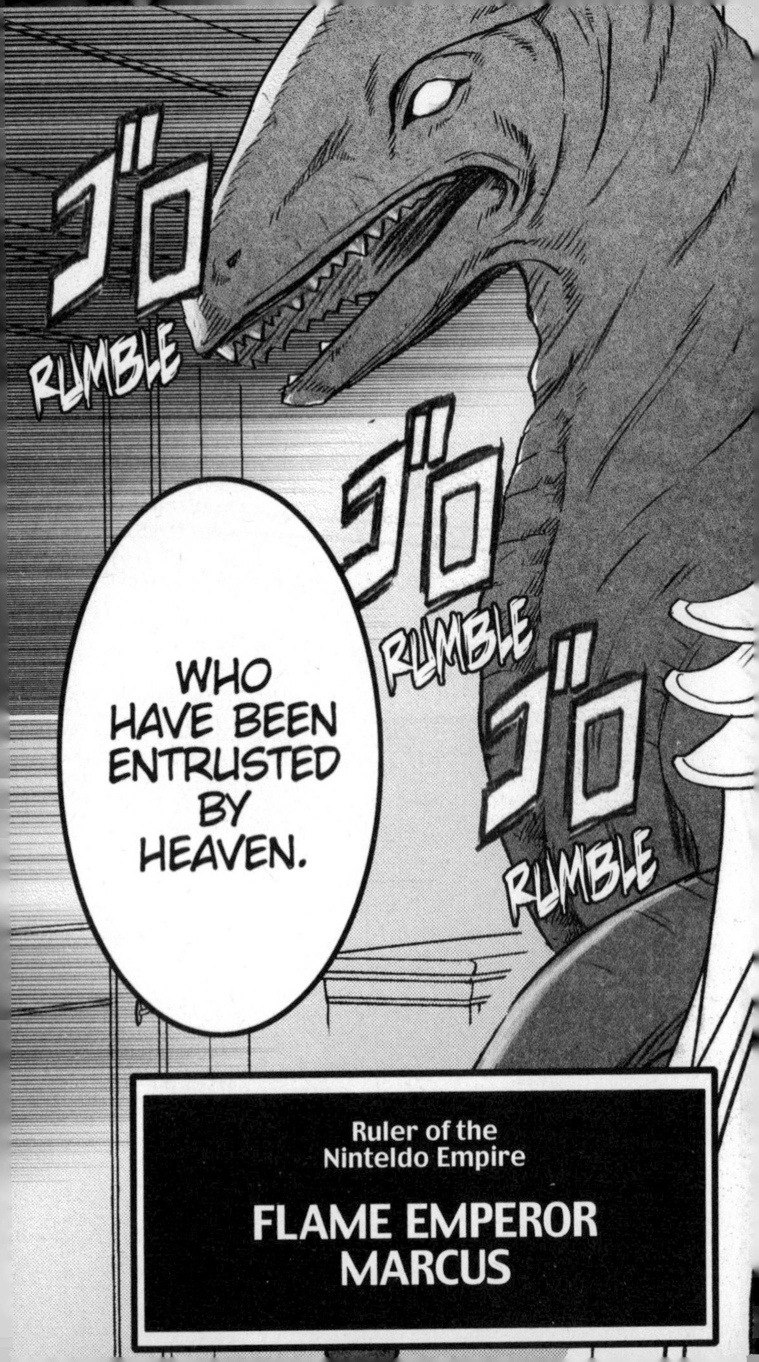
ゴロ
RUMBLE
ゴロ
RUMBLE
ゴロ
RUMBLE
WHO HAVE BEEN ENTRUSTED BY HEAVEN.
Ruler of the Ninteldo Empire
FLAME EMPEROR MARCUS

ON THE EDGE OF THE BLUE WORLD

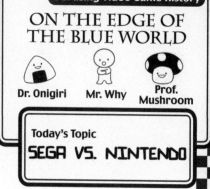

Dr. Onigiri
Mr. Why
Prof. Mushroom

Today's Topic

SEGA VS. NINTENDO

Mr. Why: Tell me about the console war between Nintendo and Sega!

Dr. Onigiri: Well, *that* question is about as blunt as a hammer to the forehead.

Prof. Mushroom: People call it a "war," but there weren't any battles or killin' or anything. Ever heard of the NES*?

Mr. Why: Yeah.

Dr. Onigiri: Okay, how about the SG-1000?

Mr. Why: Nope.

Dr. Onigiri: Oof. Okay, the SG-1000 was the game console Sega launched in 1983, the same year Nintendo launched the NES. Sega made it by taking the game functions out of the SC-3000 home computer and throwing them into a dedicated box.

Prof. Mushroom: Long story short, the SG-1000 was Sega's rival for the NES.

Dr. Onigiri: So both companies began to compete in the console game market, using various strategies to get the better of each other. People eventually referred to this competition as the "console wars."

Mr. Why: But I've never heard of the SG-1000.

Dr. Onigiri: Yeah, Sega was in a bad spot, right from the beginning. The SG-1000 was outmatched by the NES in terms of color palette, sound quality, distribution channels, and plenty of other areas. But then in 1985, they debuted the Sega Mark III (the original version of what would become the Sega Master System).

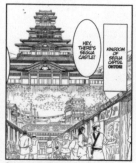

KINGDOM OF SEGUA CAPITAL OHTORI
HEY, THERE'S SEGUA CASTLE!

Segua's capital of Ohtori is always bustling with life.

*NES = Short for the Nintendo Entertainment System, a game console first released by Nintendo of Japan as the Nintendo Family Computer (Famicom) on July 15th, 1983.

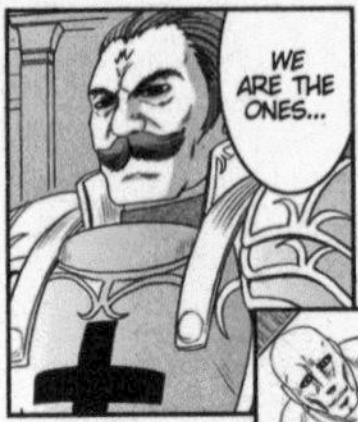
WE ARE THE ONES...

The Flame Emperor, Marcus. He is powerful, wise, and skilled.

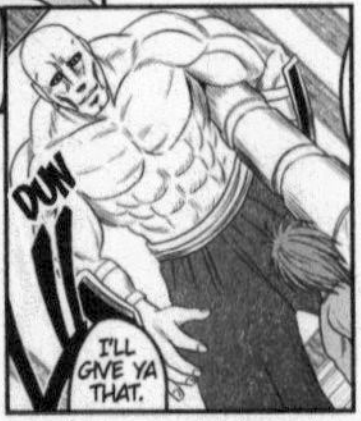
DUN
I'LL GIVE YA THAT.

Segua's strongest warrior, Harris. He fights using a huge pillar.

Mr. Why: The "Mark Three"?

Prof. Mushroom: Yep! It wasn't able to steal back a meaningful share of the market from NES, though.

Prof. Mushroom: 'Specially since in September of 1985, Nintendo released their smash hit *Super Mario Bros.* Once that was released, "Nintendo" and "game console" were used interchangeably.

Dr. Onigiri: Sega, on the other hand, ported some of their most popular arcade games, like *Space Harrier*, onto their consoles. Those grabbed attention, but weren't enough to loosen Nintendo's grip on the market.

However, it was about that time that the game magazine *Beep* started running articles on Sega games, birthing a small, but rabid Sega fanbase. Even today, some of them worship Sega's HQ in Otorii (a ward of Tokyo) as holy ground.

Then in 1987, Sega launched *Phantasy Star*, their first big original RPG. The fans loved it. In fact, they loved it so much that the long-eared purple-haired Nei, a character in *Phantasy Star II* for the Sega Genesis console, became an idol for the whole fan community.

Prof. Mushroom: Nowadays, she'd be called *moe.*

Mr. Why: Wow, Sega released a whole lot more games than those I knew about. What other games did they produce?

Dr. Onigiri: Great question! We'll get into that one, next time.

TO BE CONTINUED...

HISTORY OF SEGA GAME CONSOLES - PART 1

July 1983
SG-1000

● Sega's first home entertainment system. Retailed for 15,000 yen.

July 1984
SG-1000 II

● A mild upgrade from the SG-1000, it featured a remodeled case and joystick design. Retailed for 15,000 yen.

October 1985
Sega Mark III

● Still retailing for 15,000 yen, it featured improved graphics. The FM Sound Unit, sold separately, improved sound quality.

November 1987
Sega Master System

● A mild upgrade from the Sega Mark III, it included an onboard FM sound chip and a rapid fire unit. Retailed for 16,800 yen.

October 1988
Sega Genesis/Sega Mega Drive

● Retailing for 21,000 yen, the Genesis was Japan's first 16-bit console. It featured drastic improvements in graphics and processing power. It was on this system that Sonic the Hedgehog debuted.

WORLD WAR BLUE

CHARACTER INTRODUCTION

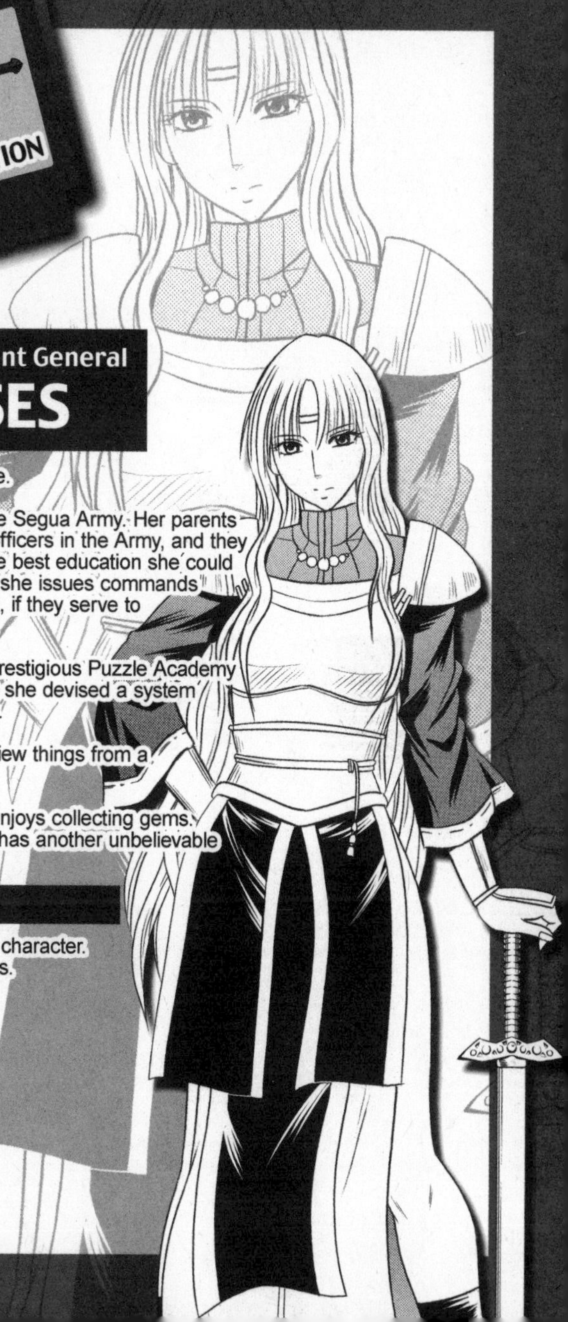

Segua's Lieutenant General

RAMSES

Kingdom of Segua native.

Lieutenant General of the Segua Army. Her parents were also high-ranking officers in the Army, and they ensured she received the best education she could get. A talented tactician, she issues commands with cold, cruel precision, if they serve to advance Segua's cause.

Ramses studied at the prestigious Puzzle Academy along with Tejirov, where she devised a system for rapid-fire spellcasting.

She has a tendency to view things from a diagonal point of view.

HOBBY: Publicly, she enjoys collecting gems. However, in private, she has another unbelievable and unspeakable hobby.

Author Comment

The experienced female character. She is in her late twenties.

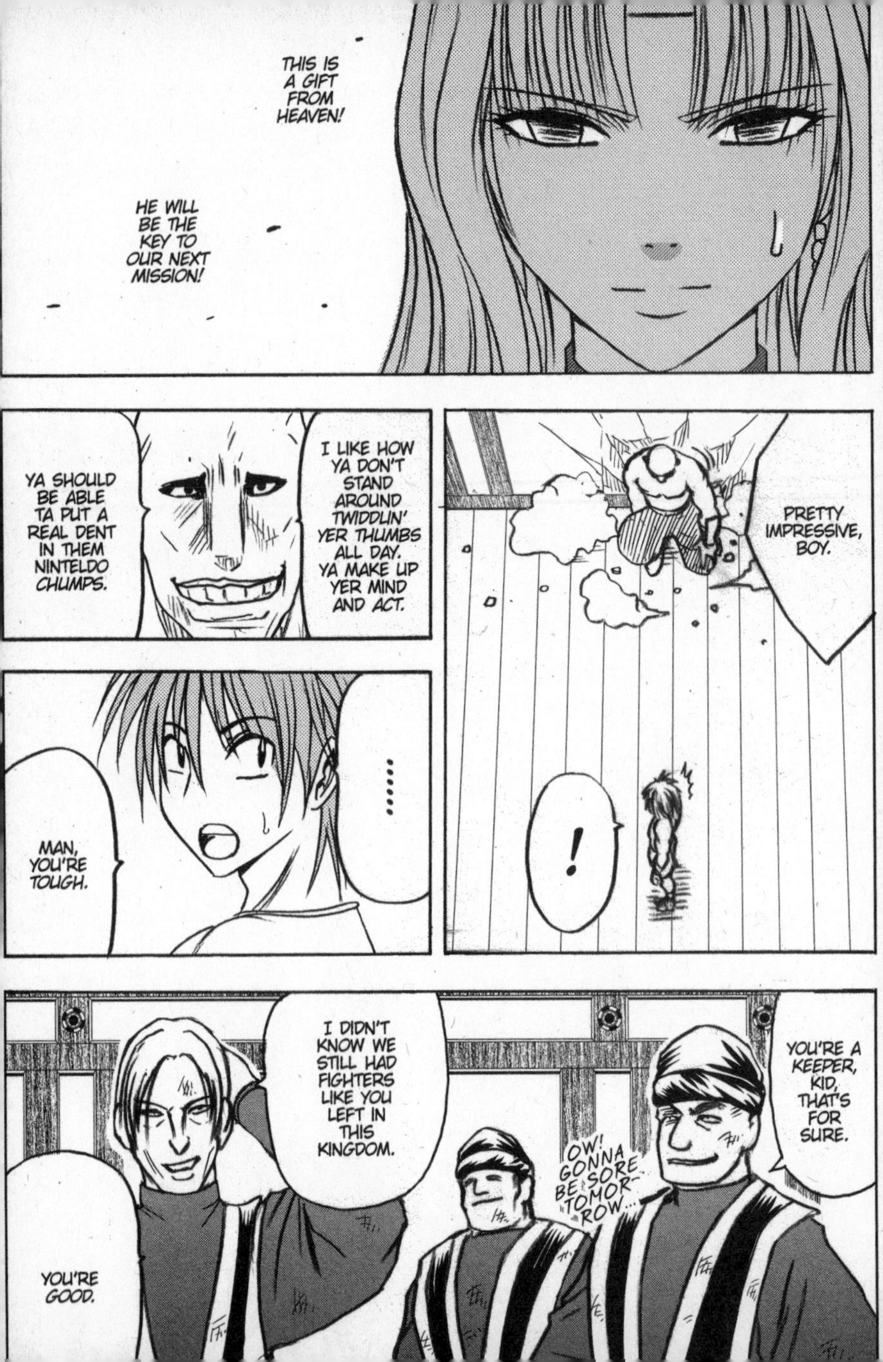
THIS IS A GIFT FROM HEAVEN!
HE WILL BE THE KEY TO OUR NEXT MISSION!
PRETTY IMPRESSIVE, BOY.
!
I LIKE HOW YA DON'T STAND AROUND TWIDDLIN' YER THUMBS ALL DAY. YA MAKE UP YER MIND AND ACT.
YA SHOULD BE ABLE TA PUT A REAL DENT IN THEM NINTELDO CHUMPS.
......
MAN, YOU'RE TOUGH.
YOU'RE A KEEPER, KID, THAT'S FOR SURE.
OW! GONNA BE SORE TOMORROW...
I DIDN'T KNOW WE STILL HAD FIGHTERS LIKE YOU LEFT IN THIS KINGDOM.
YOU'RE GOOD.

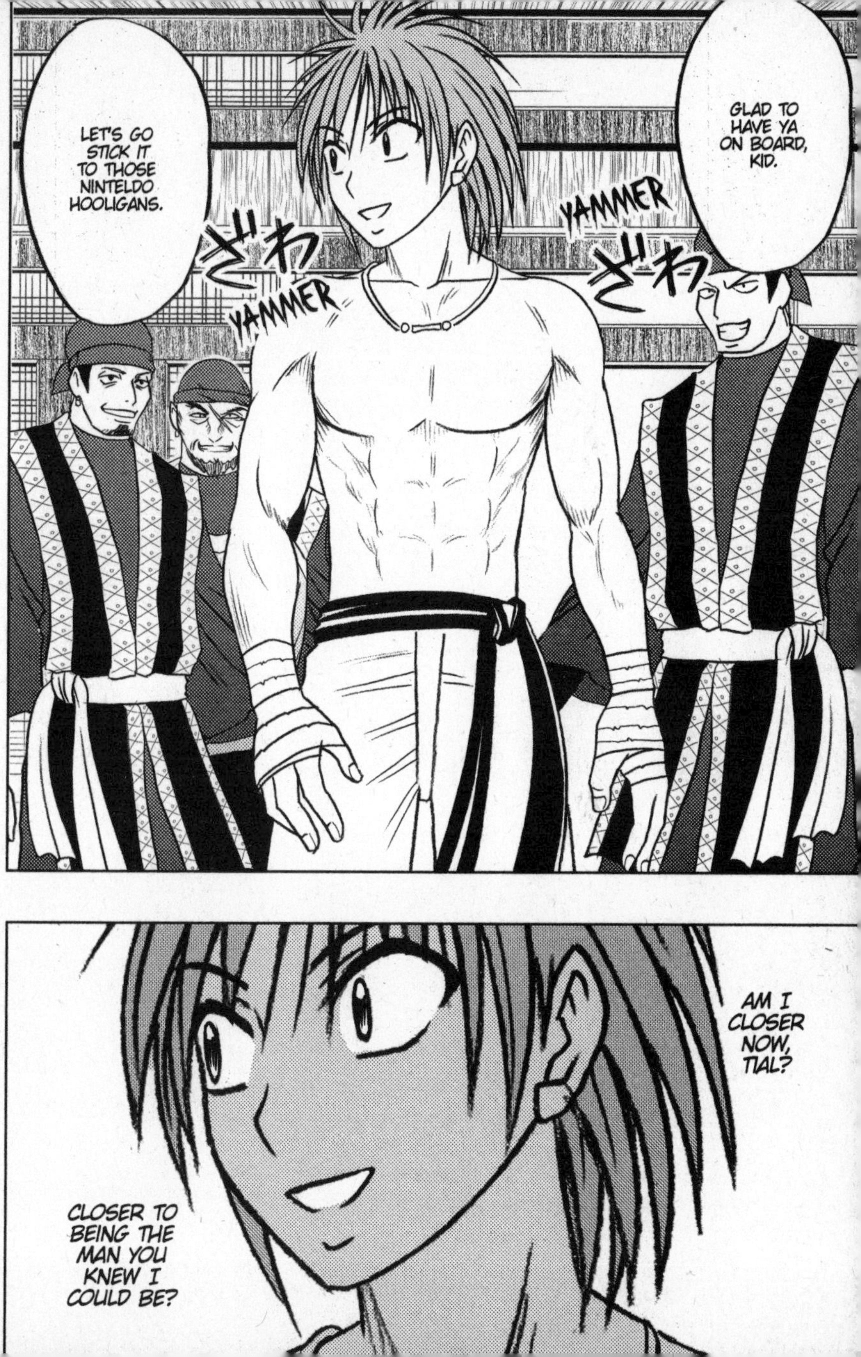
GLAD TO HAVE YA ON BOARD, KID.
ざわ
YAMMER
LET'S GO STICK IT TO THOSE NINTELDO HOOLIGANS.
ざわ
YAMMER
AM I CLOSER NOW, TIAL?
CLOSER TO BEING THE MAN YOU KNEW I COULD BE?

CHAPTER 3

YADAYO
(I don't like you.)

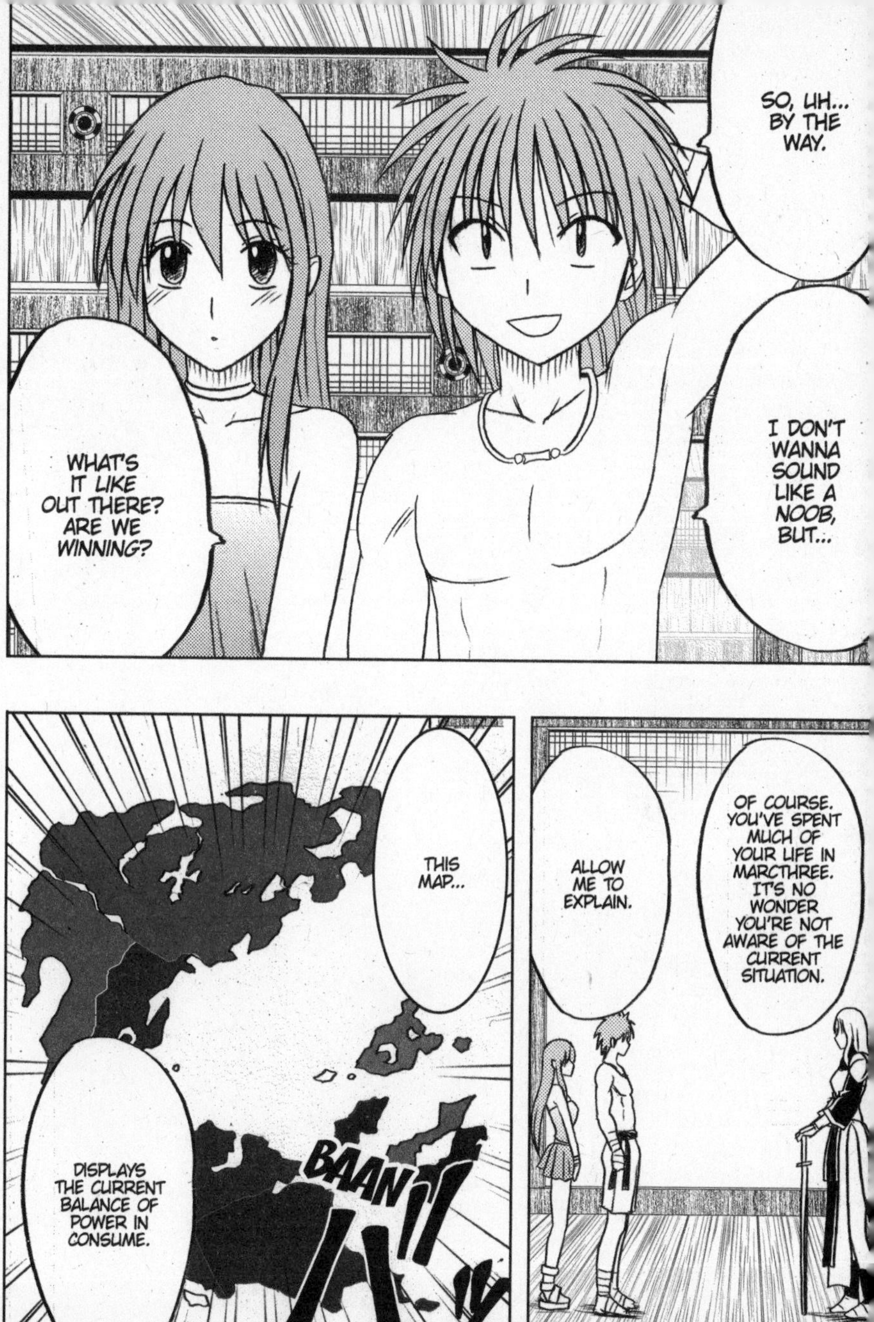
SO, UH... BY THE WAY.
I DON'T WANNA SOUND LIKE A NOOB, BUT...
WHAT'S IT LIKE OUT THERE? ARE WE WINNING?
OF COURSE. YOU'VE SPENT MUCH OF YOUR LIFE IN MARCTHREE. IT'S NO WONDER YOU'RE NOT AWARE OF THE CURRENT SITUATION.
ALLOW ME TO EXPLAIN.
THIS MAP...
BAAN
DISPLAYS THE CURRENT BALANCE OF POWER IN CONSUME.

CONSUME, YEAR 977 – BATTLE LINES

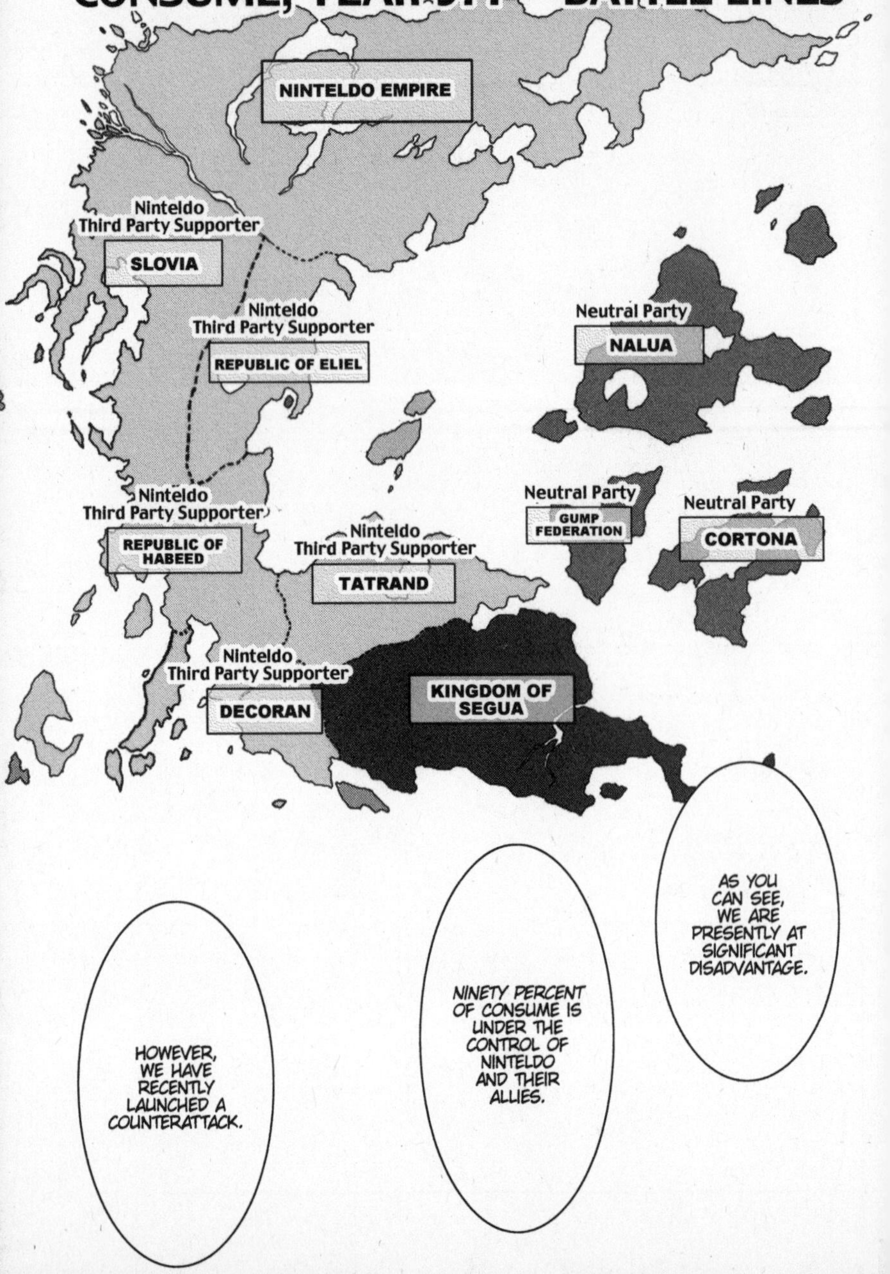
NINTELDO EMPIRE
Ninteldo Third Party Supporter
SLOVIA
Ninteldo Third Party Supporter
REPUBLIC OF ELIEL
Neutral Party
NALUA
Ninteldo Third Party Supporter
REPUBLIC OF HABEED
Neutral Party
GUMP FEDERATION
Neutral Party
CORTONA
Ninteldo Third Party Supporter
TATRAND
Ninteldo Third Party Supporter
DECORAN
KINGDOM OF SEGUA

AS YOU CAN SEE, WE ARE PRESENTLY AT SIGNIFICANT DISADVANTAGE.

NINETY PERCENT OF CONSUME IS UNDER THE CONTROL OF NINTELDO AND THEIR ALLIES.

HOWEVER, WE HAVE RECENTLY LAUNCHED A COUNTERATTACK.

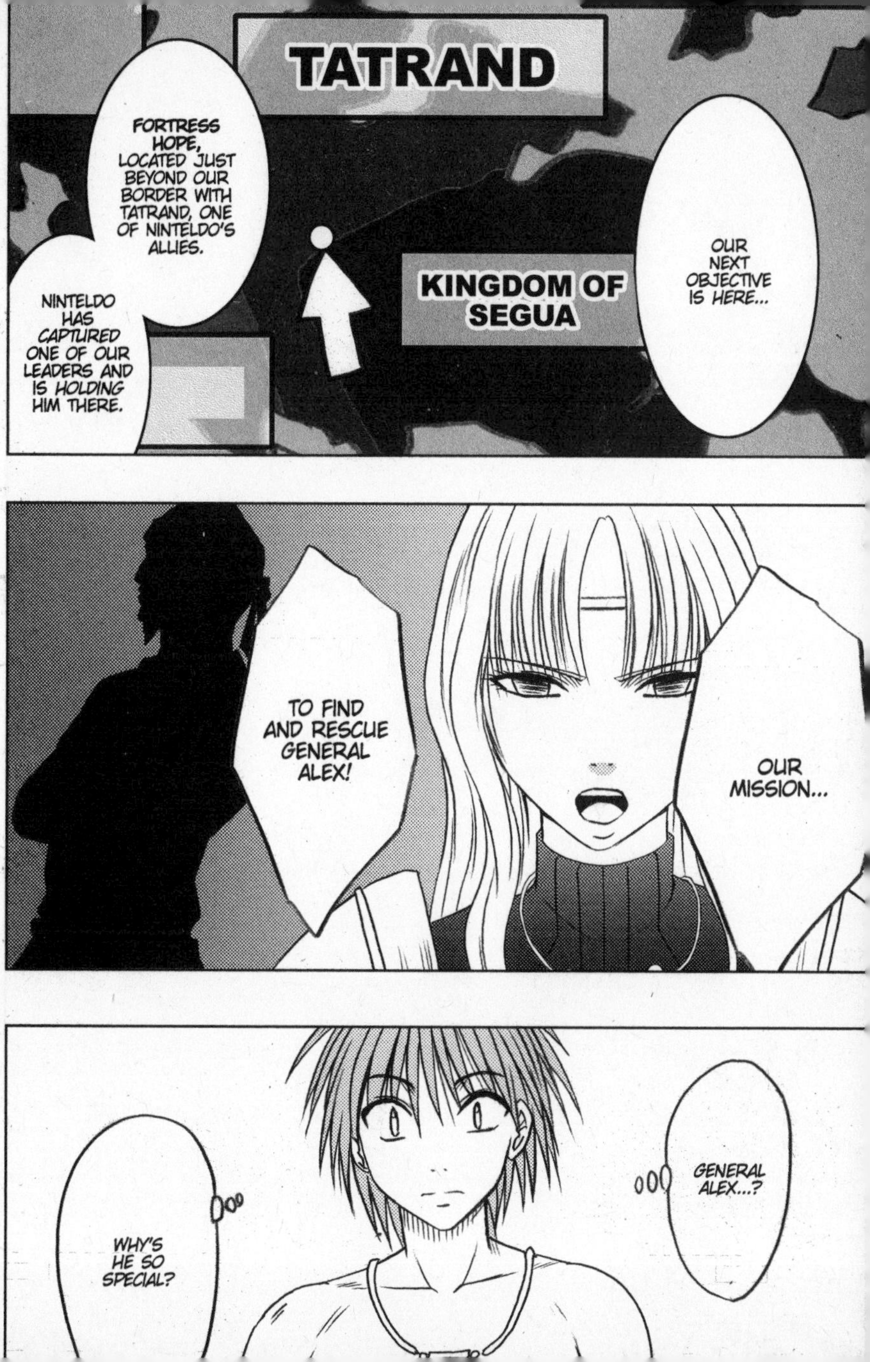
OUR NEXT OBJECTIVE IS HERE...
KINGDOM OF SEGUA
TATRAND
FORTRESS HOPE, LOCATED JUST BEYOND OUR BORDER WITH TATRAND, ONE OF NINTELDO'S ALLIES.
NINTELDO HAS CAPTURED ONE OF OUR LEADERS AND IS HOLDING HIM THERE.
OUR MISSION...
TO FIND AND RESCUE GENERAL ALEX!
GENERAL ALEX...?
WHY'S HE SO SPECIAL?

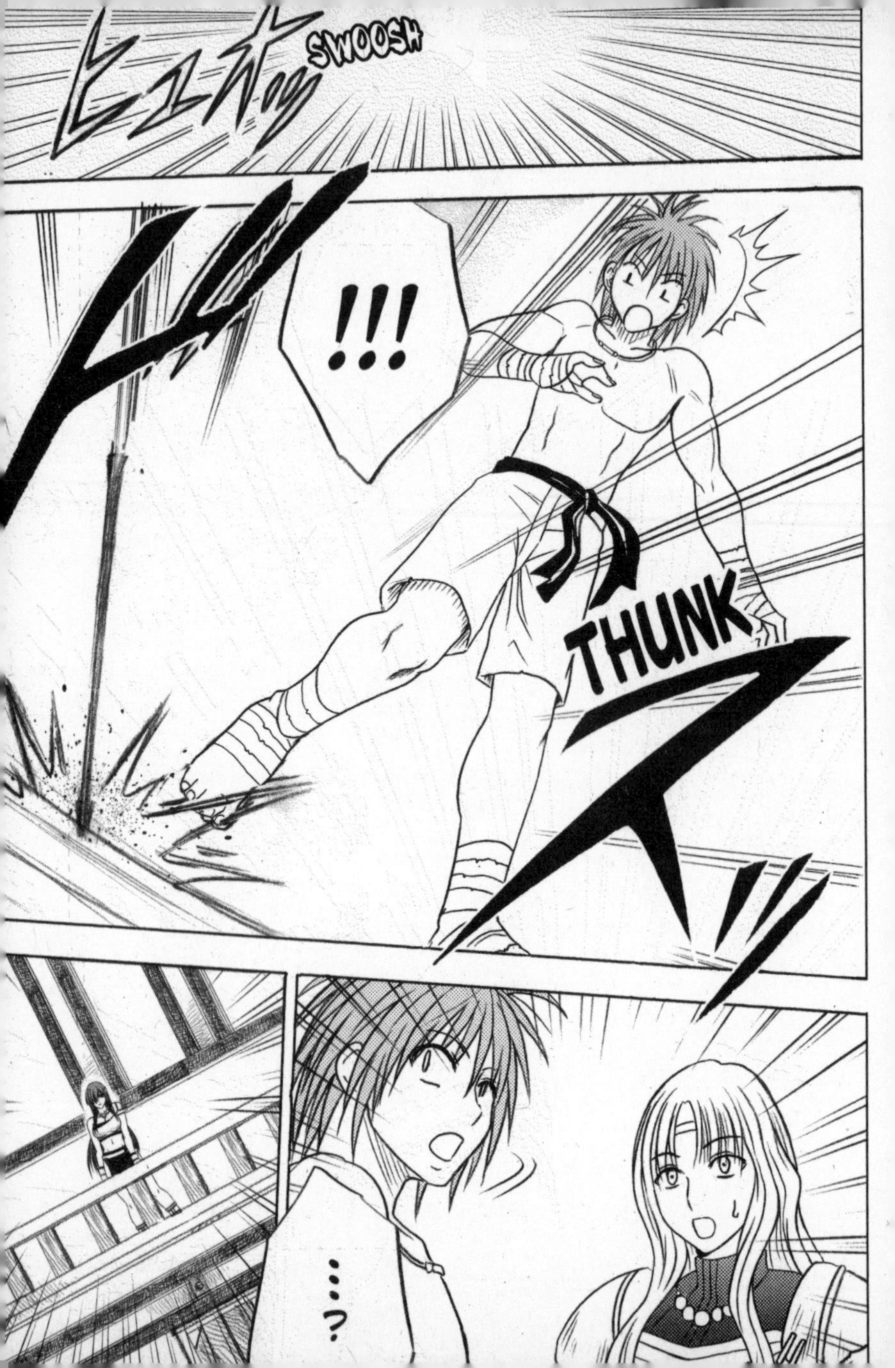
SWOOSH
!!!
THUNK
…っ？

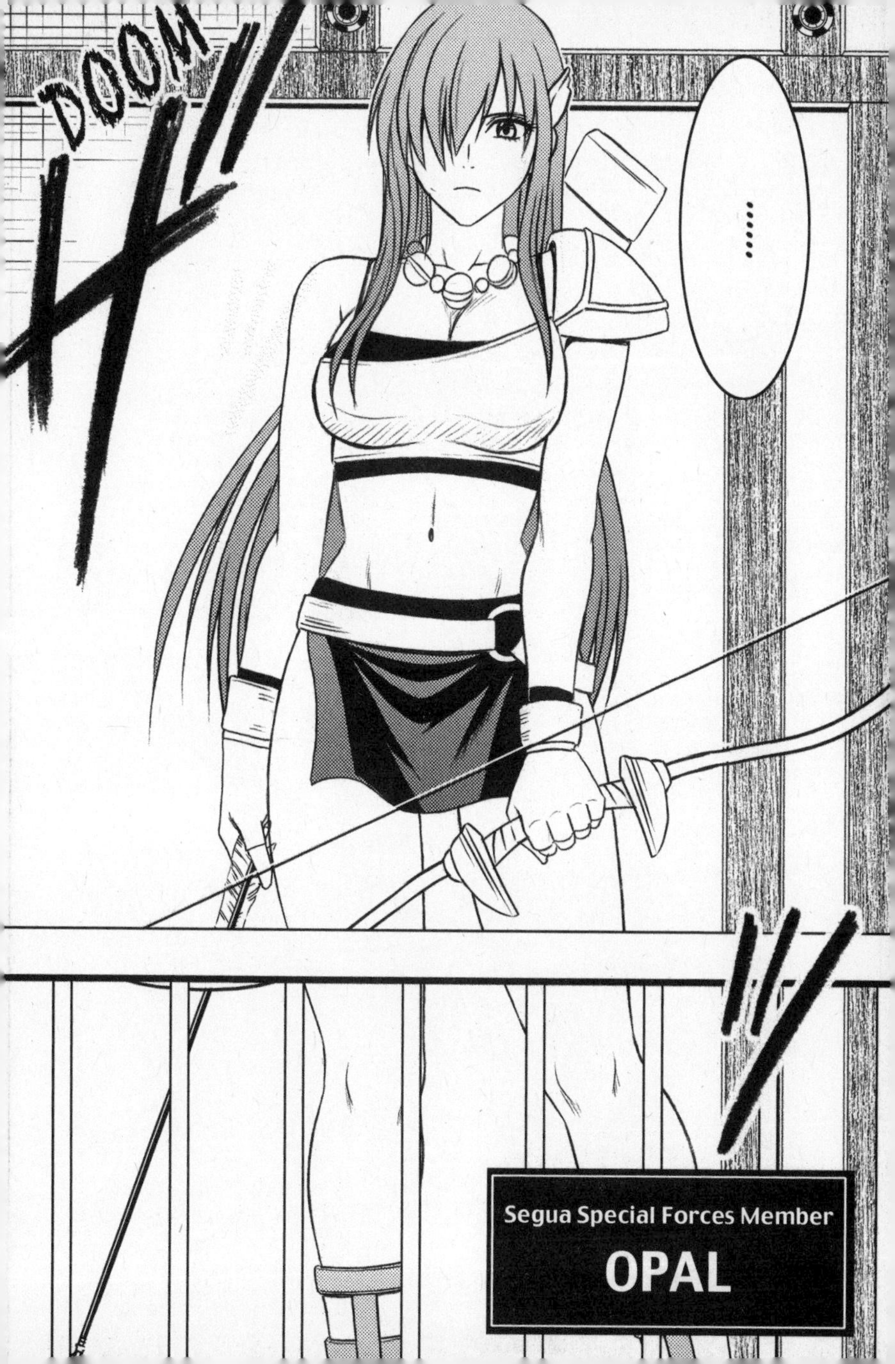

DOOM
......
Segua Special Forces Member
OPAL

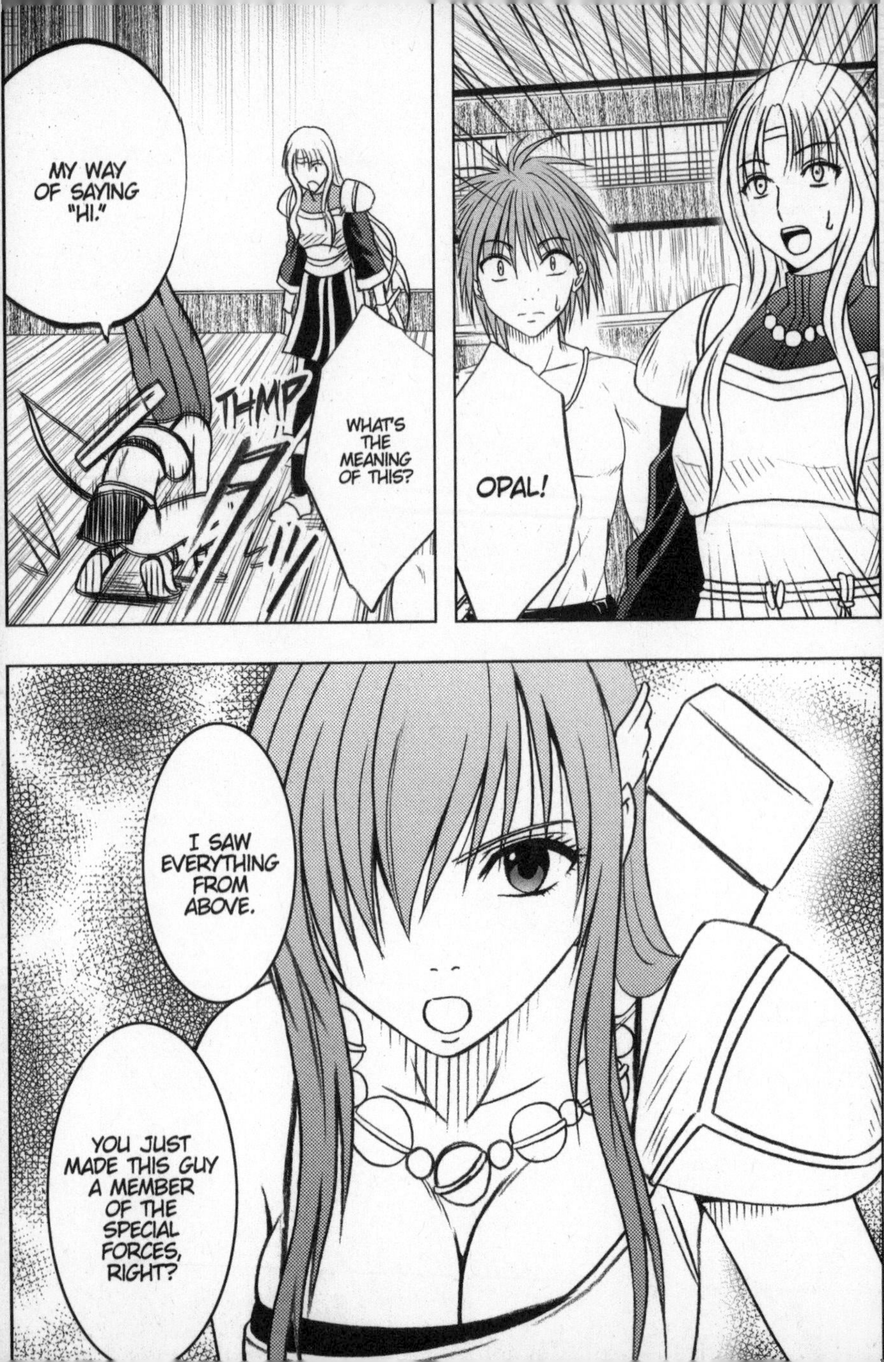
OPAL!
THMP
WHAT'S THE MEANING OF THIS?
MY WAY OF SAYING "HI."
I SAW EVERYTHING FROM ABOVE.
YOU JUST MADE THIS GUY A MEMBER OF THE SPECIAL FORCES, RIGHT?

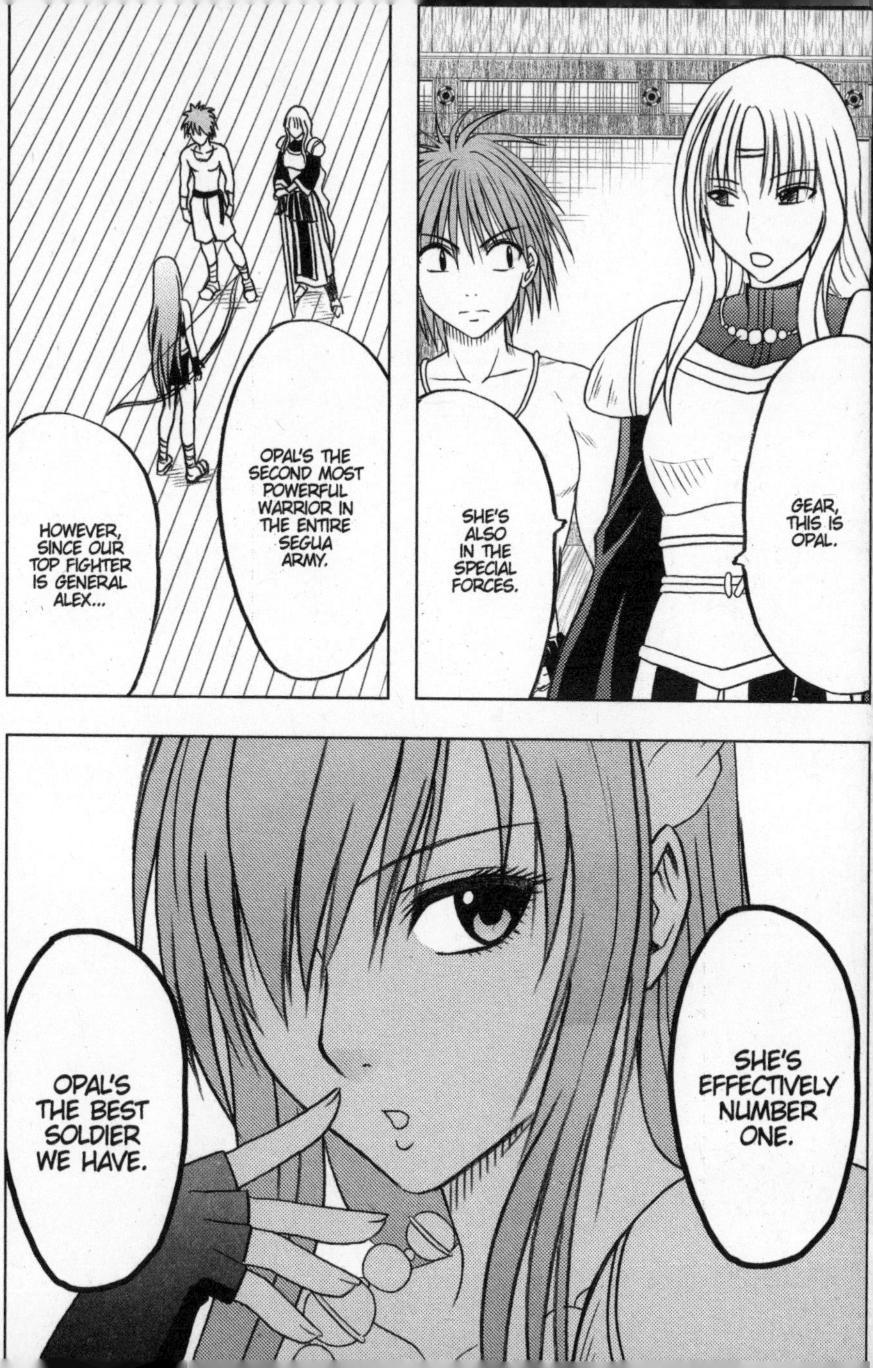
GEAR, THIS IS OPAL.
SHE'S ALSO IN THE SPECIAL FORCES.
OPAL'S THE SECOND MOST POWERFUL WARRIOR IN THE ENTIRE SEGUA ARMY.
HOWEVER, SINCE OUR TOP FIGHTER IS GENERAL ALEX...
SHE'S EFFECTIVELY NUMBER ONE.
OPAL'S THE BEST SOLDIER WE HAVE.

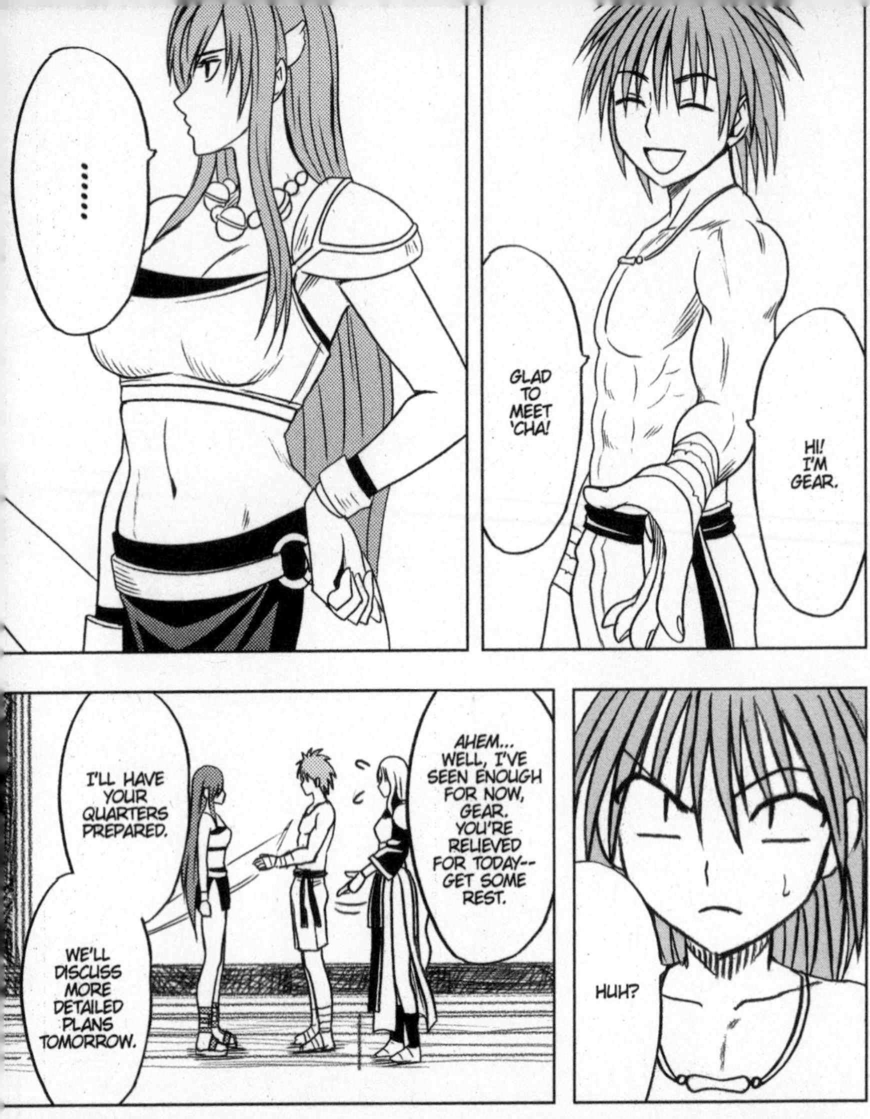
HI! I'M GEAR.
GLAD TO MEET 'CHA!
......
HUH?
AHEM... WELL, I'VE SEEN ENOUGH FOR NOW, GEAR. YOU'RE RELIEVED FOR TODAY--GET SOME REST.
I'LL HAVE YOUR QUARTERS PREPARED.
WE'LL DISCUSS MORE DETAILED PLANS TOMORROW.

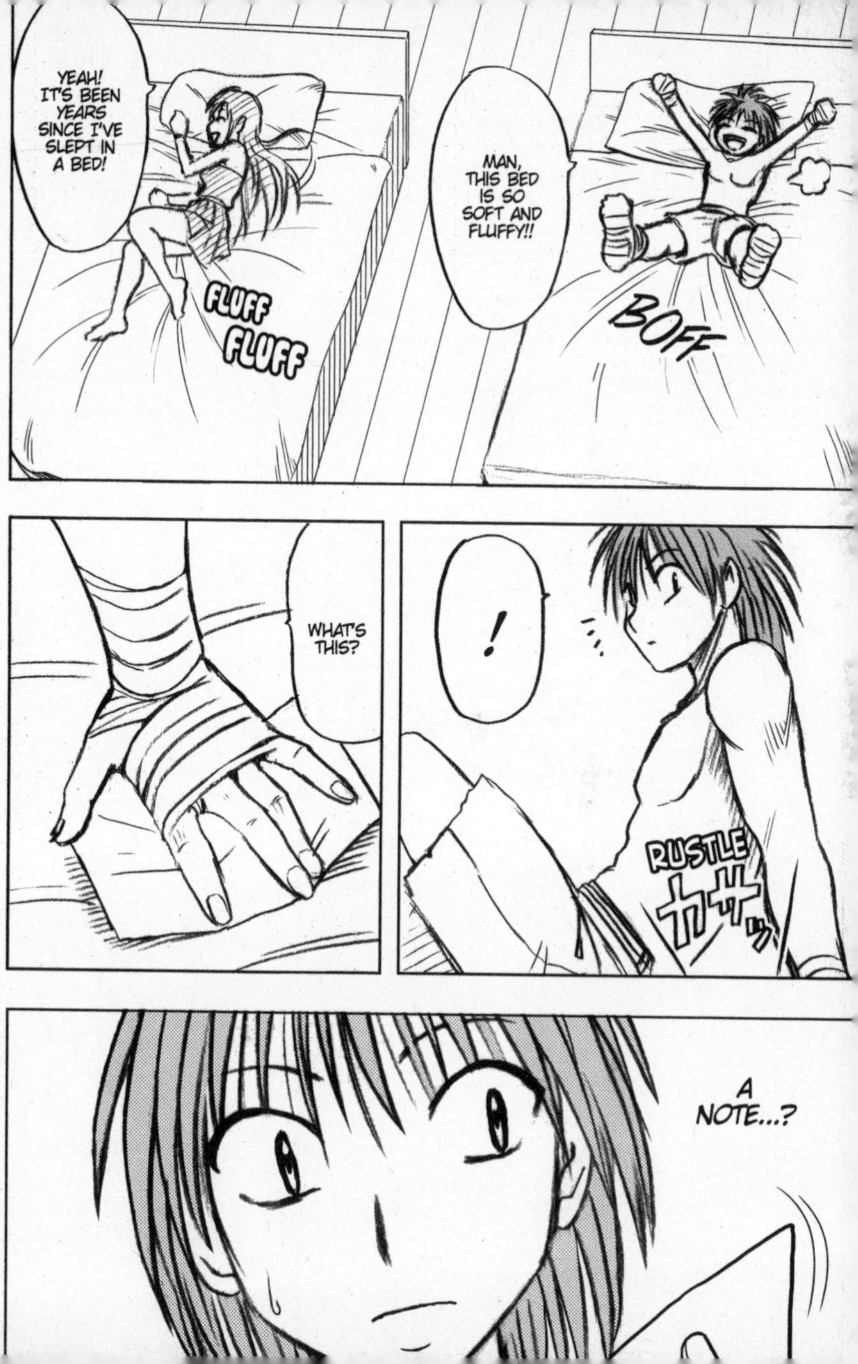
MAN, THIS BED IS SO SOFT AND FLUFFY!!
BOFF
YEAH! IT'S BEEN YEARS SINCE I'VE SLEPT IN A BED!
FLUFF FLUFF
!
RUSTLE
カサッ
WHAT'S THIS?
A NOTE...?

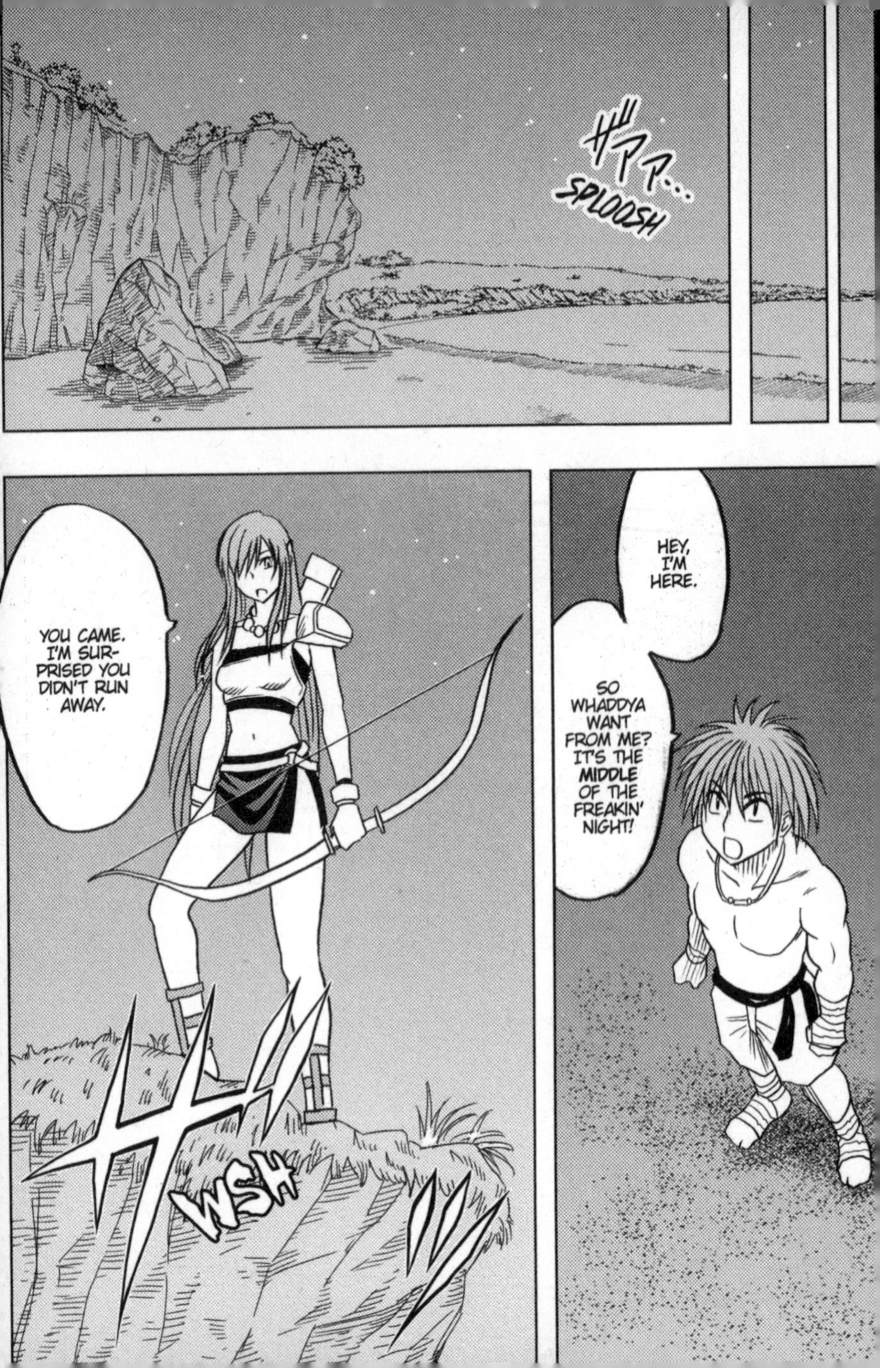
ザァァ…
SPLOOSH
HEY, I'M HERE.
SO WHADDYA WANT FROM ME? IT'S THE MIDDLE OF THE FREAKIN' NIGHT!
YOU CAME. I'M SURPRISED YOU DIDN'T RUN AWAY.
WSH

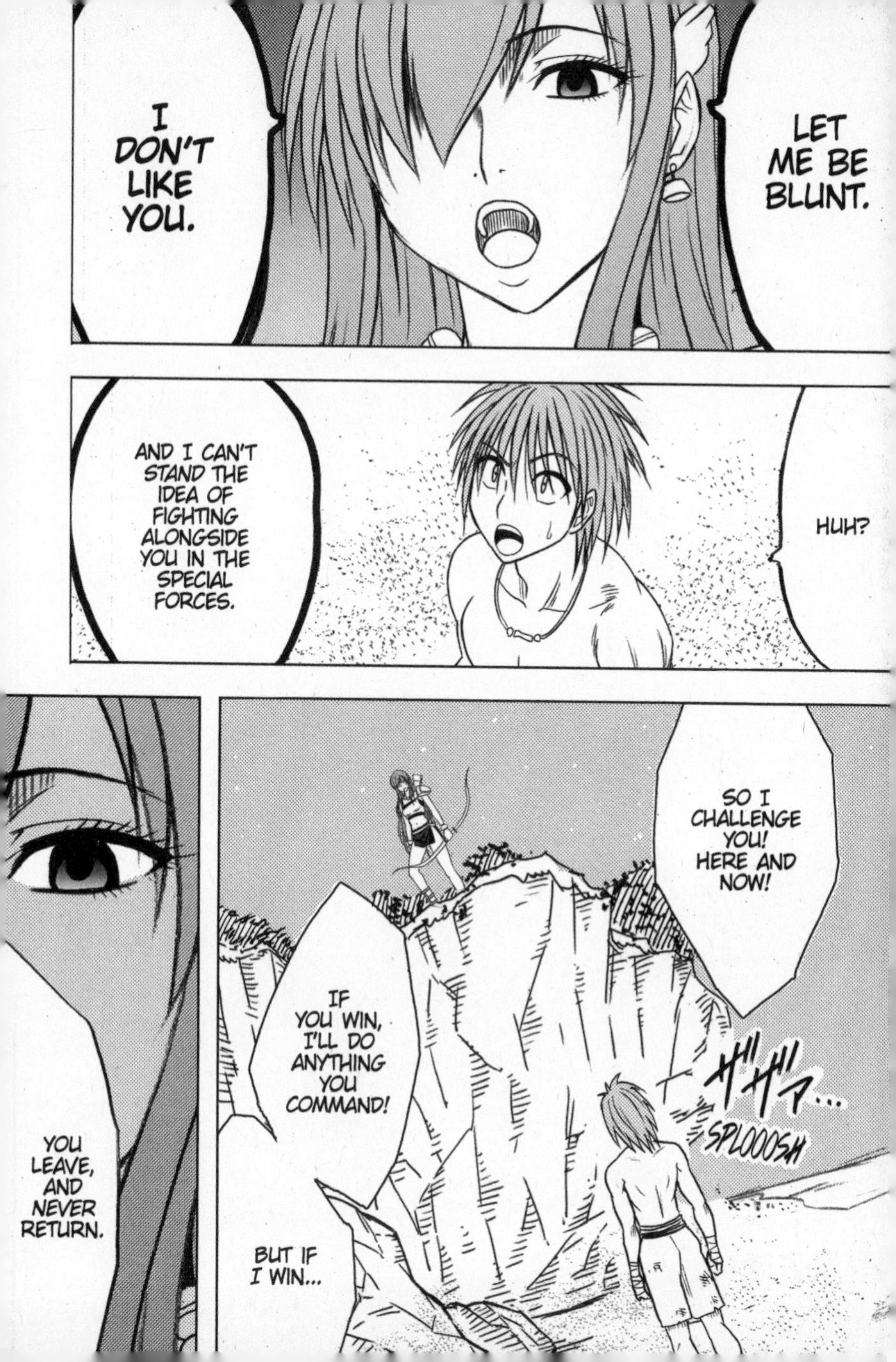
LET ME BE BLUNT.
I DON'T LIKE YOU.
AND I CAN'T STAND THE IDEA OF FIGHTING ALONGSIDE YOU IN THE SPECIAL FORCES.
HUH?
SO I CHALLENGE YOU! HERE AND NOW!
IF YOU WIN, I'LL DO ANYTHING YOU COMMAND!
ザザァ…
SPLOOOSH
BUT IF I WIN...
YOU LEAVE, AND NEVER RETURN.

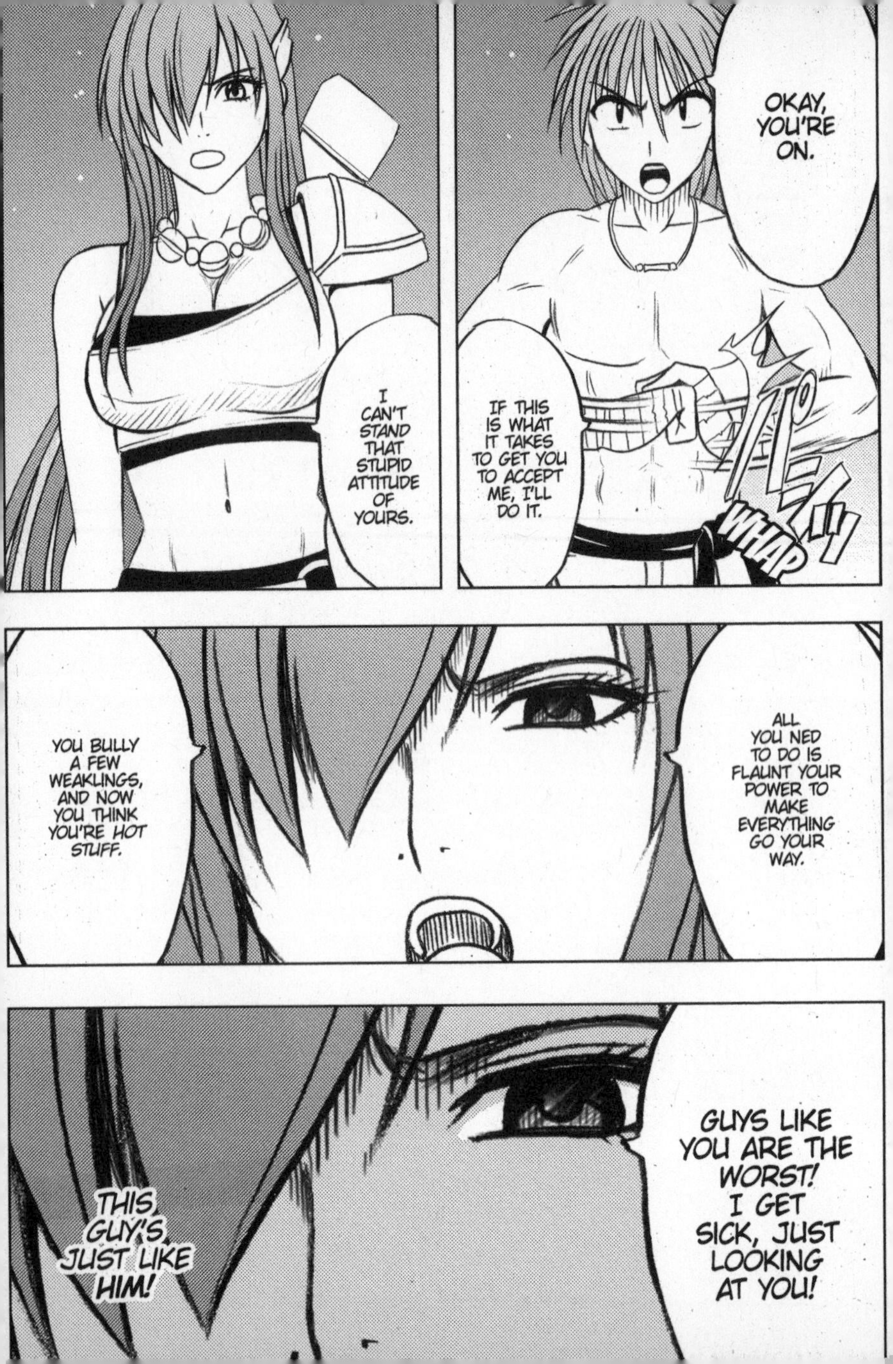
OKAY, YOU'RE ON.
IF THIS IS WHAT IT TAKES TO GET YOU TO ACCEPT ME, I'LL DO IT.
WHAP
I CAN'T STAND THAT STUPID ATTITUDE OF YOURS.
ALL YOU NED TO DO IS FLAUNT YOUR POWER TO MAKE EVERYTHING GO YOUR WAY.
YOU BULLY A FEW WEAKLINGS, AND NOW YOU THINK YOU'RE HOT STUFF.
GUYS LIKE YOU ARE THE WORST! I GET SICK, JUST LOOKING AT YOU!
THIS GUY'S JUST LIKE HIM!

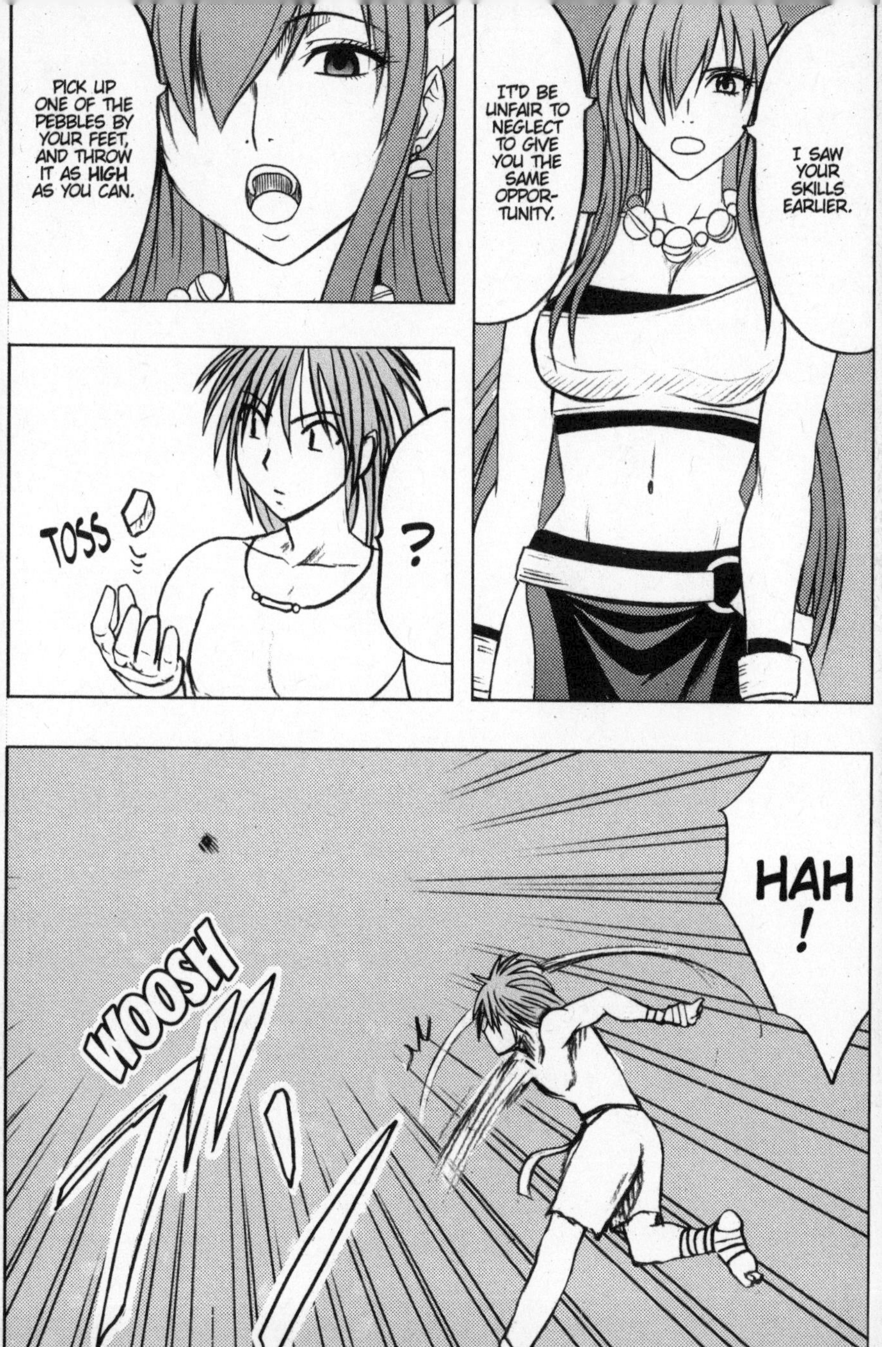
I SAW YOUR SKILLS EARLIER.
IT'D BE UNFAIR TO NEGLECT TO GIVE YOU THE SAME OPPOR-TUNITY.
PICK UP ONE OF THE PEBBLES BY YOUR FEET, AND THROW IT AS HIGH AS YOU CAN.
?
TOSS
HAH!
WOOSH

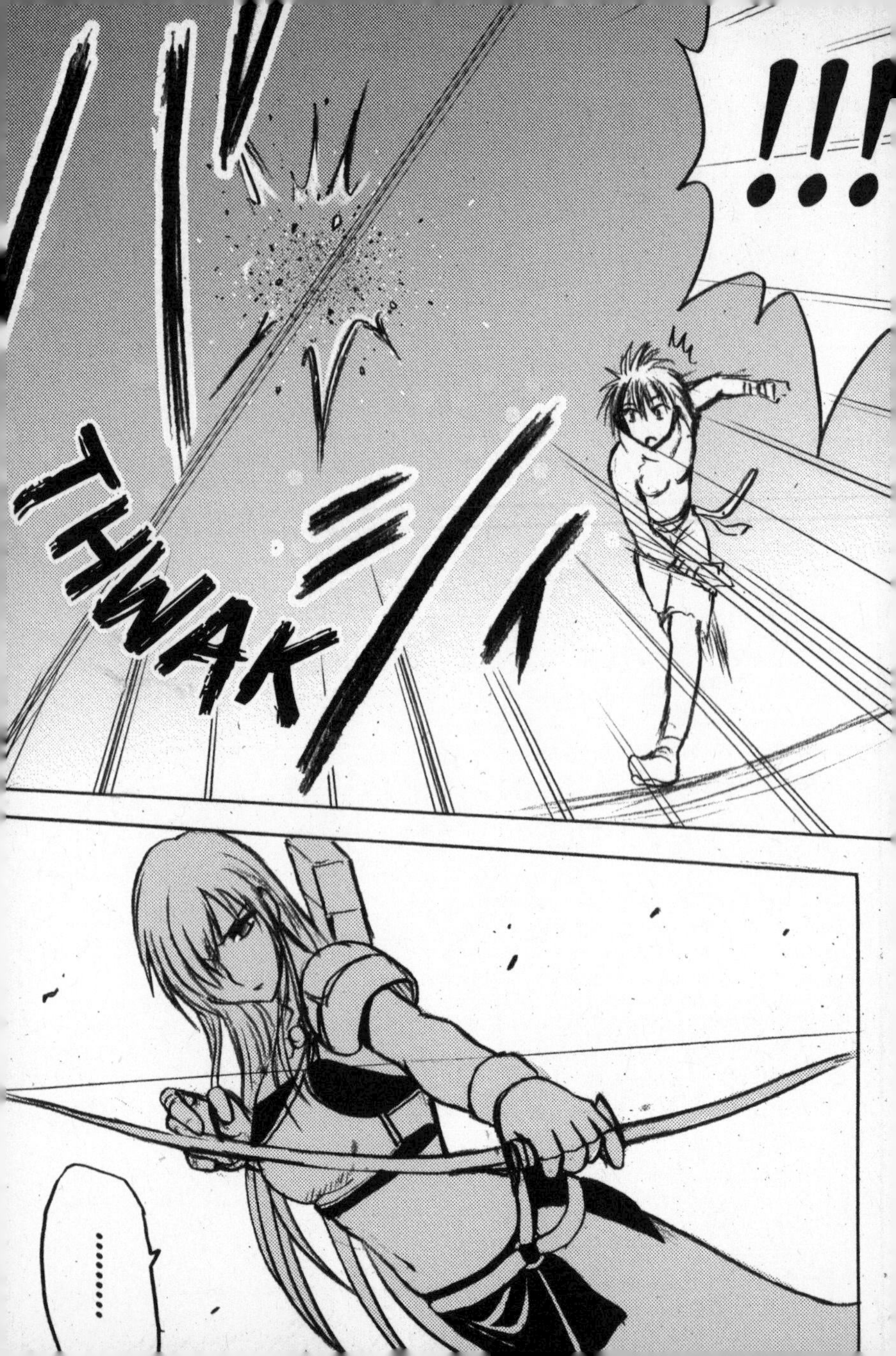
!!!
THWAK
....

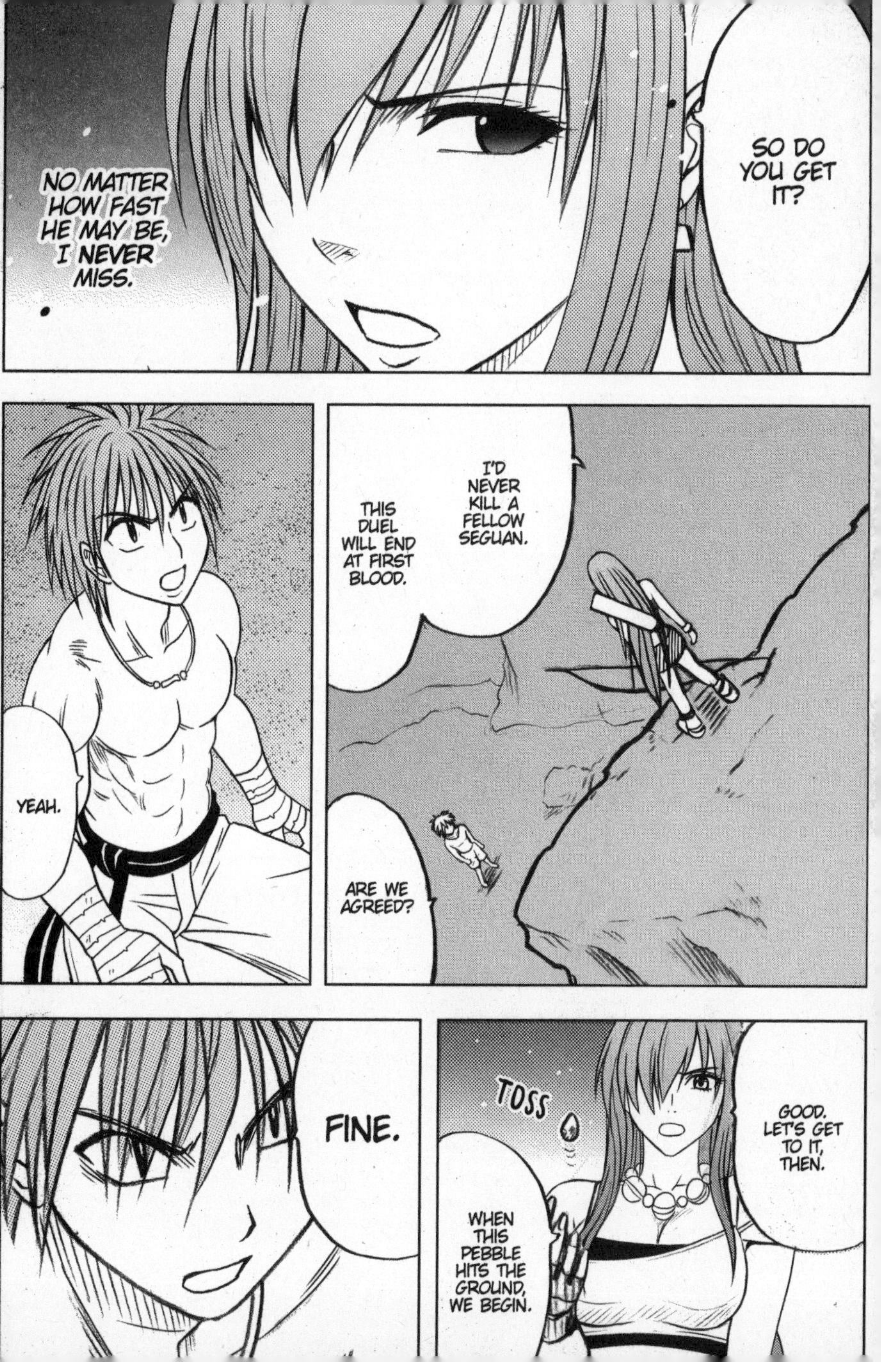
SO DO YOU GET IT?
NO MATTER HOW FAST HE MAY BE, I NEVER MISS.
I'D NEVER KILL A FELLOW SEGUAN.
THIS DUEL WILL END AT FIRST BLOOD.
ARE WE AGREED?
YEAH.
GOOD. LET'S GET TO IT, THEN.
TOSS
WHEN THIS PEBBLE HITS THE GROUND, WE BEGIN.
FINE.

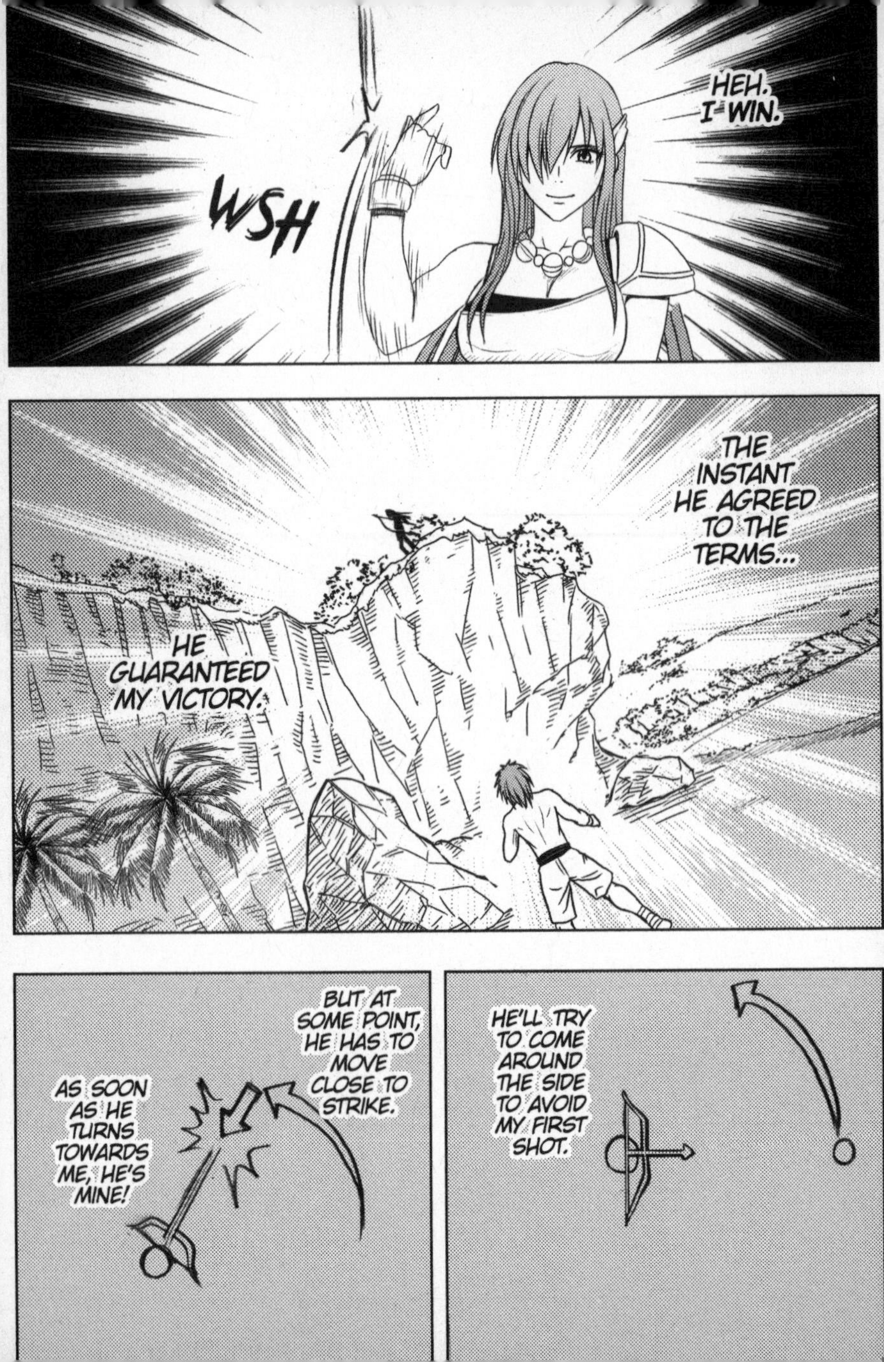
HEH. I WIN.
WSH
THE INSTANT HE AGREED TO THE TERMS...
HE GUARANTEED MY VICTORY.
HE'LL TRY TO COME AROUND THE SIDE TO AVOID MY FIRST SHOT.
BUT AT SOME POINT, HE HAS TO MOVE CLOSE TO STRIKE.
AS SOON AS HE TURNS TOWARDS ME, HE'S MINE!

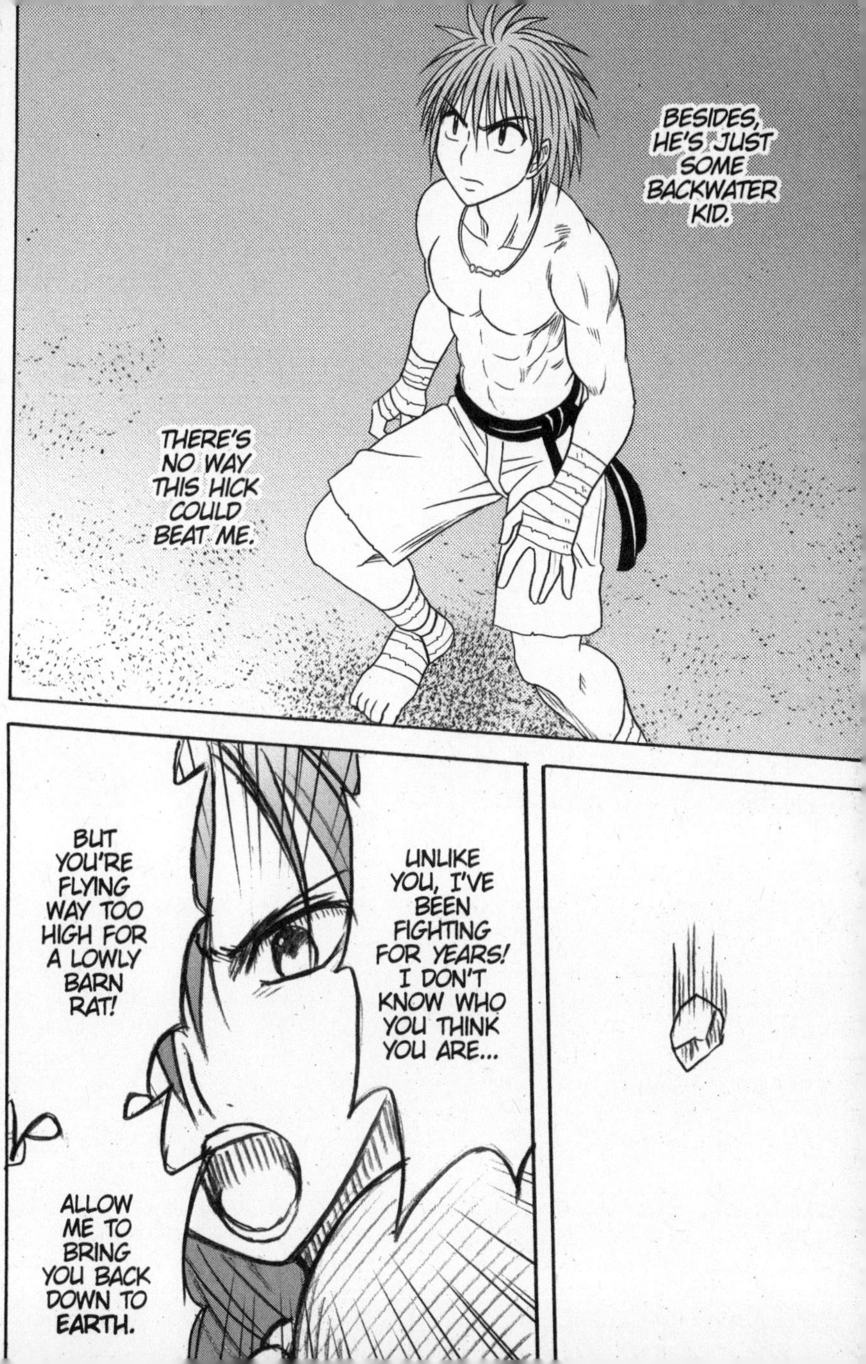
BESIDES, HE'S JUST SOME BACKWATER KID.
THERE'S NO WAY THIS HICK COULD BEAT ME.
UNLIKE YOU, I'VE BEEN FIGHTING FOR YEARS! I DON'T KNOW WHO YOU THINK YOU ARE...
BUT YOU'RE FLYING WAY TOO HIGH FOR A LOWLY BARN RAT!
ALLOW ME TO BRING YOU BACK DOWN TO EARTH.

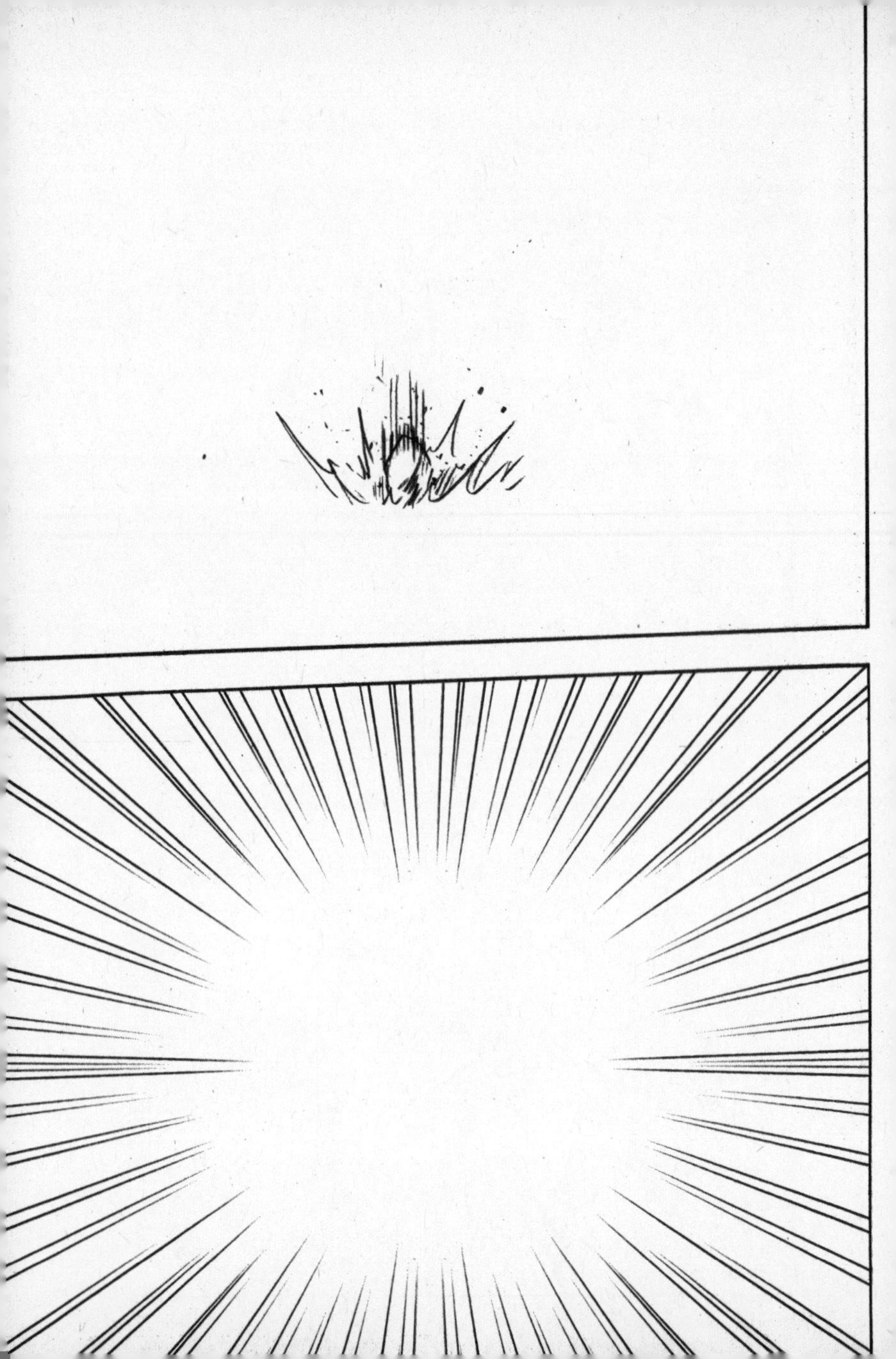

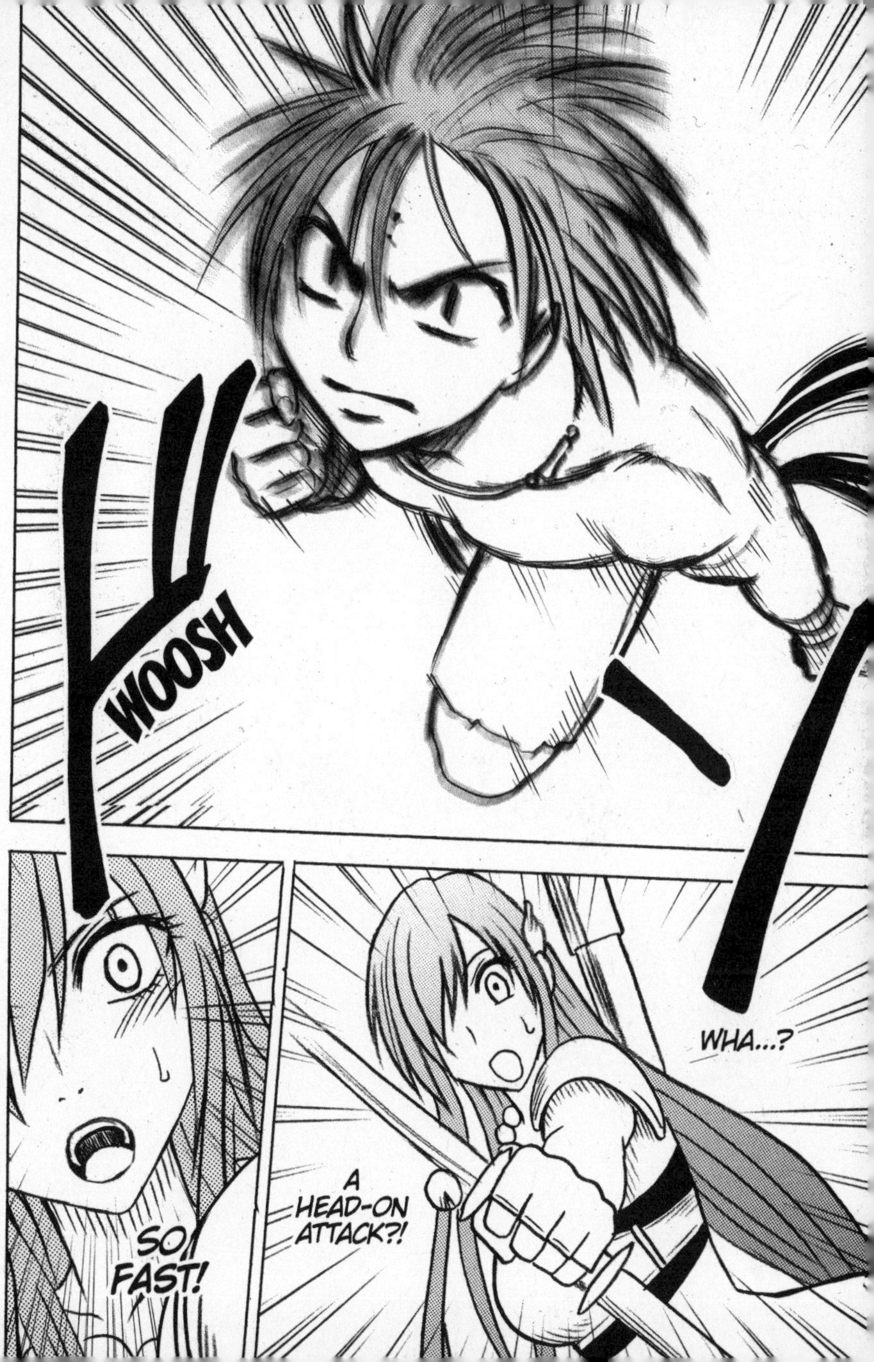
WOOSH
WHA...?
A HEAD-ON ATTACK?!
SO FAST!

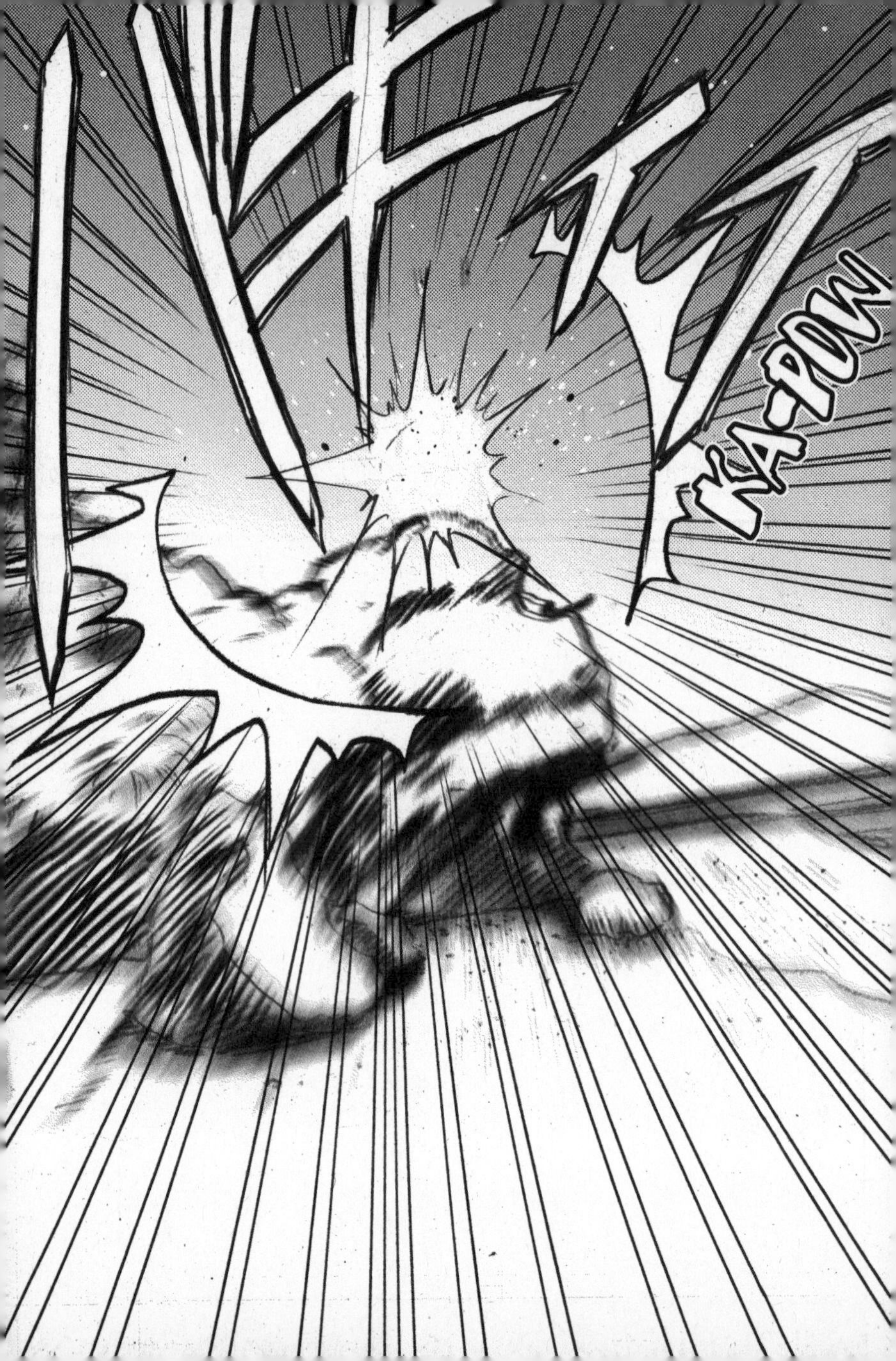
KA-POW!

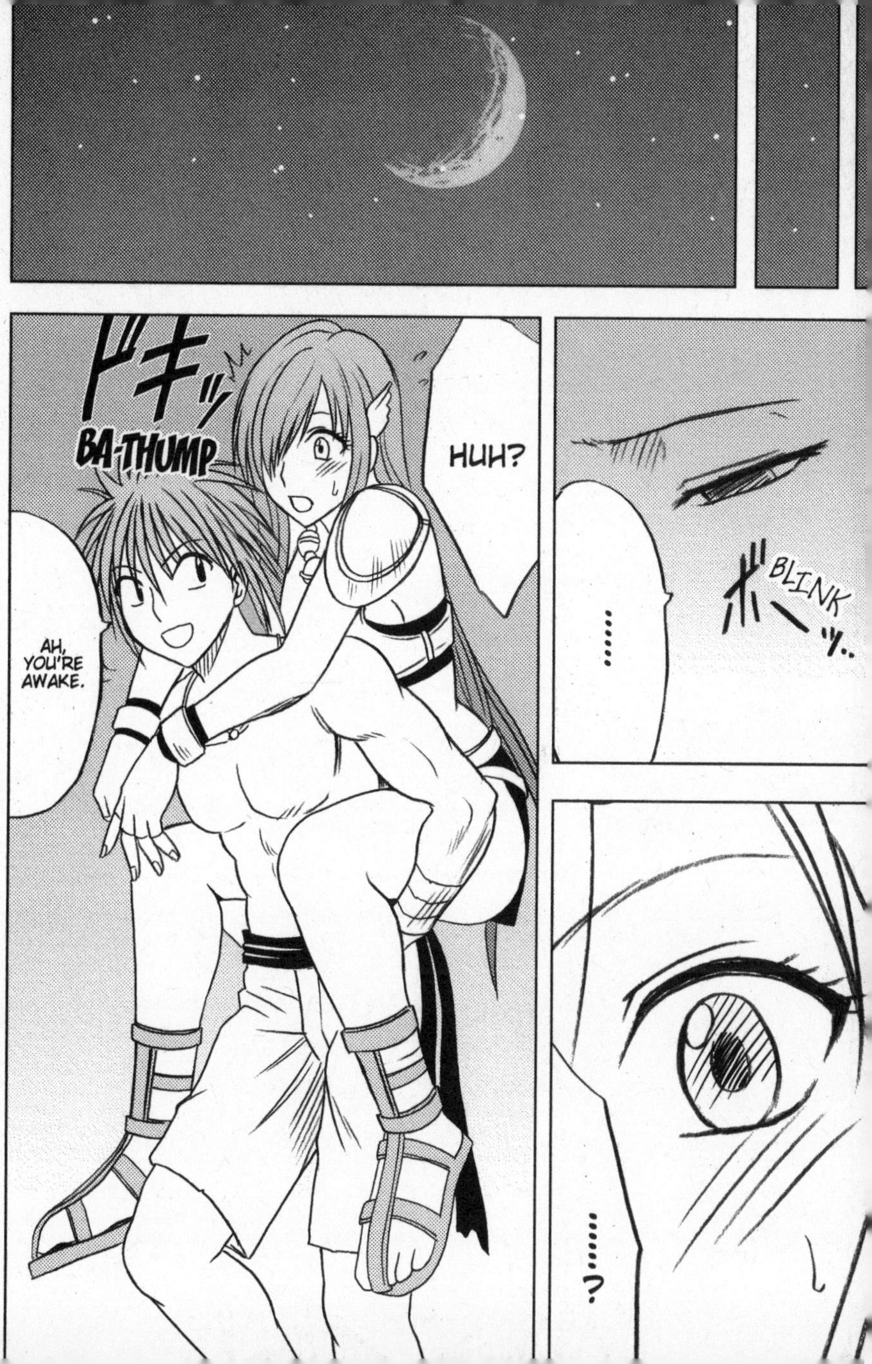

ボーッ..
BLINK
......
ッ......
HUH?
ドキッ
BA-THUMP
AH, YOU'RE AWAKE.

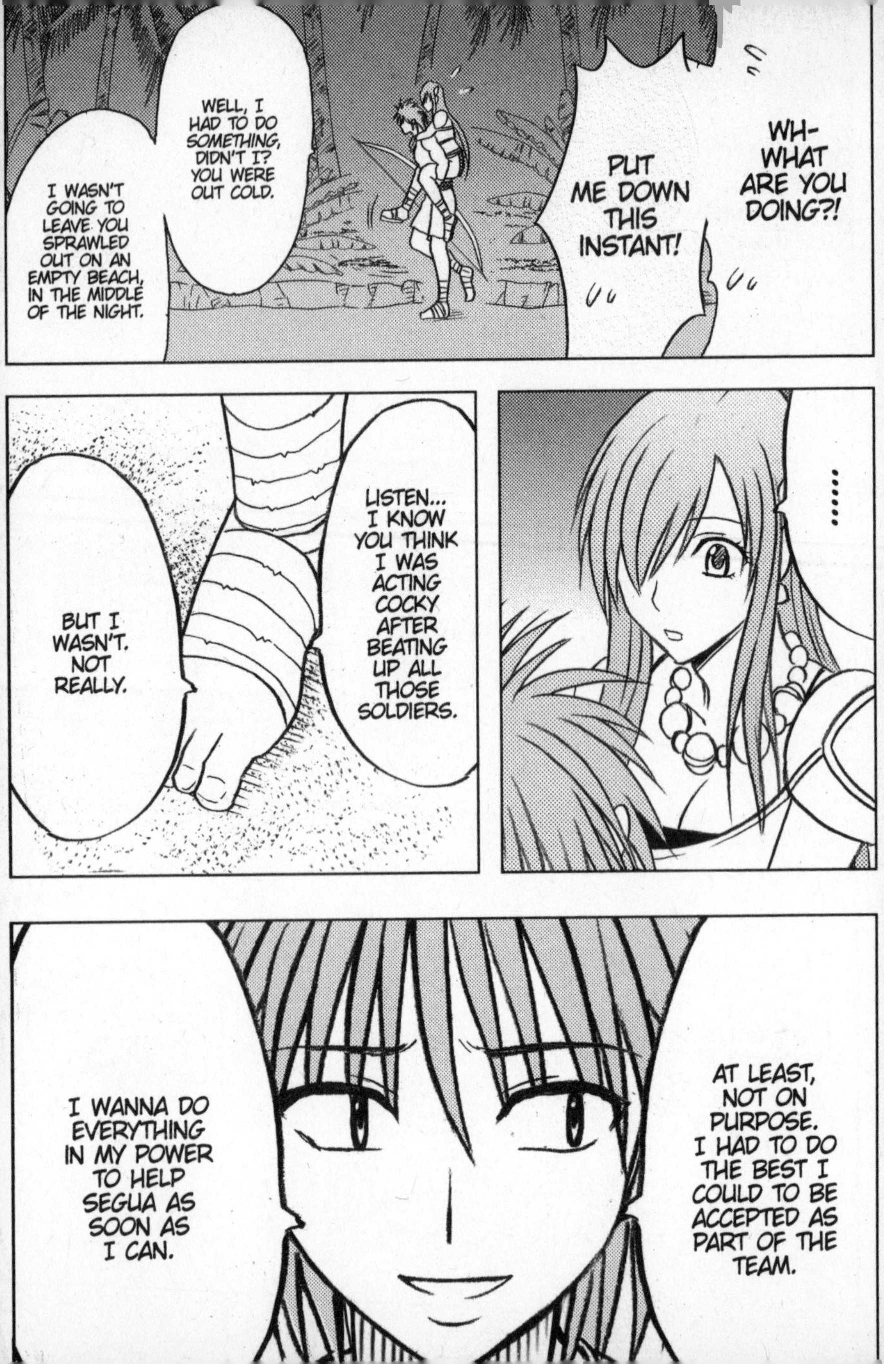
WH- WHAT ARE YOU DOING?!
PUT ME DOWN THIS INSTANT!
WELL, I HAD TO DO SOMETHING, DIDN'T I? YOU WERE OUT COLD.
I WASN'T GOING TO LEAVE YOU SPRAWLED OUT ON AN EMPTY BEACH, IN THE MIDDLE OF THE NIGHT.
......
LISTEN... I KNOW YOU THINK I WAS ACTING COCKY AFTER BEATING UP ALL THOSE SOLDIERS.
BUT I WASN'T. NOT REALLY.
AT LEAST, NOT ON PURPOSE. I HAD TO DO THE BEST I COULD TO BE ACCEPTED AS PART OF THE TEAM.
I WANNA DO EVERYTHING IN MY POWER TO HELP SEGUA AS SOON AS I CAN.

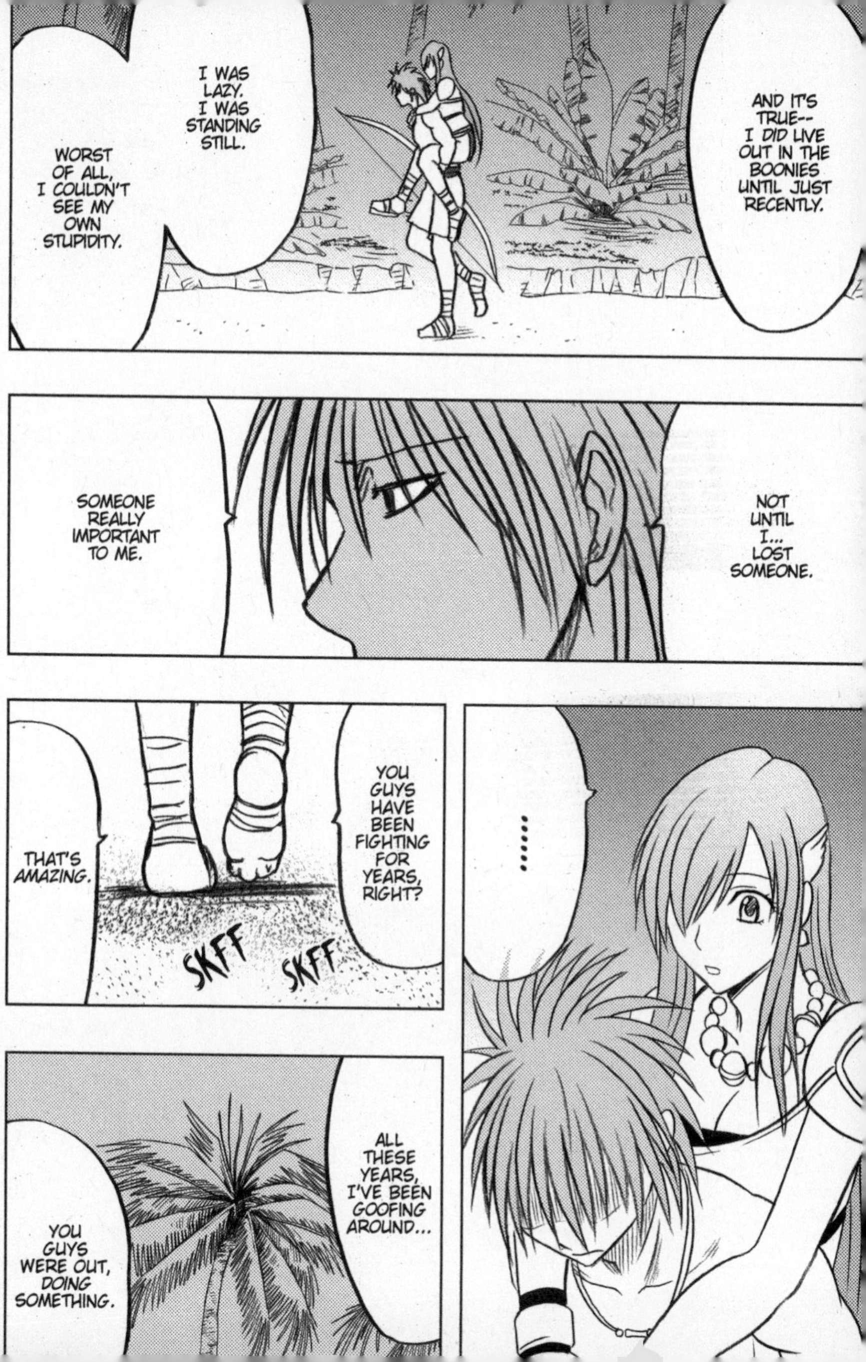
AND IT'S TRUE-- I DID LIVE OUT IN THE BOONIES UNTIL JUST RECENTLY.
I WAS LAZY. I WAS STANDING STILL.
WORST OF ALL, I COULDN'T SEE MY OWN STUPIDITY.
NOT UNTIL I... LOST SOMEONE.
SOMEONE REALLY IMPORTANT TO ME.
......
YOU GUYS HAVE BEEN FIGHTING FOR YEARS, RIGHT?
THAT'S AMAZING.
SKFF
SKFF
ALL THESE YEARS, I'VE BEEN GOOFING AROUND...
YOU GUYS WERE OUT, DOING SOMETHING.

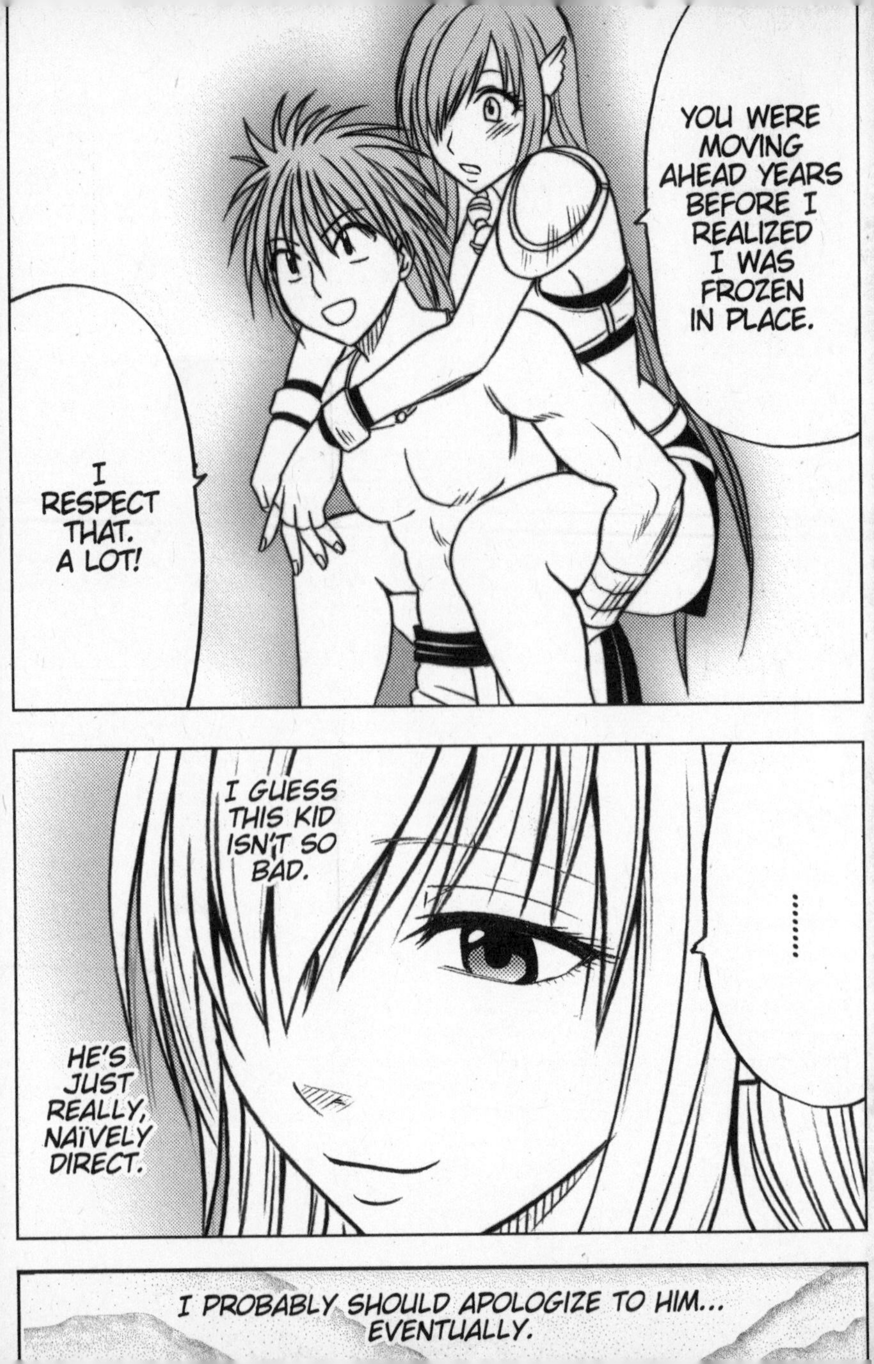
YOU WERE MOVING AHEAD YEARS BEFORE I REALIZED I WAS FROZEN IN PLACE.
I RESPECT THAT. A LOT!
......
I GUESS THIS KID ISN'T SO BAD.
HE'S JUST REALLY, NAÏVELY DIRECT.
I PROBABLY SHOULD APOLOGIZE TO HIM... EVENTUALLY.

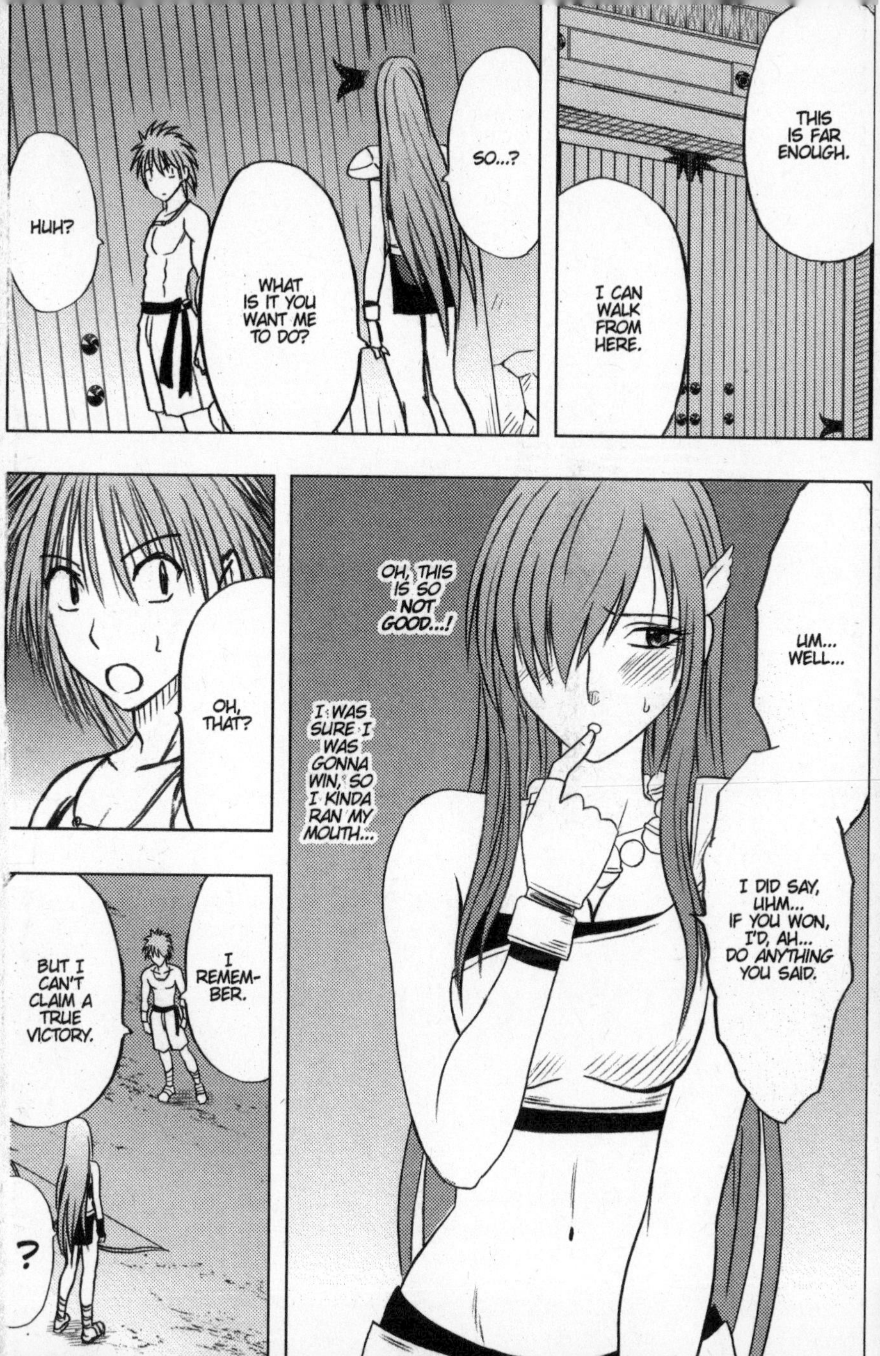
THIS IS FAR ENOUGH.
I CAN WALK FROM HERE.
SO...?
WHAT IS IT YOU WANT ME TO DO?
HUH?
UM... WELL...
I DID SAY, UHM... IF YOU WON, I'D, AH... DO ANYTHING YOU SAID.
OH, THIS IS SO NOT GOOD...!
I WAS SURE I WAS GONNA WIN, SO I KINDA RAN MY MOUTH...
OH, THAT?
I REMEMBER.
BUT I CAN'T CLAIM A TRUE VICTORY.
?

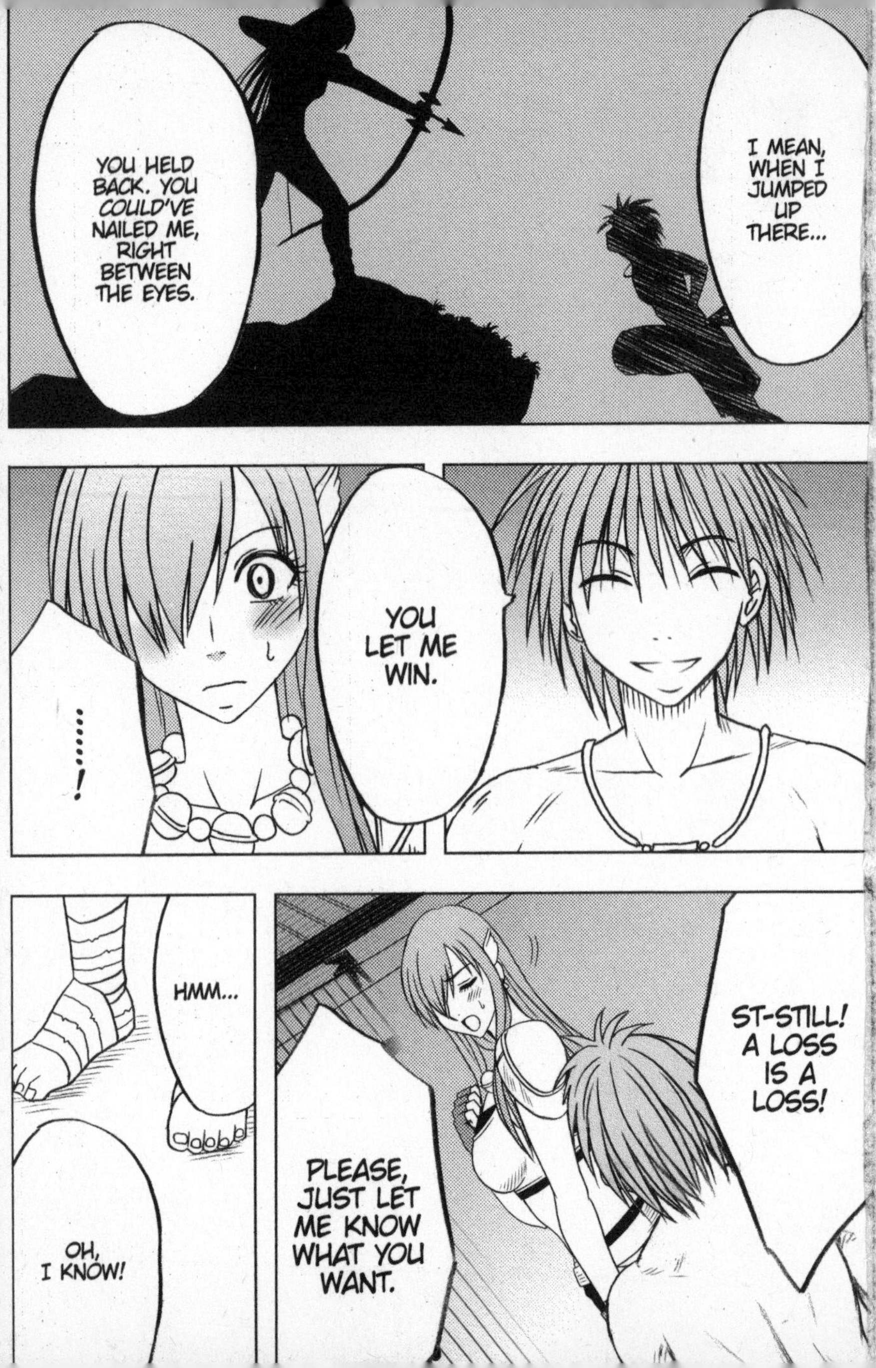
I MEAN, WHEN I JUMPED UP THERE...
YOU HELD BACK. YOU COULD'VE NAILED ME, RIGHT BETWEEN THE EYES.
YOU LET ME WIN.
......!
ST-STILL! A LOSS IS A LOSS!
PLEASE, JUST LET ME KNOW WHAT YOU WANT.
HMM...
OH, I KNOW!

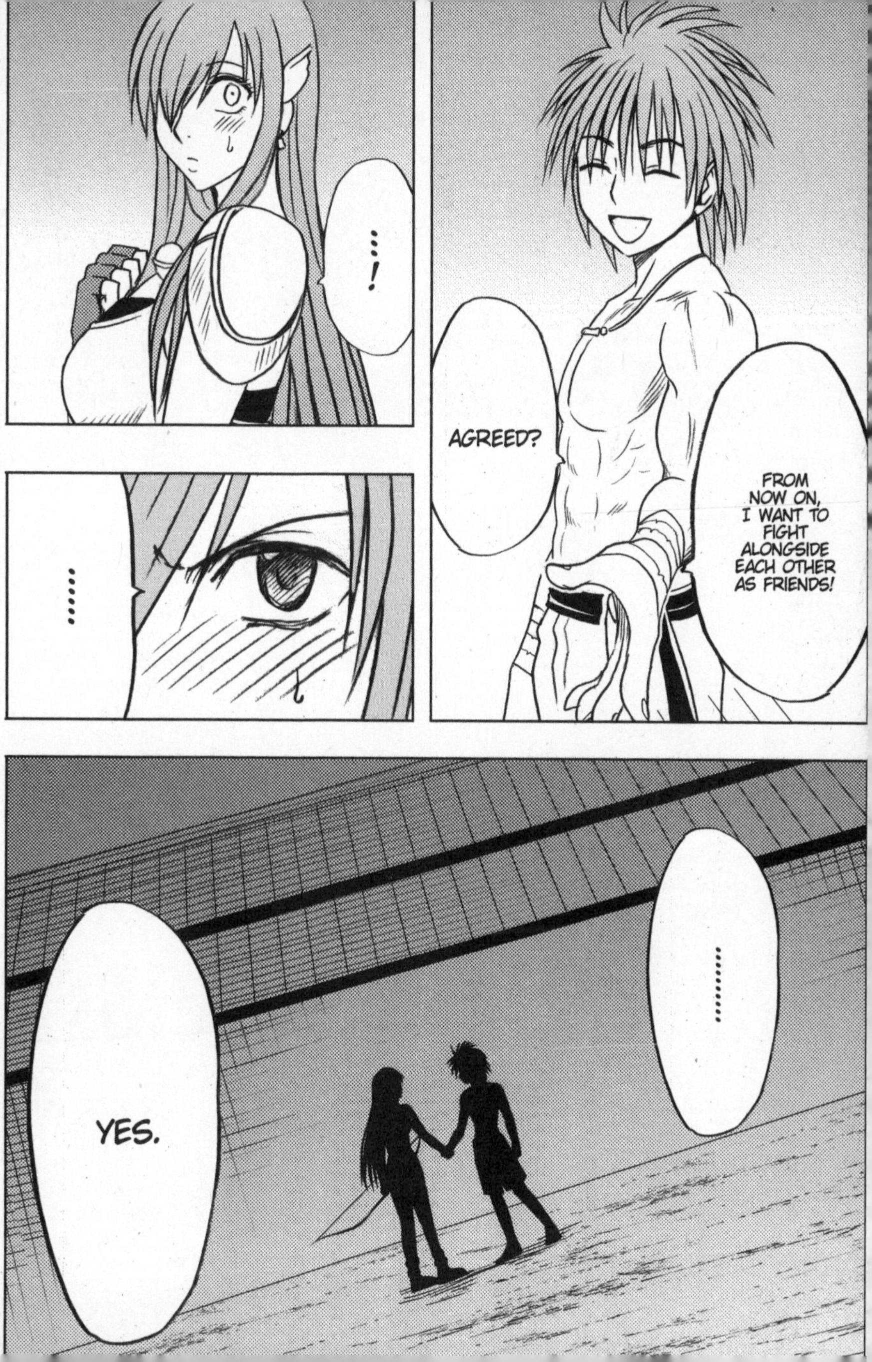
FROM NOW ON, I WANT TO FIGHT ALONGSIDE EACH OTHER AS FRIENDS!
AGREED?
...!
......
......
YES.

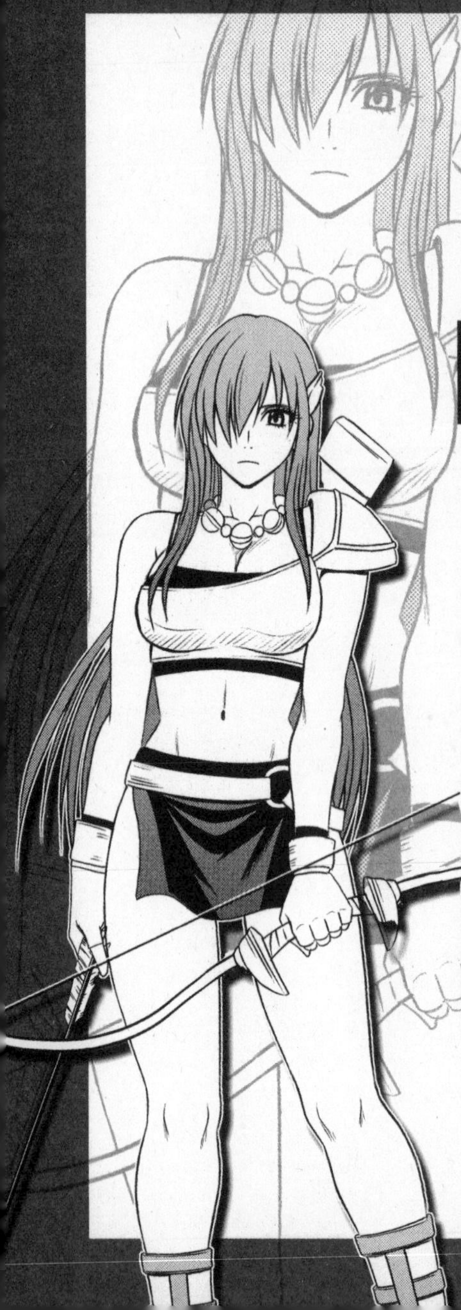

WORLD WAR BLUE
CHARACTER INTRODUCTION

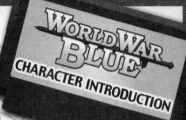

The Beautiful Hunter
OPAL

Native of the Kingdom of Segua.

The Segua Army's second best fighter.

No one knows why she came to join the Army, or what her life was like before then. She prefers solitude, often staying apart from the other soldiers. She has no close ties to anyone.

An excellent archer, she never misses her target, even while moving quickly across the battlefield.

Bad habits include nibbling on her fingertips when thinking and rashly deciding she doesn't like things. Worst of all, she has a tendency to make terrible puns.

HOBBY: Shopping. She especially loves buying different kinds of shoulder-plates for her armor.

Author Comment

I have an easy time drawing asymmetrical designs, so Opal is my favorite character to draw.

Perusing Video Game History

ON THE EDGE OF THE BLUE WORLD

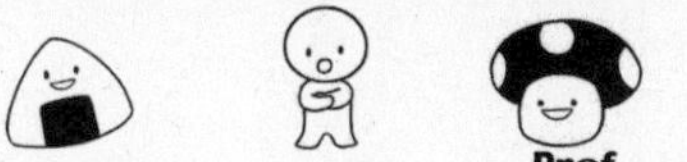

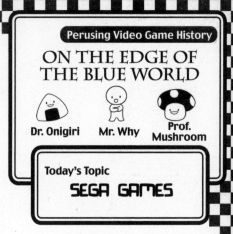

Dr. Onigiri
Mr. Why
Prof. Mushroom

Today's Topic

SEGA GAMES

Mr. Why: This time, I wanna hear all about Sega games!

Dr. Onigiri: Perfect! I wanna tell you all about Sega games!

Prof. Mushroom: Great. I ain't gonna get a chance to say much in this segment.

Dr. Onigiri: Okay, as I mentioned last time, Sega had already released a whole bunch of arcade games. They ported many of those over onto their consoles, and therefore, much of their popularity originated from fans of shooters and action games.

Prof. Mushroom: See, at the time, the big draw of consoles was getting to play arcade games in your own home. Even the NES gained popularity by porting big hits like *Donkey Kong* and *Super Mario Bros.*

Mr. Why: So what were Sega's big games?

Dr. Onigiri: They had quite a few hits, but let's start with *Fantasy Zone*, released for the Sega Mark III in 1986. Players controlled Opa-Opa, a protagonist who looked like a pod with wings, as he flew around, destroying enemy bases. Defeating enemies earned you coins, which could then be spent in a shop to buy upgrades. That's a staple of RPG games, but for it to show up in a shooter was very innovative at the time.

Mr. Why: Neat! You could go shopping, right inside the game!

Dr. Onigiri: Yeah, you could buy fun stuff like extra lives, otherwise known as a **1-up**, the **7-Way Shot**, which did spread-damage, or the **Heavy Bomb**, which could shoot huge bullets that looked like 16-ton weights.

Mr. Why: Wow, that sounds cool!

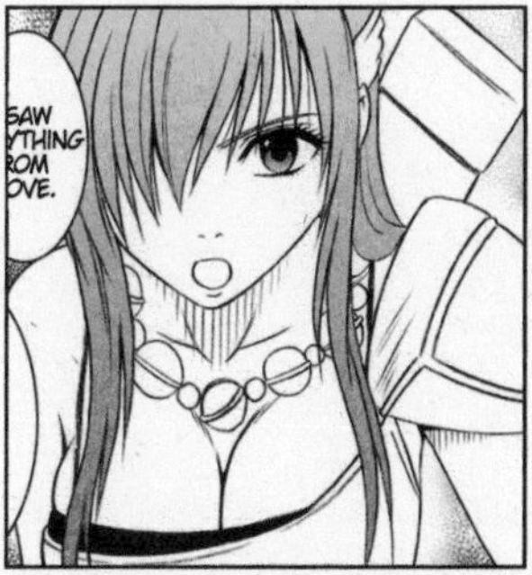

SAW YTHING ROM OVE.

Opal, the beautiful huntress. She never misses her mark.

Opal's earrings have a unique design.

The elite of Segua Army. They're fairly decent!

Dr. Onigiri: It sure was! Speaking of cool stuff, the background music even had vocals!

Mr. Why: What, there was someone singing?

Dr. Onigiri: Not precisely. The technology at the time wasn't capable of having actual voices in the music. However, a game magazine published the lyrics to the in-game song, and after reading them, whenever you played the game, you could fit the words you read to the music.

Mr. Why: Ooh! What kind of song was it? Tell me! Tell me!

Dr. Onigiri: Well, there were two tracks in the main part of the game with lyrics, but the most famous song was the tune used in the final boss stage, "YA-DA-YO."

Mr. Why: Sing it for me! Sing it for me!

Dr. Onigiri: No.

Mr Why: Awww! Scrooge! Meany-pants!

Dr. Onigiri: Anyway, *Fantasy Zone* had other cool features, but I'll have to tell you about them later. Just don't forget what I've taught you so far.

Mr. Why: C'mon, why can't you tell me more now?

Dr. Onigiri: No.

Prof. Mushroom: Anyway, ain't it time for you to start talking about some *other* games?

Dr. Onigiri: Sure! There's *Shinobi*, an action game where you control a ninja. There's *Aztec Adventure* and its iconic cowboy hat. There was also a port of the arcade game *Quartet*, which was famous for letting 4 players play at once—in the arcade, at least. The console only supported two players: a girl and a bald guy with sunglasses, so they renamed it *Double Target*. Oh, and don't forget the puzzle game *Columns*, either.

Prof. Mushroom: Hey, how about we make *Columns* our topic for next time?

TO BE CONTINUED...

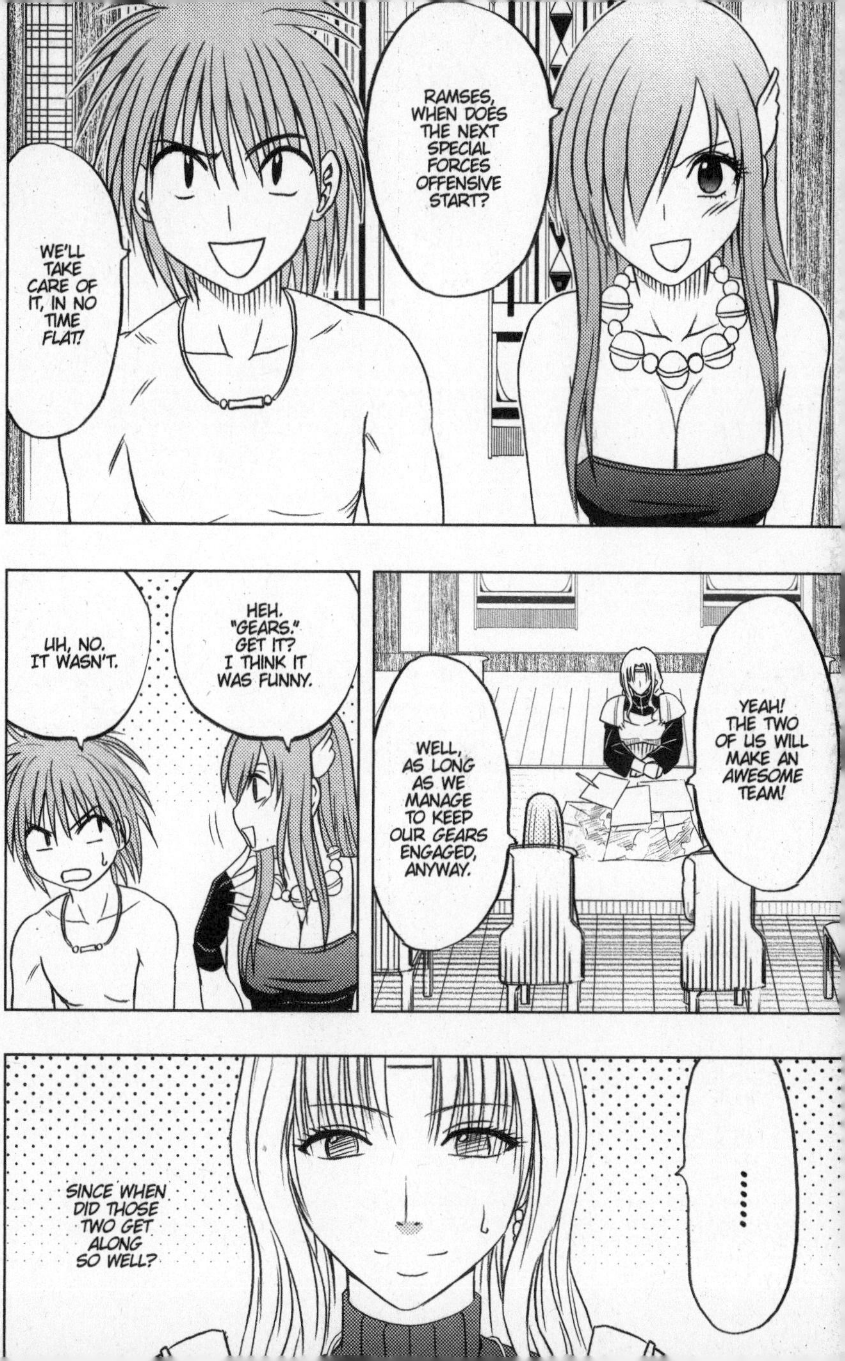
RAMSES, WHEN DOES THE NEXT SPECIAL FORCES OFFENSIVE START?
WE'LL TAKE CARE OF IT, IN NO TIME FLAT!
YEAH! THE TWO OF US WILL MAKE AN AWESOME TEAM!
WELL, AS LONG AS WE MANAGE TO KEEP OUR GEARS ENGAGED, ANYWAY.
HEH. "GEARS." GET IT? I THINK IT WAS FUNNY.
UH, NO. IT WASN'T.
......
SINCE WHEN DID THOSE TWO GET ALONG SO WELL?

CHAPTER 4

FOR EVERY BUMP THERE IS A DIVOT, FOR EVERY HOLE, THERE IS A ROD.

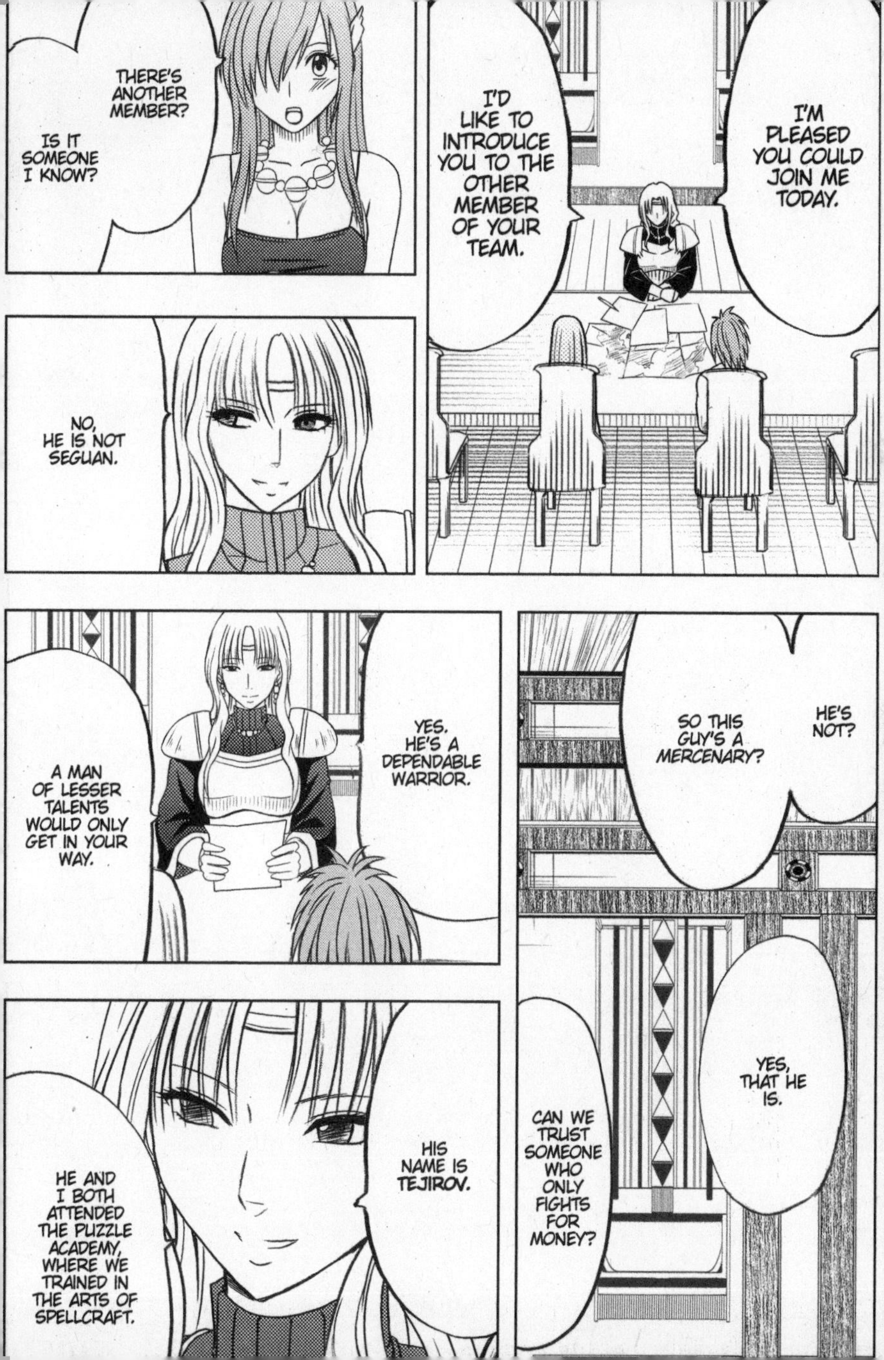
I'M PLEASED YOU COULD JOIN ME TODAY.
I'D LIKE TO INTRODUCE YOU TO THE OTHER MEMBER OF YOUR TEAM.
THERE'S ANOTHER MEMBER?
IS IT SOMEONE I KNOW?
NO, HE IS NOT SEGUAN.
HE'S NOT?
SO THIS GUY'S A MERCENARY?
YES, THAT HE IS.
CAN WE TRUST SOMEONE WHO ONLY FIGHTS FOR MONEY?
YES. HE'S A DEPENDABLE WARRIOR.
A MAN OF LESSER TALENTS WOULD ONLY GET IN YOUR WAY.
HIS NAME IS TEJIROV.
HE AND I BOTH ATTENDED THE PUZZLE ACADEMY, WHERE WE TRAINED IN THE ARTS OF SPELLCRAFT.

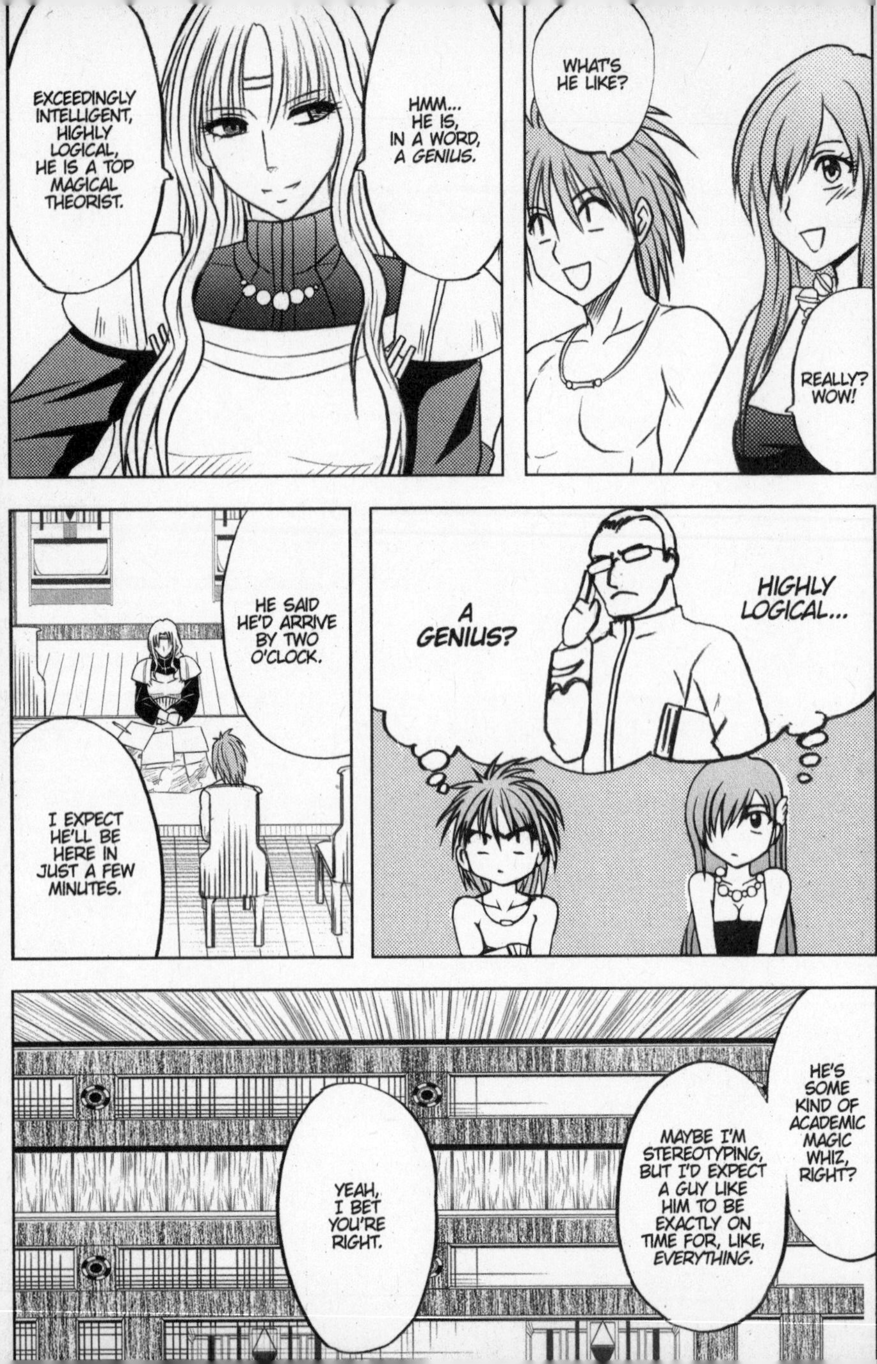
WHAT'S HE LIKE?
REALLY? WOW!
HMM... HE IS, IN A WORD, A GENIUS.
EXCEEDINGLY INTELLIGENT, HIGHLY LOGICAL, HE IS A TOP MAGICAL THEORIST.
HIGHLY LOGICAL...
A GENIUS?
HE SAID HE'D ARRIVE BY TWO O'CLOCK.
I EXPECT HE'LL BE HERE IN JUST A FEW MINUTES.
HE'S SOME KIND OF ACADEMIC MAGIC WHIZ, RIGHT?
MAYBE I'M STEREOTYPING, BUT I'D EXPECT A GUY LIKE HIM TO BE EXACTLY ON TIME FOR, LIKE, EVERYTHING.
YEAH, I BET YOU'RE RIGHT.

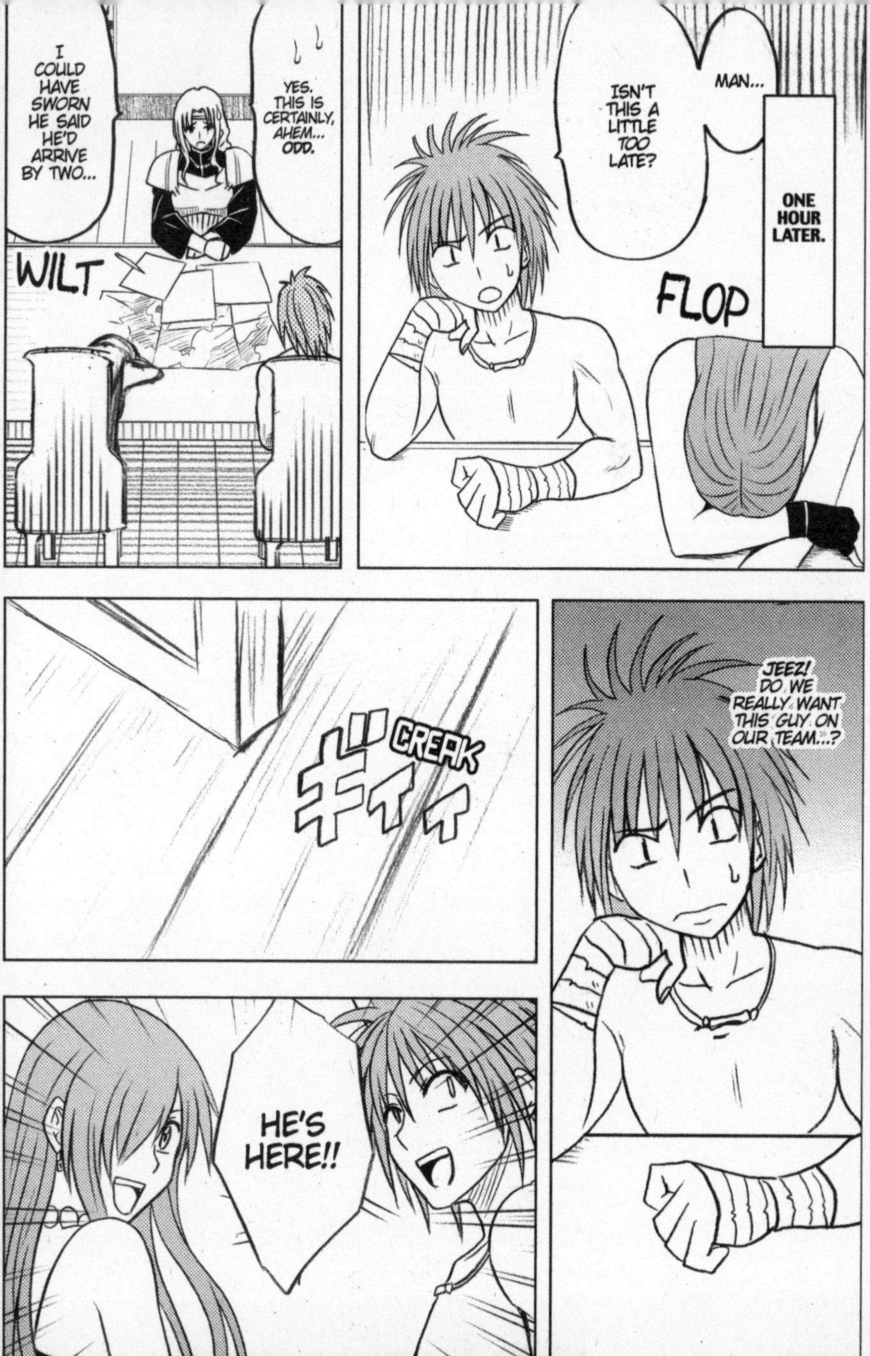
ONE HOUR LATER.
MAN... ISN'T THIS A LITTLE TOO LATE?
FLOP
YES. THIS IS CERTAINLY, AHEM... ODD.
I COULD HAVE SWORN HE SAID HE'D ARRIVE BY TWO...
WILT
JEEZ! DO WE REALLY WANT THIS GUY ON OUR TEAM...?
ギィィ
CREAK
HE'S HERE!!

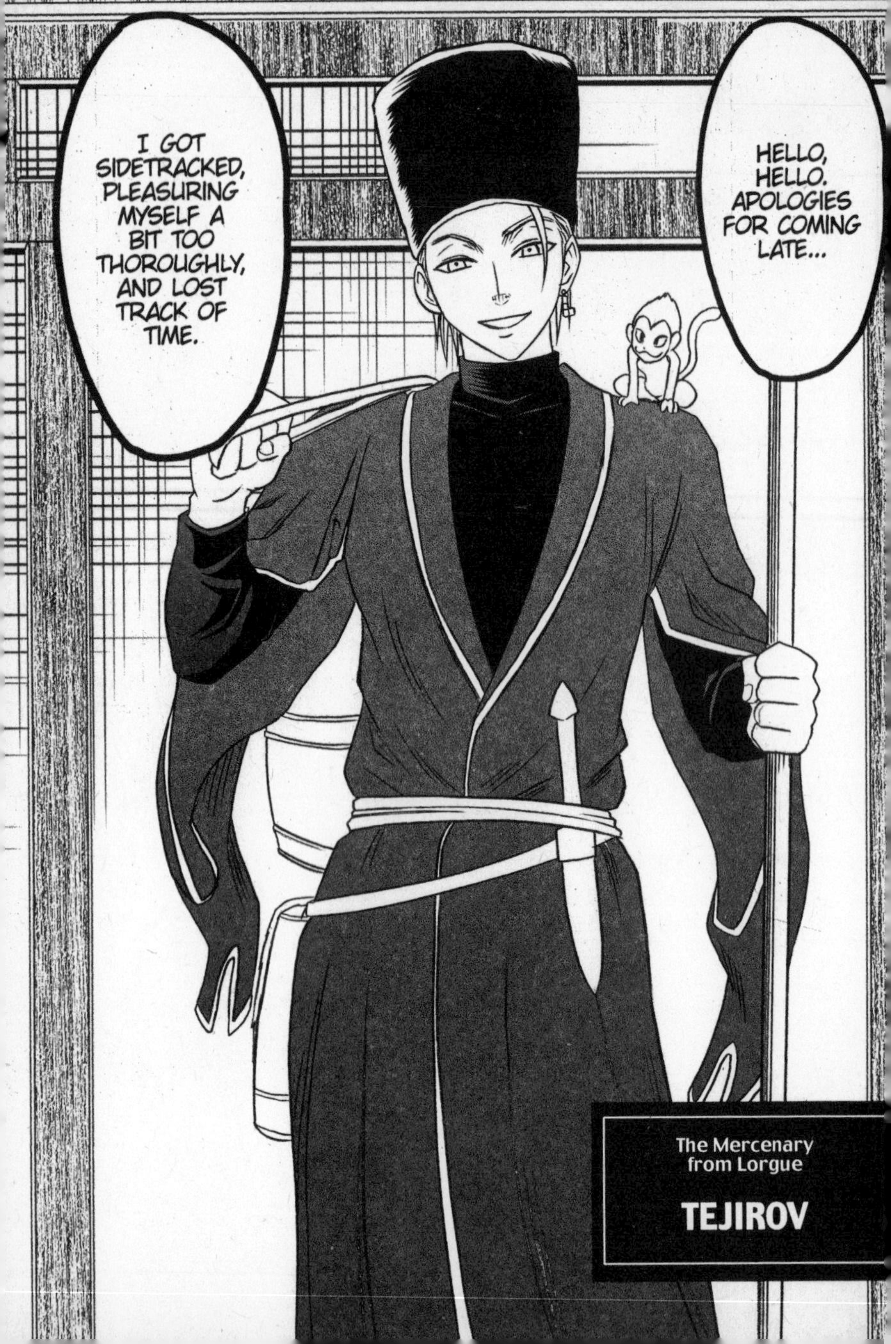
HELLO, HELLO. APOLOGIES FOR COMING LATE...
I GOT SIDETRACKED, PLEASURING MYSELF A BIT TOO THOROUGHLY, AND LOST TRACK OF TIME.
The Mercenary from Lorgue
TEJIROV

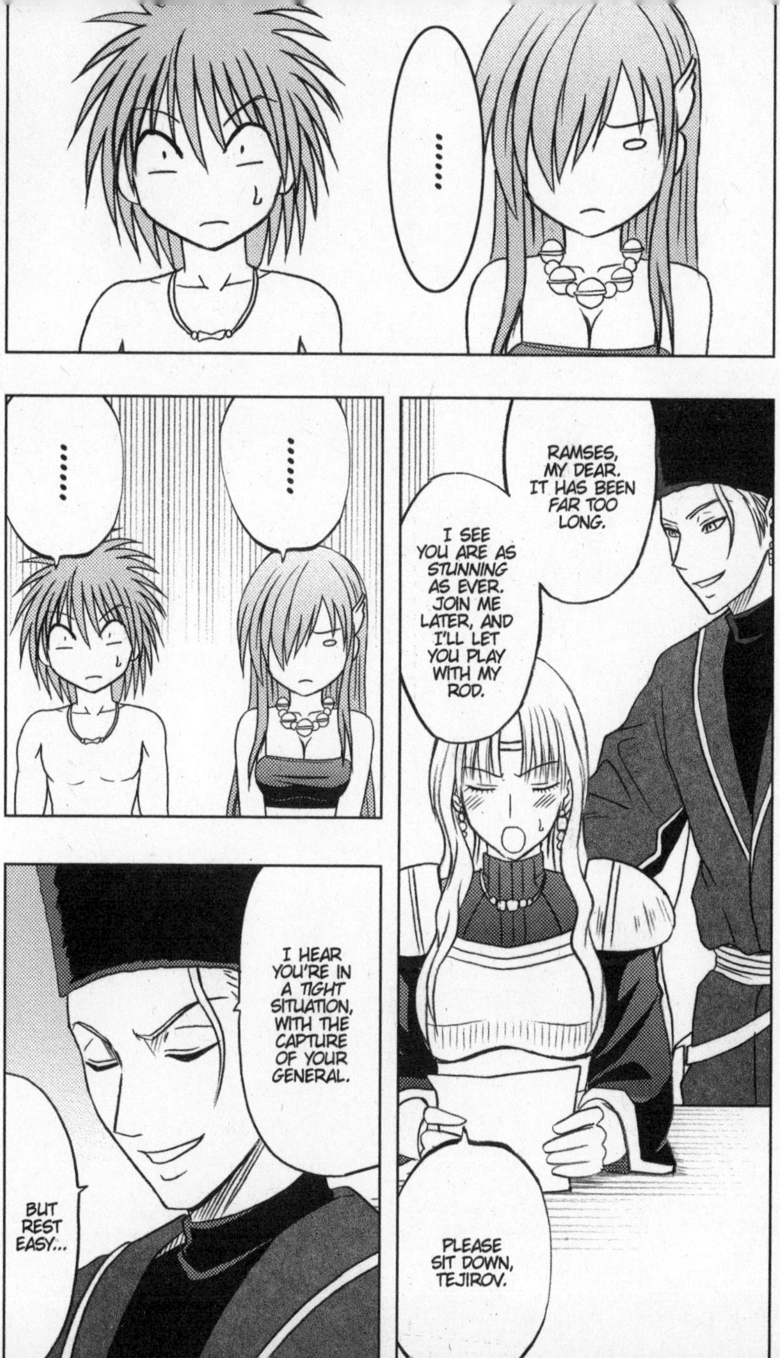
……
RAMSES, MY DEAR. IT HAS BEEN FAR TOO LONG.
I SEE YOU ARE AS STUNNING AS EVER. JOIN ME LATER, AND I'LL LET YOU PLAY WITH MY ROD.
PLEASE SIT DOWN, TEJIROV.
……
……
I HEAR YOU'RE IN A TIGHT SITUATION, WITH THE CAPTURE OF YOUR GENERAL.
BUT REST EASY...

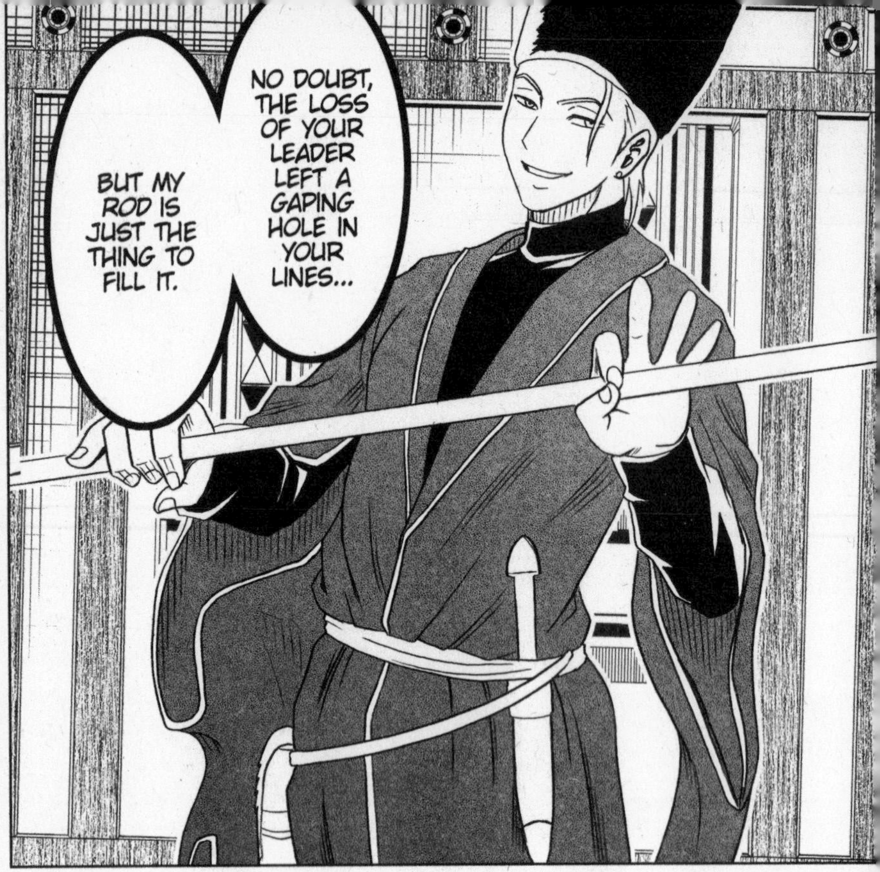
NO DOUBT, THE LOSS OF YOUR LEADER LEFT A GAPING HOLE IN YOUR LINES...
BUT MY ROD IS JUST THE THING TO FILL IT.

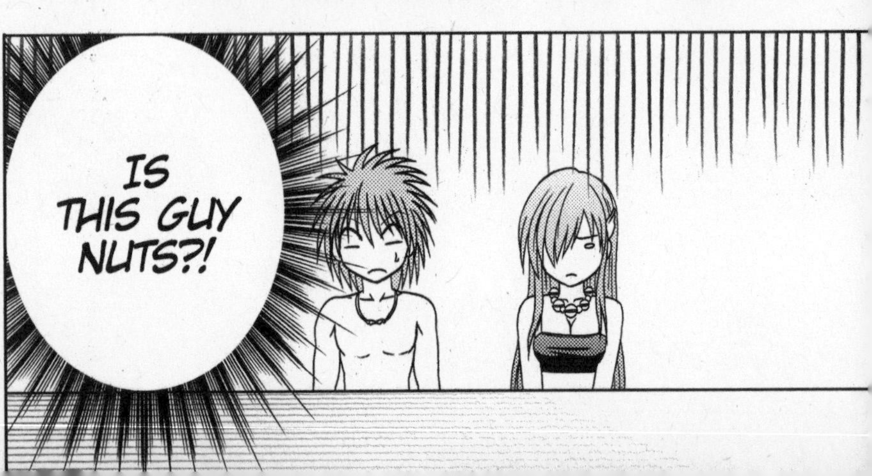
IS THIS GUY NUTS?!

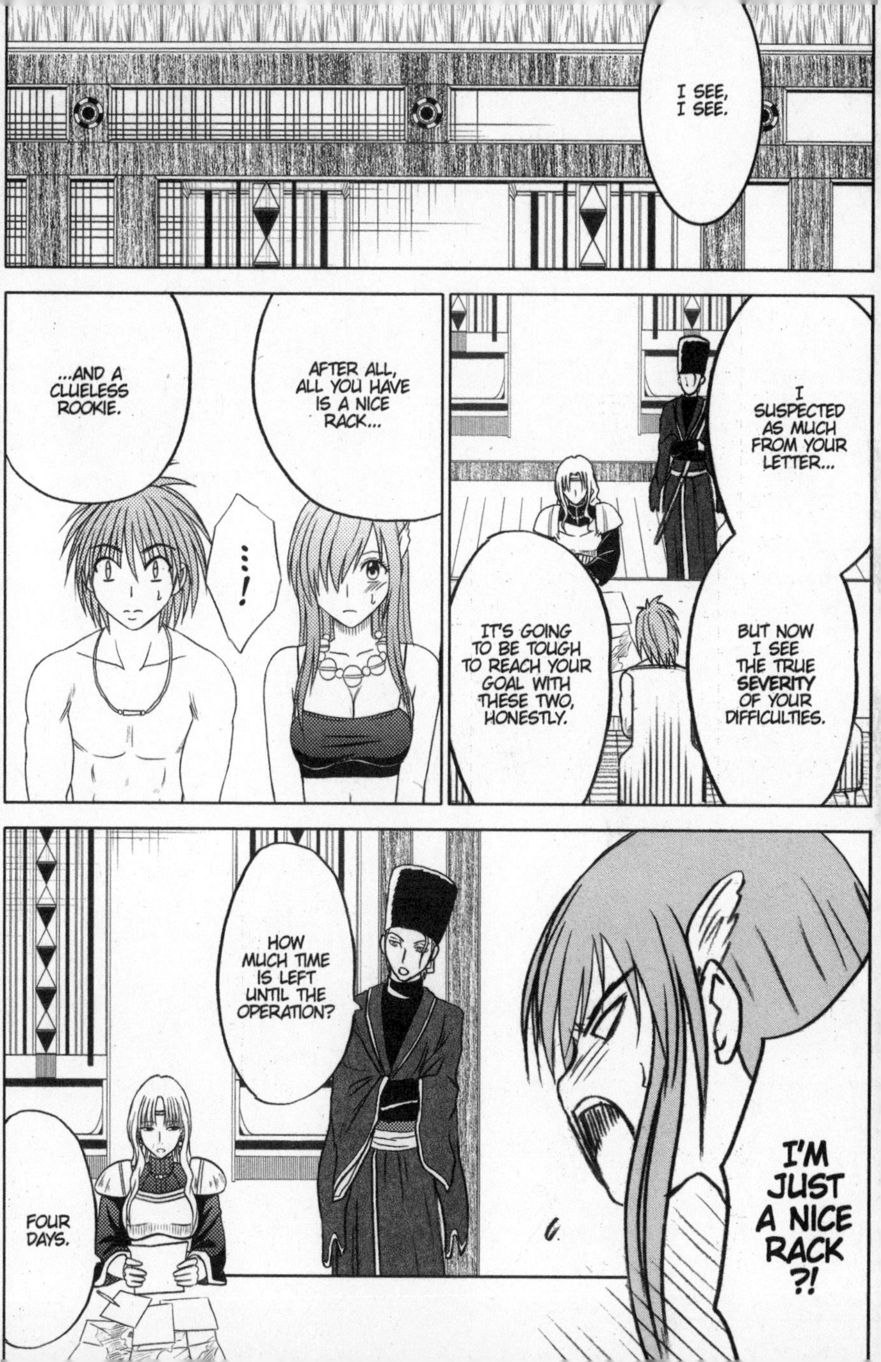
I SEE, I SEE.
I SUSPECTED AS MUCH FROM YOUR LETTER...
BUT NOW I SEE THE TRUE SEVERITY OF YOUR DIFFICULTIES.
IT'S GOING TO BE TOUGH TO REACH YOUR GOAL WITH THESE TWO, HONESTLY.
AFTER ALL, ALL YOU HAVE IS A NICE RACK...
...!
...AND A CLUELESS ROOKIE.
I'M JUST A NICE RACK ?!
HOW MUCH TIME IS LEFT UNTIL THE OPERATION?
FOUR DAYS.

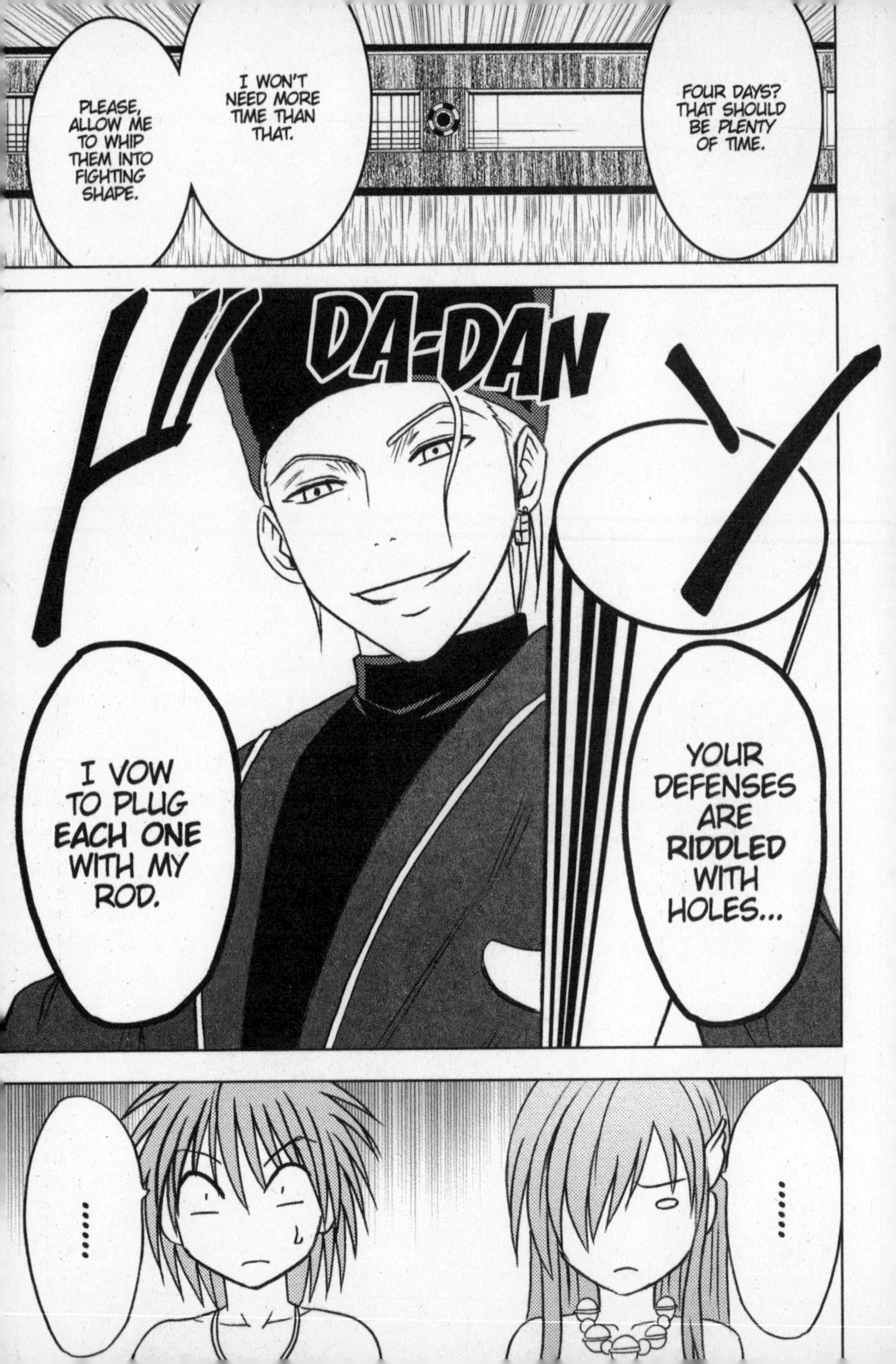
FOUR DAYS? THAT SHOULD BE PLENTY OF TIME.
I WON'T NEED MORE TIME THAN THAT.
PLEASE, ALLOW ME TO WHIP THEM INTO FIGHTING SHAPE.
DA-DAN
YOUR DEFENSES ARE RIDDLED WITH HOLES...
I VOW TO PLUG EACH ONE WITH MY ROD.
......
......

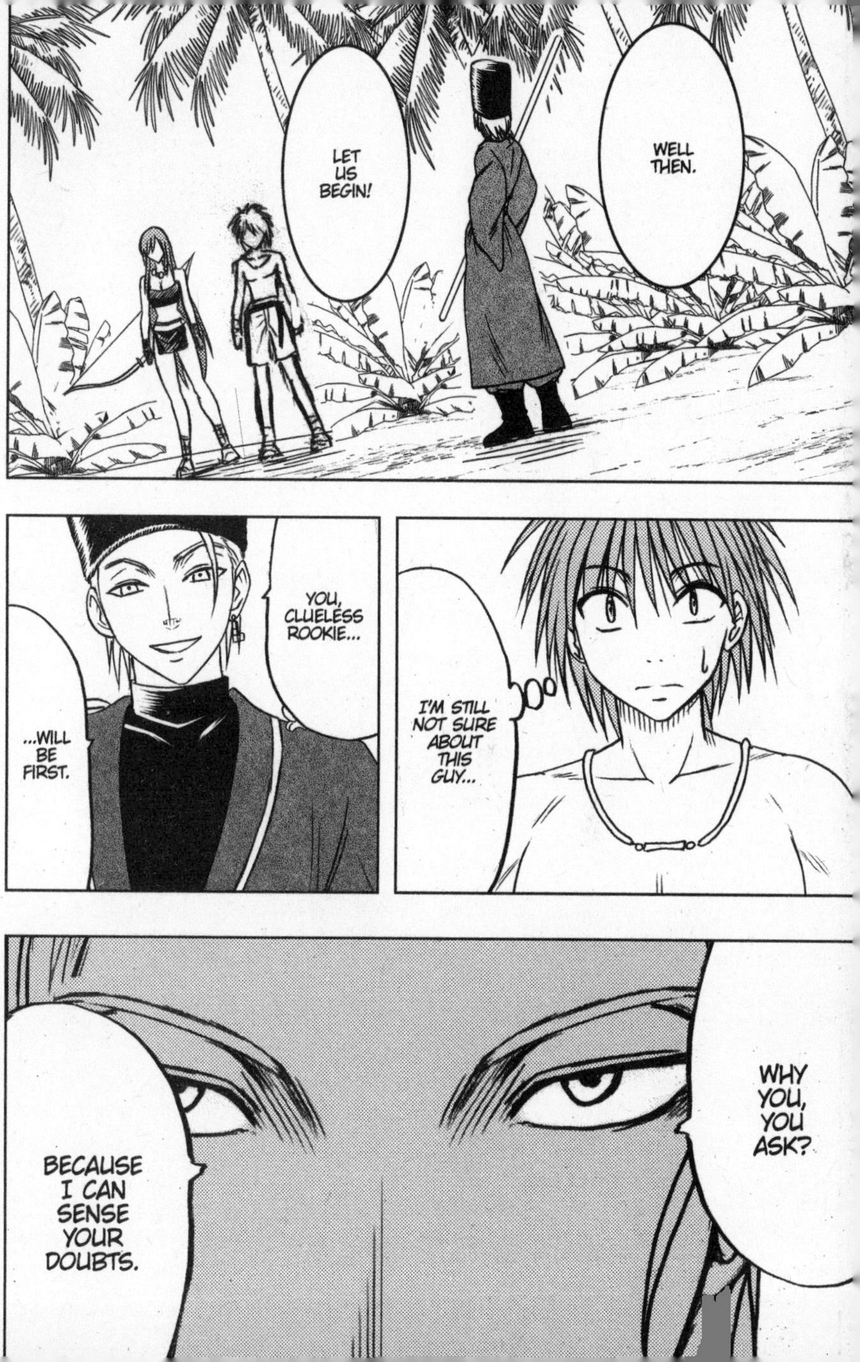
WELL THEN.
LET US BEGIN!
I'M STILL NOT SURE ABOUT THIS GUY...
YOU, CLUELESS ROOKIE...
...WILL BE FIRST.
WHY YOU, YOU ASK?
BECAUSE I CAN SENSE YOUR DOUBTS.

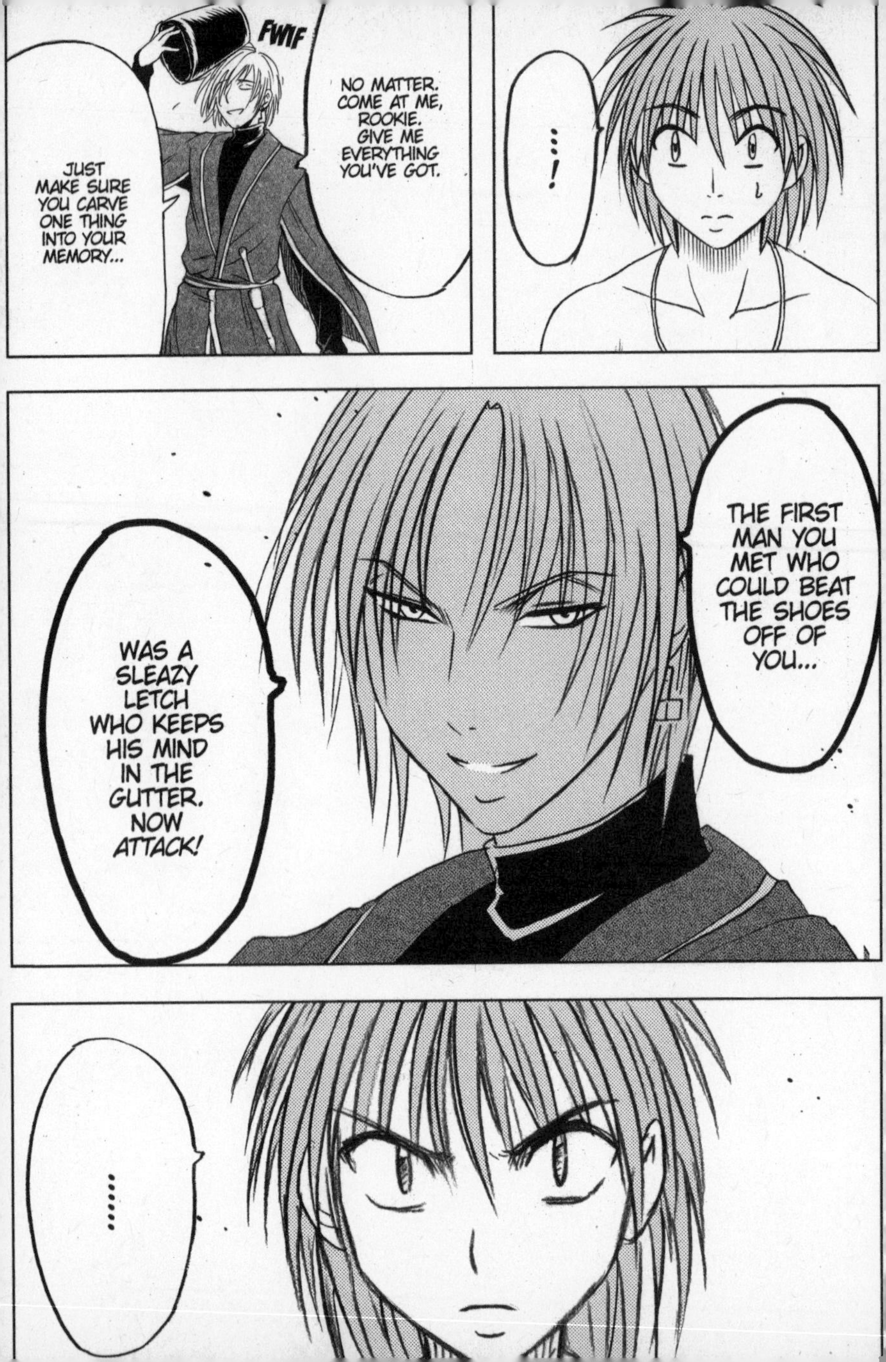
...!
FWIF
NO MATTER. COME AT ME, ROOKIE. GIVE ME EVERYTHING YOU'VE GOT.
JUST MAKE SURE YOU CARVE ONE THING INTO YOUR MEMORY...
THE FIRST MAN YOU MET WHO COULD BEAT THE SHOES OFF OF YOU...
WAS A SLEAZY LETCH WHO KEEPS HIS MIND IN THE GUTTER. NOW ATTACK!
......

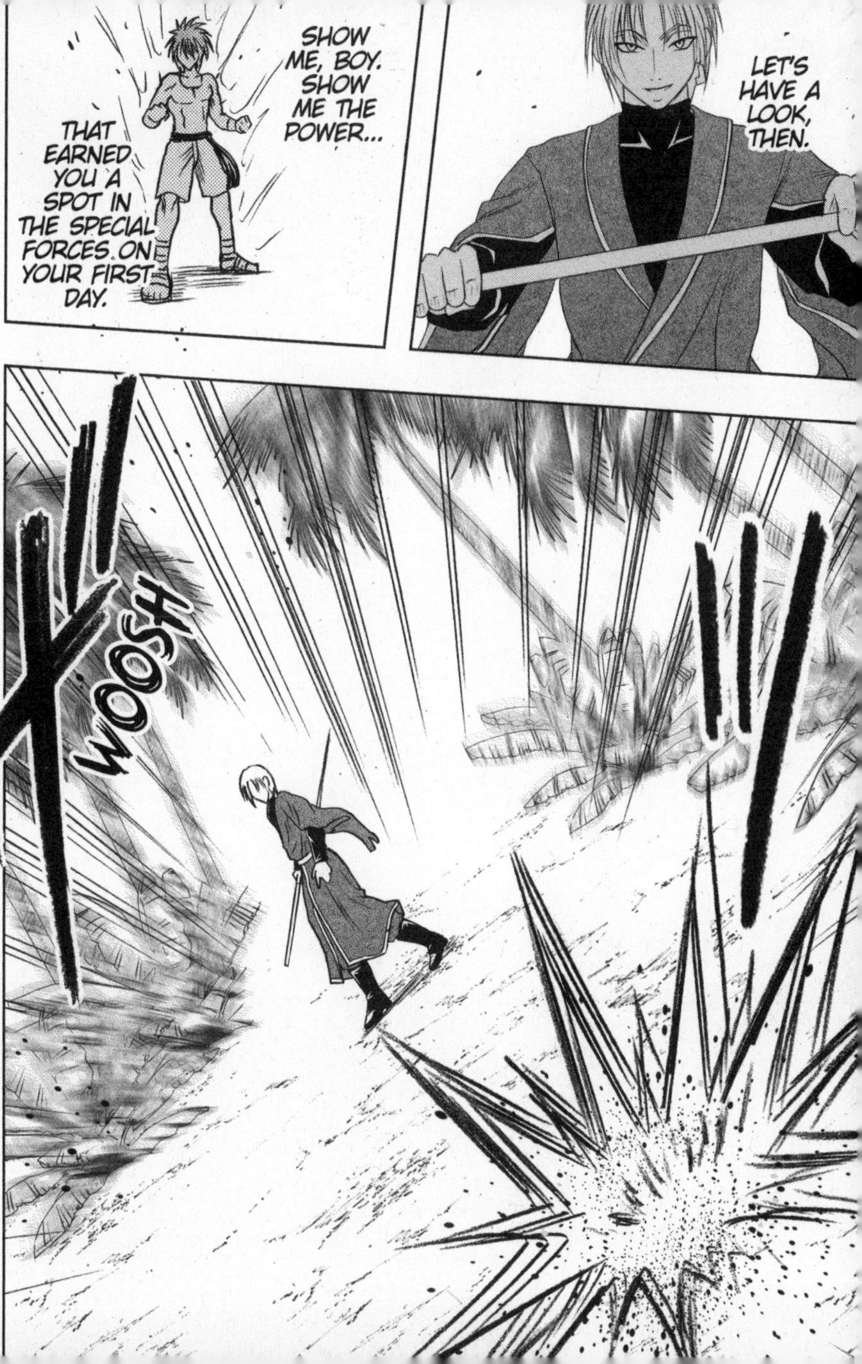
LET'S HAVE A LOOK, THEN.
SHOW ME, BOY. SHOW ME THE POWER...
THAT EARNED YOU A SPOT IN THE SPECIAL FORCES ON YOUR FIRST DAY.
WOOSH

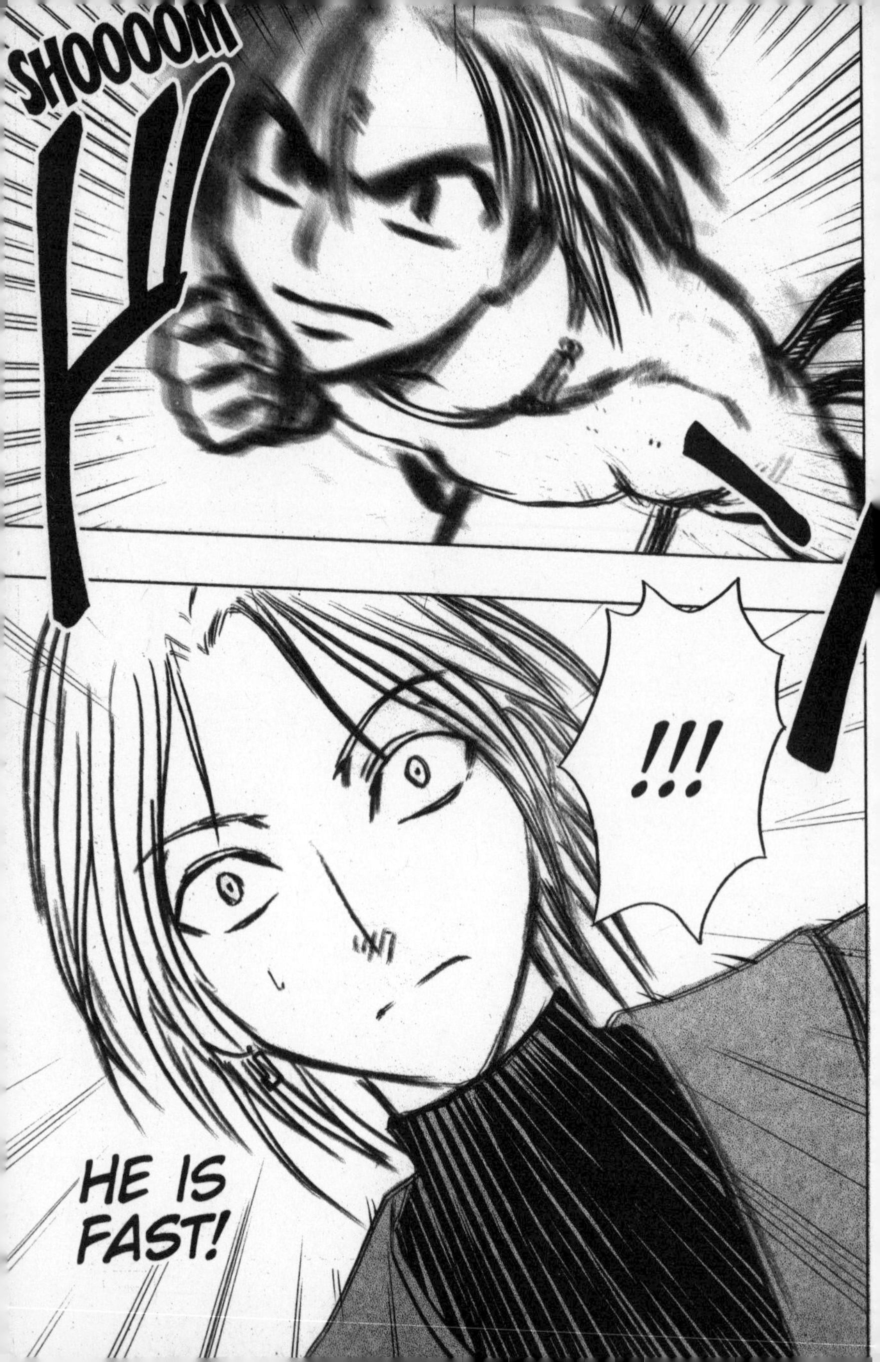
SHOOOOM
!!!
HE IS FAST!

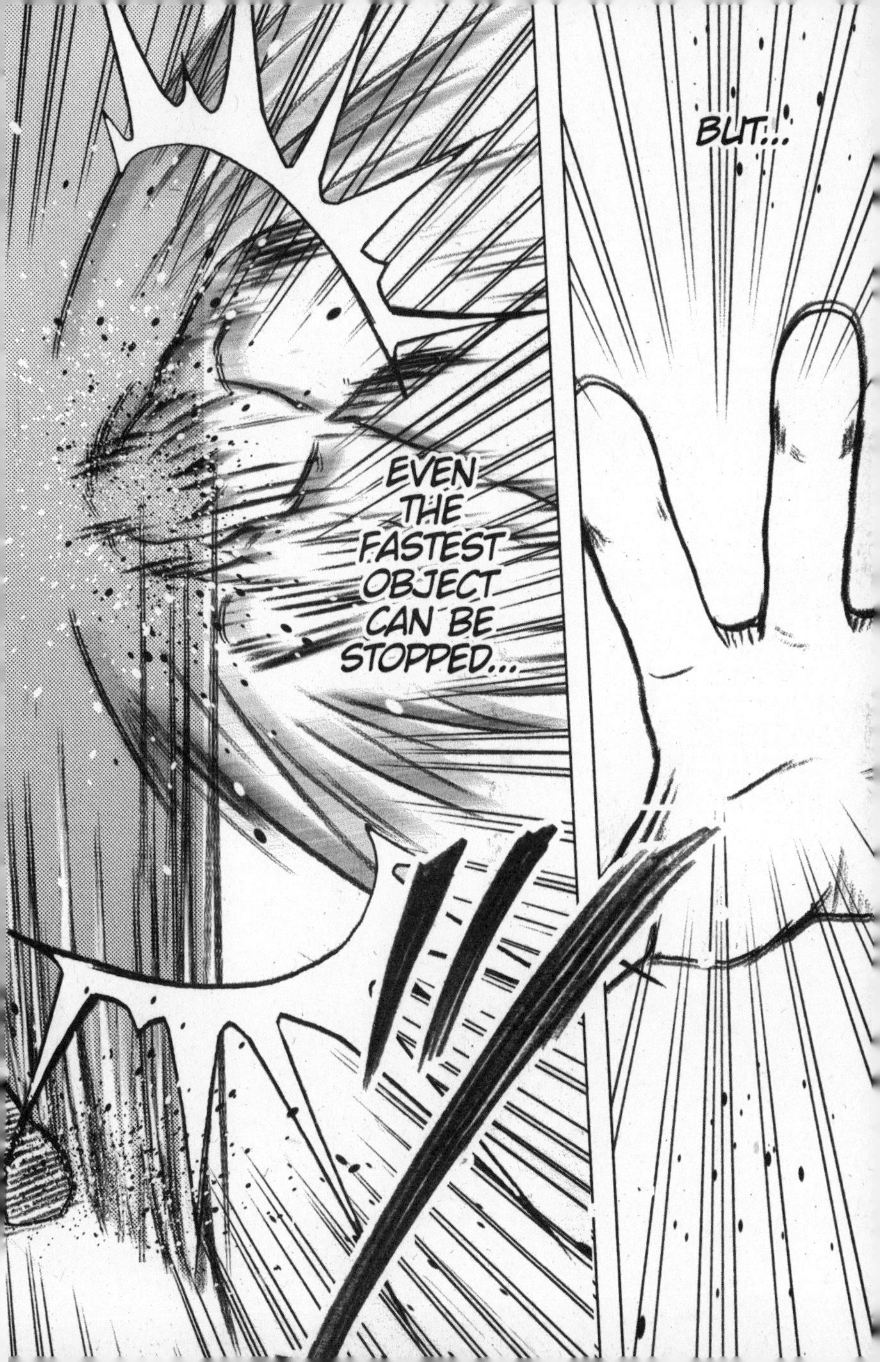
BUT...
EVEN THE FASTEST OBJECT CAN BE STOPPED...

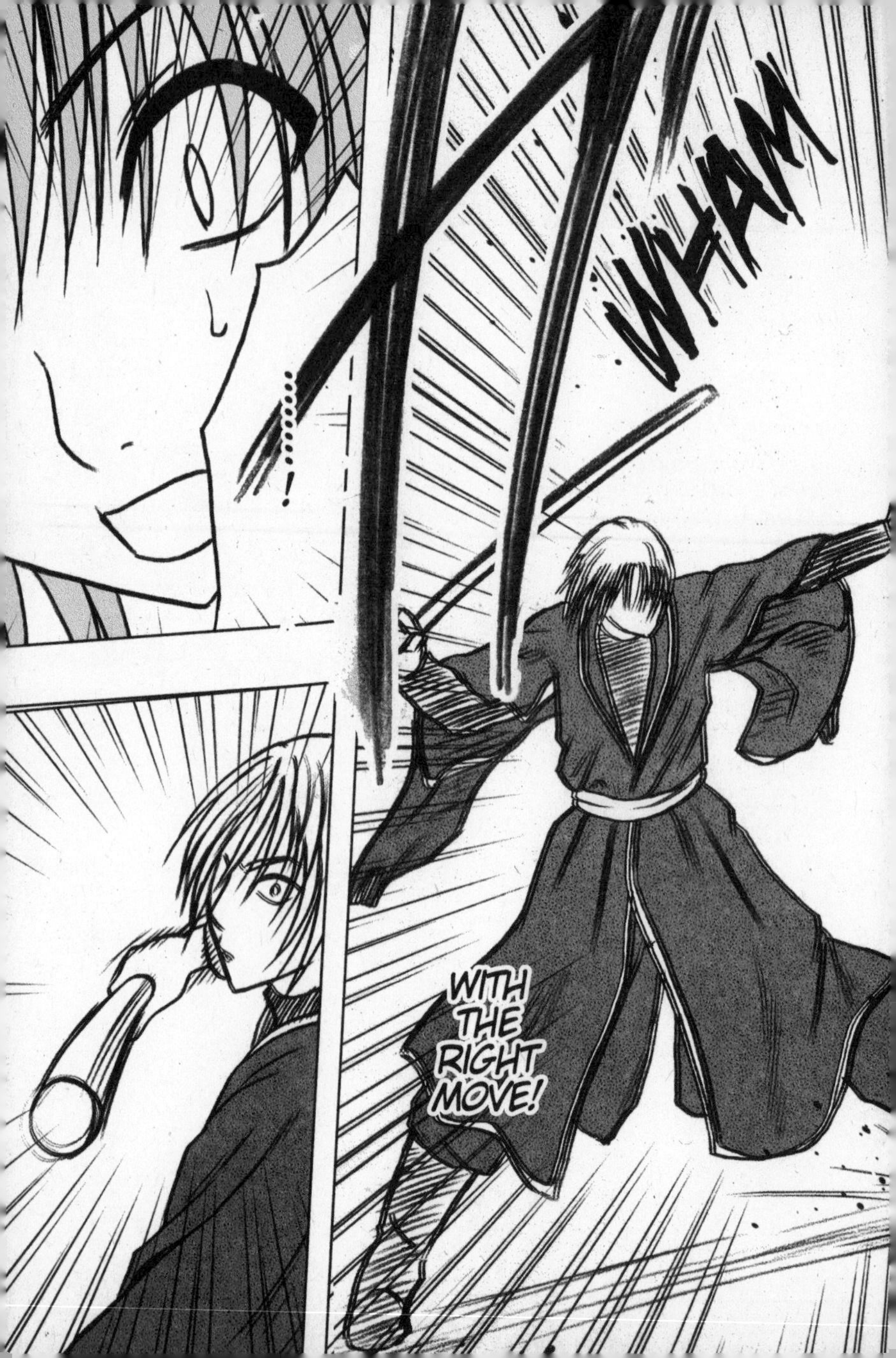
WHAM
WITH THE RIGHT MOVE!
......!

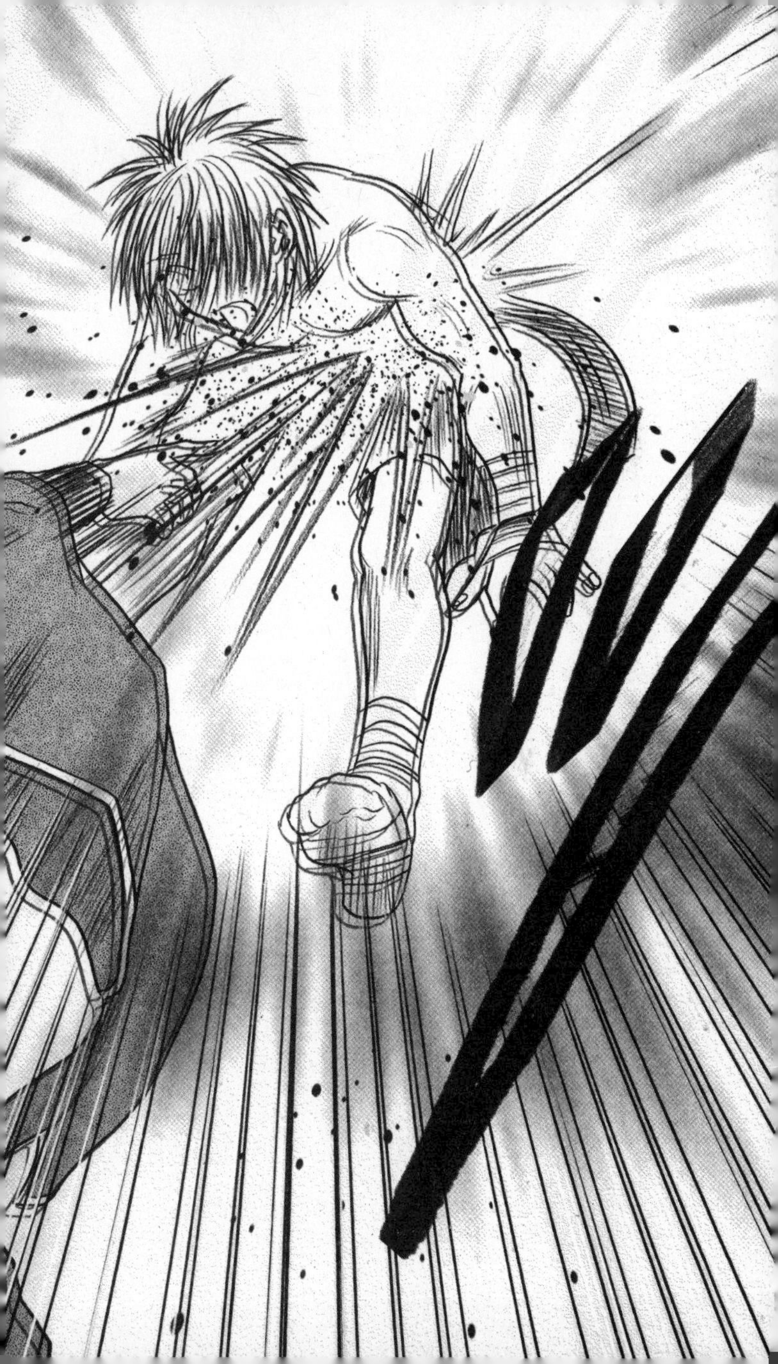

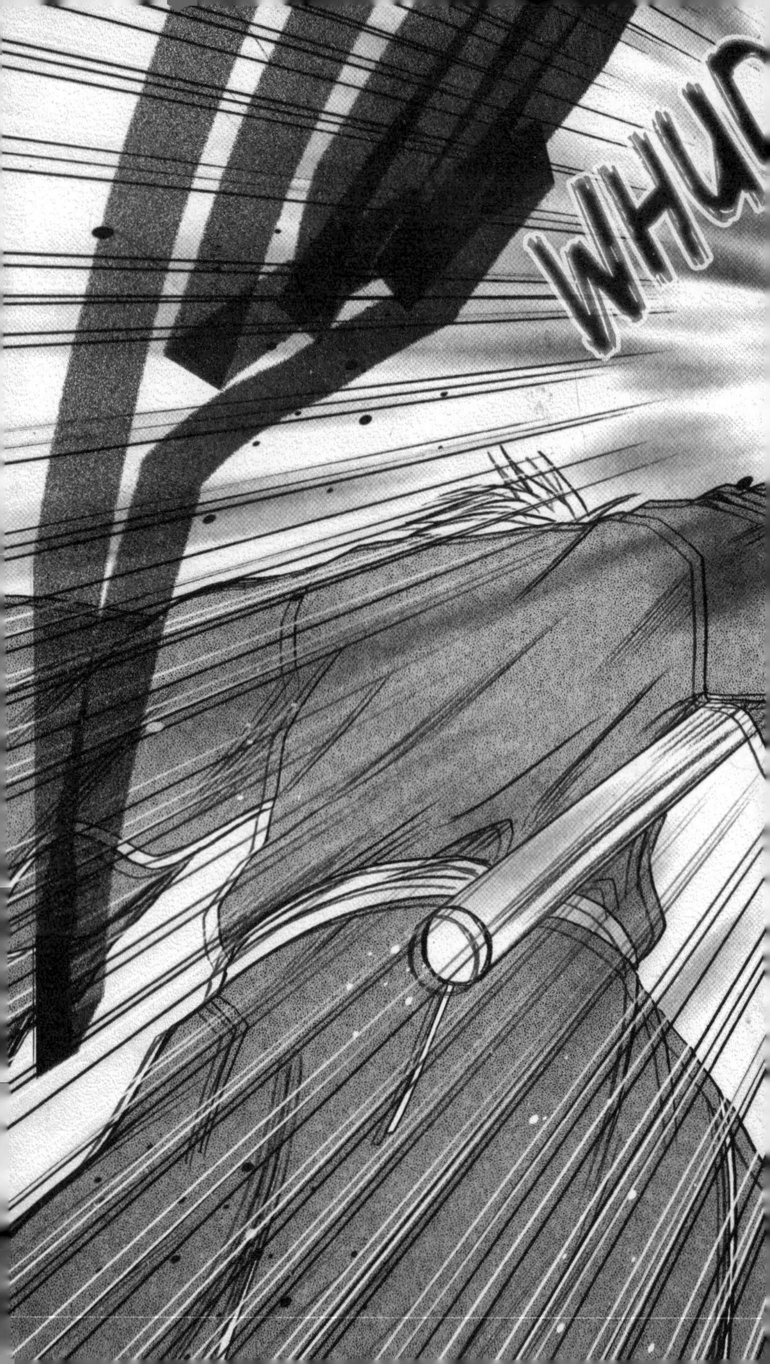
WHU

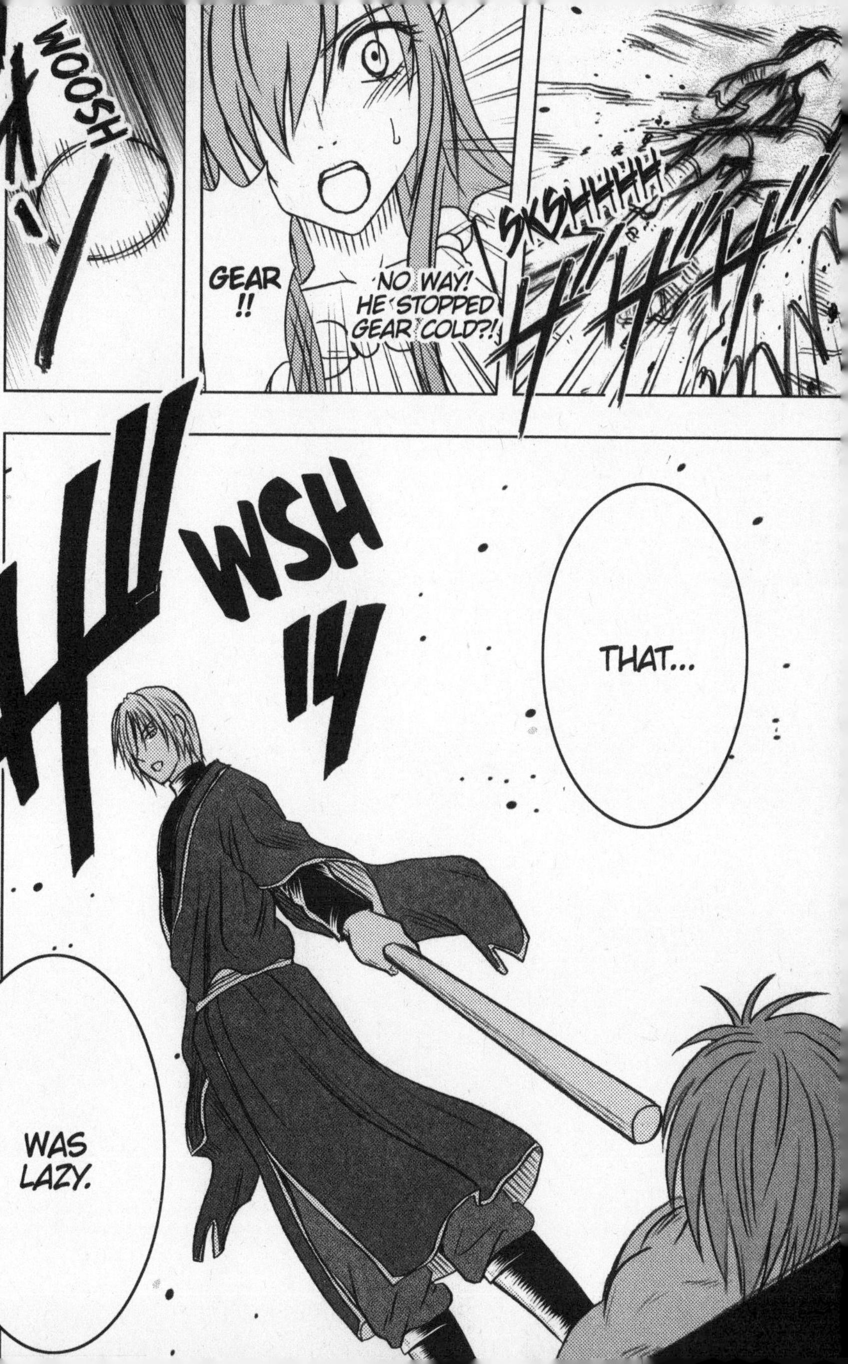
SKSHHHHH
NO WAY! HE STOPPED GEAR COLD?!
GEAR !!
WOOSH
THAT...
WSH
WAS LAZY.

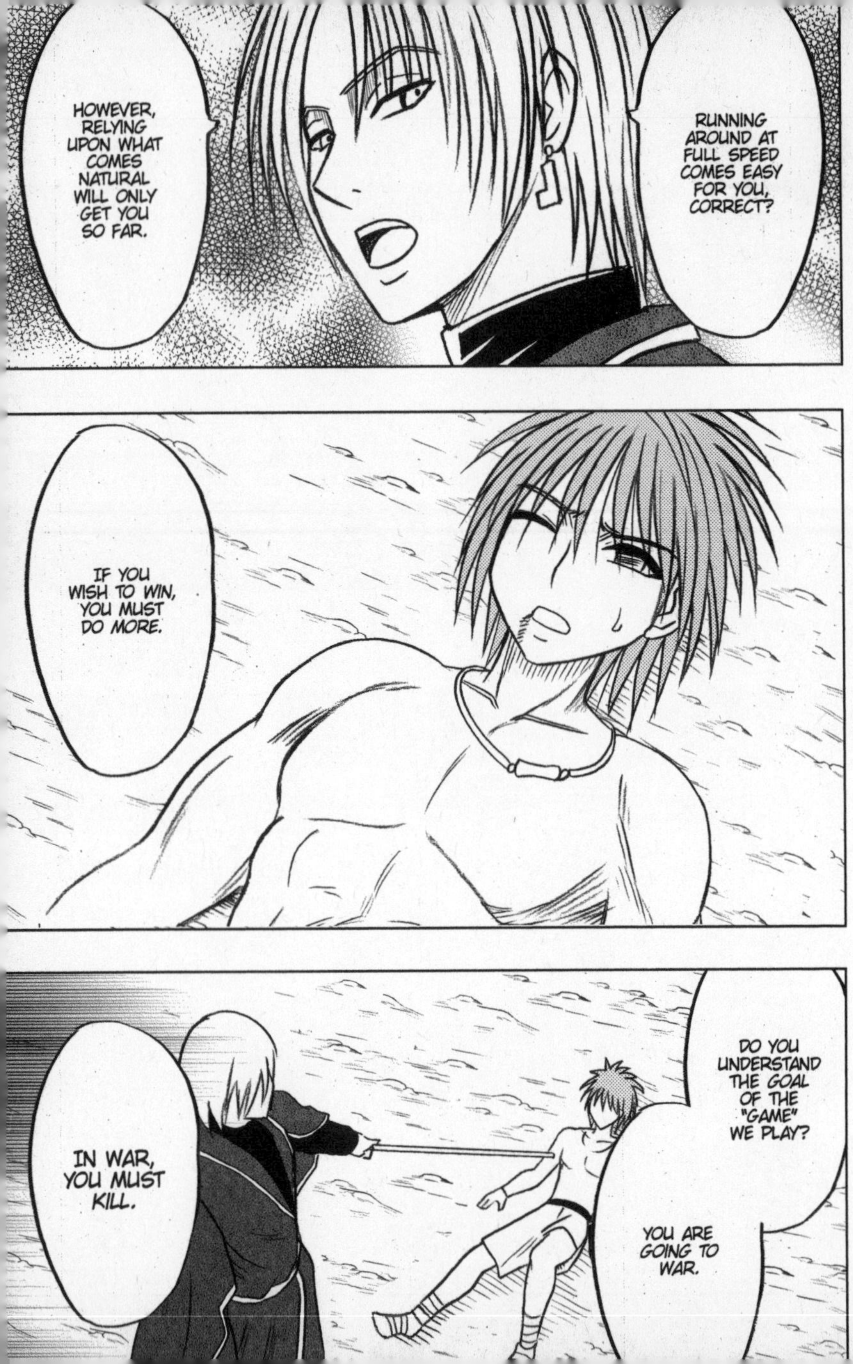
RUNNING AROUND AT FULL SPEED COMES EASY FOR YOU, CORRECT?
HOWEVER, RELYING UPON WHAT COMES NATURAL WILL ONLY GET YOU SO FAR.
IF YOU WISH TO WIN, YOU MUST DO MORE.
DO YOU UNDERSTAND THE GOAL OF THE "GAME" WE PLAY?
YOU ARE GOING TO WAR.
IN WAR, YOU MUST KILL.

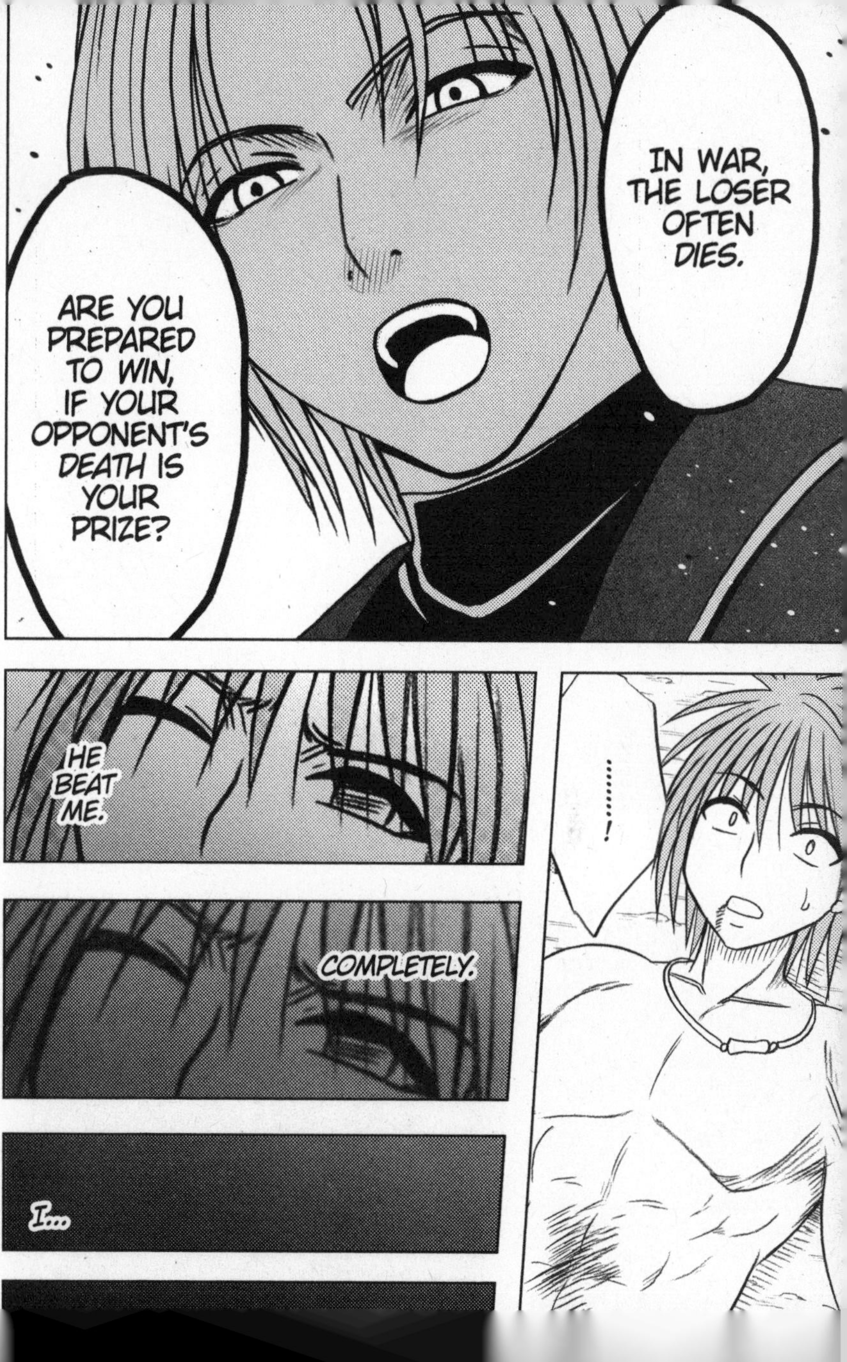
IN WAR, THE LOSER OFTEN DIES.
ARE YOU PREPARED TO WIN, IF YOUR OPPONENT'S DEATH IS YOUR PRIZE?
......!
HE BEAT ME.
COMPLETELY.
I...

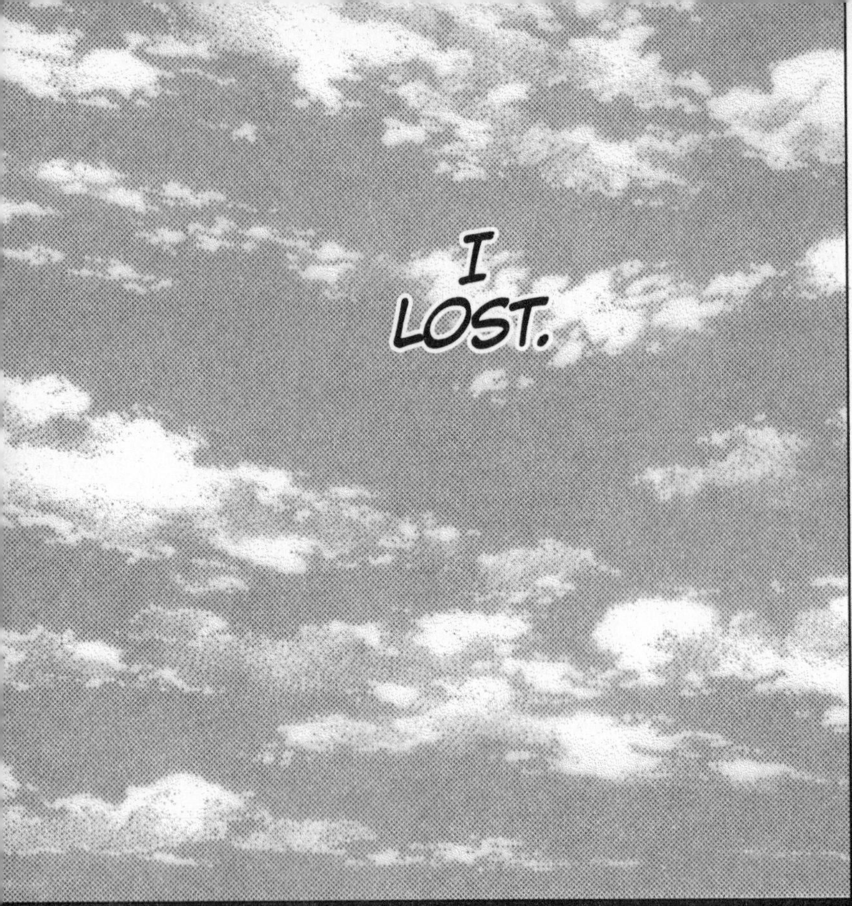
I LOST.
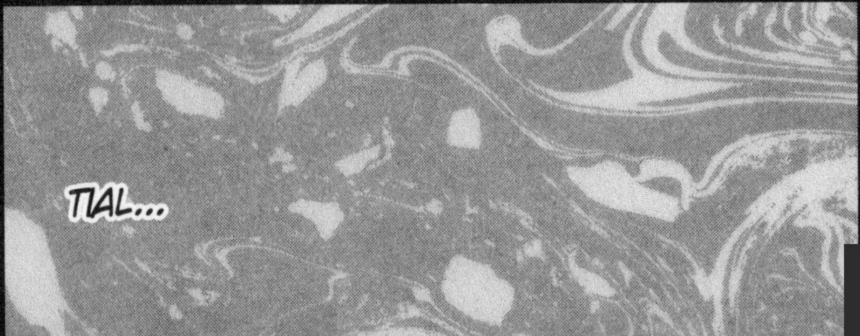
TIAL...

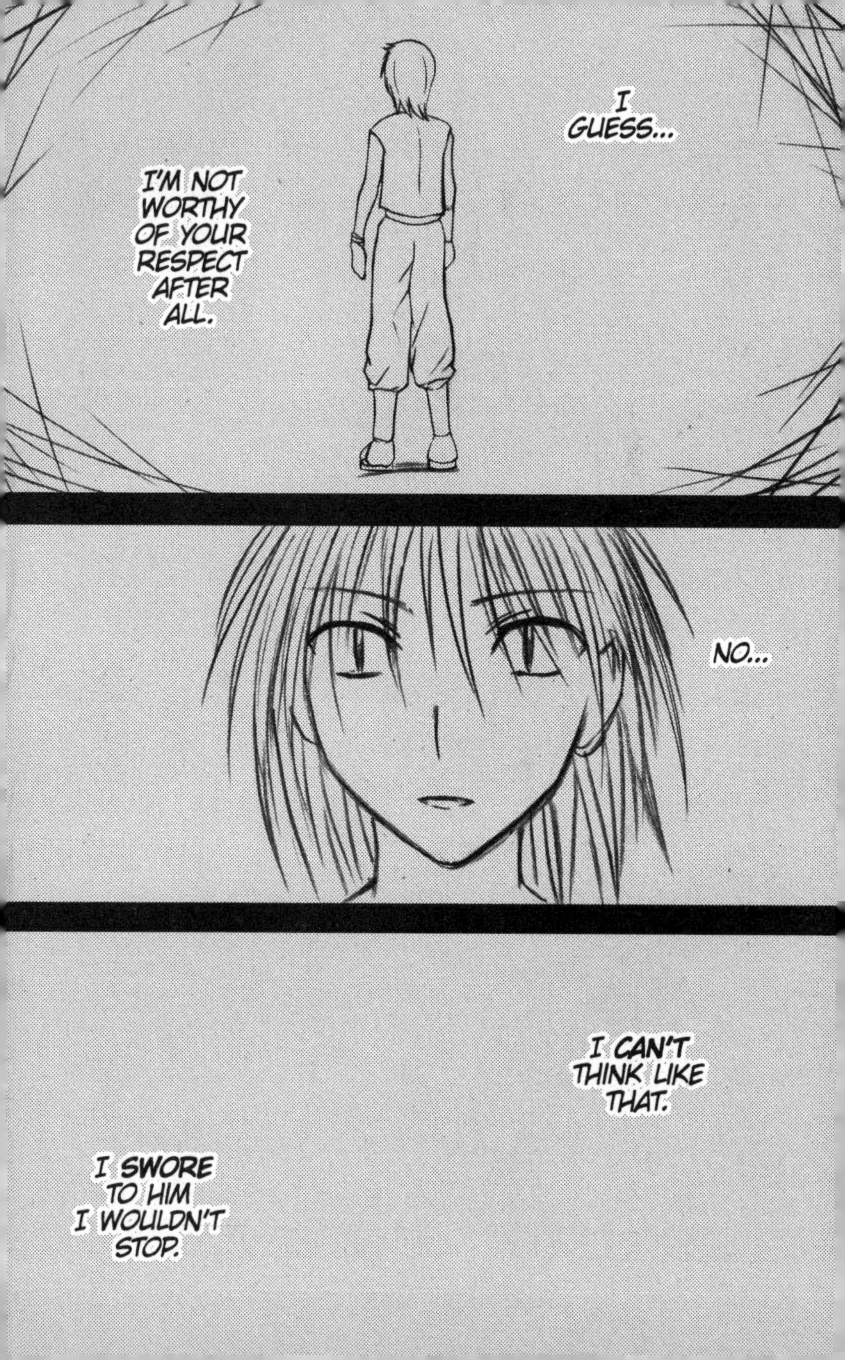
I GUESS...
I'M NOT WORTHY OF YOUR RESPECT AFTER ALL.
NO...
I CAN'T THINK LIKE THAT.
I SWORE TO HIM I WOULDN'T STOP.

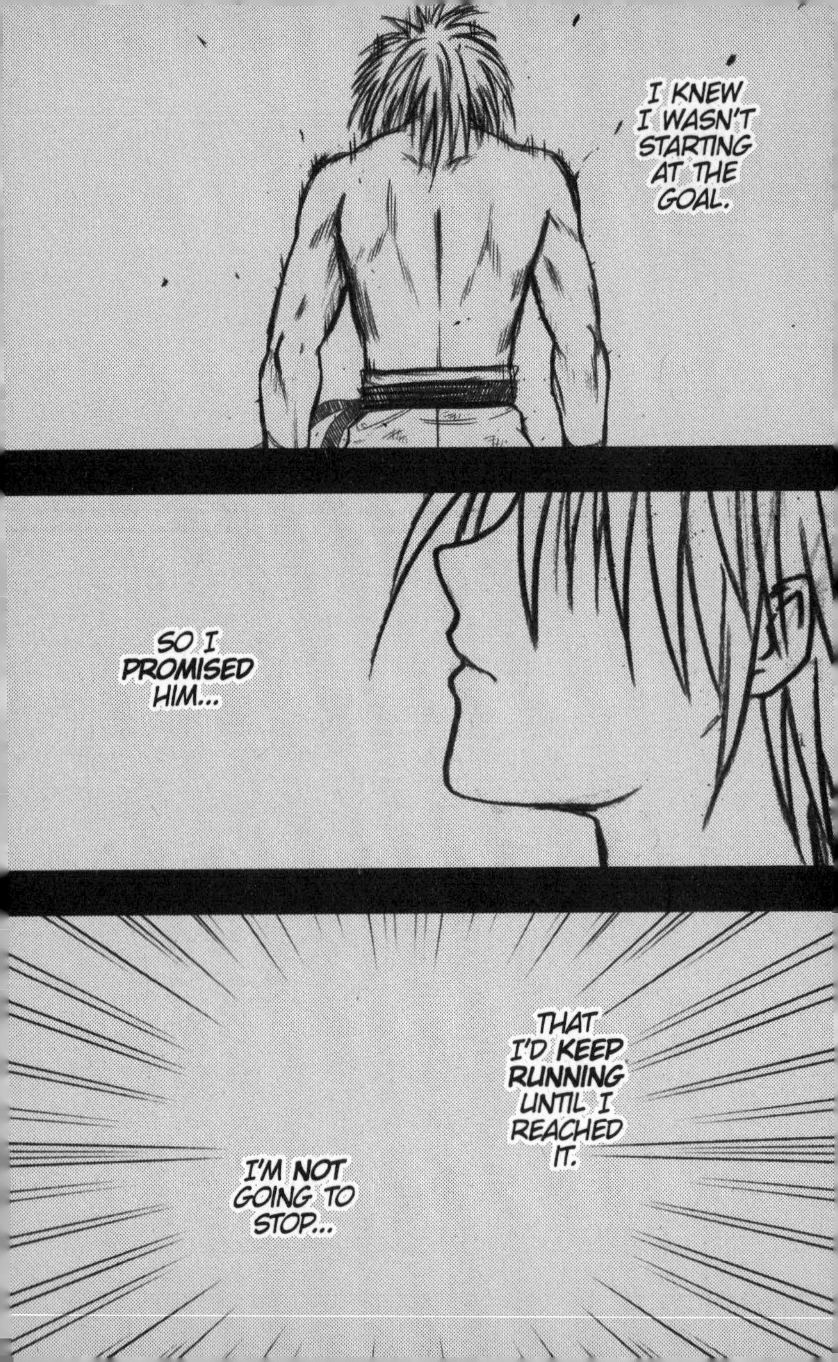
I KNEW I WASN'T STARTING AT THE GOAL.
SO I PROMISED HIM...
THAT I'D KEEP RUNNING UNTIL I REACHED IT.
I'M NOT GOING TO STOP...

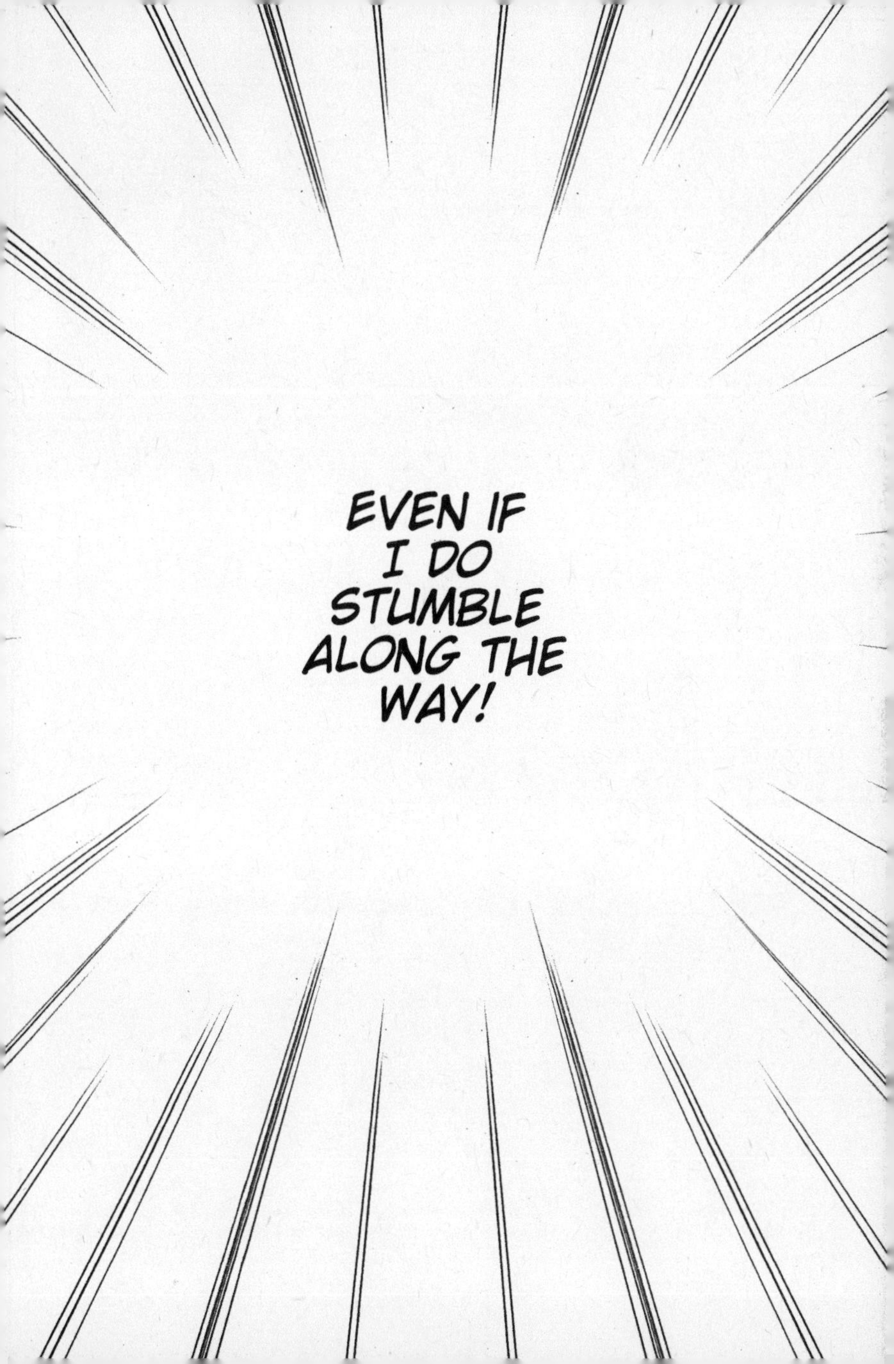
EVEN IF I DO STUMBLE ALONG THE WAY!

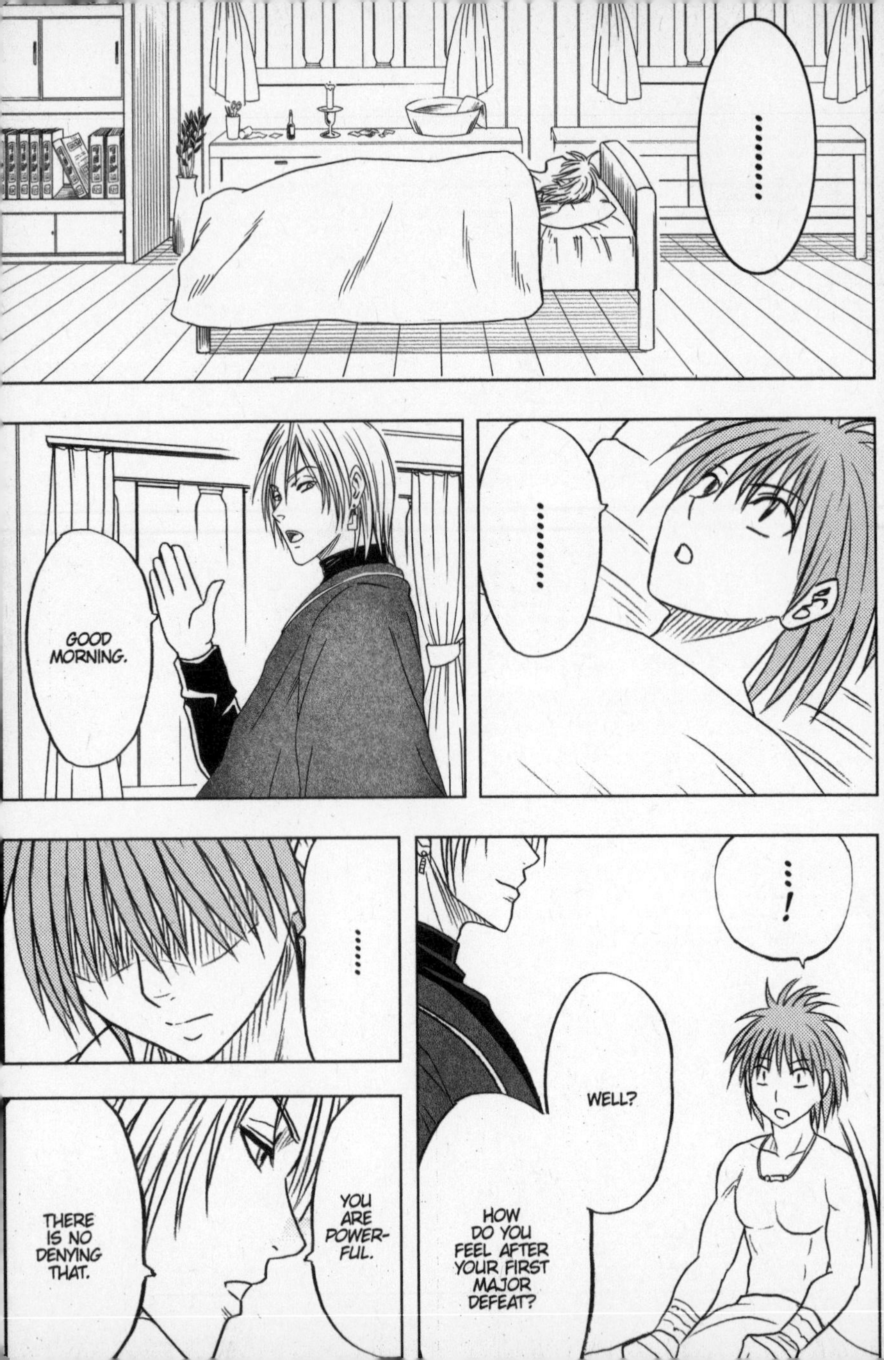
......
....
GOOD MORNING.
...!
WELL?
HOW DO YOU FEEL AFTER YOUR FIRST MAJOR DEFEAT?
.....
YOU ARE POWERFUL.
THERE IS NO DENYING THAT.

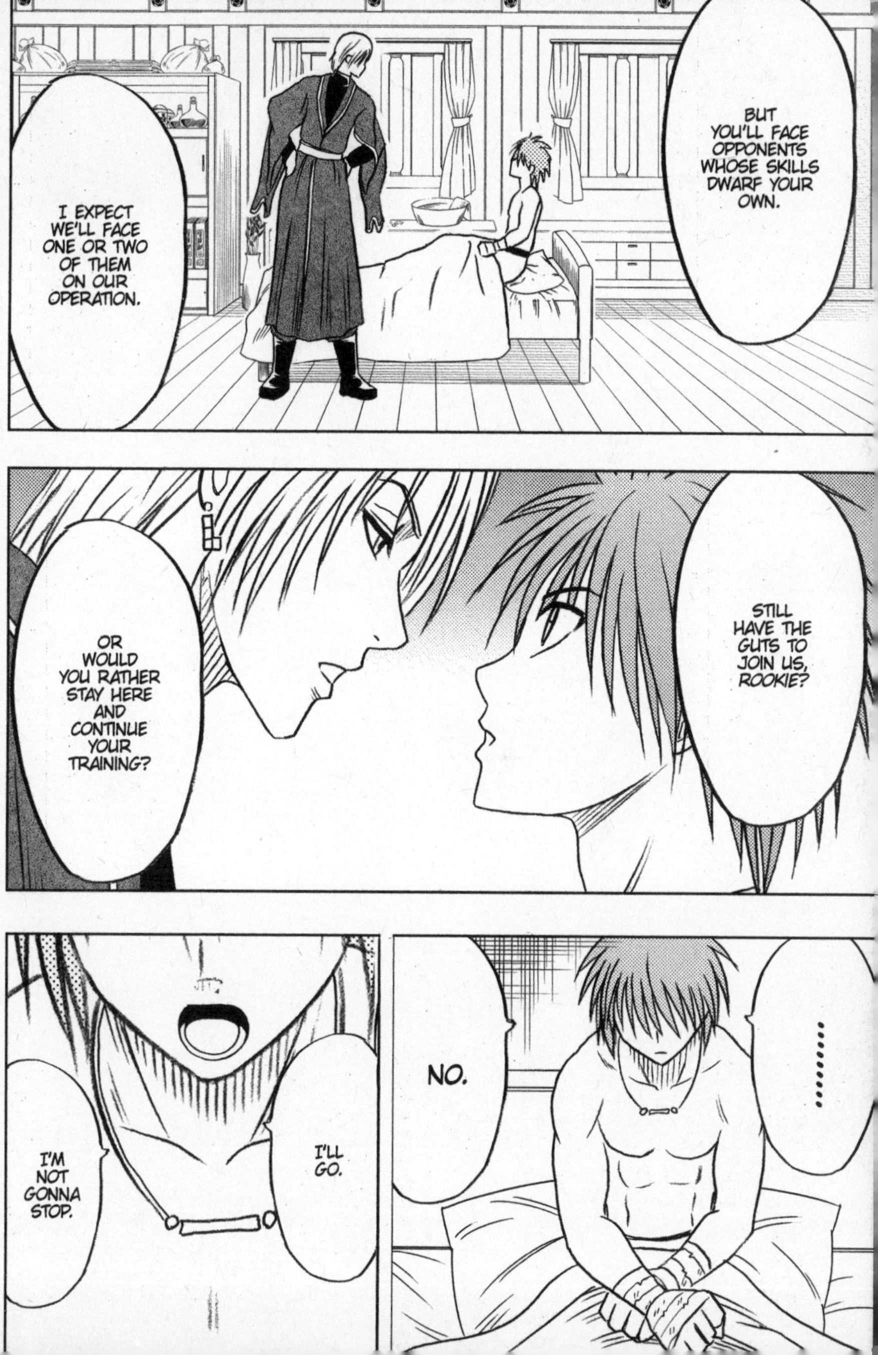
BUT YOU'LL FACE OPPONENTS WHOSE SKILLS DWARF YOUR OWN.
I EXPECT WE'LL FACE ONE OR TWO OF THEM ON OUR OPERATION.
STILL HAVE THE GUTS TO JOIN US, ROOKIE?
OR WOULD YOU RATHER STAY HERE AND CONTINUE YOUR TRAINING?
……
NO.
I'LL GO.
I'M NOT GONNA STOP.

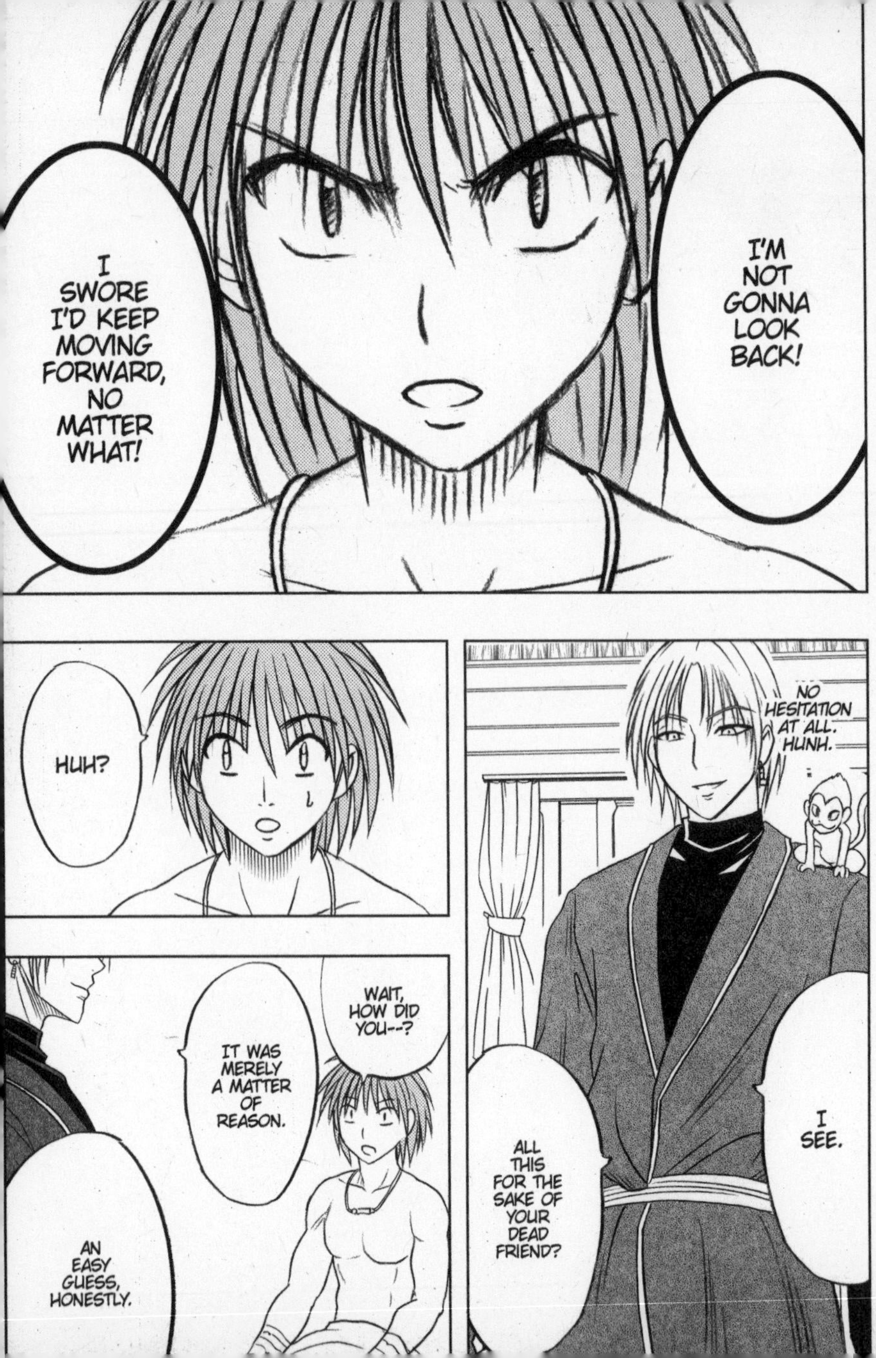
I'M NOT GONNA LOOK BACK!
I SWORE I'D KEEP MOVING FORWARD, NO MATTER WHAT!
NO HESITATION AT ALL. HUNH.
I SEE.
ALL THIS FOR THE SAKE OF YOUR DEAD FRIEND?
HUH?
WAIT, HOW DID YOU--?
IT WAS MERELY A MATTER OF REASON.
AN EASY GUESS, HONESTLY.

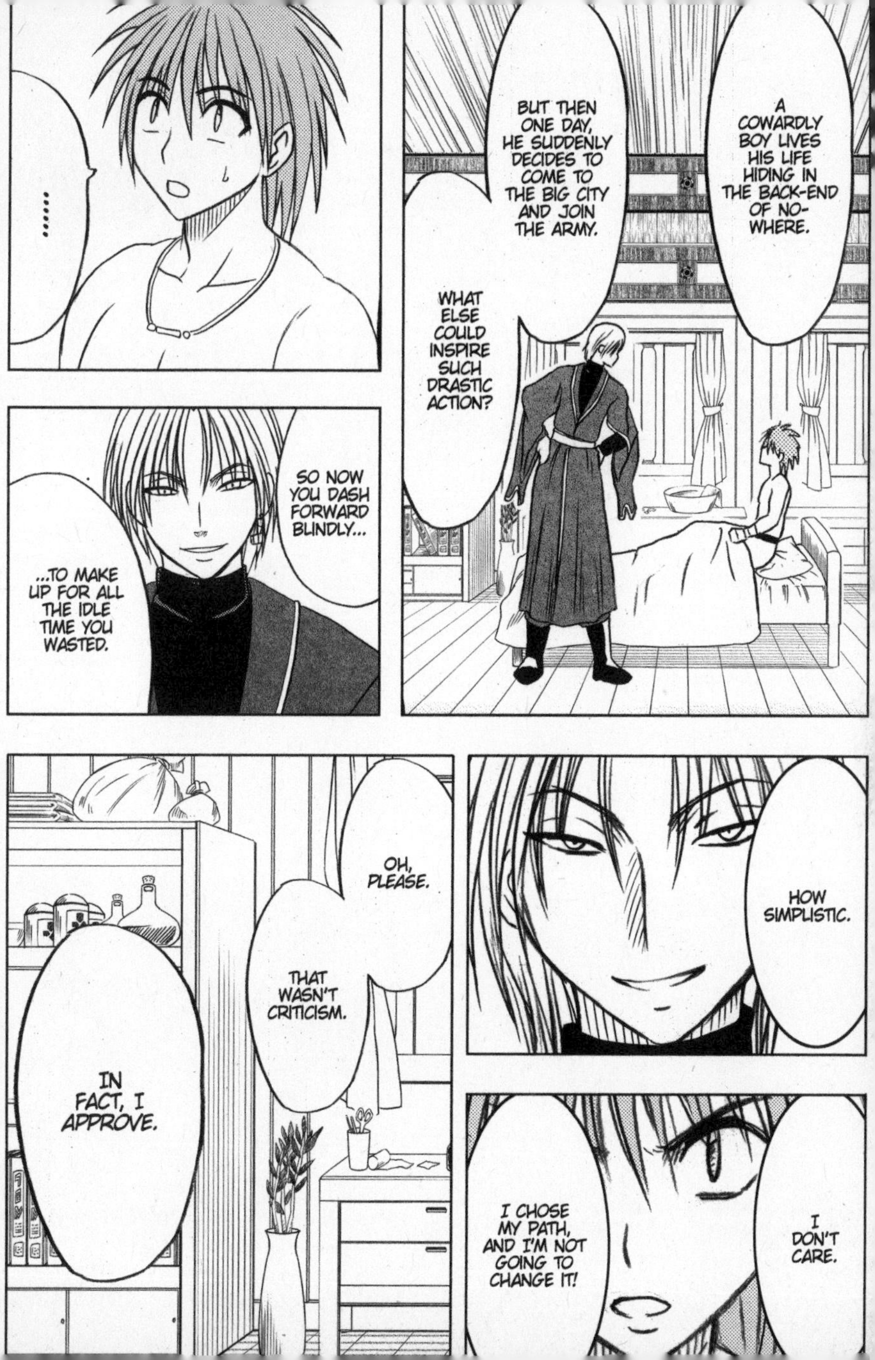
A COWARDLY BOY LIVES HIS LIFE HIDING IN THE BACK-END OF NO-WHERE.
BUT THEN ONE DAY, HE SUDDENLY DECIDES TO COME TO THE BIG CITY AND JOIN THE ARMY.
WHAT ELSE COULD INSPIRE SUCH DRASTIC ACTION?
......
SO NOW YOU DASH FORWARD BLINDLY...
...TO MAKE UP FOR ALL THE IDLE TIME YOU WASTED.
HOW SIMPLISTIC.
I DON'T CARE.
I CHOSE MY PATH, AND I'M NOT GOING TO CHANGE IT!
OH, PLEASE.
THAT WASN'T CRITICISM.
IN FACT, I APPROVE.

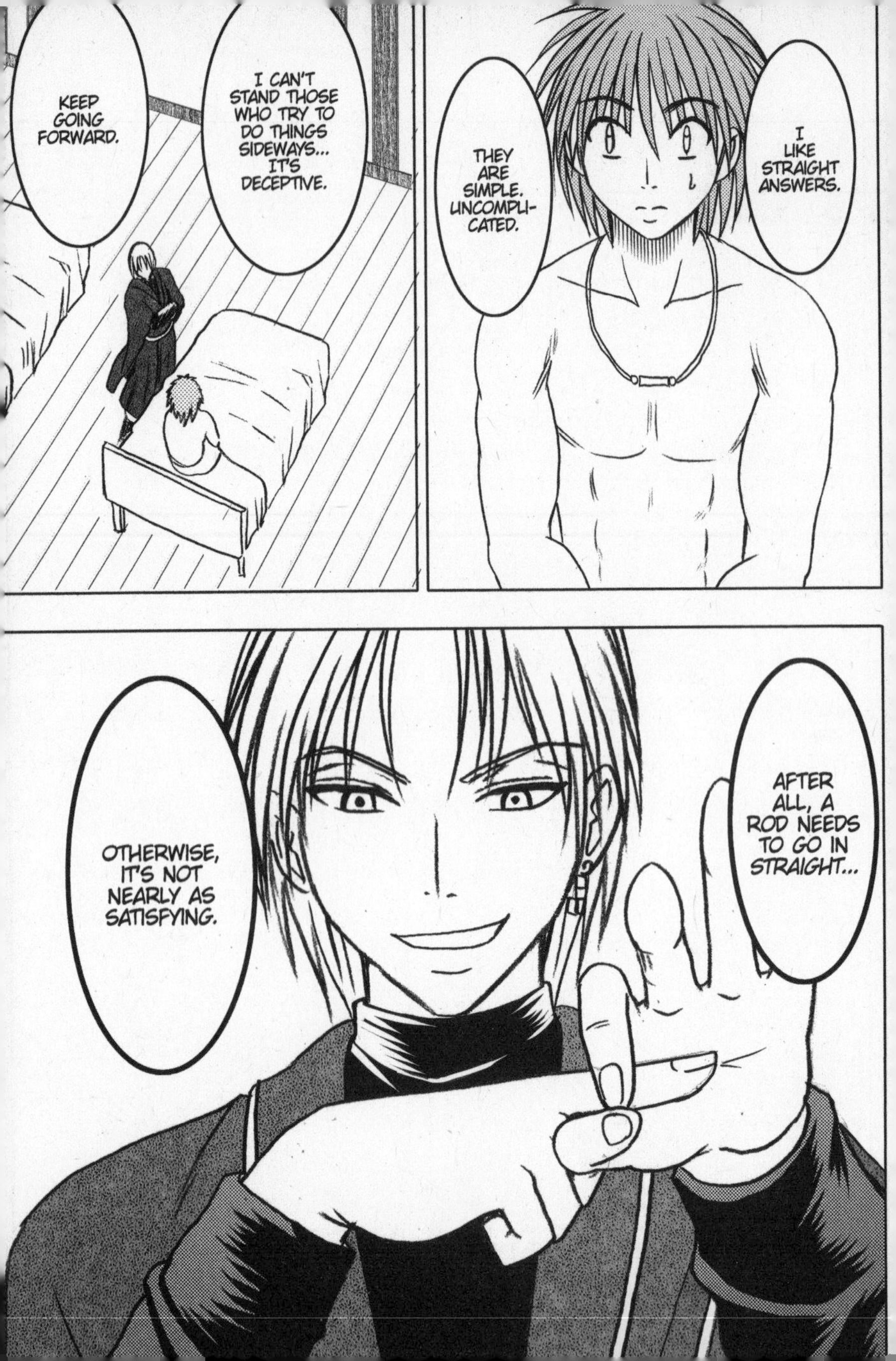
I LIKE STRAIGHT ANSWERS.
THEY ARE SIMPLE. UNCOMPLI-CATED.
I CAN'T STAND THOSE WHO TRY TO DO THINGS SIDEWAYS... IT'S DECEPTIVE.
KEEP GOING FORWARD.
AFTER ALL, A ROD NEEDS TO GO IN STRAIGHT...
OTHERWISE, IT'S NOT NEARLY AS SATISFYING.

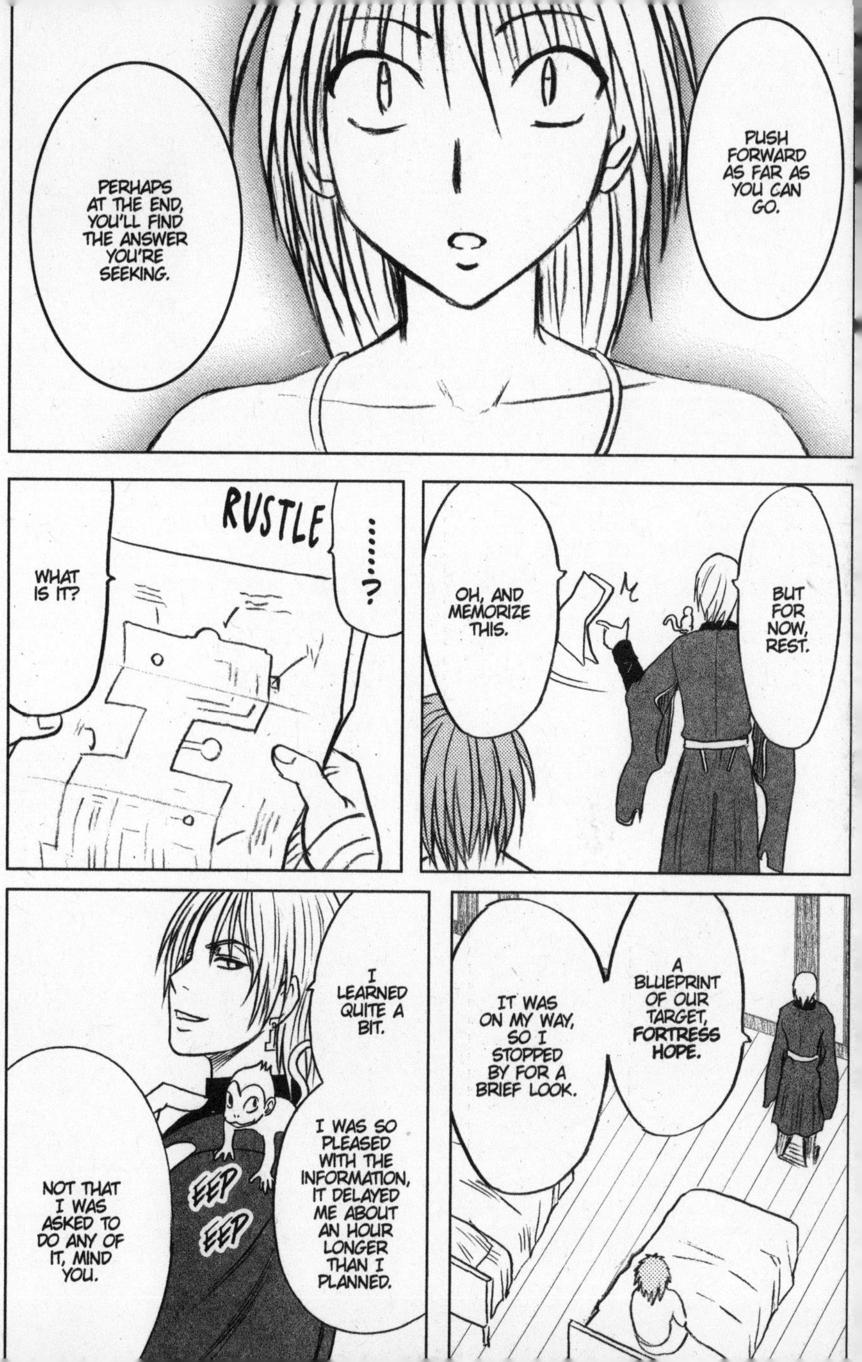
PUSH FORWARD AS FAR AS YOU CAN GO.
PERHAPS AT THE END, YOU'LL FIND THE ANSWER YOU'RE SEEKING.
BUT FOR NOW, REST.
OH, AND MEMORIZE THIS.
......?
RUSTLE
WHAT IS IT?
A BLUEPRINT OF OUR TARGET, FORTRESS HOPE.
IT WAS ON MY WAY, SO I STOPPED BY FOR A BRIEF LOOK.
I LEARNED QUITE A BIT.
I WAS SO PLEASED WITH THE INFORMATION, IT DELAYED ME ABOUT AN HOUR LONGER THAN I PLANNED.
EEP
EEP
NOT THAT I WAS ASKED TO DO ANY OF IT, MIND YOU.

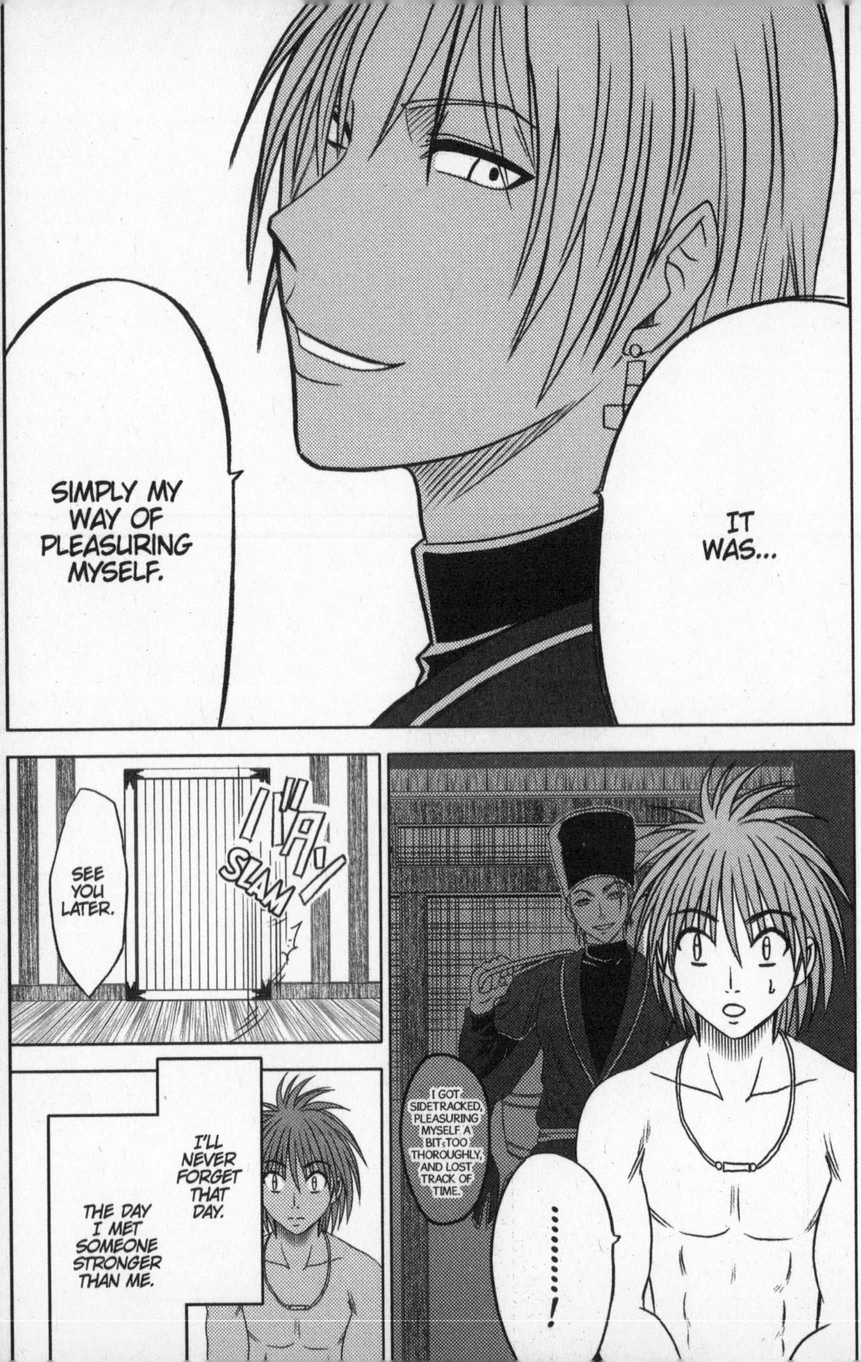
IT WAS...
SIMPLY MY WAY OF PLEASURING MYSELF.
I GOT SIDETRACKED, PLEASURING MYSELF A BIT TOO THOROUGHLY, AND LOST TRACK OF TIME.
......!
SEE YOU LATER.
SLAM
I'LL NEVER FORGET THAT DAY.
THE DAY I MET SOMEONE STRONGER THAN ME.

HE WAS A
WISE MAN,
SMART AND
STRONG AND
BOLD.

HE
EXPOSED
ME TO NEW
IDEAS.

HE WAS
ALSO A
PERVERT,
WITH A MIND
PERMANENTLY
DRAGGING
THROUGH THE
GUTTER.

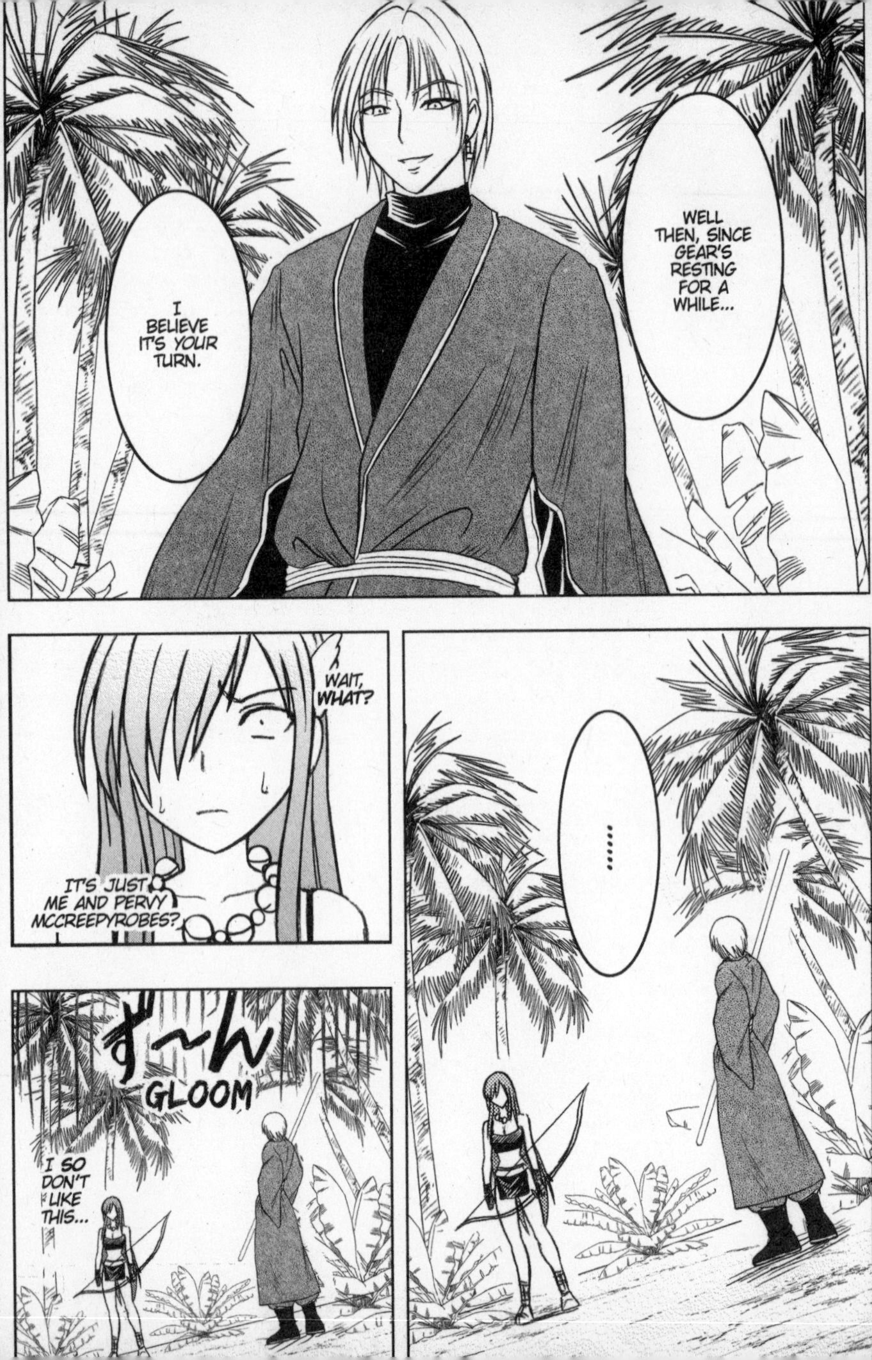
WELL THEN, SINCE GEAR'S RESTING FOR A WHILE...
I BELIEVE IT'S YOUR TURN.
......
WAIT, WHAT?
IT'S JUST ME AND PERVY MCCREEPYROBES?
ず～ん
GLOOM
I SO DON'T LIKE THIS...

WORLD WAR BLUE

CHARACTER INTRODUCTION

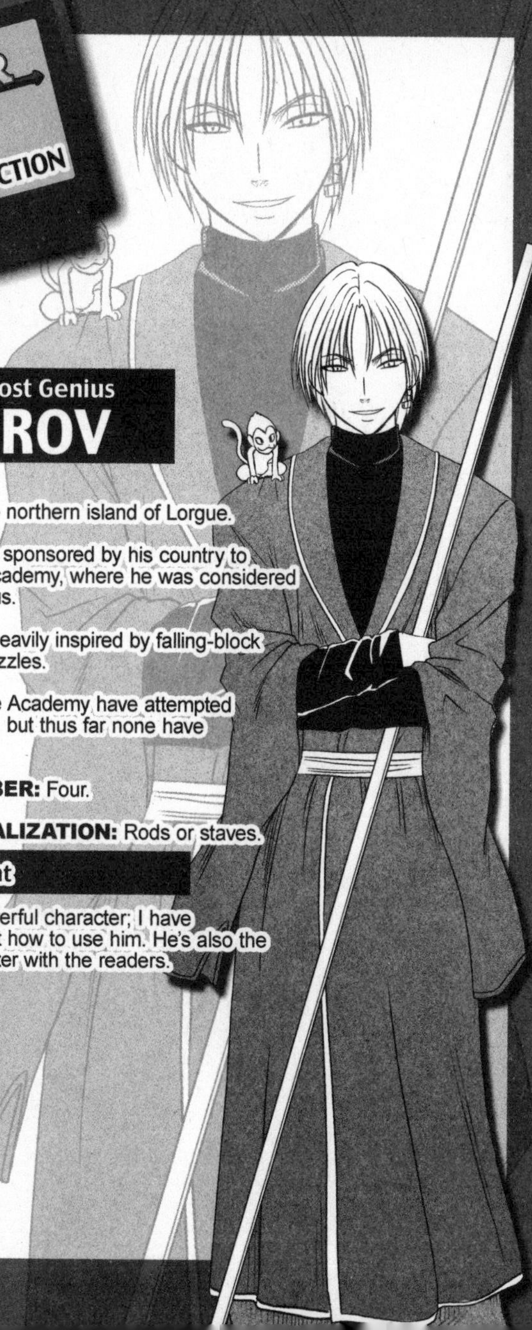

Heaven's Lost Genius

TEJIROV

Tejirov hails from the northern island of Lorgue.

This mercenary was sponsored by his country to attend the Puzzle Academy, where he was considered a revolutionary genius.

His fighting style is heavily inspired by falling-block and tile-matching puzzles.

Many students at the Academy have attempted to duplicate his style, but thus far none have succeeded.

FAVORITE NUMBER: Four.

WEAPON SPECIALIZATION: Rods or staves.

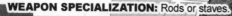

Author Comment

Tejirov is such a powerful character; I have problems figuring out how to use him. He's also the most popular character with the readers.

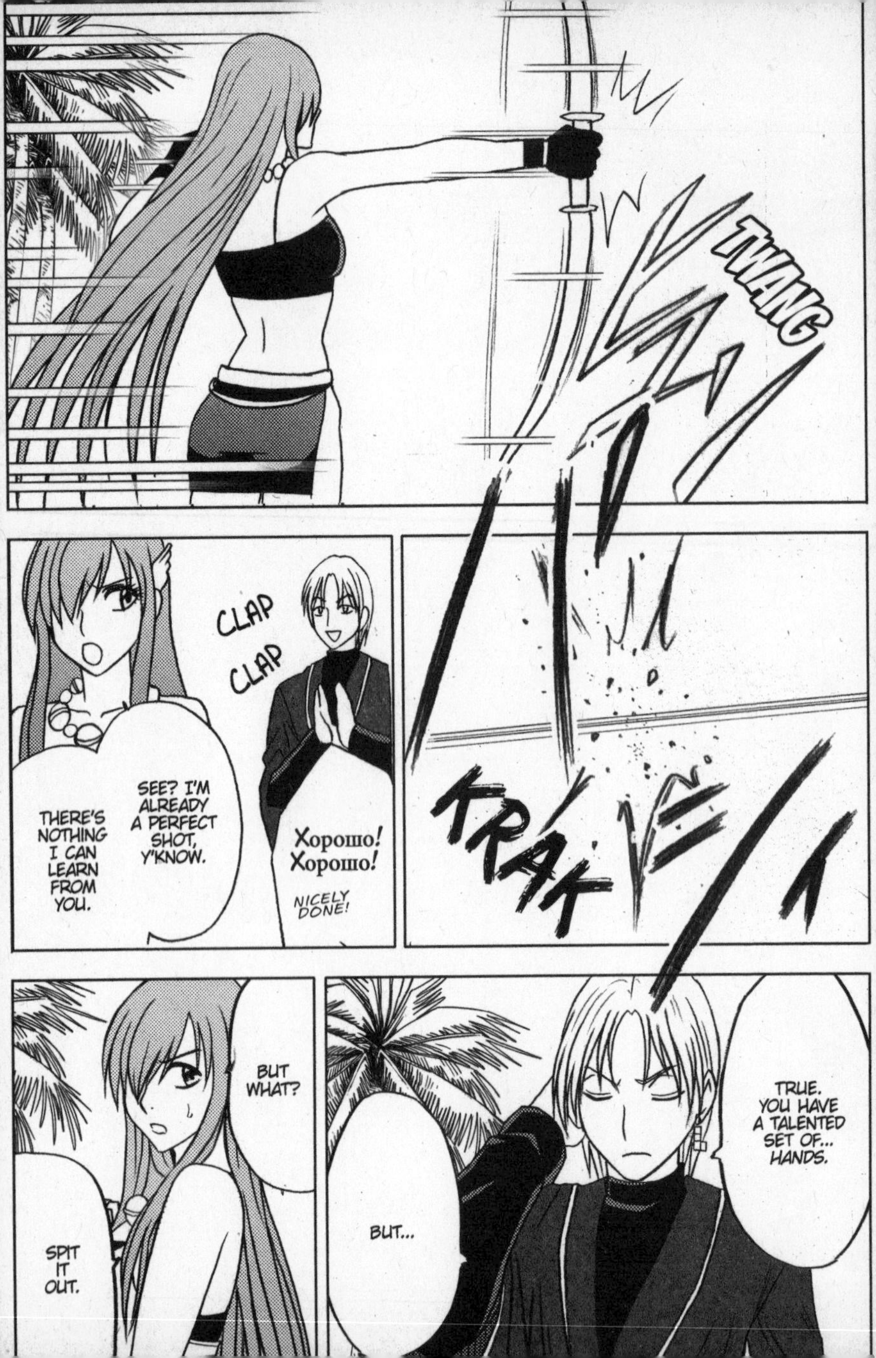
TWANG
KRAK
CLAP
CLAP
Хорошо! Хорошо!
NICELY DONE!
SEE? I'M ALREADY A PERFECT SHOT, Y'KNOW.
THERE'S NOTHING I CAN LEARN FROM YOU.
TRUE. YOU HAVE A TALENTED SET OF... HANDS.
BUT...
BUT WHAT?
SPIT IT OUT.

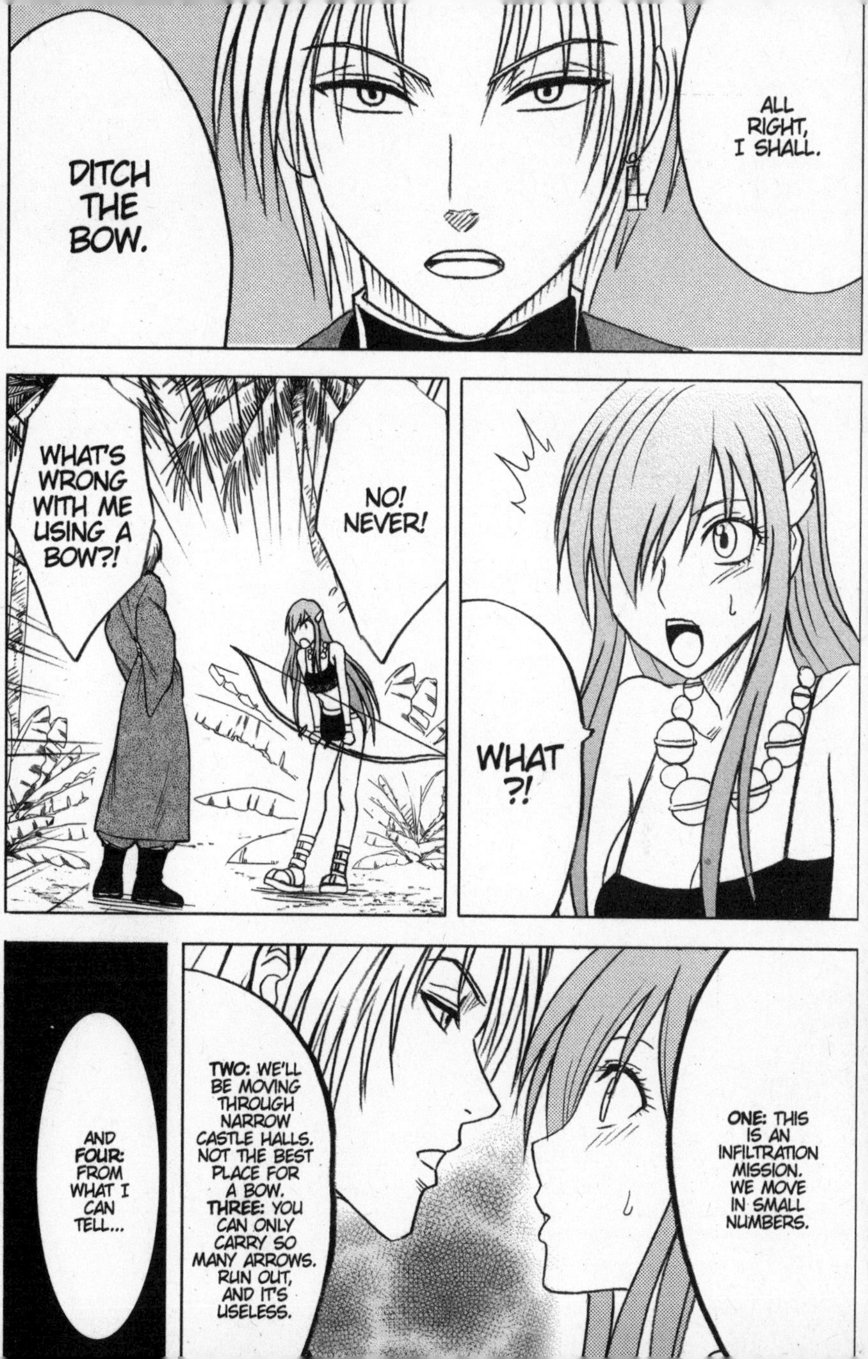
ALL RIGHT, I SHALL.
DITCH THE BOW.
WHAT?!
NO! NEVER!
WHAT'S WRONG WITH ME USING A BOW?!
ONE: THIS IS AN INFILTRATION MISSION. WE MOVE IN SMALL NUMBERS.
TWO: WE'LL BE MOVING THROUGH NARROW CASTLE HALLS. NOT THE BEST PLACE FOR A BOW. THREE: YOU CAN ONLY CARRY SO MANY ARROWS. RUN OUT, AND IT'S USELESS.
AND FOUR: FROM WHAT I CAN TELL...

CHAPTER 5

GET READY!

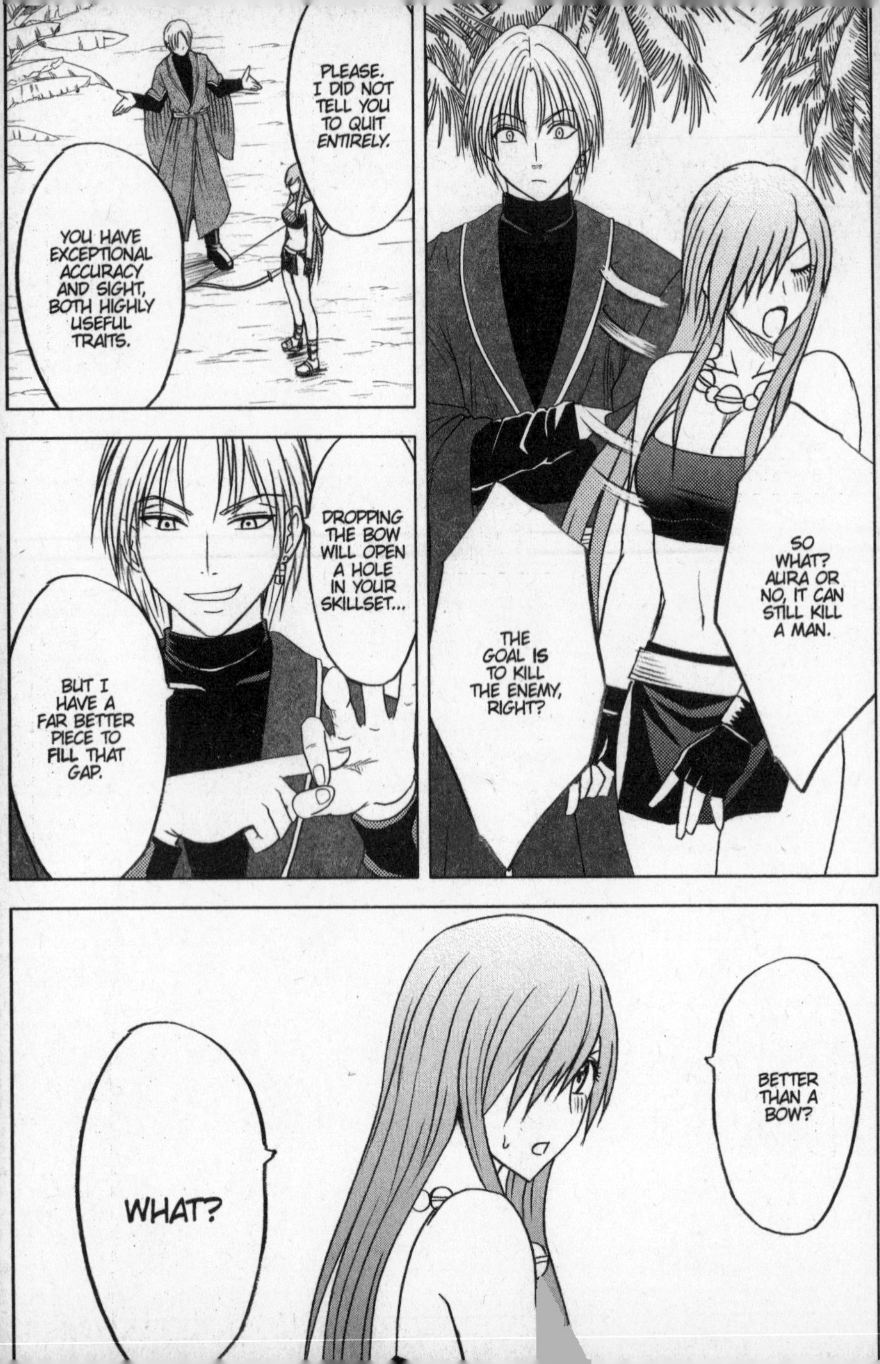
SO WHAT? AURA OR NO, IT CAN STILL KILL A MAN.
THE GOAL IS TO KILL THE ENEMY, RIGHT?
PLEASE. I DID NOT TELL YOU TO QUIT ENTIRELY.
YOU HAVE EXCEPTIONAL ACCURACY AND SIGHT, BOTH HIGHLY USEFUL TRAITS.
DROPPING THE BOW WILL OPEN A HOLE IN YOUR SKILLSET...
BUT I HAVE A FAR BETTER PIECE TO FILL THAT GAP.
BETTER THAN A BOW?
WHAT?

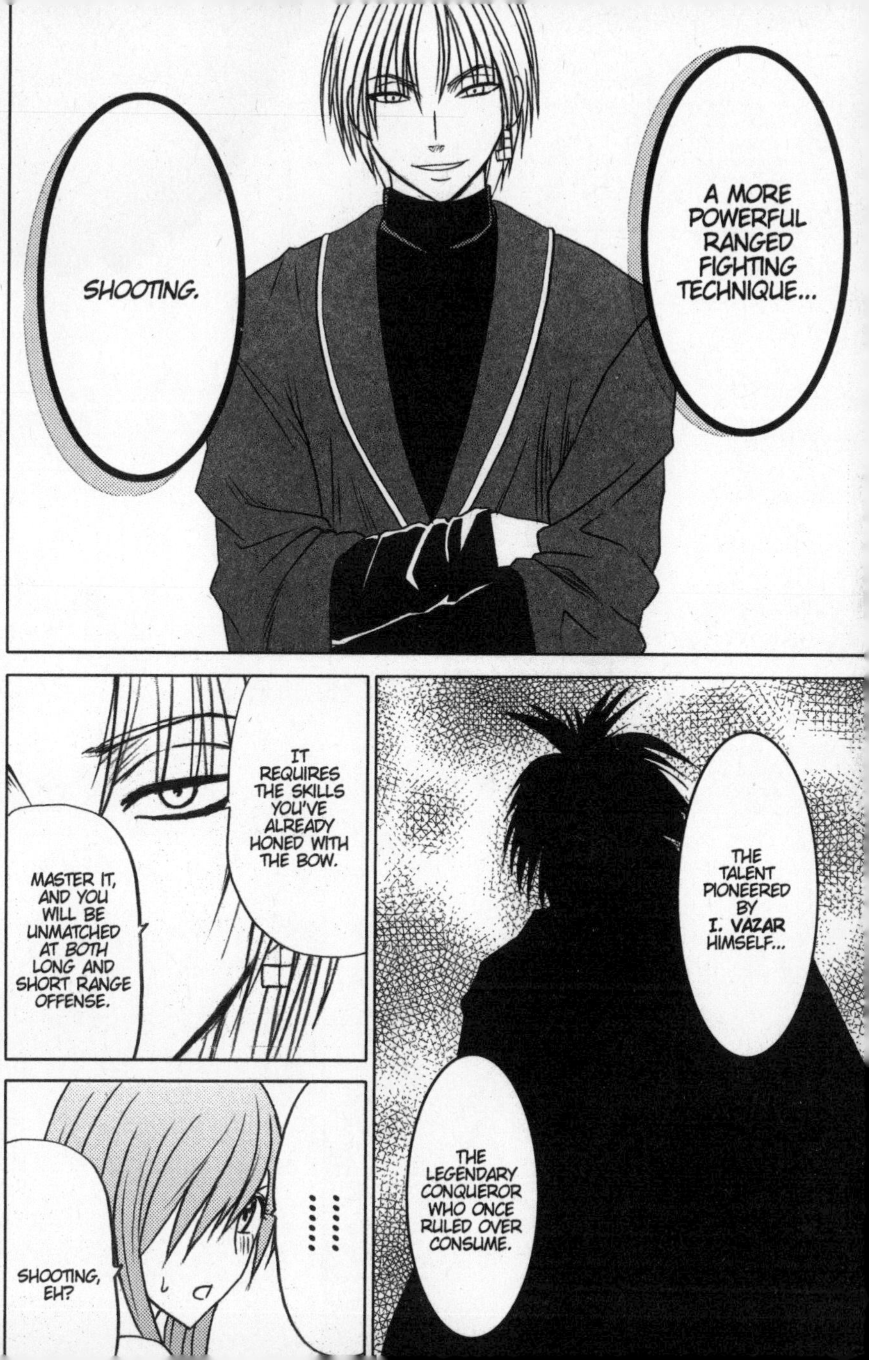
A MORE POWERFUL RANGED FIGHTING TECHNIQUE...
SHOOTING.
THE TALENT PIONEERED BY I. VAZAR HIMSELF...
THE LEGENDARY CONQUEROR WHO ONCE RULED OVER CONSUME.
IT REQUIRES THE SKILLS YOU'VE ALREADY HONED WITH THE BOW.
MASTER IT, AND YOU WILL BE UNMATCHED AT BOTH LONG AND SHORT RANGE OFFENSE.
......
SHOOTING, EH?

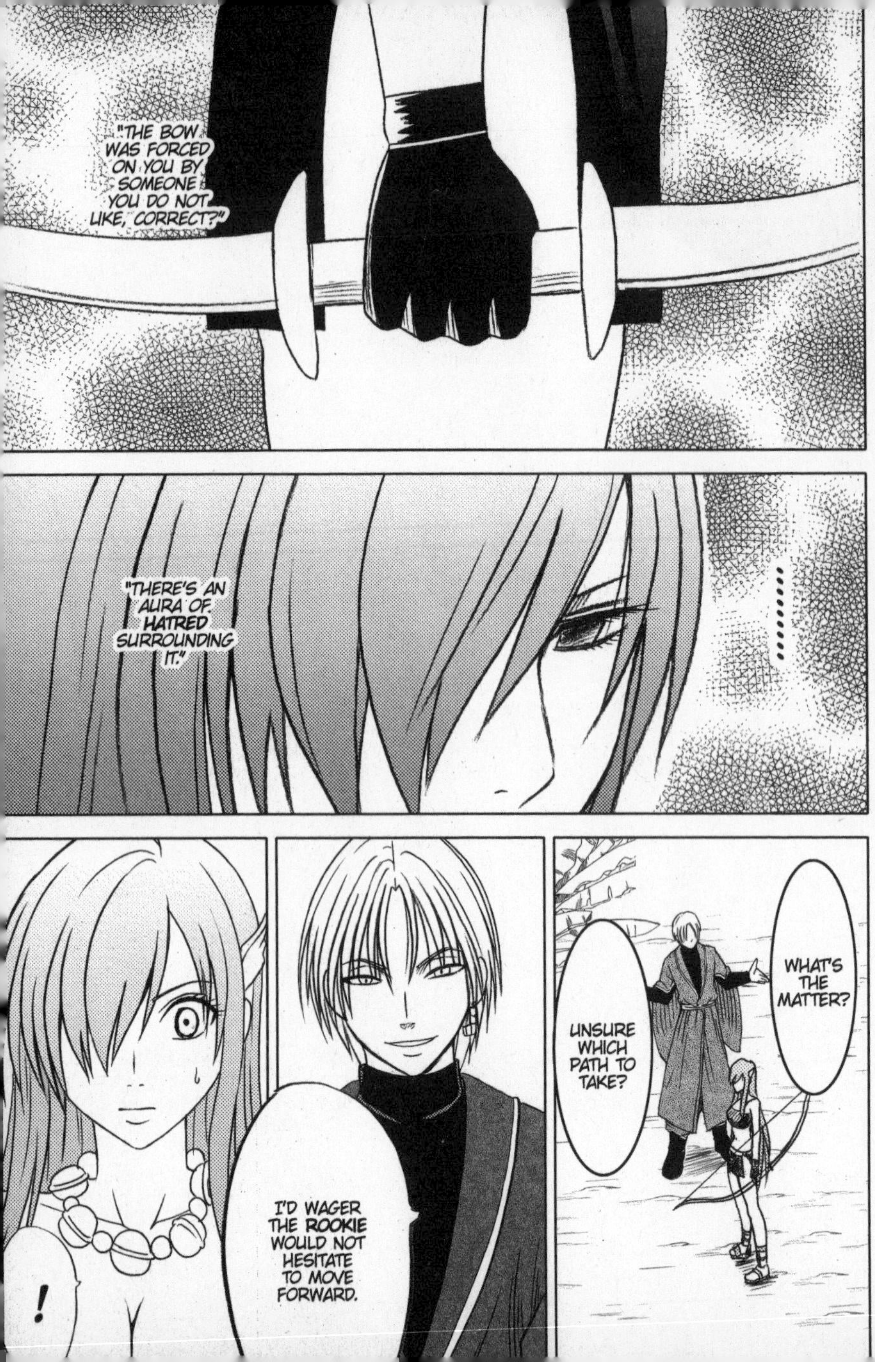
"THE BOW WAS FORCED ON YOU BY SOMEONE YOU DO NOT LIKE, CORRECT?"
......
"THERE'S AN AURA OF HATRED SURROUNDING IT."
WHAT'S THE MATTER?
UNSURE WHICH PATH TO TAKE?
I'D WAGER THE ROOKIE WOULD NOT HESITATE TO MOVE FORWARD.
!

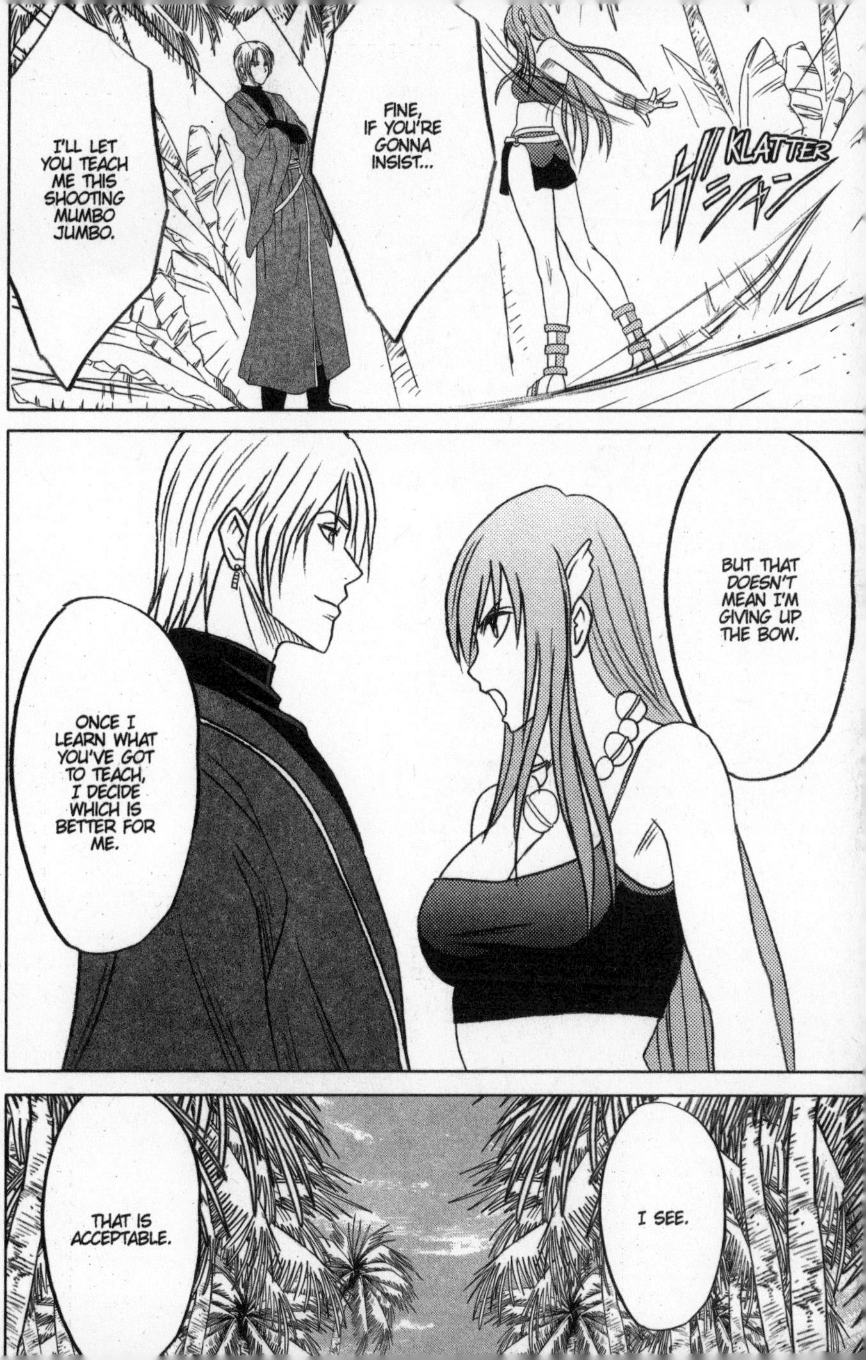
KLATTER
ガシャン
FINE, IF YOU'RE GONNA INSIST...
I'LL LET YOU TEACH ME THIS SHOOTING MUMBO JUMBO.
BUT THAT DOESN'T MEAN I'M GIVING UP THE BOW.
ONCE I LEARN WHAT YOU'VE GOT TO TEACH, I DECIDE WHICH IS BETTER FOR ME.
I SEE.
THAT IS ACCEPTABLE.

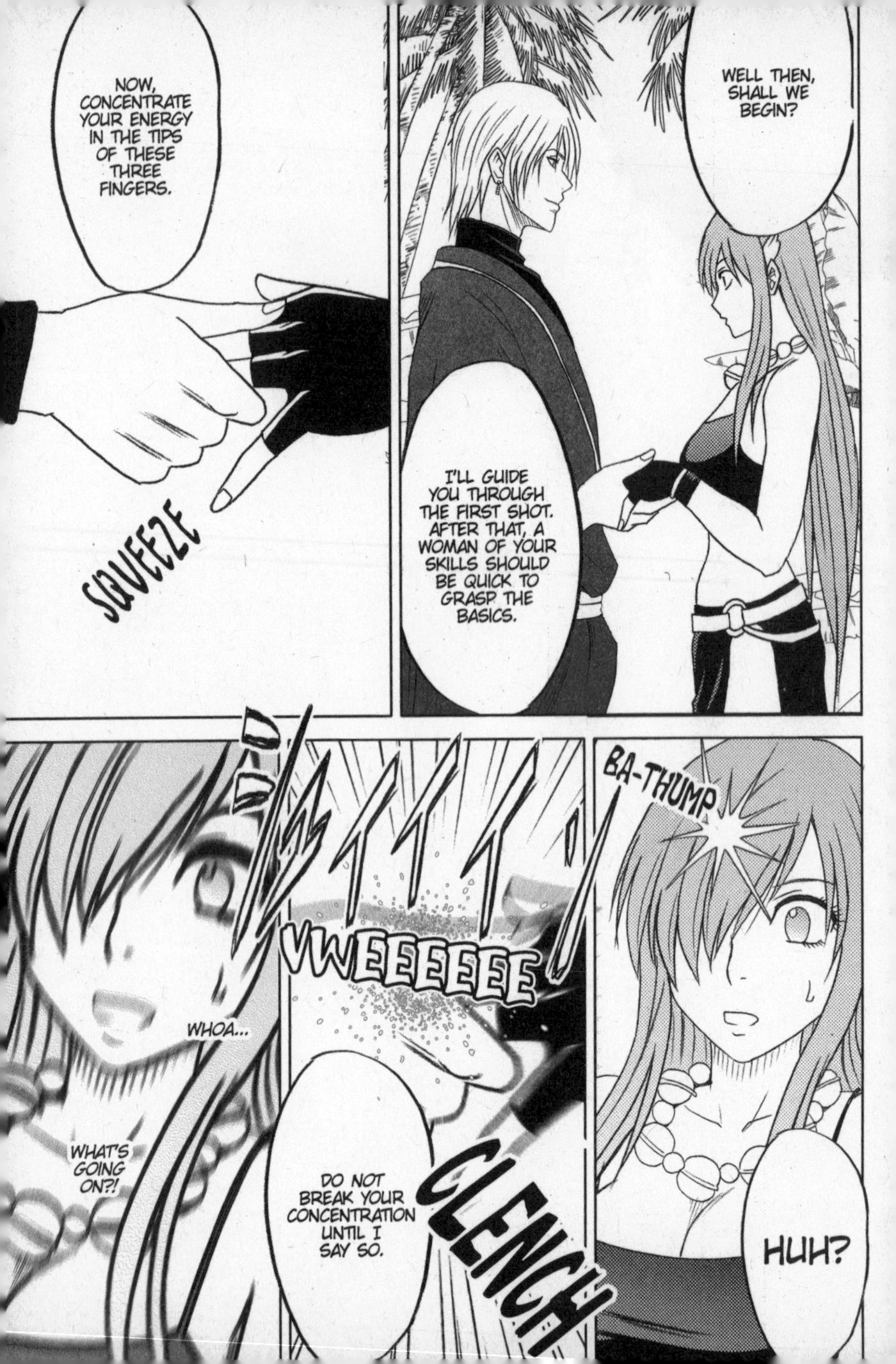
WELL THEN, SHALL WE BEGIN?
I'LL GUIDE YOU THROUGH THE FIRST SHOT. AFTER THAT, A WOMAN OF YOUR SKILLS SHOULD BE QUICK TO GRASP THE BASICS.
NOW, CONCENTRATE YOUR ENERGY IN THE TIPS OF THESE THREE FINGERS.
SQUEEZE
BA-THUMP
HUH?
VWEEEEEE
DO NOT BREAK YOUR CONCENTRATION UNTIL I SAY SO.
CLENCH
WHOA...
WHAT'S GOING ON?!

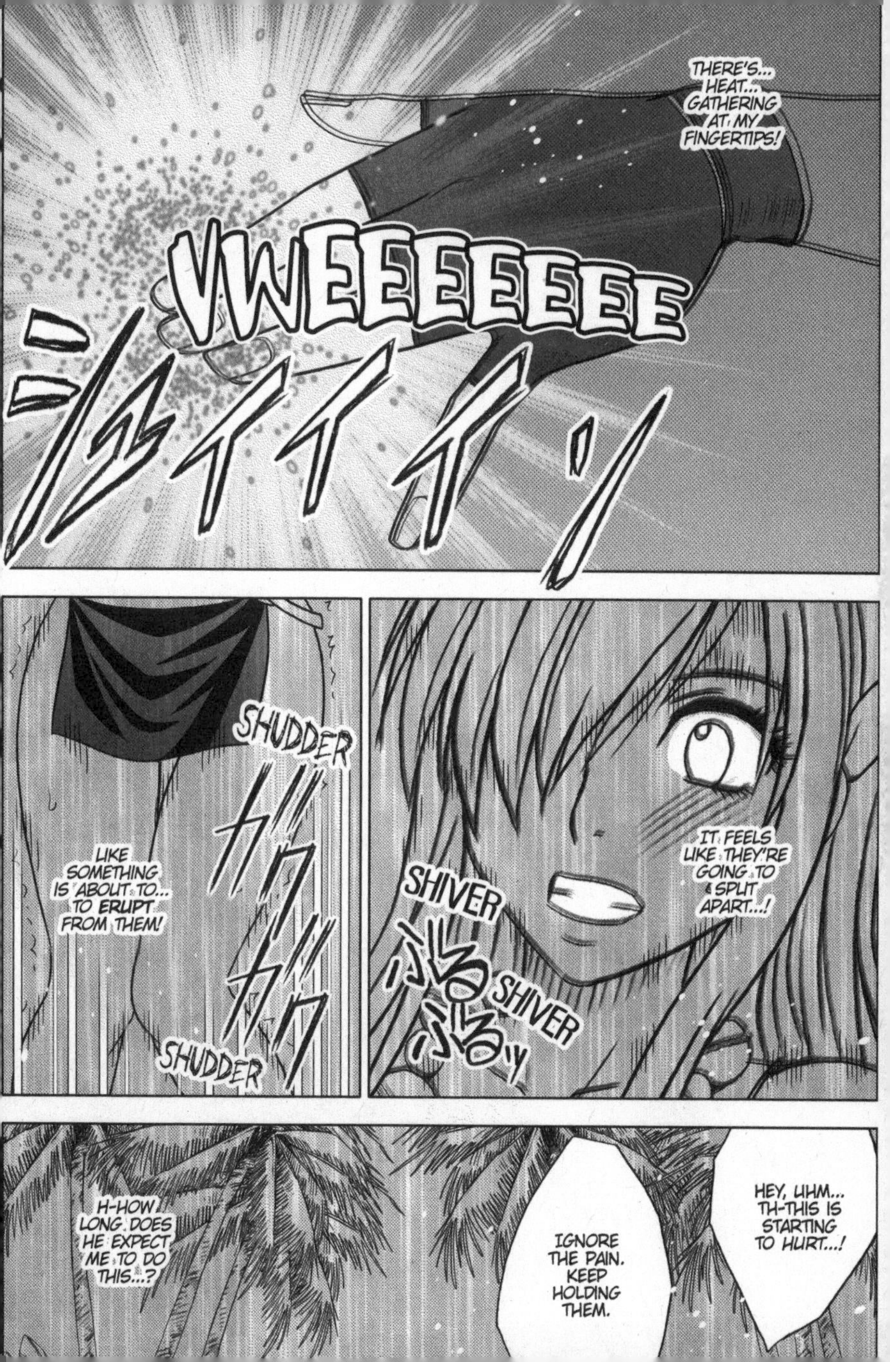
THERE'S... HEAT... GATHERING AT MY FINGERTIPS!
VWEEEEEEE
IT FEELS LIKE THEY'RE GOING TO SPLIT APART...!
SHIVER
SHIVER
SHUDDER
LIKE SOMETHING IS ABOUT TO... TO ERUPT FROM THEM!
SHUDDER
HEY, UHM... TH-THIS IS STARTING TO HURT...!
IGNORE THE PAIN. KEEP HOLDING THEM.
H-HOW LONG DOES HE EXPECT ME TO DO THIS...?

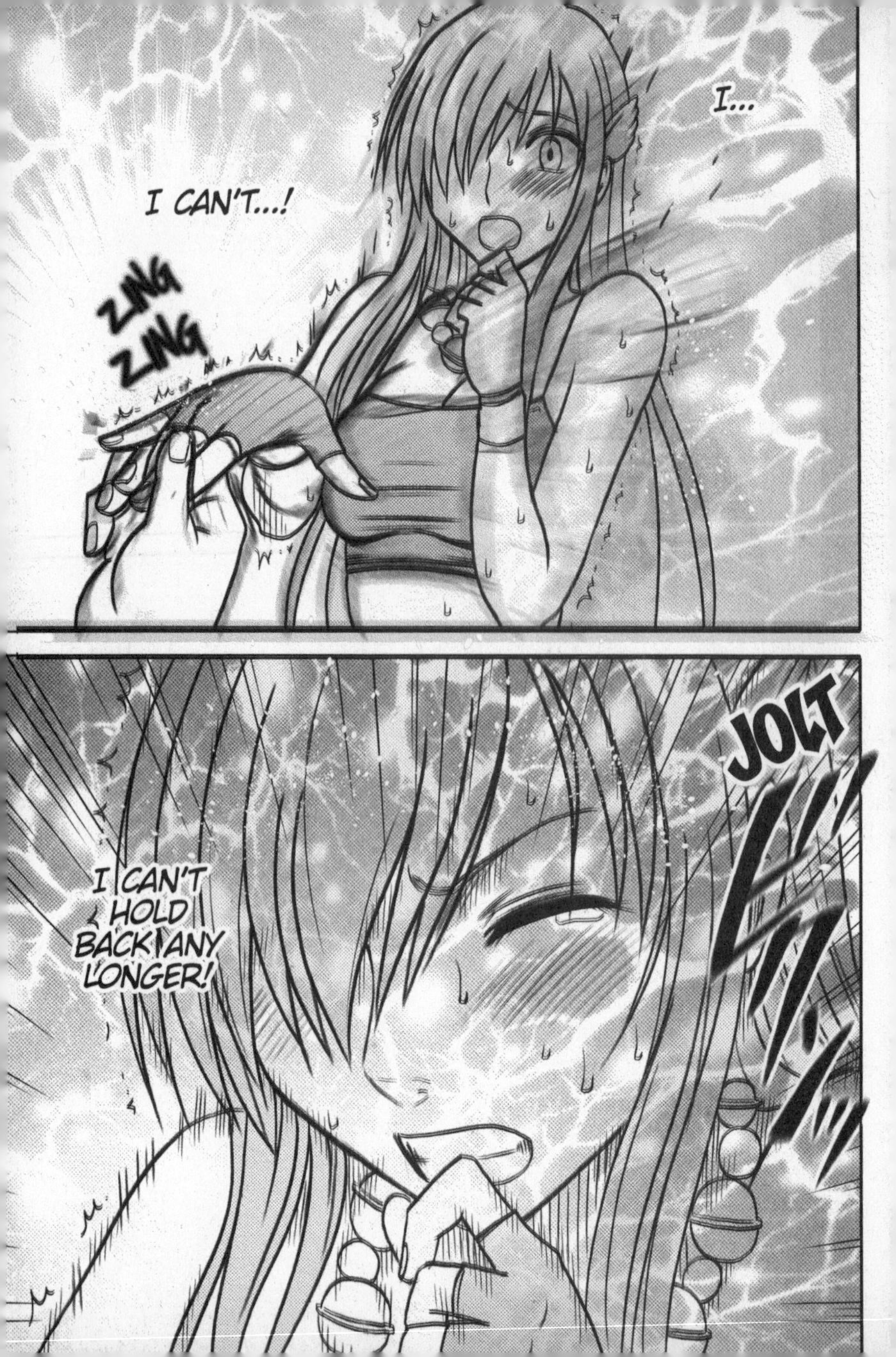
I...
I CAN'T...!
ZING ZING
JOLT
I CAN'T HOLD BACK ANY LONGER!

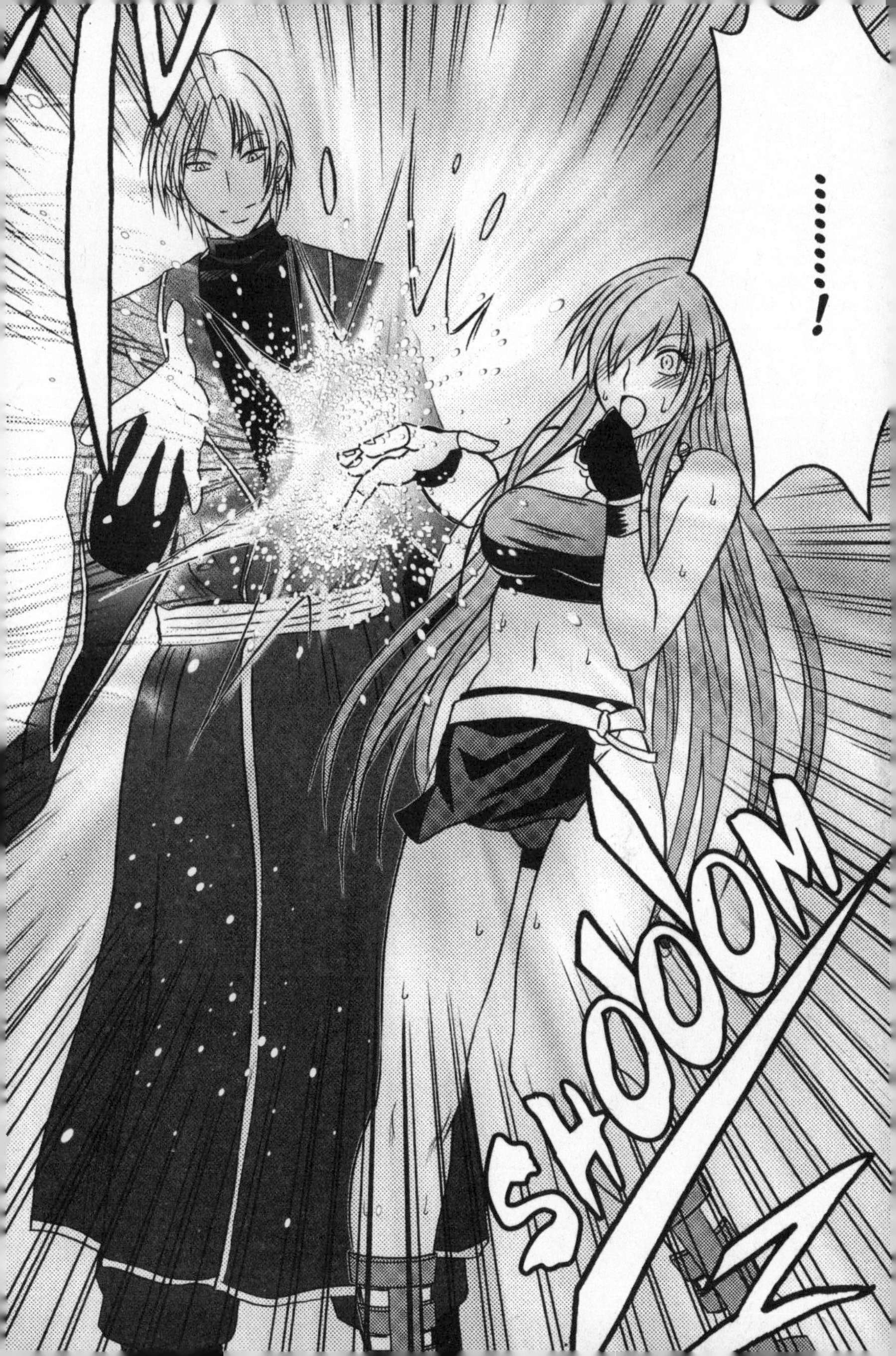
……!
SHOOOM

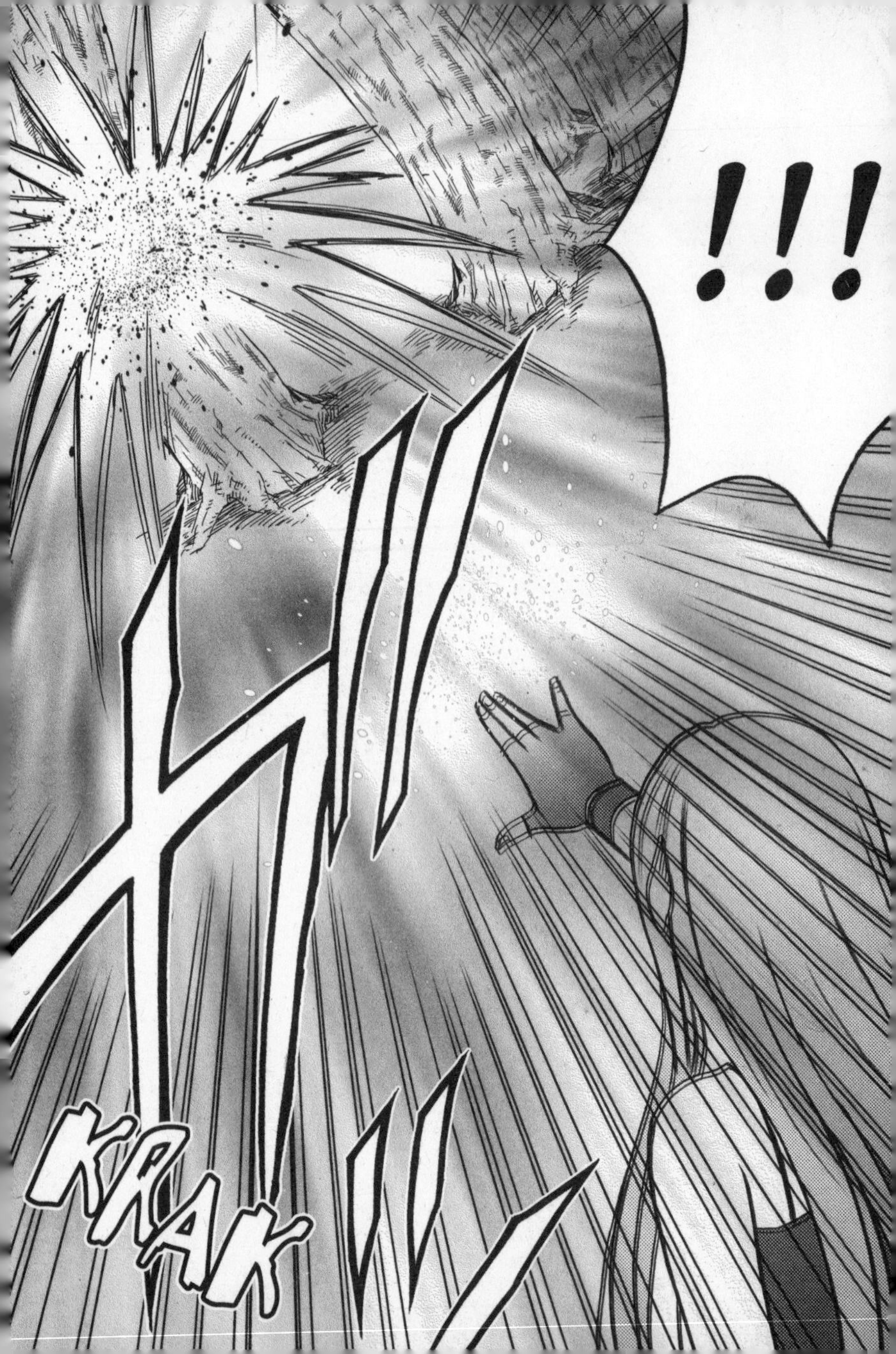
!!!
KRAK

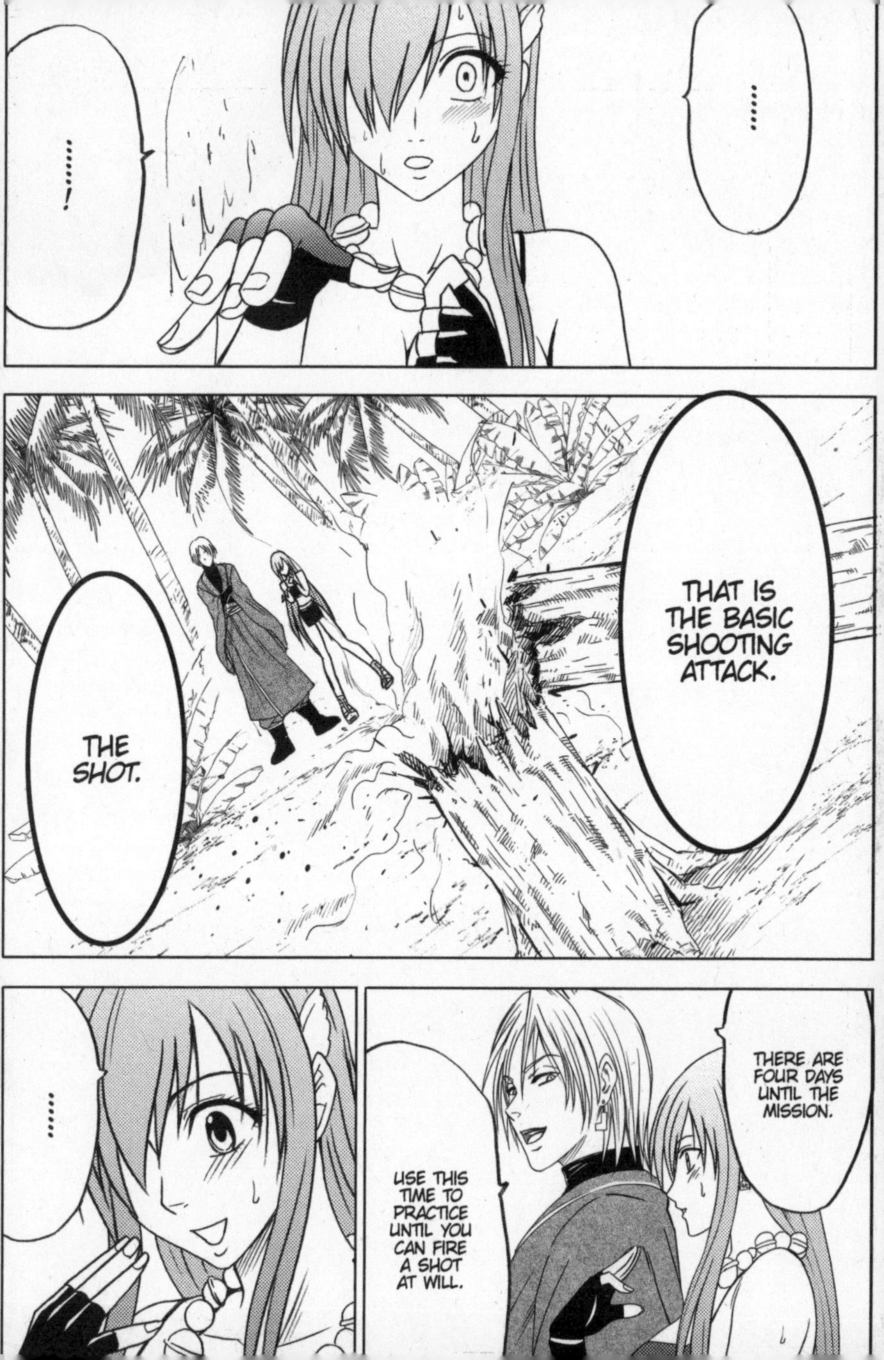
......
......!
THAT IS THE BASIC SHOOTING ATTACK.
THE SHOT.
THERE ARE FOUR DAYS UNTIL THE MISSION.
USE THIS TIME TO PRACTICE UNTIL YOU CAN FIRE A SHOT AT WILL.
......

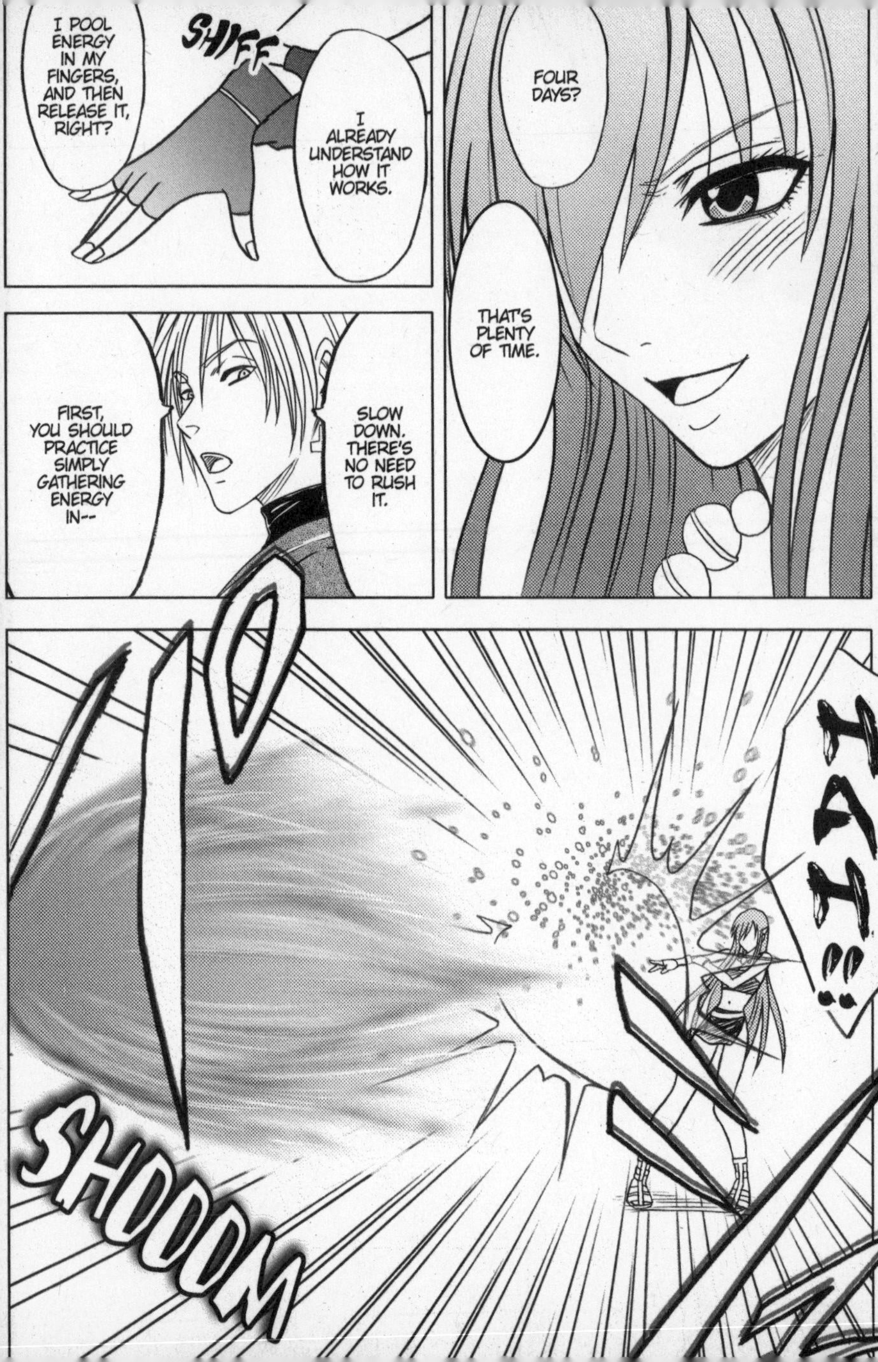
FOUR DAYS?
THAT'S PLENTY OF TIME.
SHIFF
I ALREADY UNDERSTAND HOW IT WORKS.
I POOL ENERGY IN MY FINGERS, AND THEN RELEASE IT, RIGHT?
SLOW DOWN. THERE'S NO NEED TO RUSH IT.
FIRST, YOU SHOULD PRACTICE SIMPLY GATHERING ENERGY IN--
IAI!!
SHOOOM

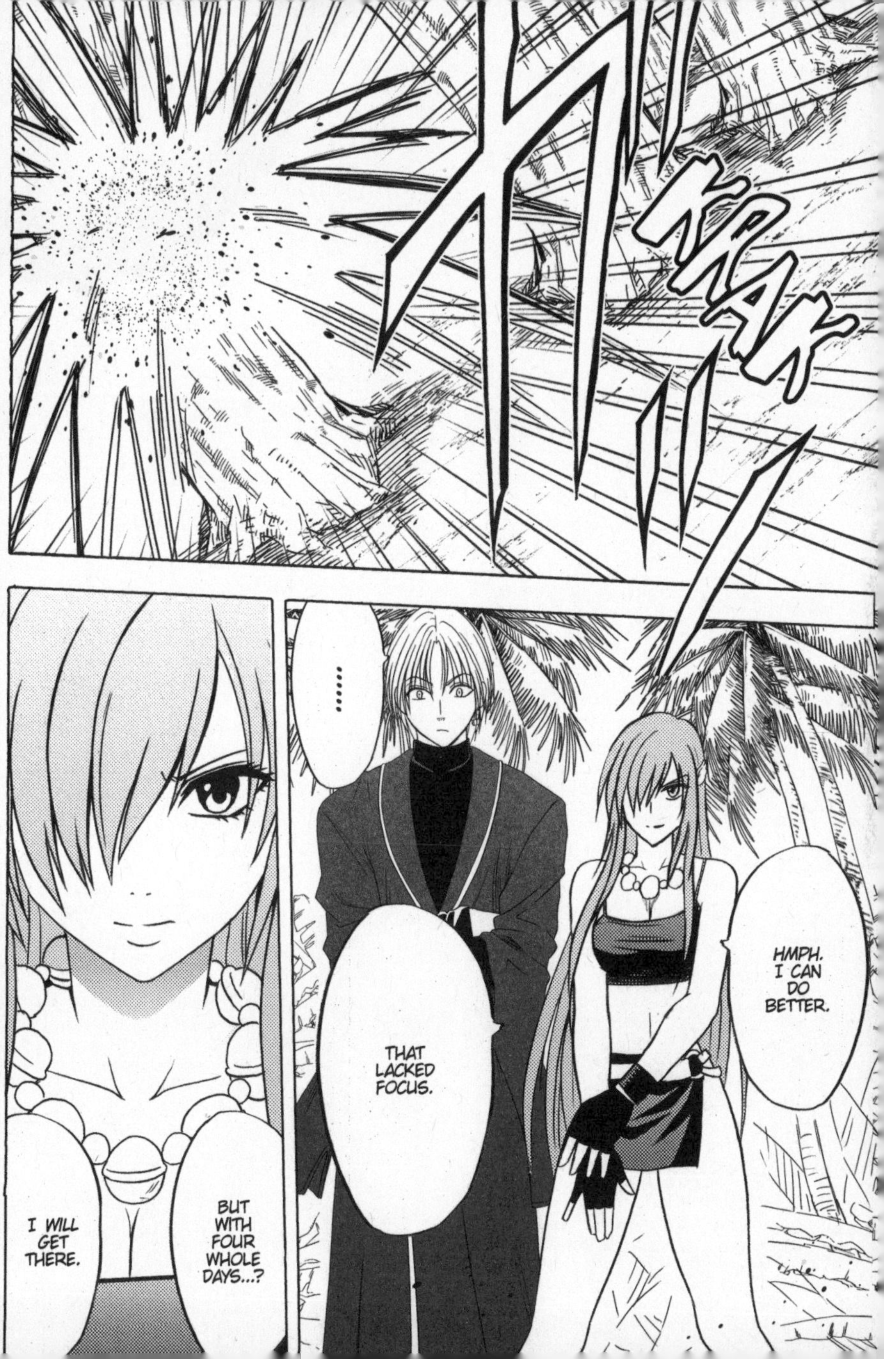
KRAK
HMPH. I CAN DO BETTER.
......
THAT LACKED FOCUS.
BUT WITH FOUR WHOLE DAYS...?
I WILL GET THERE.

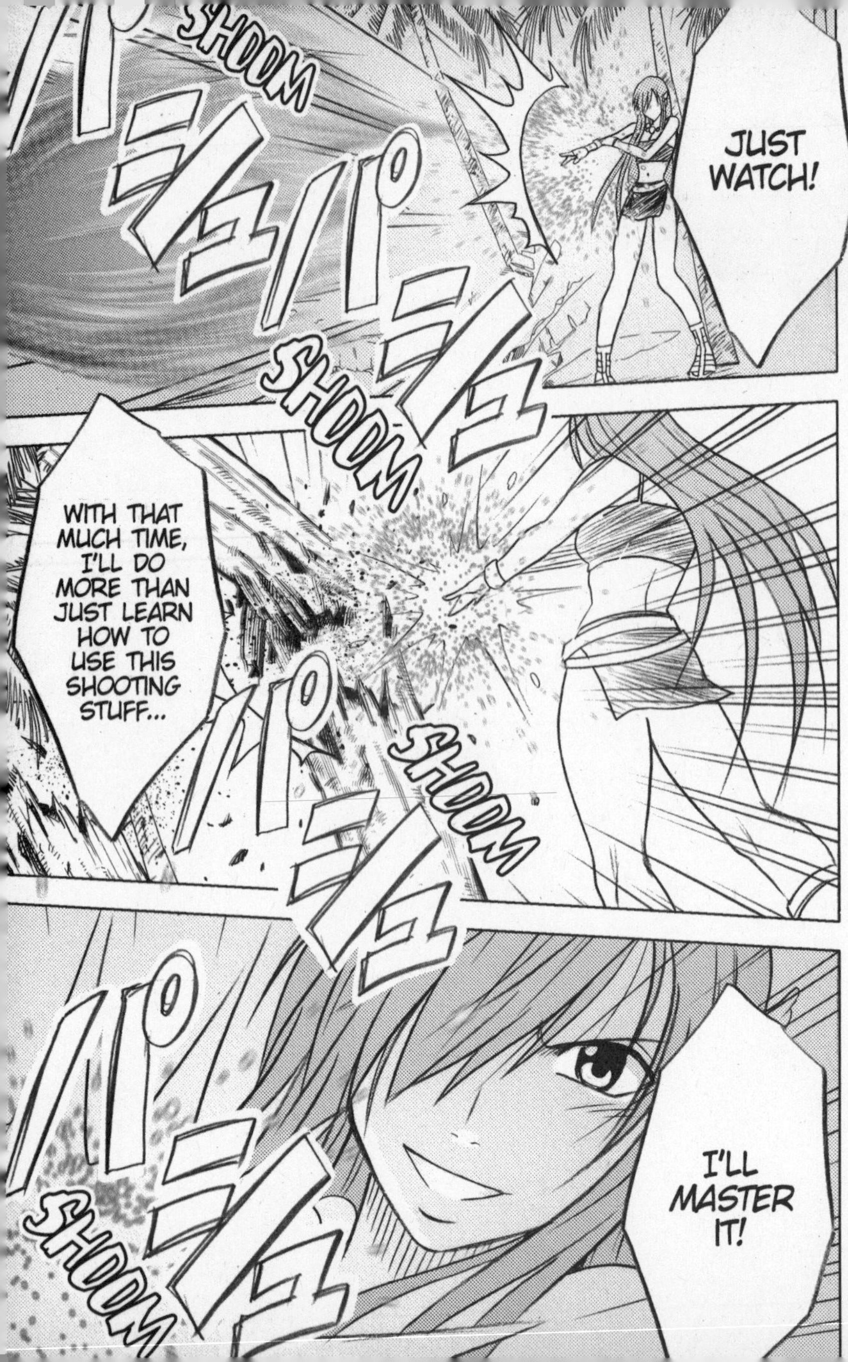
JUST WATCH!
SHOOM
SHOOM
WITH THAT MUCH TIME, I'LL DO MORE THAN JUST LEARN HOW TO USE THIS SHOOTING STUFF...
SHOOM
I'LL MASTER IT!
SHOOM

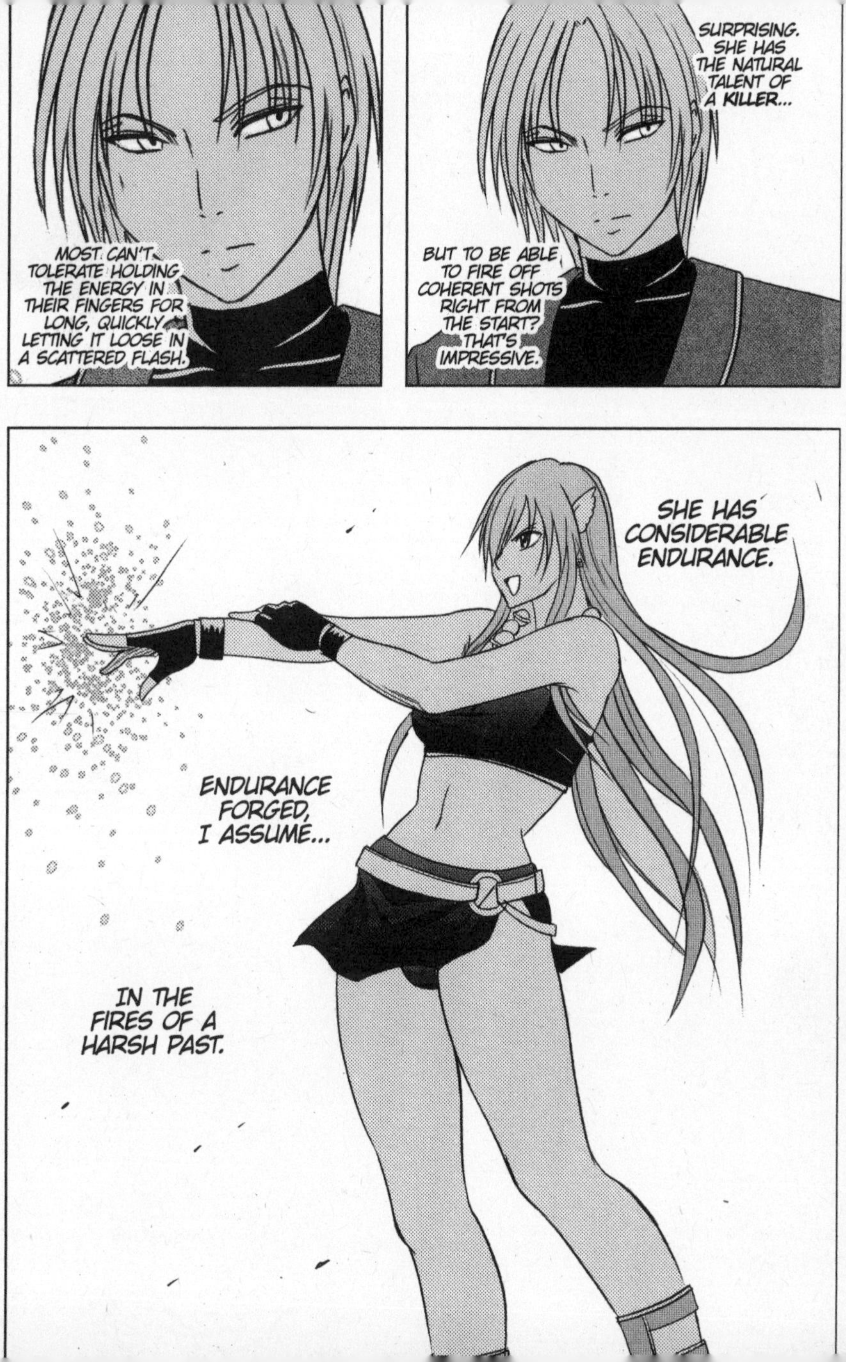
SURPRISING. SHE HAS THE NATURAL TALENT OF A KILLER...
BUT TO BE ABLE TO FIRE OFF COHERENT SHOTS RIGHT FROM THE START? THAT'S IMPRESSIVE.
MOST CAN'T TOLERATE HOLDING THE ENERGY IN THEIR FINGERS FOR LONG, QUICKLY LETTING IT LOOSE IN A SCATTERED FLASH.
SHE HAS CONSIDERABLE ENDURANCE.
ENDURANCE FORGED, I ASSUME...
IN THE FIRES OF A HARSH PAST.

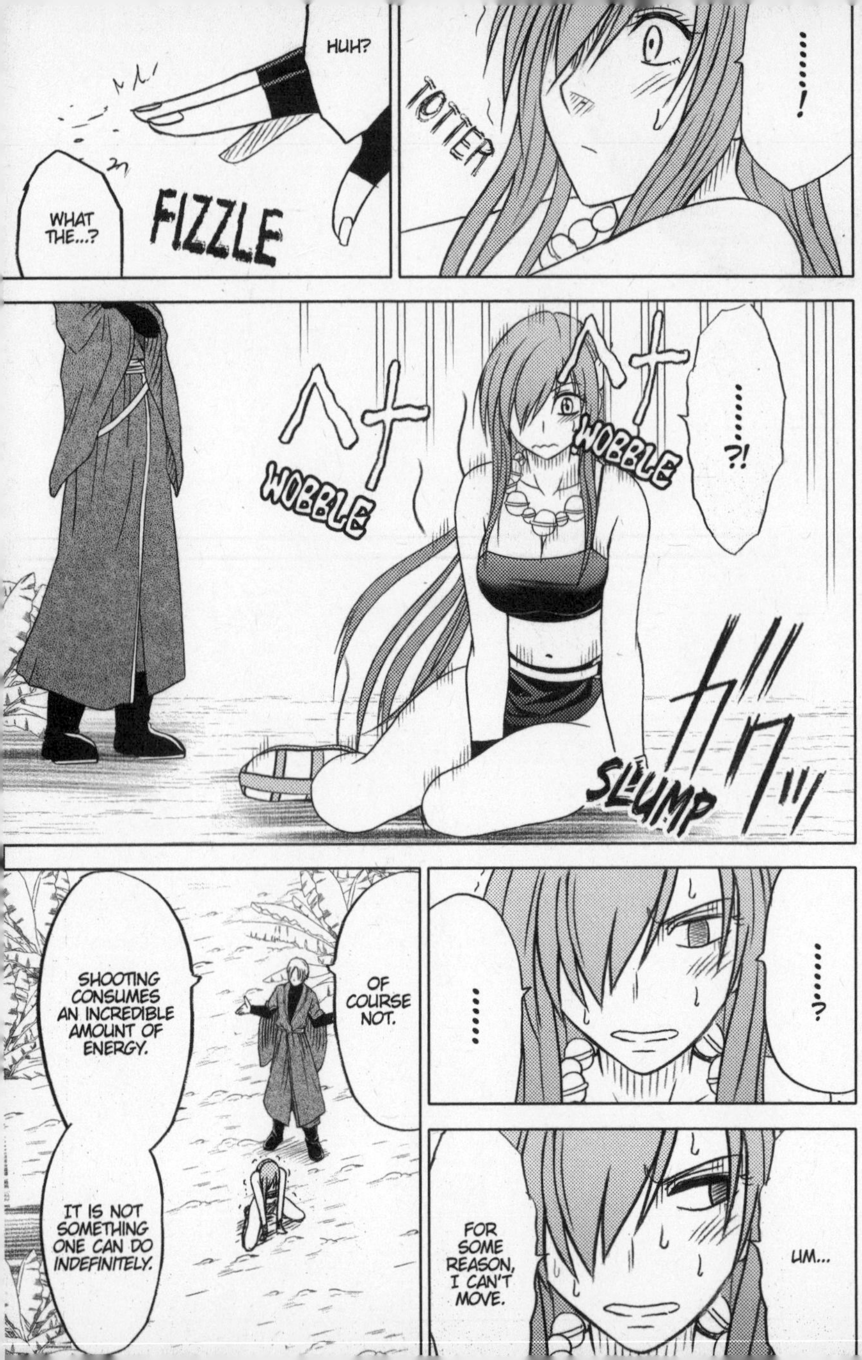
......!
TOTTER
HUH?
FIZZLE
WHAT THE...?
......?!
ヘナ
WOBBLE
ヘナ
WOBBLE
ガクッ
SLUMP
......?
......
UM...
FOR SOME REASON, I CAN'T MOVE.
OF COURSE NOT.
SHOOTING CONSUMES AN INCREDIBLE AMOUNT OF ENERGY.
IT IS NOT SOMETHING ONE CAN DO INDEFINITELY.

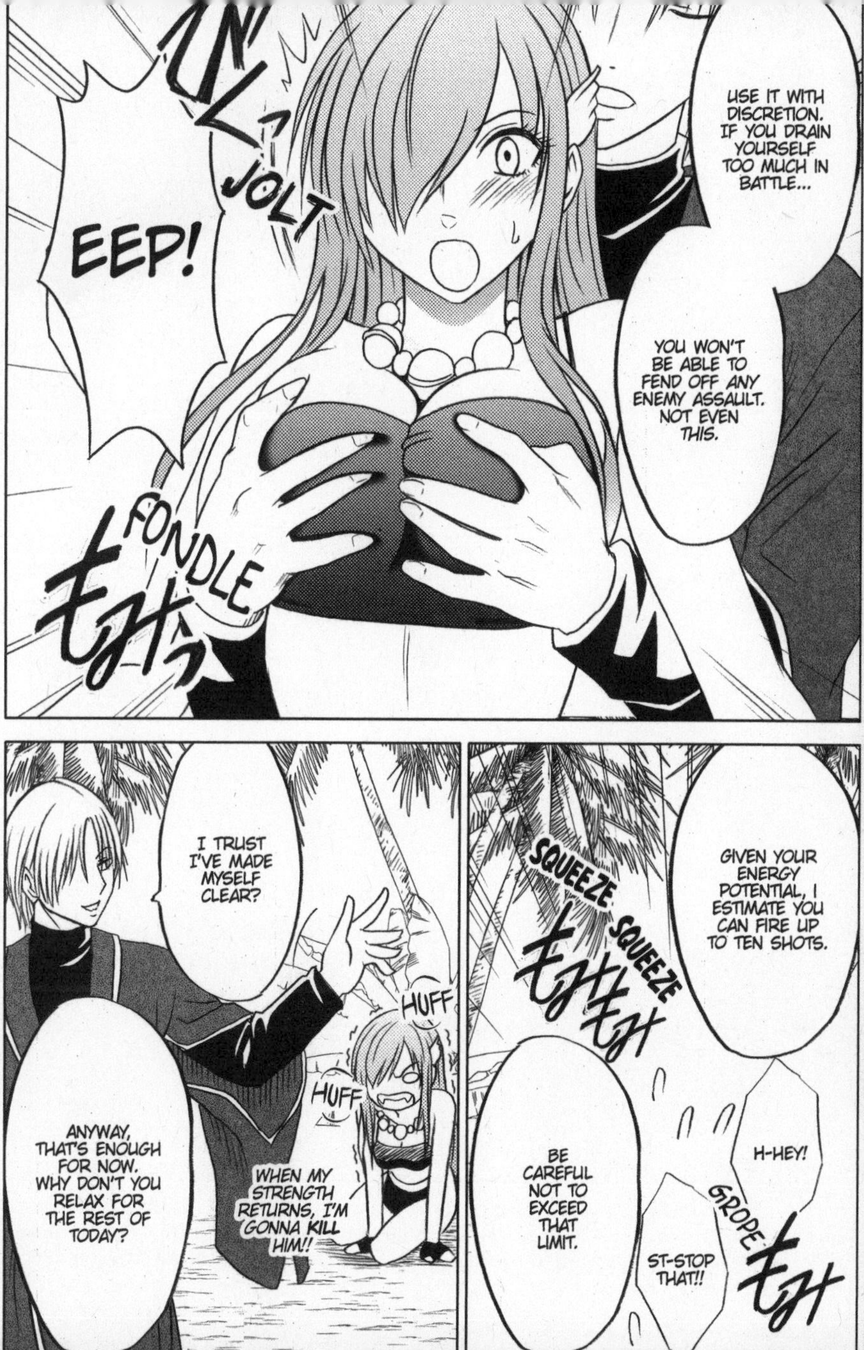
USE IT WITH DISCRETION. IF YOU DRAIN YOURSELF TOO MUCH IN BATTLE...
YOU WON'T BE ABLE TO FEND OFF ANY ENEMY ASSAULT. NOT EVEN THIS.
JOLT
EEP!
FONDLE
GIVEN YOUR ENERGY POTENTIAL, I ESTIMATE YOU CAN FIRE UP TO TEN SHOTS.
SQUEEZE
SQUEEZE
BE CAREFUL NOT TO EXCEED THAT LIMIT.
H-HEY!
GROPE
ST-STOP THAT!!
I TRUST I'VE MADE MYSELF CLEAR?
HUFF
HUFF
ANYWAY, THAT'S ENOUGH FOR NOW. WHY DON'T YOU RELAX FOR THE REST OF TODAY?
WHEN MY STRENGTH RETURNS, I'M GONNA KILL HIM!!

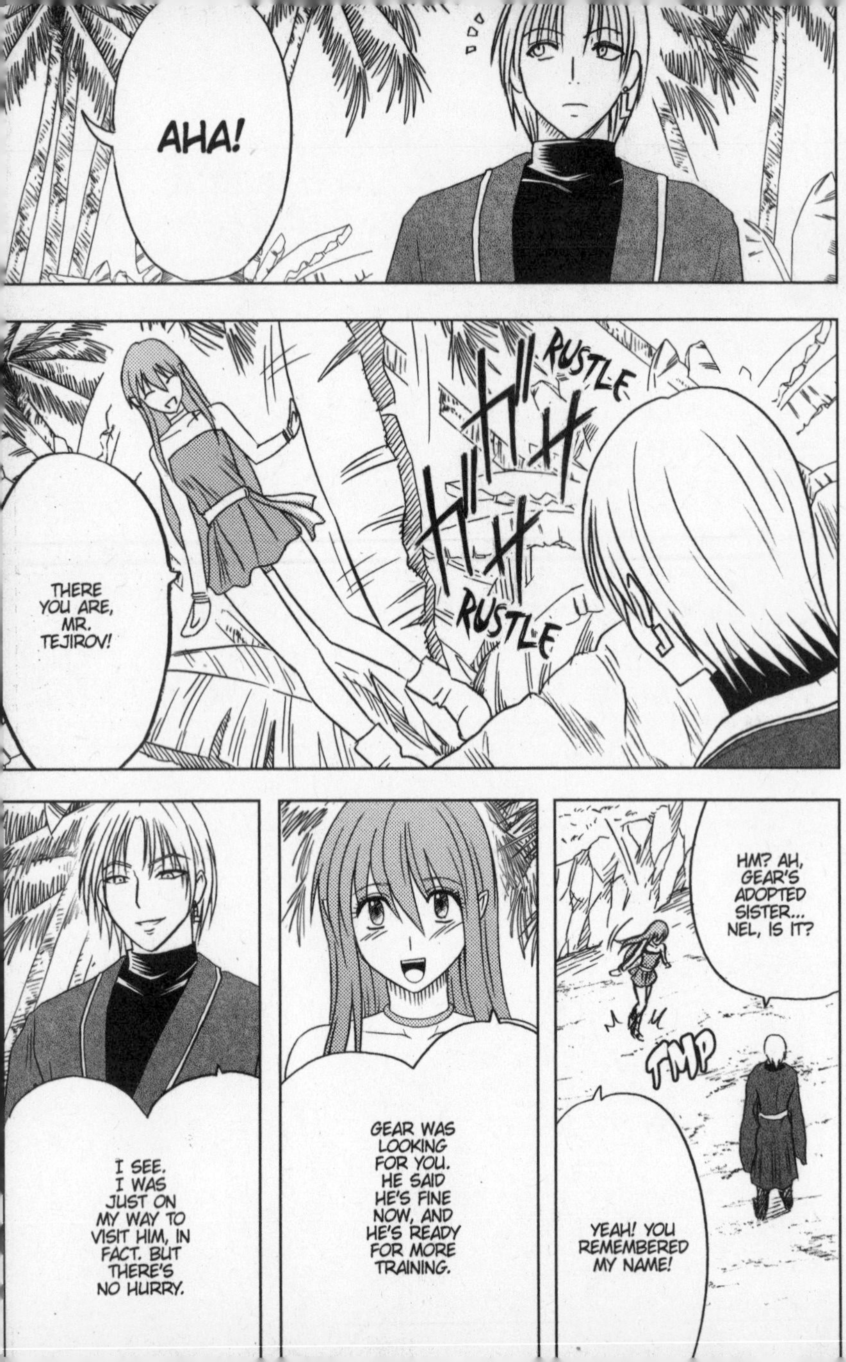
AHA!
RUSTLE
RUSTLE
THERE YOU ARE, MR. TEJIROV!
HM? AH, GEAR'S ADOPTED SISTER... NEL, IS IT?
TMP
YEAH! YOU REMEMBERED MY NAME!
GEAR WAS LOOKING FOR YOU. HE SAID HE'S FINE NOW, AND HE'S READY FOR MORE TRAINING.
I SEE. I WAS JUST ON MY WAY TO VISIT HIM, IN FACT. BUT THERE'S NO HURRY.

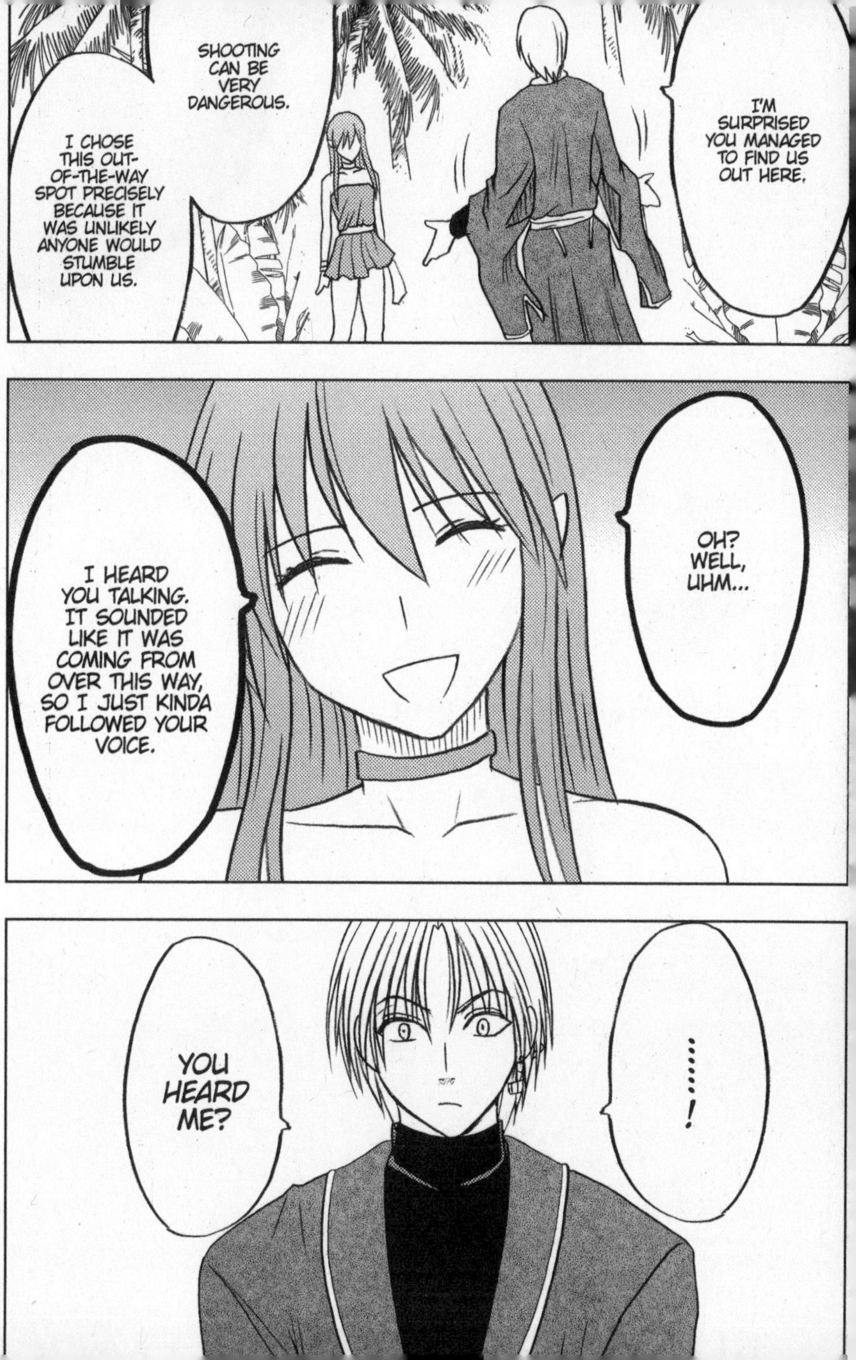
I'M SURPRISED YOU MANAGED TO FIND US OUT HERE.
SHOOTING CAN BE VERY DANGEROUS.
I CHOSE THIS OUT-OF-THE-WAY SPOT PRECISELY BECAUSE IT WAS UNLIKELY ANYONE WOULD STUMBLE UPON US.
OH? WELL, UHM...
I HEARD YOU TALKING. IT SOUNDED LIKE IT WAS COMING FROM OVER THIS WAY, SO I JUST KINDA FOLLOWED YOUR VOICE.
......!
YOU HEARD ME?

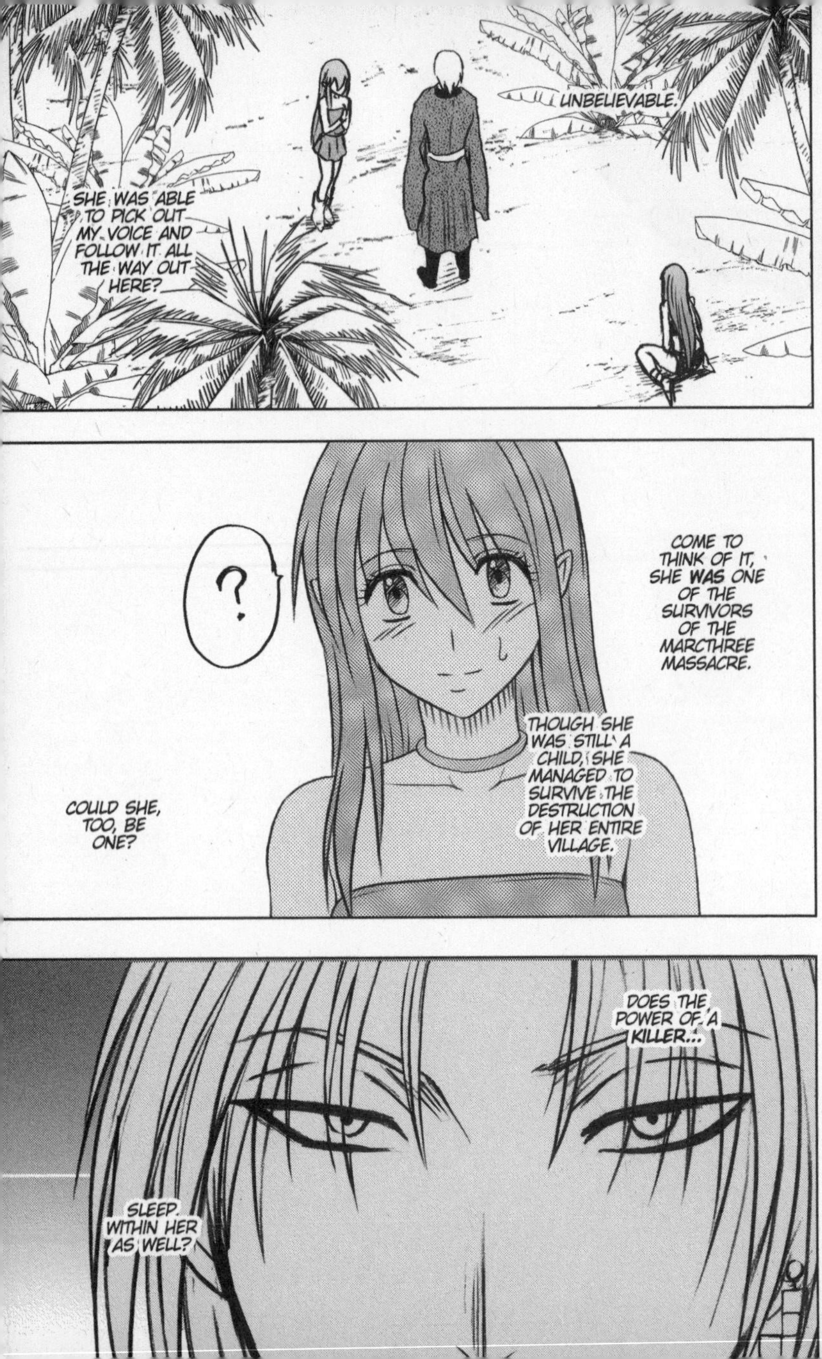
UNBELIEVABLE.
SHE WAS ABLE TO PICK OUT MY VOICE AND FOLLOW IT ALL THE WAY OUT HERE?
COME TO THINK OF IT, SHE WAS ONE OF THE SURVIVORS OF THE MARCTHREE MASSACRE.
?
THOUGH SHE WAS STILL A CHILD, SHE MANAGED TO SURVIVE THE DESTRUCTION OF HER ENTIRE VILLAGE.
COULD SHE, TOO, BE ONE?
DOES THE POWER OF A KILLER...
SLEEP WITHIN HER AS WELL?

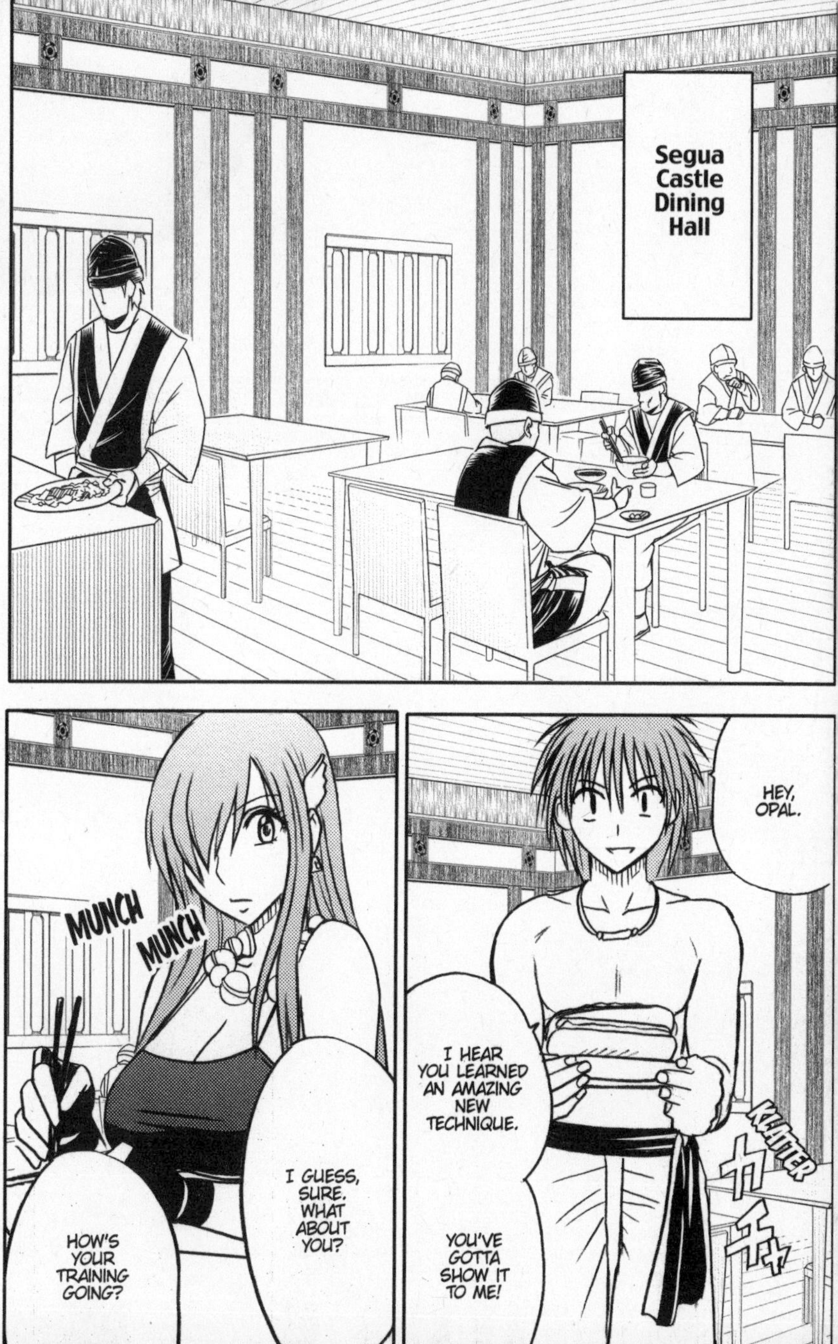

Segua Castle Dining Hall
HEY, OPAL.
I HEAR YOU LEARNED AN AMAZING NEW TECHNIQUE.
YOU'VE GOTTA SHOW IT TO ME!
KLATTER
MUNCH MUNCH
I GUESS, SURE. WHAT ABOUT YOU?
HOW'S YOUR TRAINING GOING?

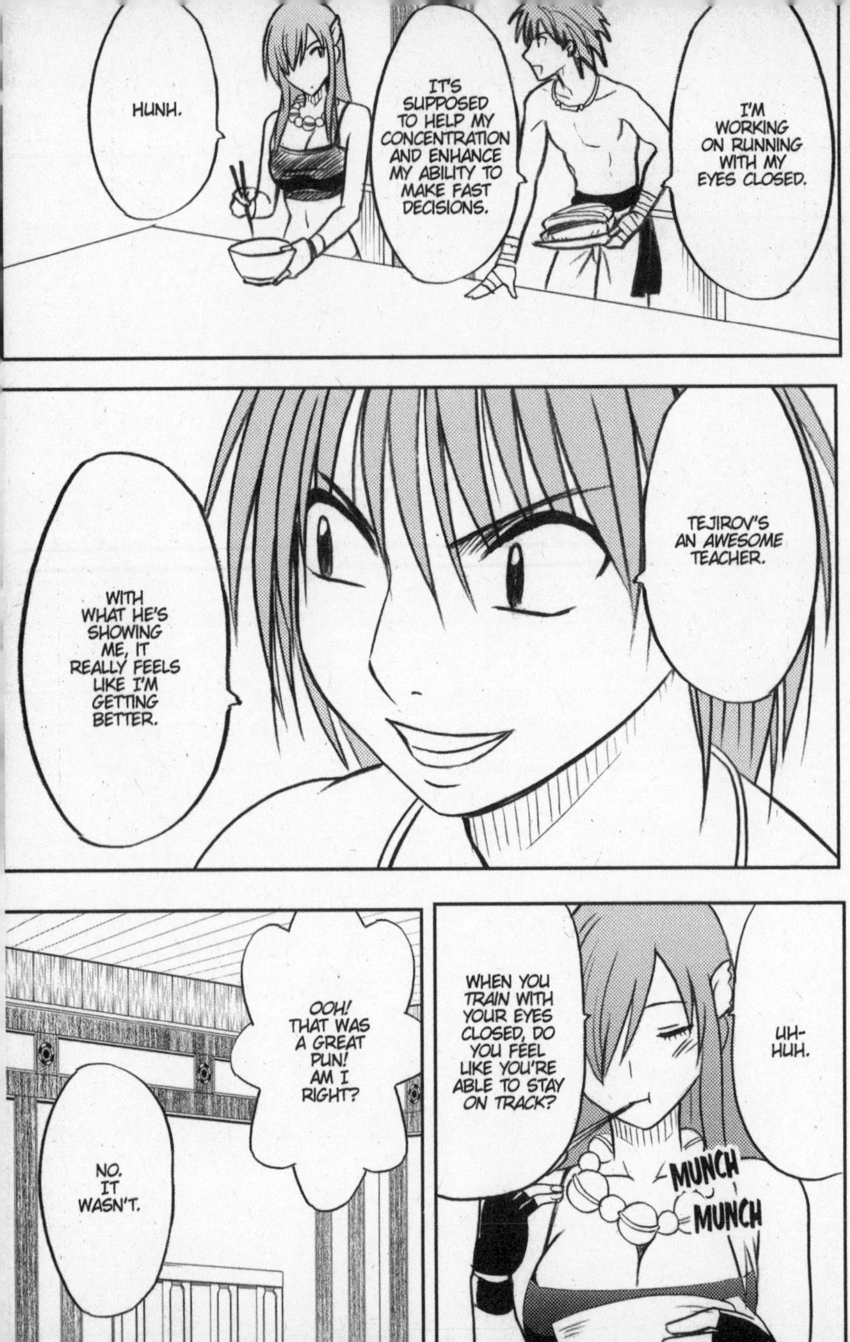
I'M WORKING ON RUNNING WITH MY EYES CLOSED.
IT'S SUPPOSED TO HELP MY CONCENTRATION AND ENHANCE MY ABILITY TO MAKE FAST DECISIONS.
HUNH.
TEJIROV'S AN *AWESOME* TEACHER.
WITH WHAT HE'S SHOWING ME, IT REALLY FEELS LIKE I'M GETTING BETTER.
UH-HUH.
WHEN YOU *TRAIN* WITH YOUR EYES CLOSED, DO YOU FEEL LIKE YOU'RE ABLE TO STAY *ON TRACK?*
MUNCH
MUNCH
OOH! THAT WAS A GREAT PUN! AM I RIGHT?
NO. IT WASN'T.

CHAPTER 6

QUARTET

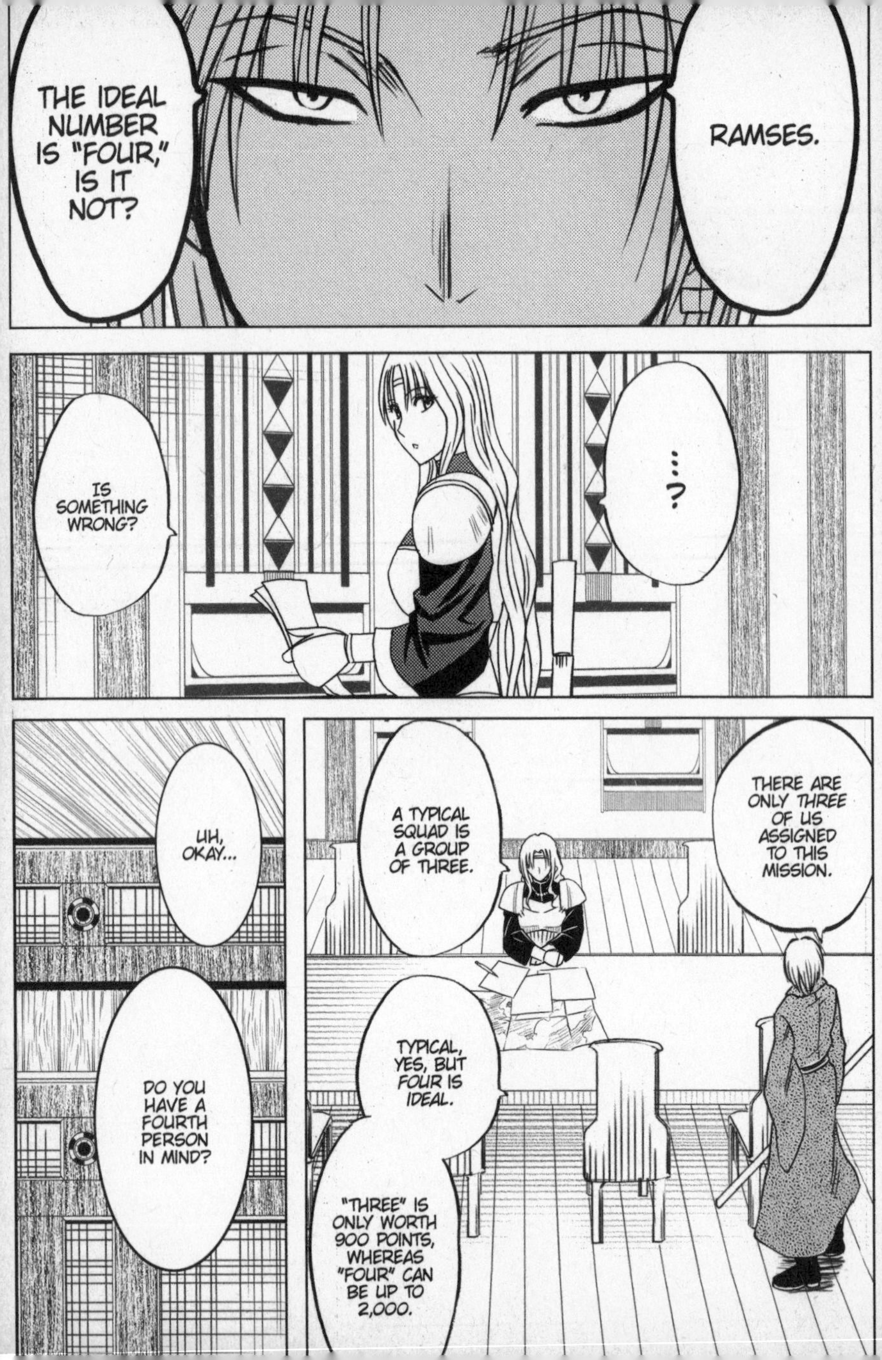
RAMSES.
THE IDEAL NUMBER IS "FOUR," IS IT NOT?
...?
IS SOMETHING WRONG?
THERE ARE ONLY THREE OF US ASSIGNED TO THIS MISSION.
A TYPICAL SQUAD IS A GROUP OF THREE.
TYPICAL, YES, BUT FOUR IS IDEAL.
"THREE" IS ONLY WORTH 900 POINTS, WHEREAS "FOUR" CAN BE UP TO 2,000.
UH, OKAY...
DO YOU HAVE A FOURTH PERSON IN MIND?

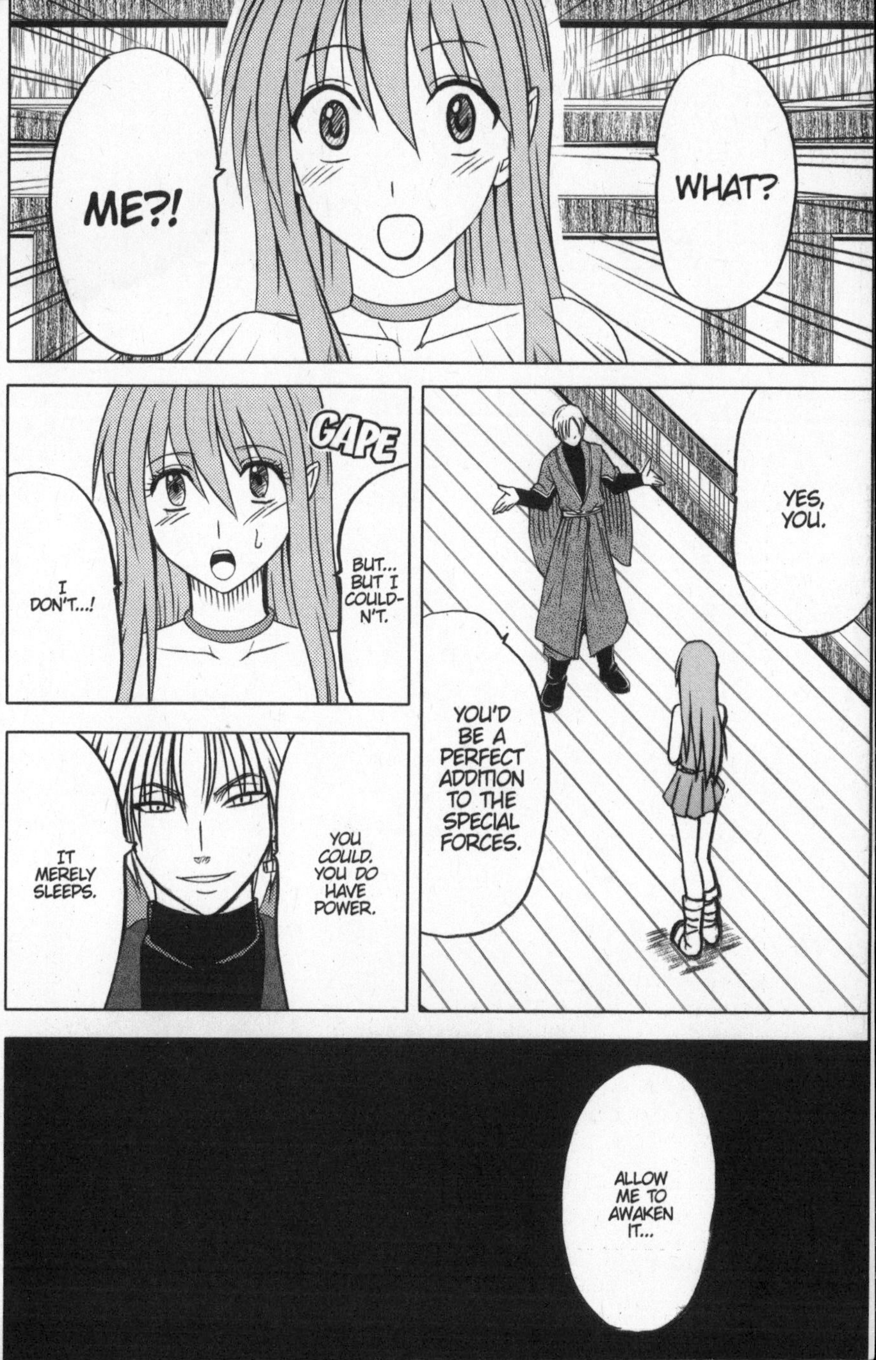
WHAT?
ME?!
YES, YOU.
YOU'D BE A PERFECT ADDITION TO THE SPECIAL FORCES.
GAPE
BUT... BUT I COULDN'T.
I DON'T...!
YOU COULD. YOU DO HAVE POWER.
IT MERELY SLEEPS.
ALLOW ME TO AWAKEN IT...

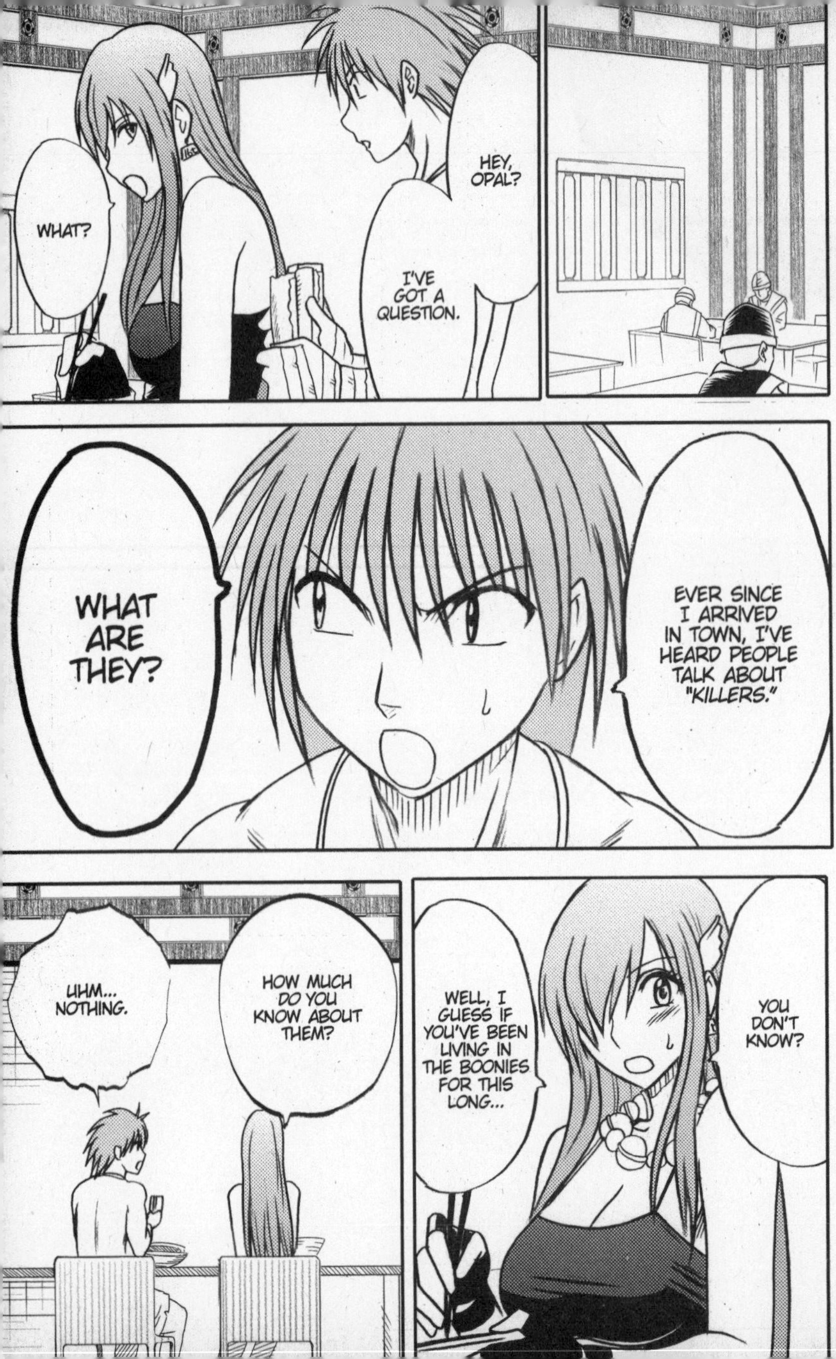
HEY, OPAL?
I'VE GOT A QUESTION.
WHAT?
EVER SINCE I ARRIVED IN TOWN, I'VE HEARD PEOPLE TALK ABOUT "KILLERS."
WHAT ARE THEY?
YOU DON'T KNOW?
WELL, I GUESS IF YOU'VE BEEN LIVING IN THE BOONIES FOR THIS LONG...
HOW MUCH DO YOU KNOW ABOUT THEM?
UHM... NOTHING.

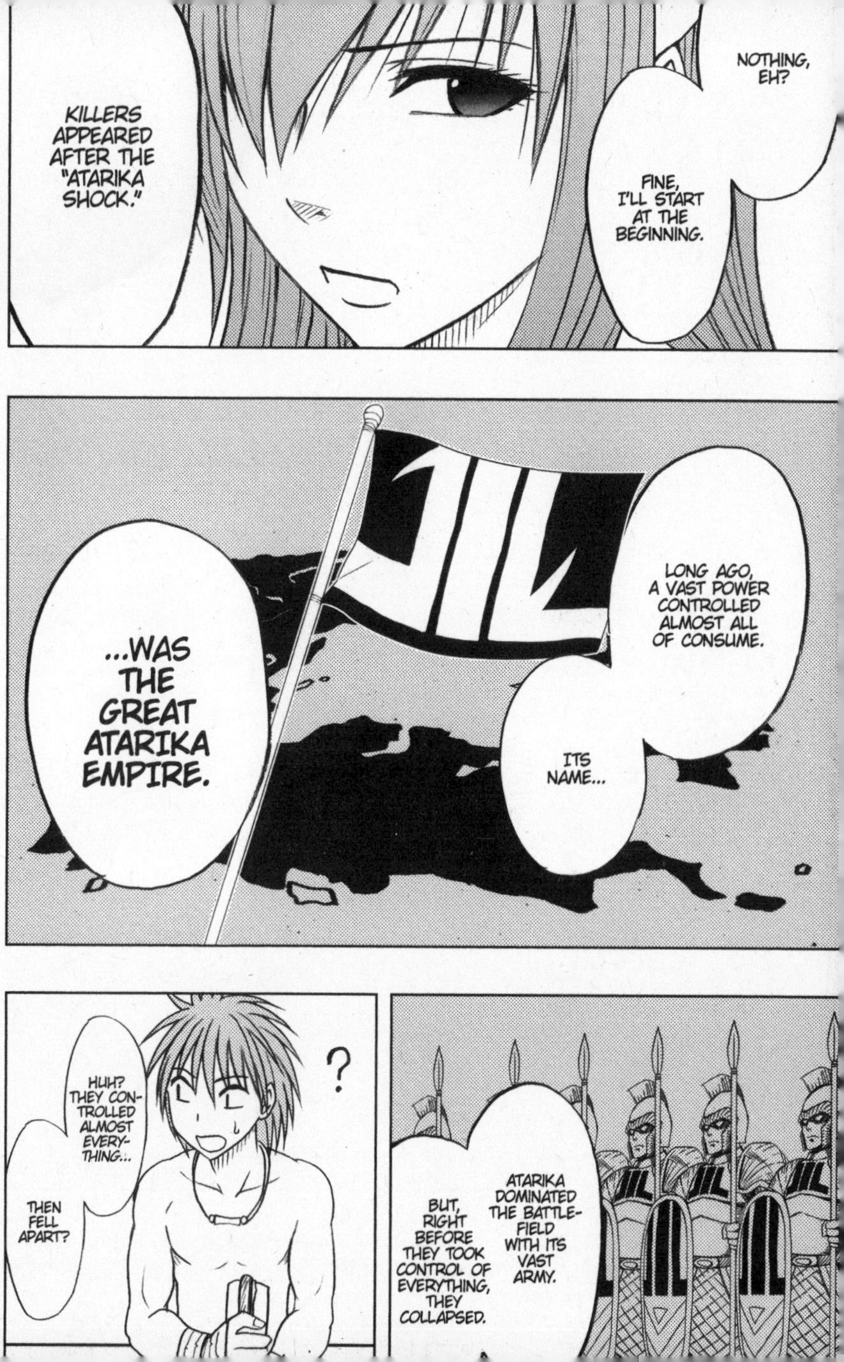
NOTHING, EH?
FINE, I'LL START AT THE BEGINNING.
KILLERS APPEARED AFTER THE "ATARIKA SHOCK."
LONG AGO, A VAST POWER CONTROLLED ALMOST ALL OF CONSUME.
ITS NAME...
...WAS THE GREAT ATARIKA EMPIRE.
ATARIKA DOMINATED THE BATTLE-FIELD WITH ITS VAST ARMY.
BUT, RIGHT BEFORE THEY TOOK CONTROL OF EVERYTHING, THEY COLLAPSED.
?
HUH? THEY CON-TROLLED ALMOST EVERY-THING...
THEN FELL APART?

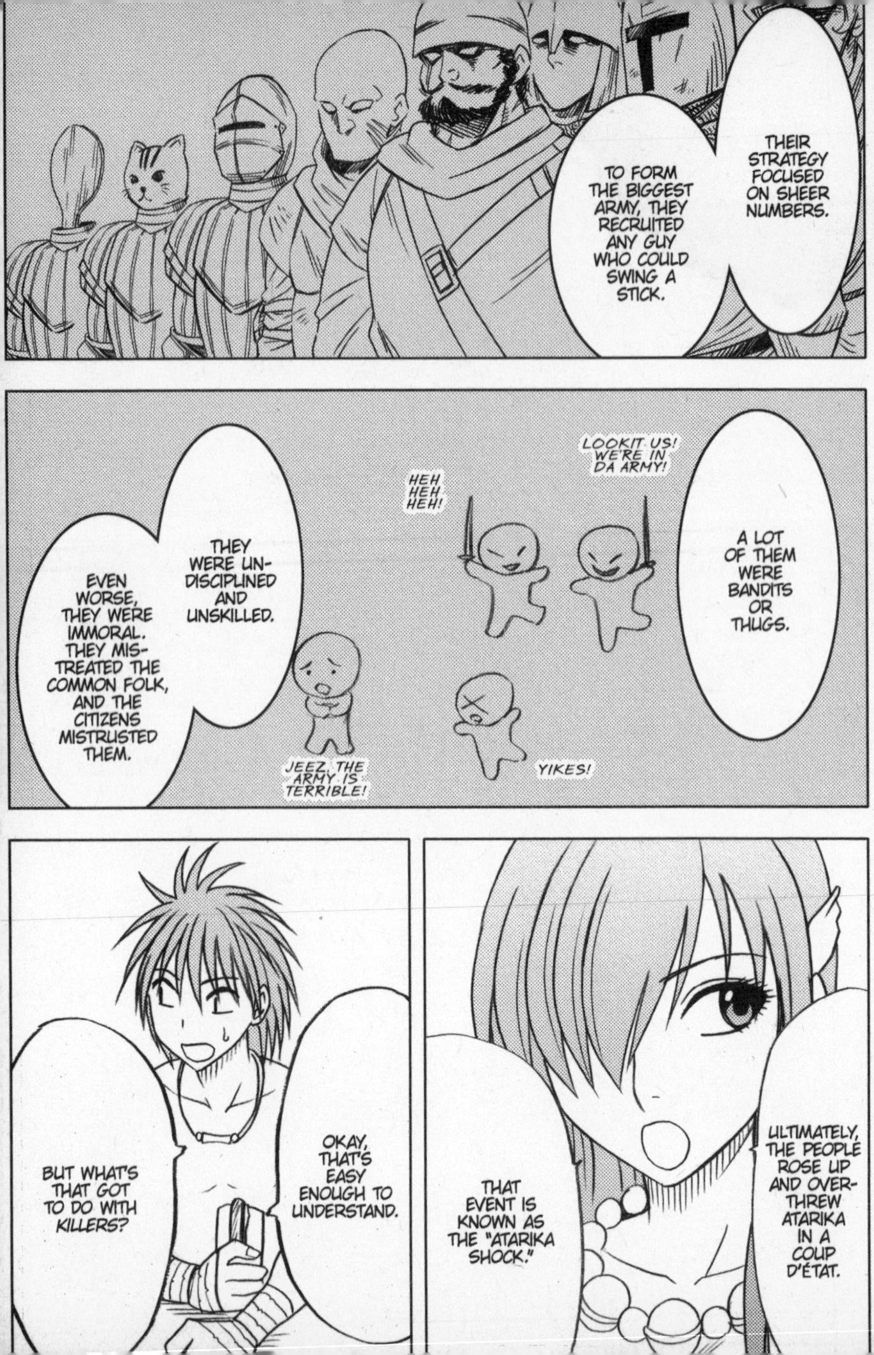
THEIR STRATEGY FOCUSED ON SHEER NUMBERS.
TO FORM THE BIGGEST ARMY, THEY RECRUITED ANY GUY WHO COULD SWING A STICK.
A LOT OF THEM WERE BANDITS OR THUGS.
LOOKIT US! WE'RE IN DA ARMY!
HEH HEH HEH!
YIKES!
JEEZ, THE ARMY IS TERRIBLE!
THEY WERE UN-DISCIPLINED AND UNSKILLED.
EVEN WORSE, THEY WERE IMMORAL. THEY MIS-TREATED THE COMMON FOLK, AND THE CITIZENS MISTRUSTED THEM.
ULTIMATELY, THE PEOPLE ROSE UP AND OVER-THREW ATARIKA IN A COUP D'ÉTAT.
THAT EVENT IS KNOWN AS THE "ATARIKA SHOCK."
OKAY, THAT'S EASY ENOUGH TO UNDERSTAND.
BUT WHAT'S THAT GOT TO DO WITH KILLERS?

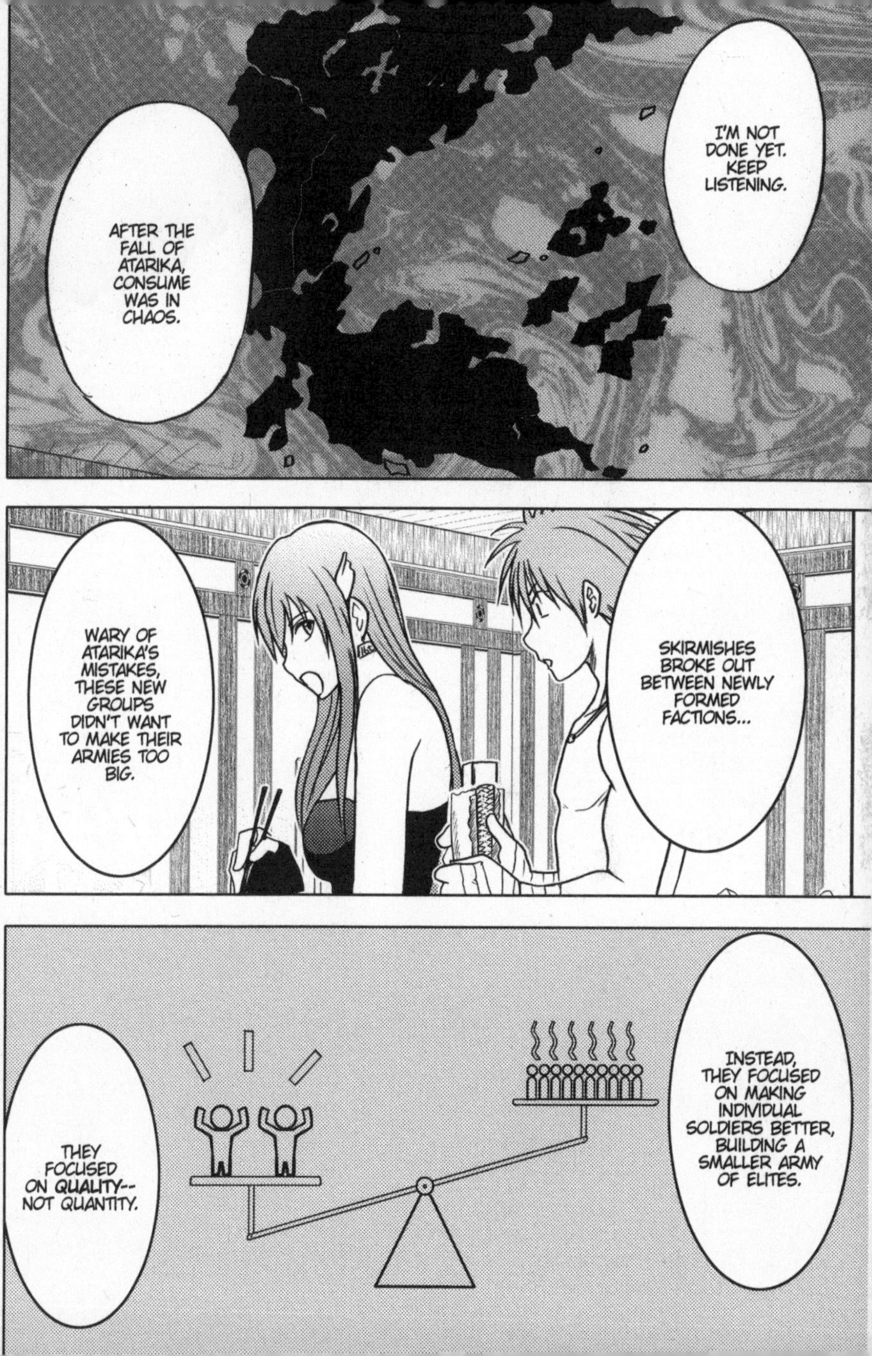
I'M NOT DONE YET. KEEP LISTENING.
AFTER THE FALL OF ATARIKA, CONSUME WAS IN CHAOS.
SKIRMISHES BROKE OUT BETWEEN NEWLY FORMED FACTIONS...
WARY OF ATARIKA'S MISTAKES, THESE NEW GROUPS DIDN'T WANT TO MAKE THEIR ARMIES TOO BIG.
INSTEAD, THEY FOCUSED ON MAKING INDIVIDUAL SOLDIERS BETTER, BUILDING A SMALLER ARMY OF ELITES.
THEY FOCUSED ON **QUALITY**-- NOT QUANTITY.

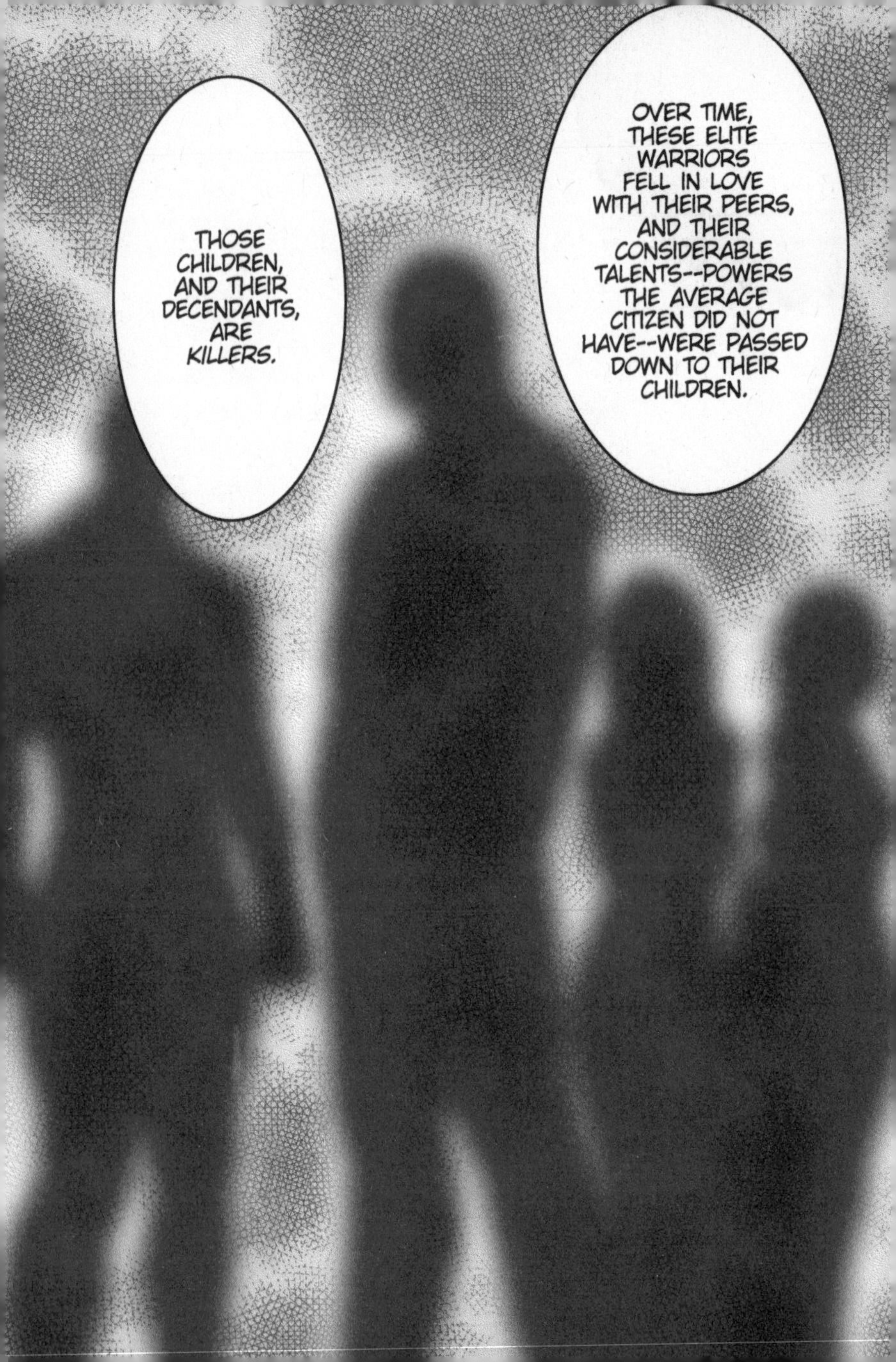
OVER TIME, THESE ELITE WARRIORS FELL IN LOVE WITH THEIR PEERS, AND THEIR CONSIDERABLE TALENTS--POWERS THE AVERAGE CITIZEN DID NOT HAVE--WERE PASSED DOWN TO THEIR CHILDREN.
THOSE CHILDREN, AND THEIR DECENDANTS, ARE KILLERS.

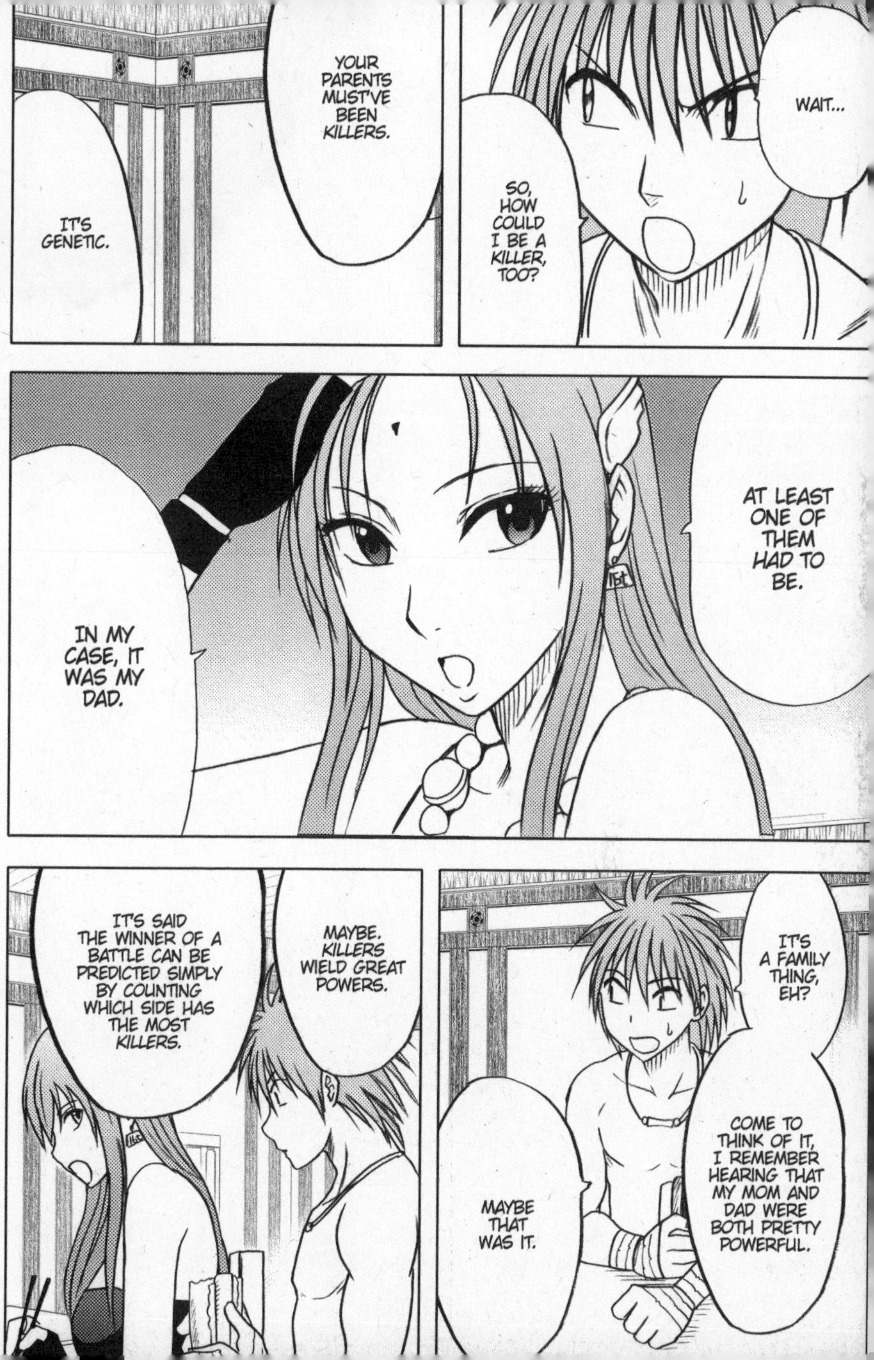
WAIT...
SO, HOW COULD I BE A KILLER, TOO?
YOUR PARENTS MUST'VE BEEN KILLERS.
IT'S GENETIC.
AT LEAST ONE OF THEM HAD TO BE.
IN MY CASE, IT WAS MY DAD.
IT'S A FAMILY THING, EH?
COME TO THINK OF IT, I REMEMBER HEARING THAT MY MOM AND DAD WERE BOTH PRETTY POWERFUL.
MAYBE THAT WAS IT.
MAYBE. KILLERS WIELD GREAT POWERS.
IT'S SAID THE WINNER OF A BATTLE CAN BE PREDICTED SIMPLY BY COUNTING WHICH SIDE HAS THE MOST KILLERS.

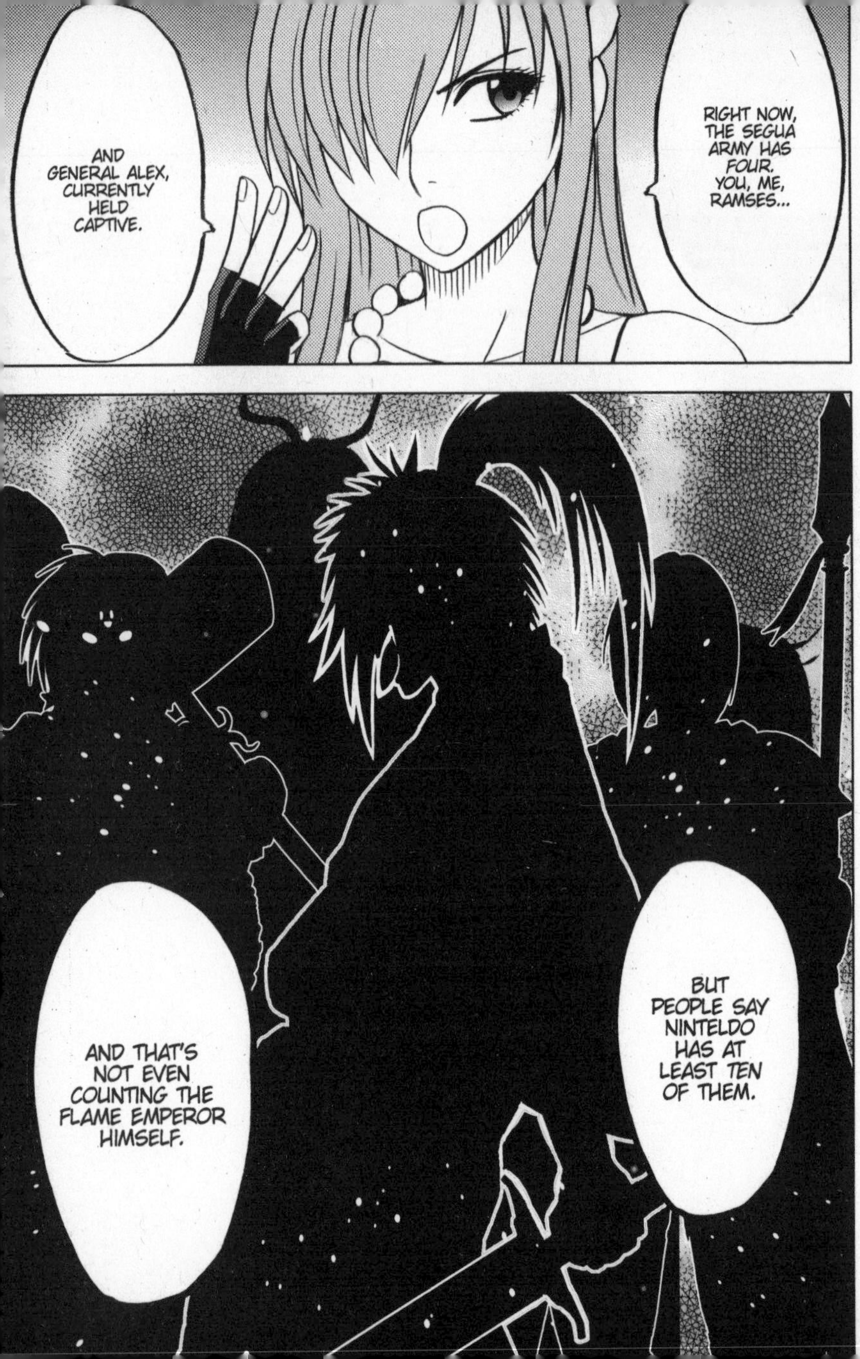
RIGHT NOW, THE SEGUA ARMY HAS FOUR. YOU, ME, RAMSES...
AND GENERAL ALEX, CURRENTLY HELD CAPTIVE.
BUT PEOPLE SAY NINTELDO HAS AT LEAST TEN OF THEM.
AND THAT'S NOT EVEN COUNTING THE FLAME EMPEROR HIMSELF.

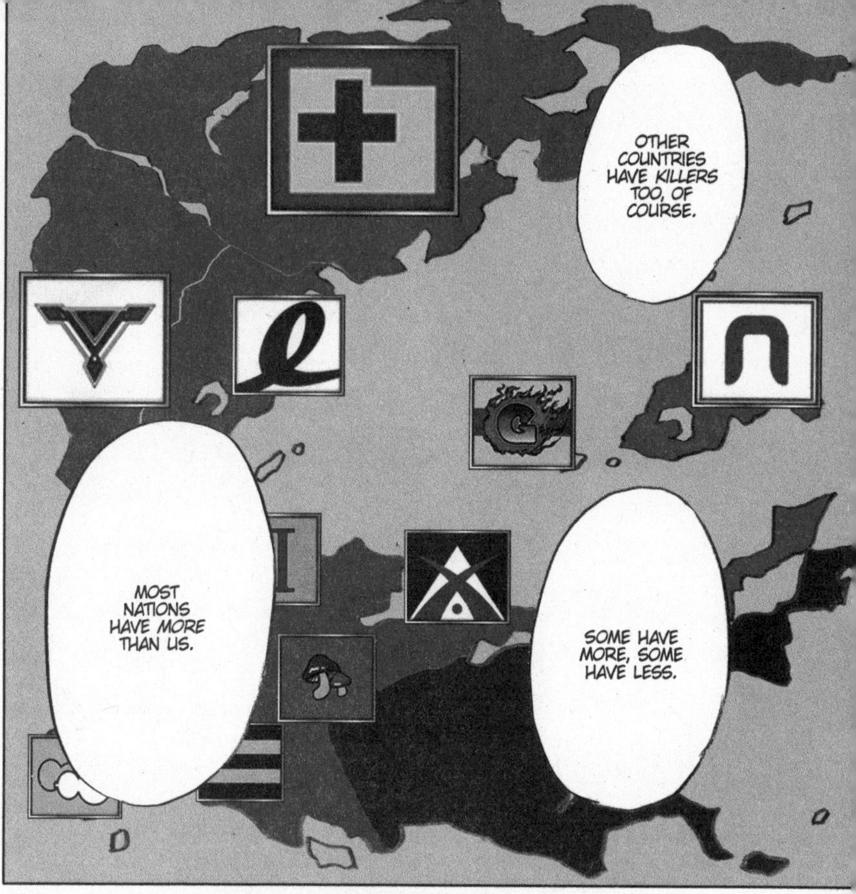
OTHER COUNTRIES HAVE KILLERS TOO, OF COURSE.
SOME HAVE MORE, SOME HAVE LESS.
MOST NATIONS HAVE MORE THAN US.
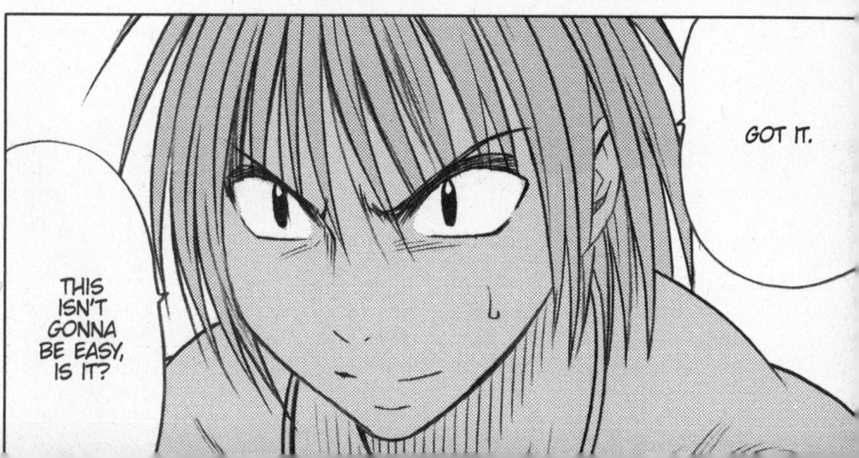
GOT IT.
THIS ISN'T GONNA BE EASY, IS IT?

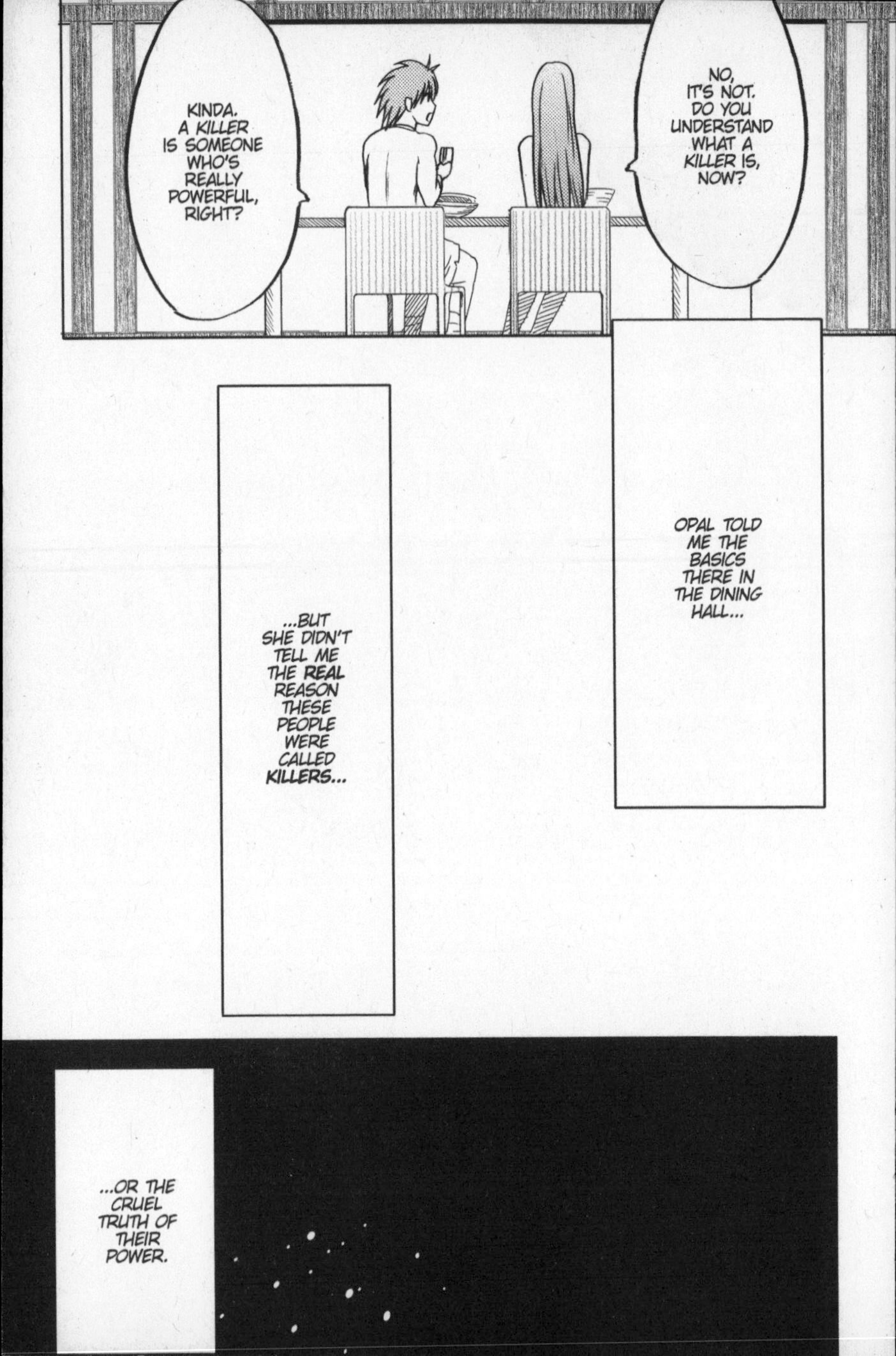
NO, IT'S NOT. DO YOU UNDERSTAND WHAT A KILLER IS, NOW?
KINDA. A KILLER IS SOMEONE WHO'S REALLY POWERFUL, RIGHT?
OPAL TOLD ME THE BASICS THERE IN THE DINING HALL...
...BUT SHE DIDN'T TELL ME THE REAL REASON THESE PEOPLE WERE CALLED KILLERS...
...OR THE CRUEL TRUTH OF THEIR POWER.

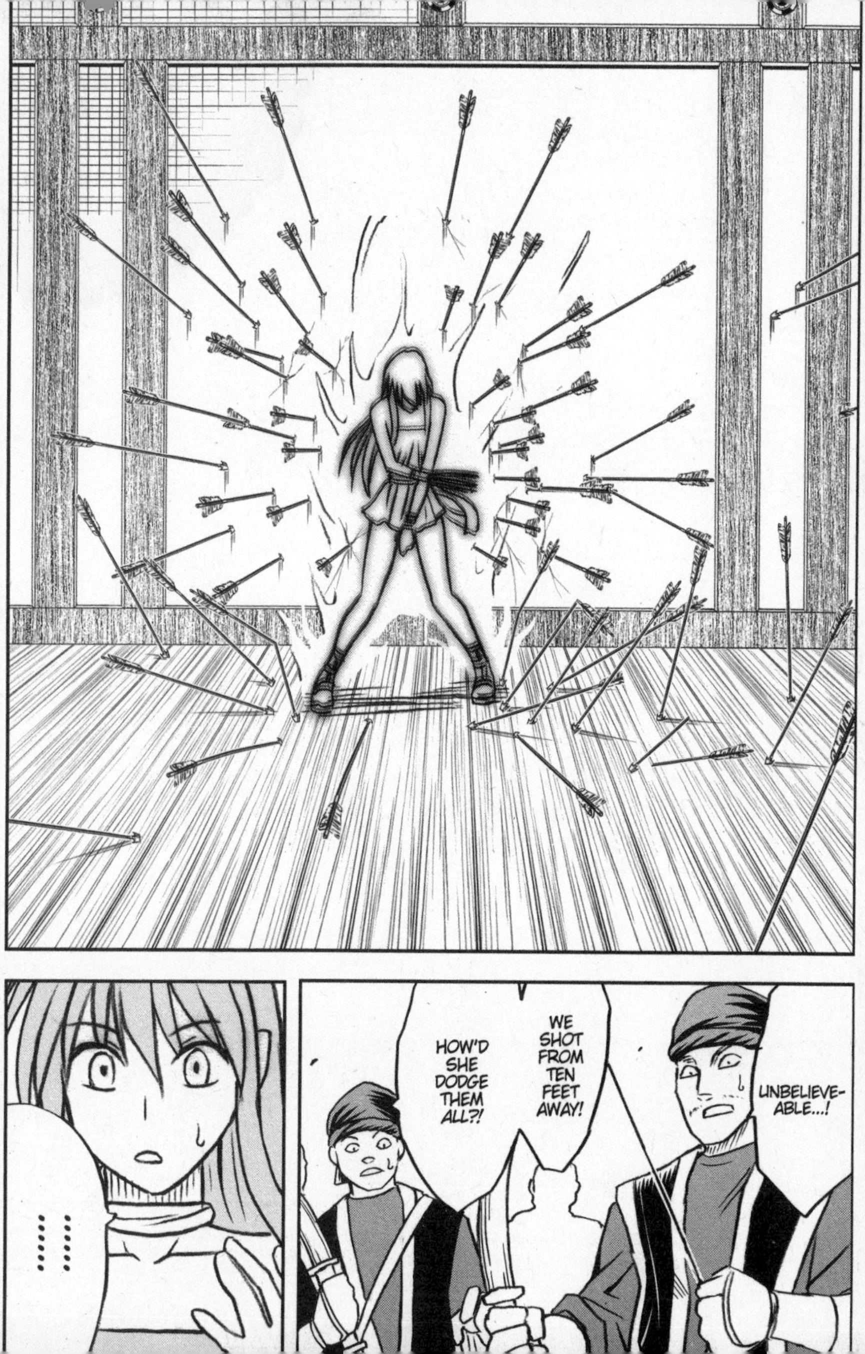
UNBELIEVE-ABLE...!
WE SHOT FROM TEN FEET AWAY!
HOW'D SHE DODGE THEM ALL?!
......

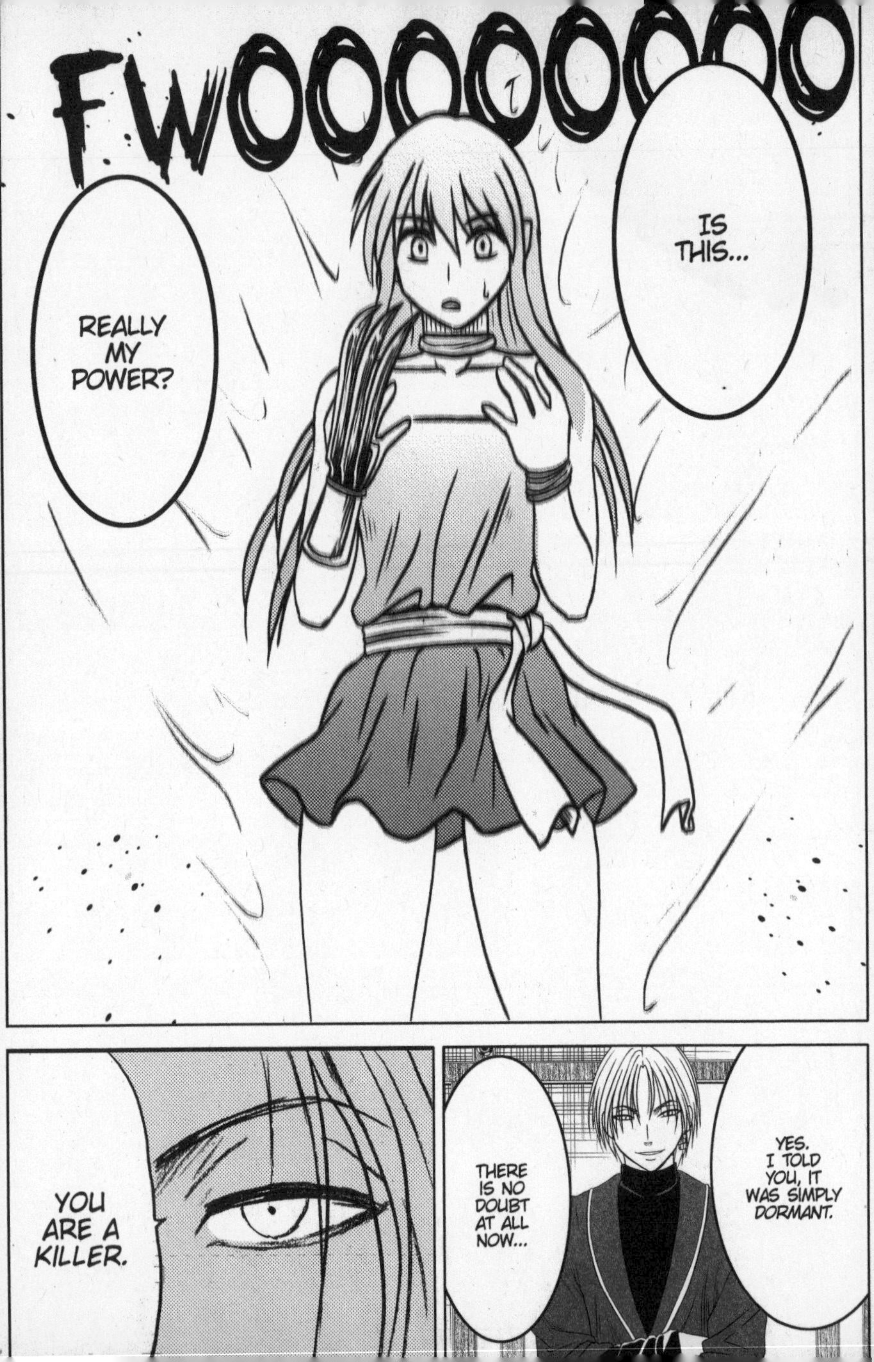
FWOOOOOOOO
IS THIS...
REALLY MY POWER?
YES. I TOLD YOU, IT WAS SIMPLY DORMANT.
THERE IS NO DOUBT AT ALL NOW...
YOU ARE A KILLER.

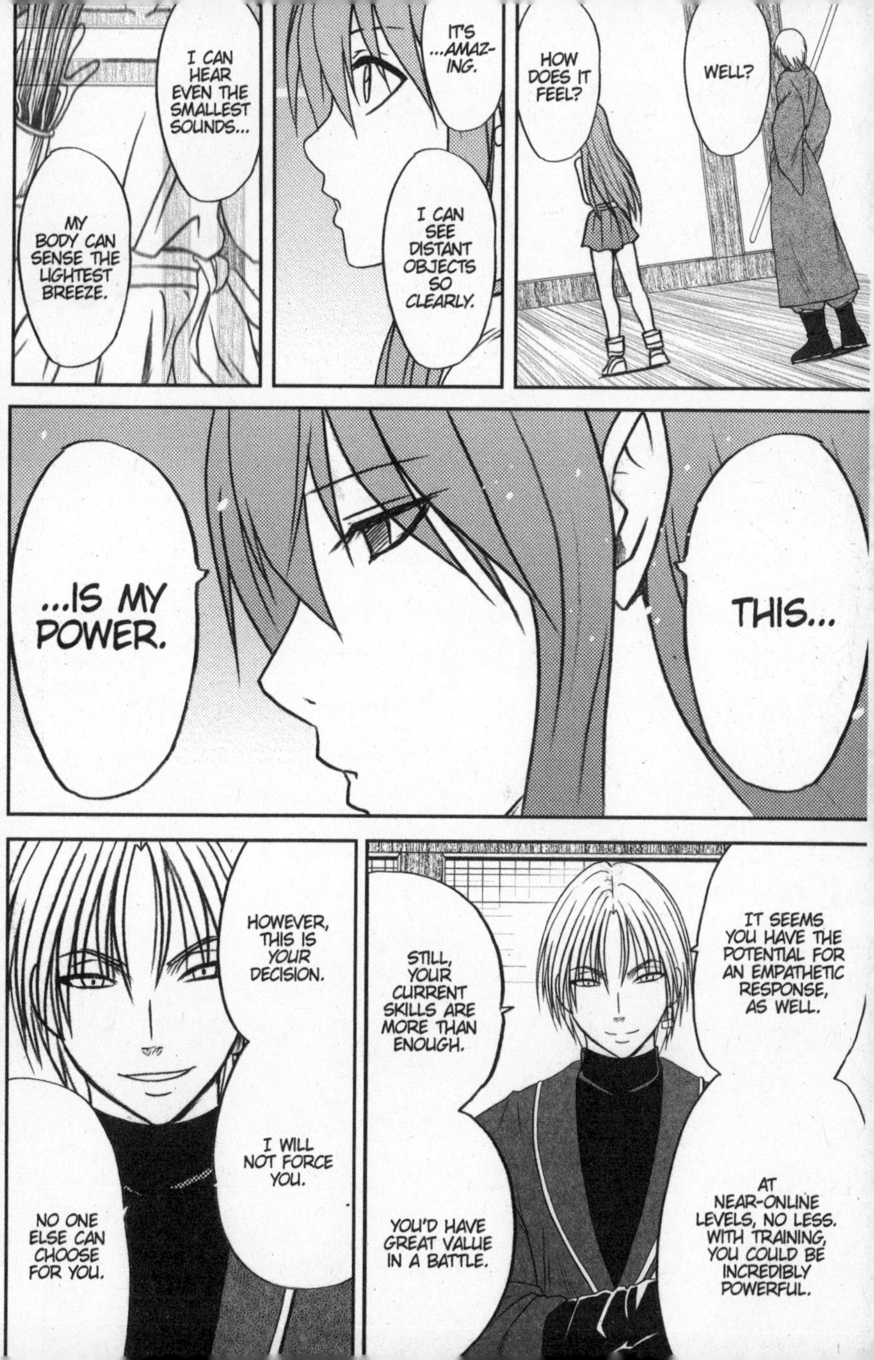
WELL?
HOW DOES IT FEEL?
IT'S ...AMAZ-ING.
I CAN SEE DISTANT OBJECTS SO CLEARLY.
I CAN HEAR EVEN THE SMALLEST SOUNDS...
MY BODY CAN SENSE THE LIGHTEST BREEZE.
THIS...
...IS MY POWER.
IT SEEMS YOU HAVE THE POTENTIAL FOR AN EMPATHETIC RESPONSE, AS WELL.
AT NEAR-ONLINE LEVELS, NO LESS. WITH TRAINING, YOU COULD BE INCREDIBLY POWERFUL.
STILL, YOUR CURRENT SKILLS ARE MORE THAN ENOUGH.
YOU'D HAVE GREAT VALUE IN A BATTLE.
HOWEVER, THIS IS *YOUR* DECISION.
I WILL NOT FORCE YOU.
NO ONE ELSE CAN CHOOSE FOR YOU.

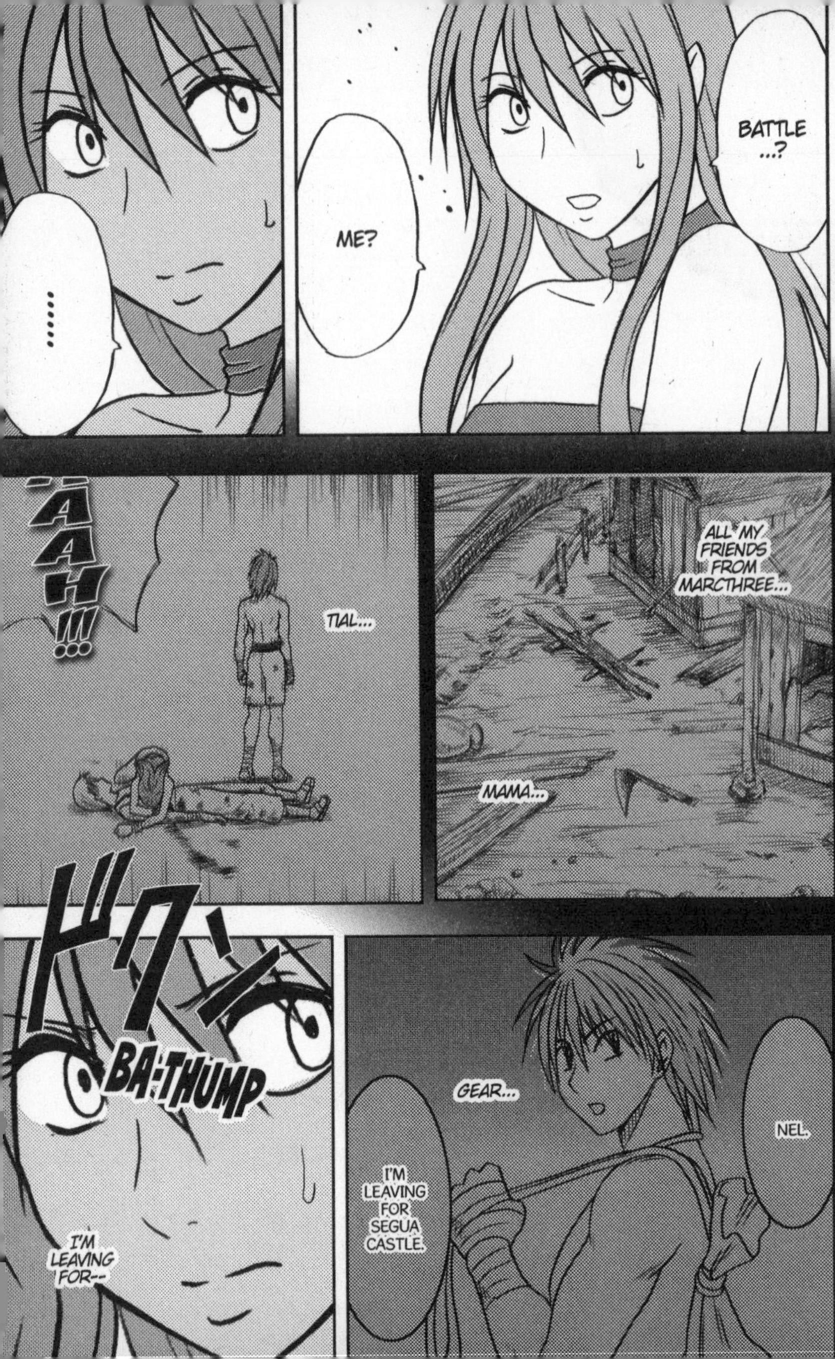
BATTLE ...?
ME?
......
ALL MY FRIENDS FROM MARCTHREE...
MAMA...
TIAL...
AAAH!!!
NEL.
GEAR...
I'M LEAVING FOR SEGUA CASTLE.
ドクン
BA-THUMP
I'M LEAVING FOR--

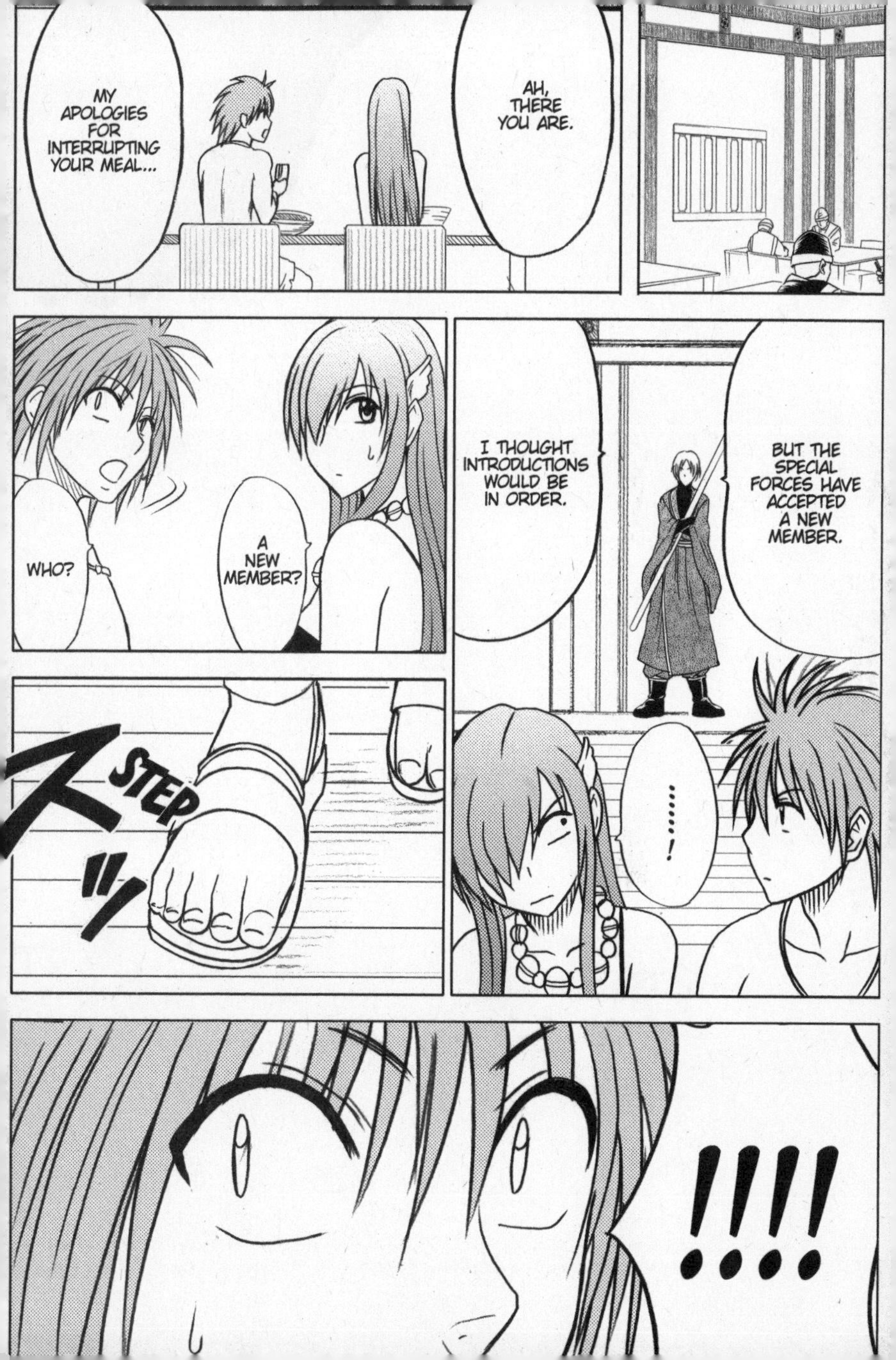

AH, THERE YOU ARE.
MY APOLOGIES FOR INTERRUPTING YOUR MEAL...
BUT THE SPECIAL FORCES HAVE ACCEPTED A NEW MEMBER.
I THOUGHT INTRODUCTIONS WOULD BE IN ORDER.
......!
A NEW MEMBER?
WHO?
STEP
!!!!

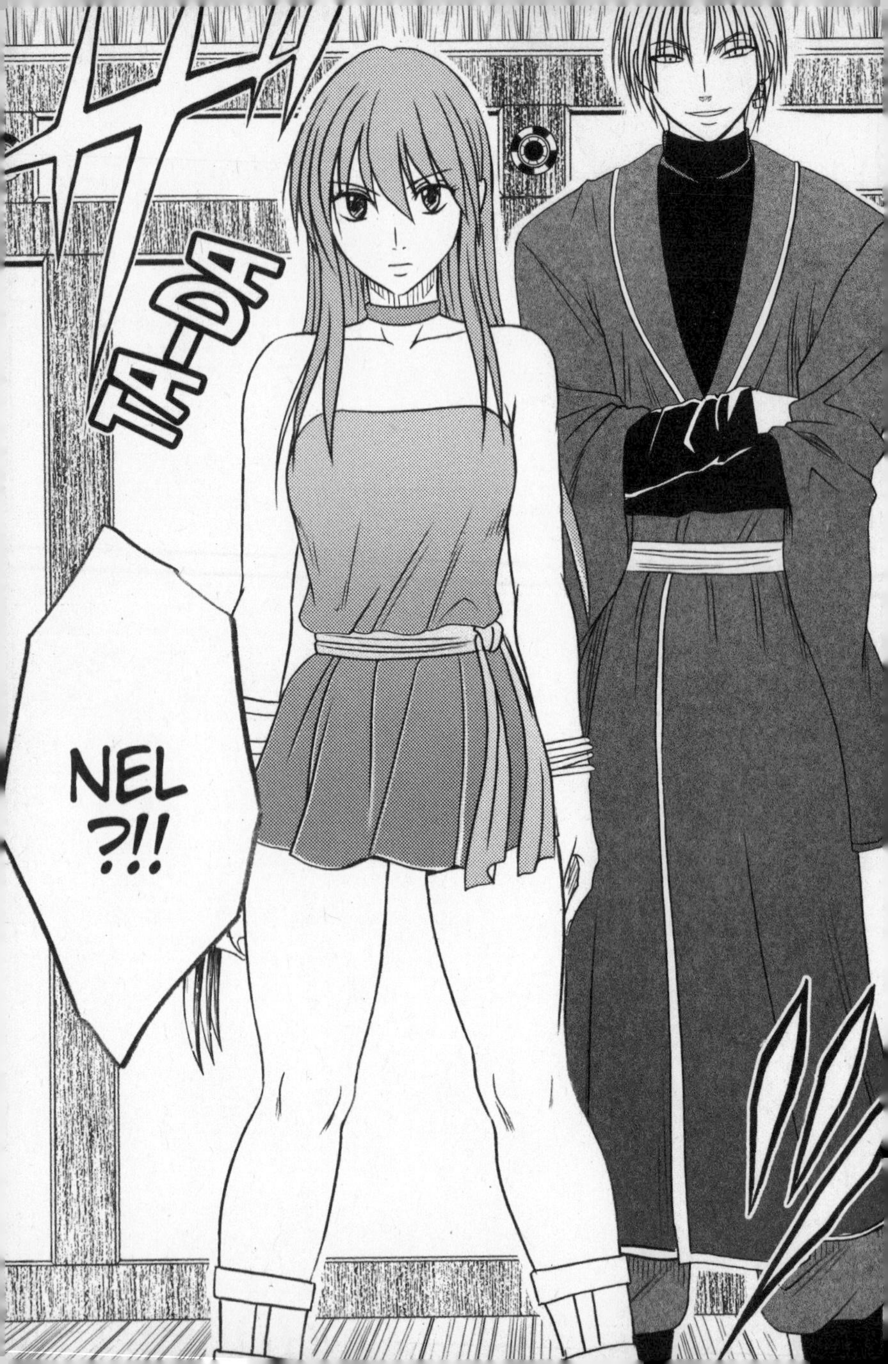
TA-DA
NEL ?!!

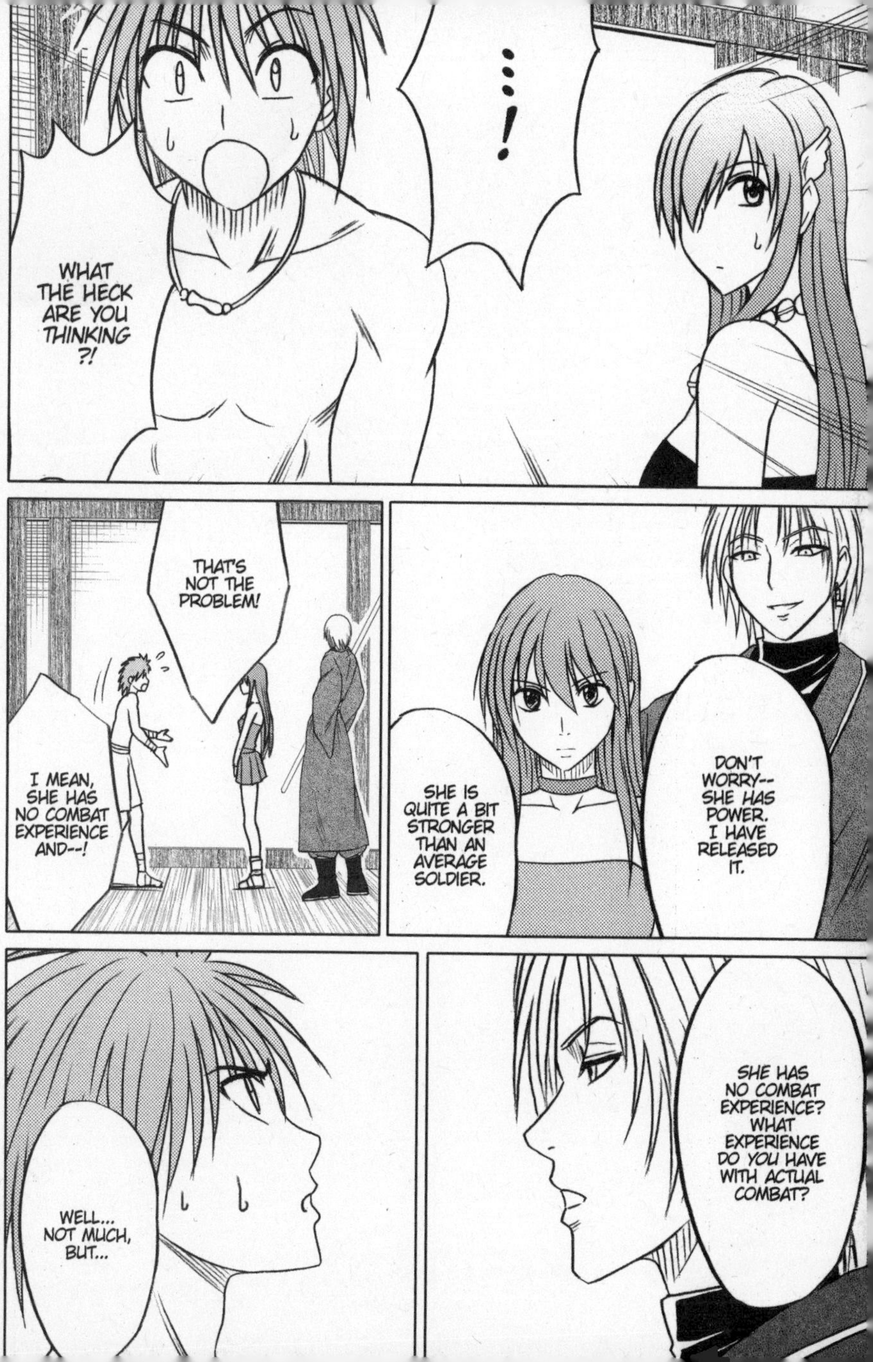
...!
WHAT THE HECK ARE YOU THINKING?!
DON'T WORRY-- SHE HAS POWER. I HAVE RELEASED IT.
SHE IS QUITE A BIT STRONGER THAN AN AVERAGE SOLDIER.
THAT'S NOT THE PROBLEM!
I MEAN, SHE HAS NO COMBAT EXPERIENCE AND--!
SHE HAS NO COMBAT EXPERIENCE? WHAT EXPERIENCE DO YOU HAVE WITH ACTUAL COMBAT?
WELL... NOT MUCH, BUT...

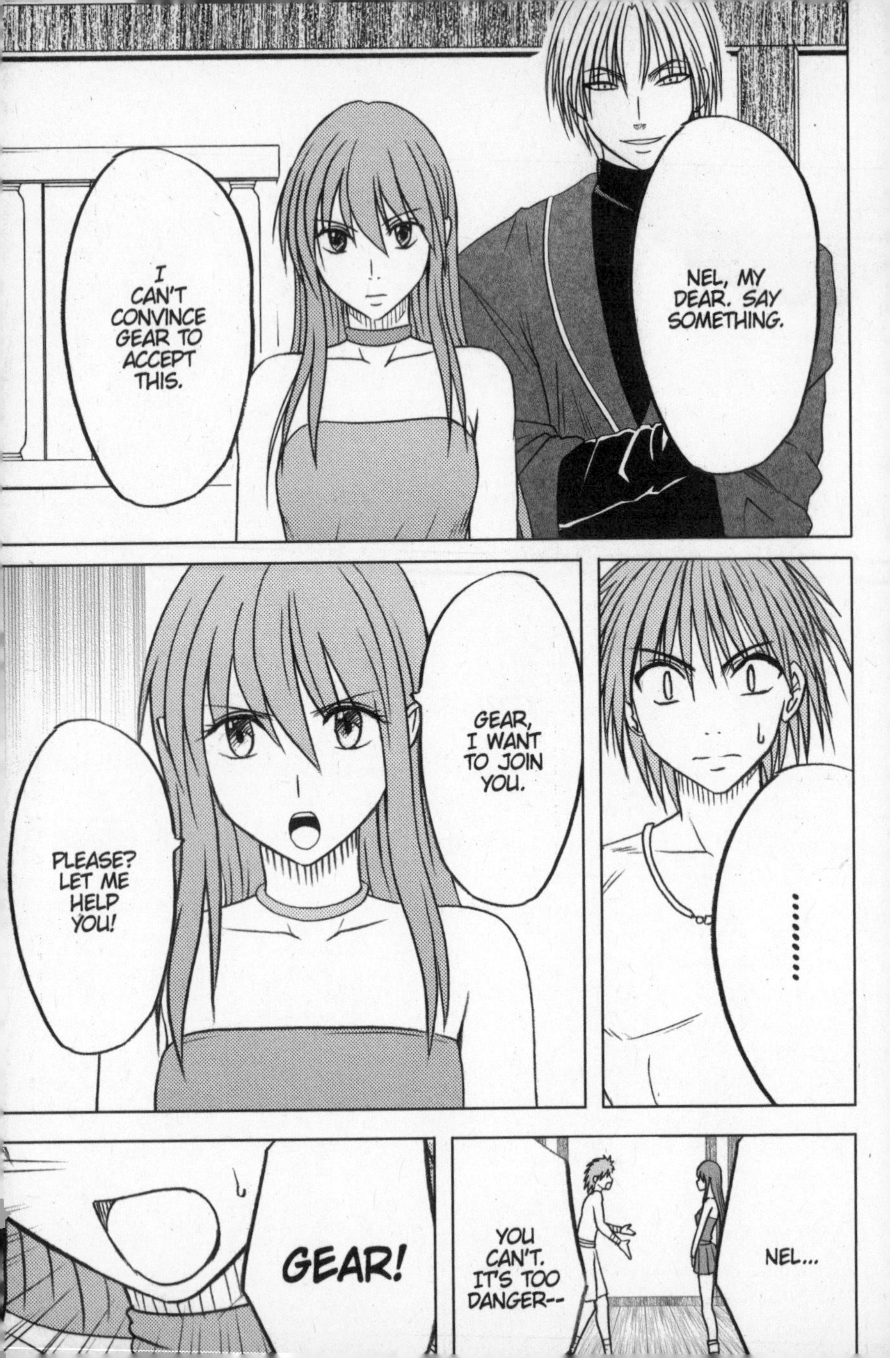
NEL, MY DEAR. SAY SOMETHING.
I CAN'T CONVINCE GEAR TO ACCEPT THIS.
......
GEAR, I WANT TO JOIN YOU.
PLEASE? LET ME HELP YOU!
NEL...
YOU CAN'T. IT'S TOO DANGER--
GEAR!

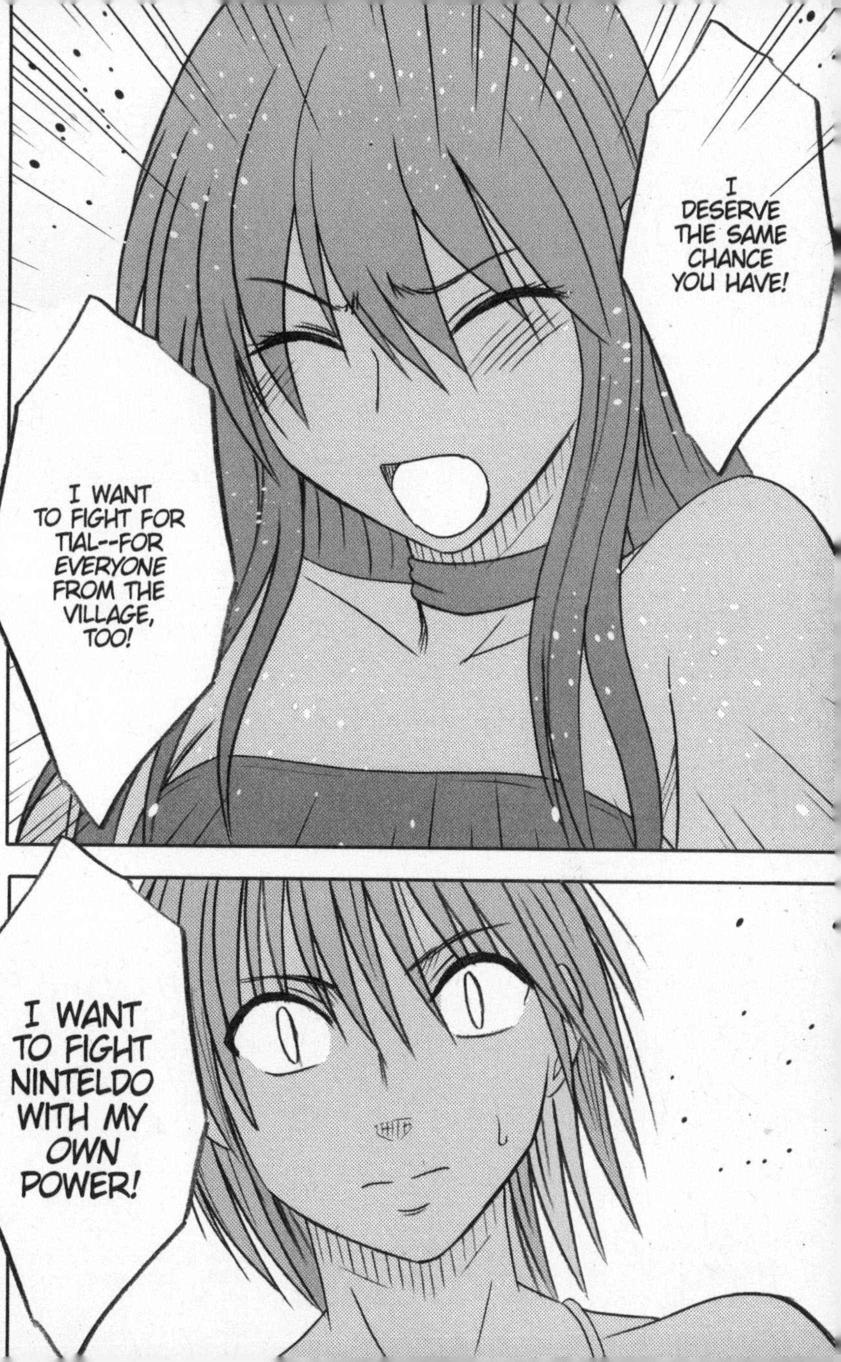
I DESERVE THE SAME CHANCE YOU HAVE!
I WANT TO FIGHT FOR TIAL--FOR EVERYONE FROM THE VILLAGE, TOO!
I WANT TO FIGHT NINTELDO WITH MY OWN POWER!

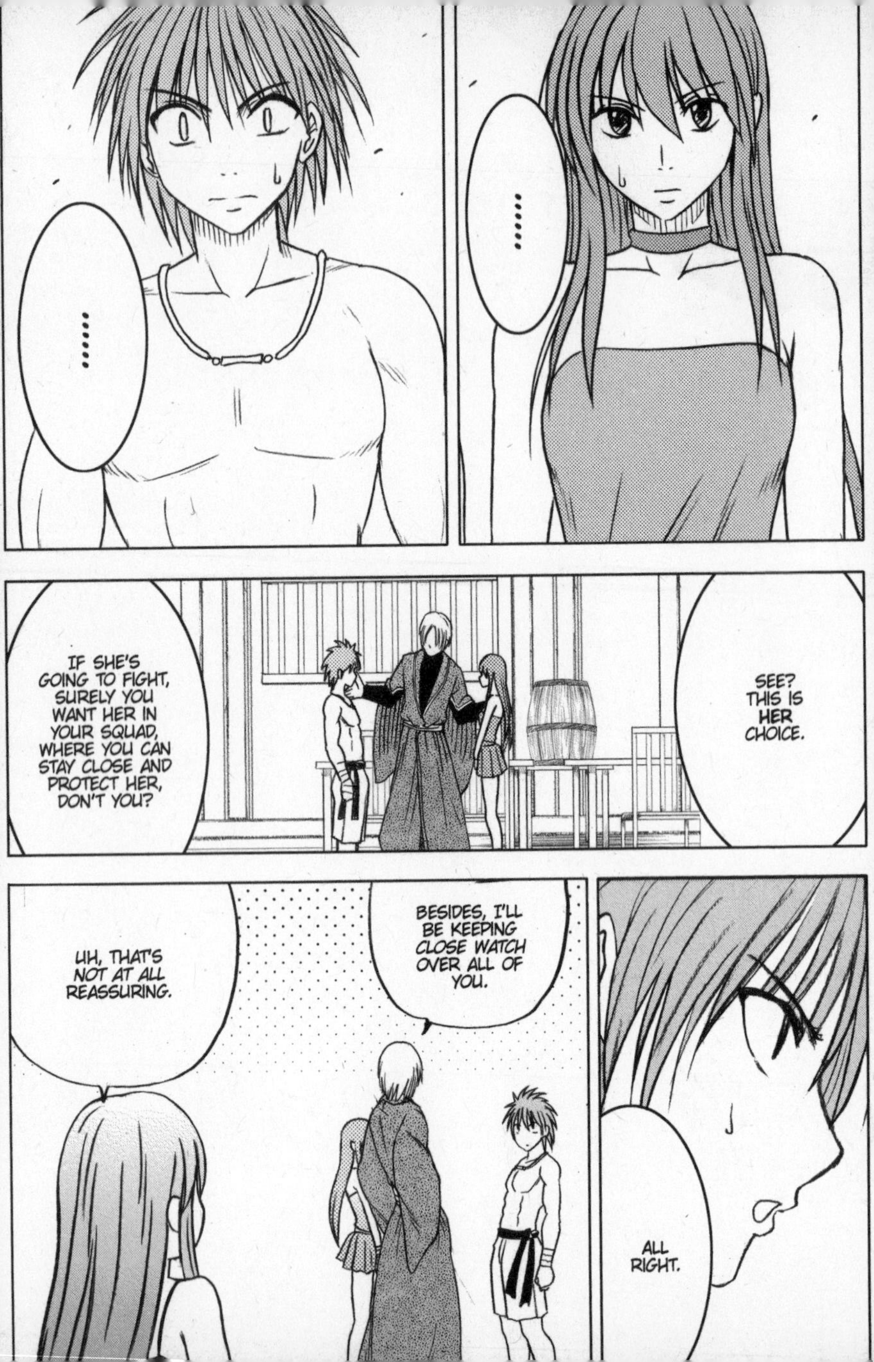
......
......
SEE? THIS IS HER CHOICE.
IF SHE'S GOING TO FIGHT, SURELY YOU WANT HER IN YOUR SQUAD, WHERE YOU CAN STAY CLOSE AND PROTECT HER, DON'T YOU?
ALL RIGHT.
BESIDES, I'LL BE KEEPING CLOSE WATCH OVER ALL OF YOU.
UH, THAT'S NOT AT ALL REASSURING.

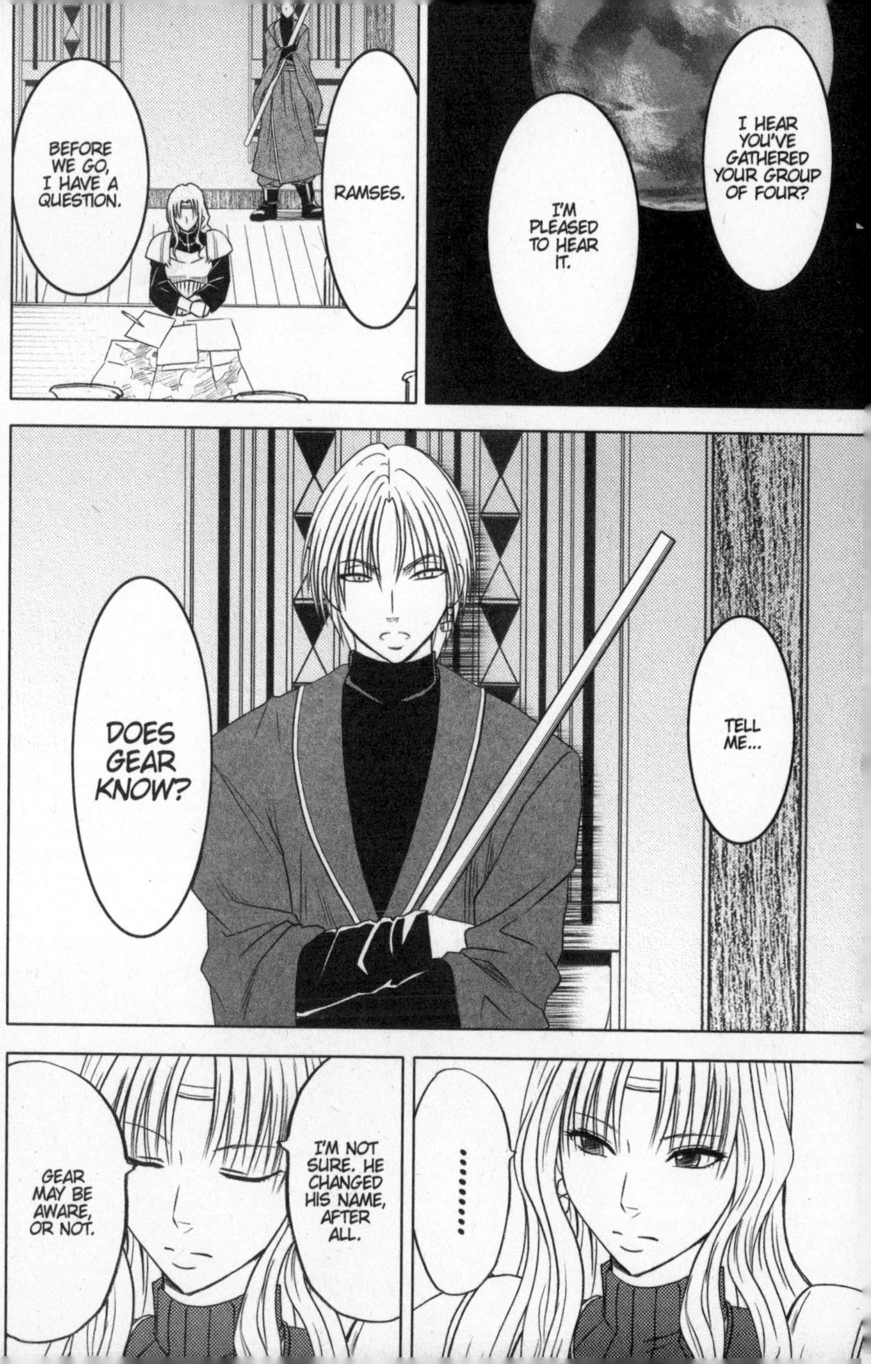
I HEAR YOU'VE GATHERED YOUR GROUP OF FOUR?
I'M PLEASED TO HEAR IT.
RAMSES.
BEFORE WE GO, I HAVE A QUESTION.
TELL ME...
DOES GEAR KNOW?
......
I'M NOT SURE. HE CHANGED HIS NAME, AFTER ALL.
GEAR MAY BE AWARE, OR NOT.

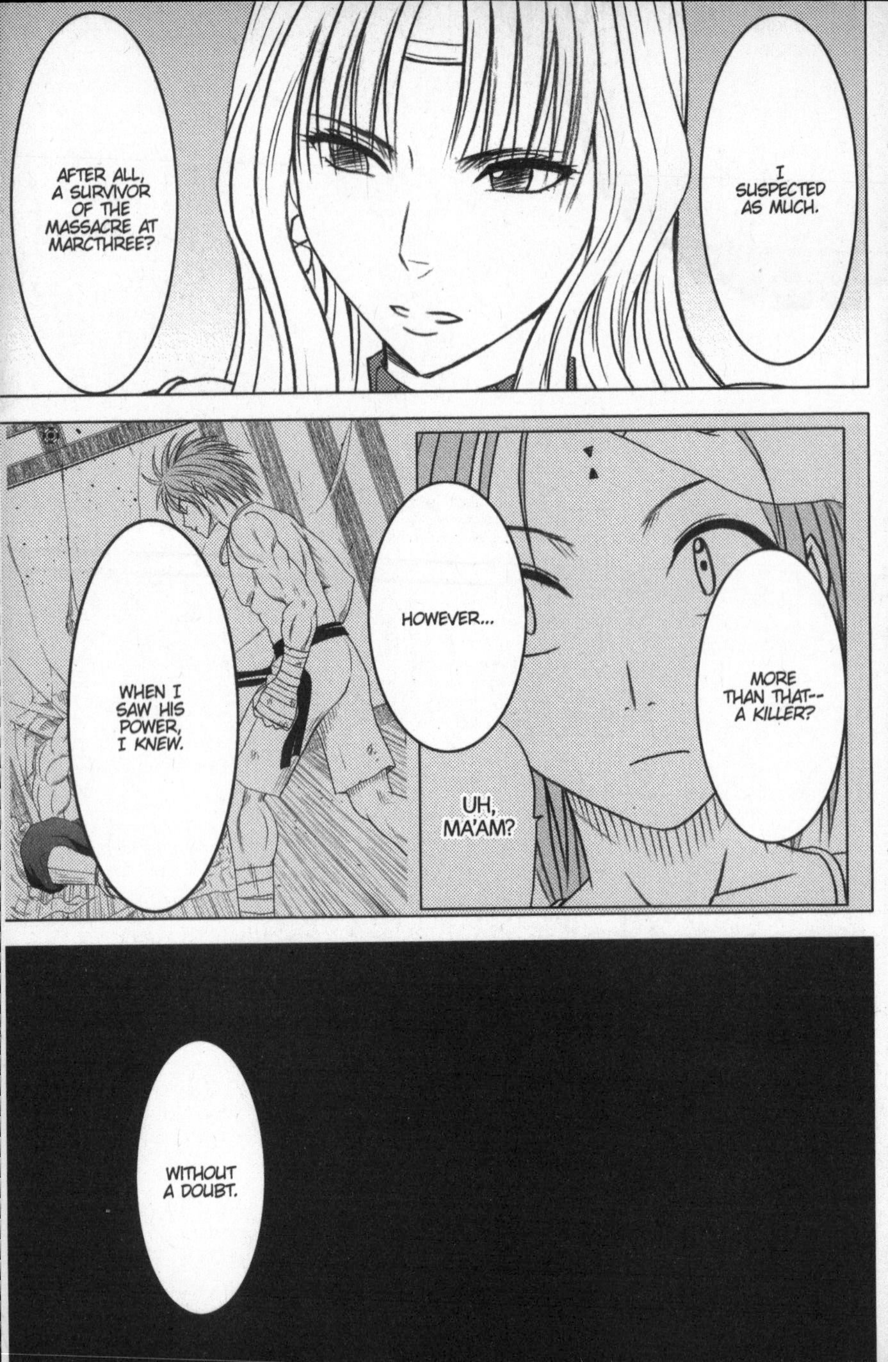
I SUSPECTED AS MUCH.
AFTER ALL, A SURVIVOR OF THE MASSACRE AT MARCHTHREE?
MORE THAN THAT-- A KILLER?
UH, MA'AM?
HOWEVER...
WHEN I SAW HIS POWER, I KNEW.
WITHOUT A DOUBT.

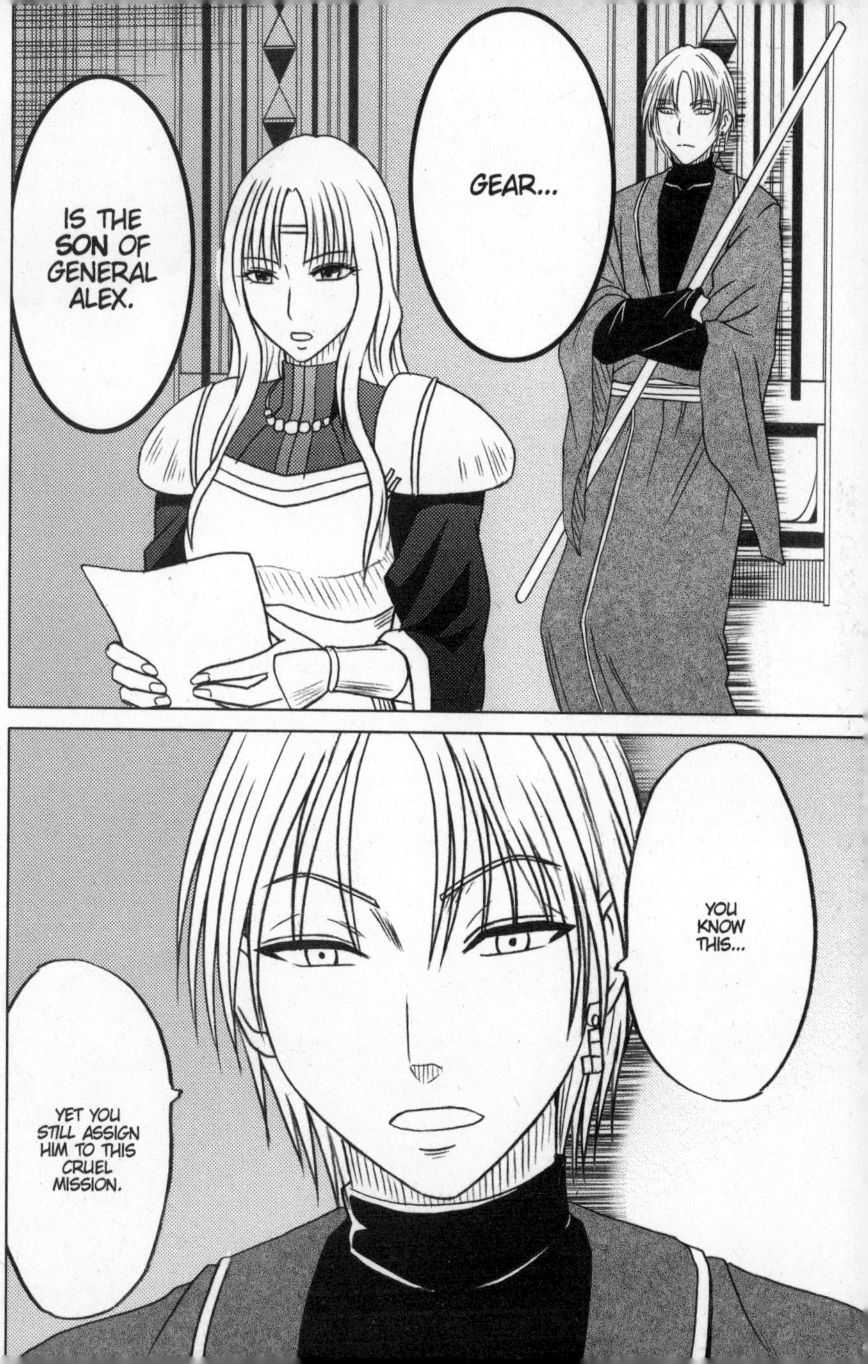
GEAR...
IS THE SON OF GENERAL ALEX.
YOU KNOW THIS...
YET YOU STILL ASSIGN HIM TO THIS CRUEL MISSION.

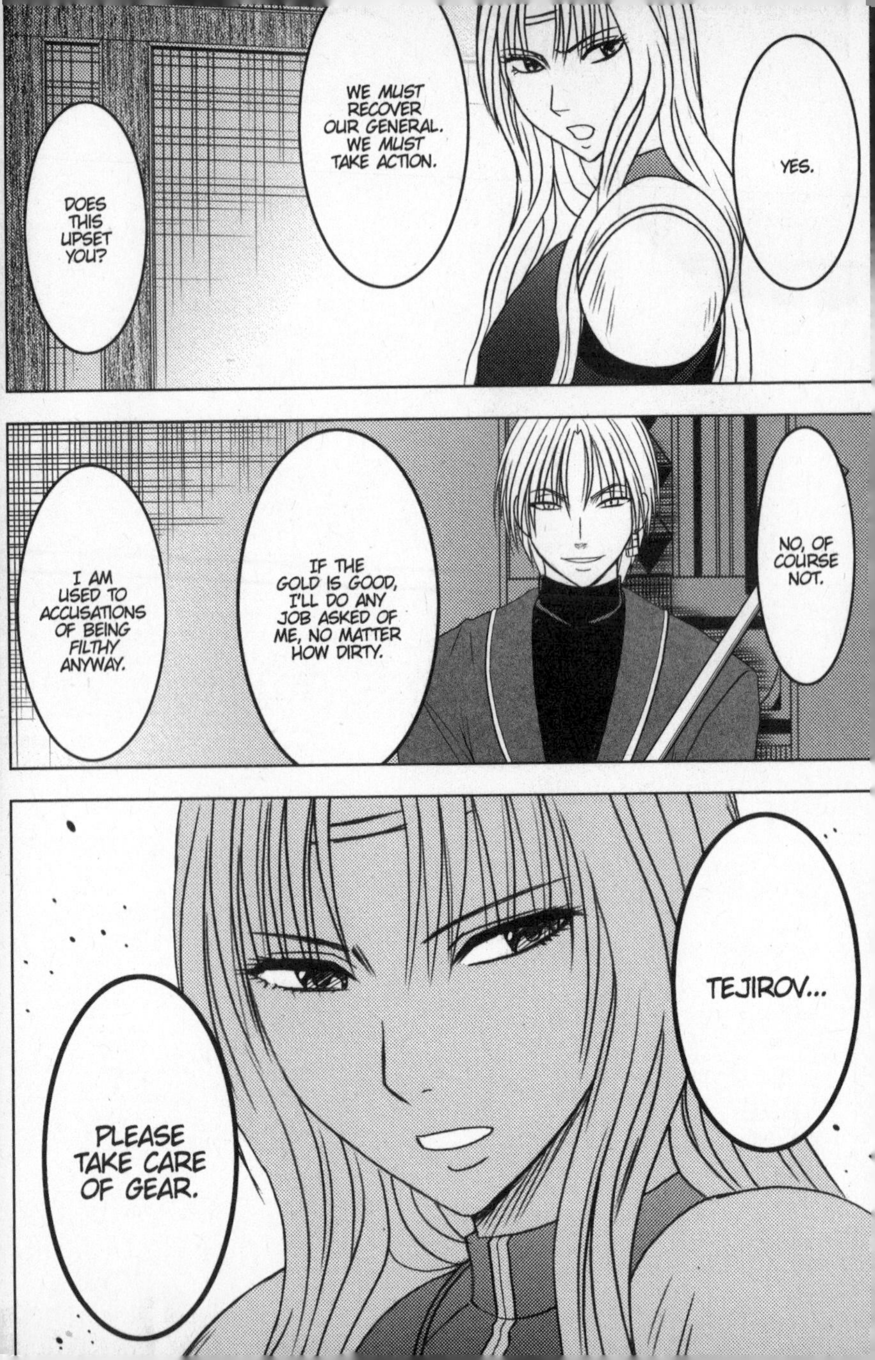
YES.
WE MUST RECOVER OUR GENERAL. WE MUST TAKE ACTION.
DOES THIS UPSET YOU?
NO, OF COURSE NOT.
IF THE GOLD IS GOOD, I'LL DO ANY JOB ASKED OF ME, NO MATTER HOW DIRTY.
I AM USED TO ACCUSATIONS OF BEING FILTHY ANYWAY.
TEJIROV...
PLEASE TAKE CARE OF GEAR.

Perusing Video Game History

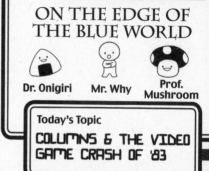

ON THE EDGE OF THE BLUE WORLD

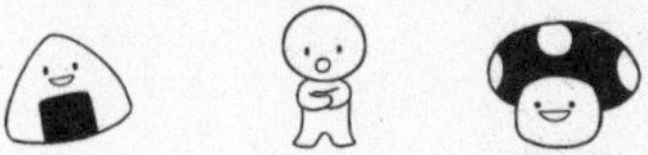

Dr. Onigiri Mr. Why Prof. Mushroom

Today's Topic

COLUMNS & THE VIDEO GAME CRASH OF '83

Mr. Why: So this time we're talking about *Columns*, right?

Dr. Onigiri: Yep. *Columns* was another arcade port. It's a type of "falling-block" puzzle game. You can't mention a "falling-block" puzzler without referencing *Tetris*, the first and greatest of that genre. However, *Columns* was popular enough to stand shoulder-to-shoulder with its predecessor.

Mr. Why: How's *Columns* different from *Tetris*?

Dr. Onigiri: Well, in *Columns*, gems fall from the top, not blocks. And the aim isn't to fill a horizontal row to make it disappear. In this game, the goal is to get three of the same colored gems next to each other vertically, horizontally, or diagonally to make them vanish. When the gems fall to fill in the cleared space, if three of a kind line up again, they vanish, too, creating a combo. Later falling-block games which used that idea, like *Puyo Puyo,* were all inspired by *Columns*. It's fair to say *Columns* had just as much influence on the puzzle genre as *Tetris* did.

Prof. Mushroom: Ya got that right. Even today, I can go to an arcade in Japan and find a Sega *Columns* machine there, complete with little monkey doin' the explaining on the demo screen. It's amazing.

Mr. Why: Wow. That reminds me of all those little pocket versions of those types of games. They usually came attached to key chains. Those were really popular, too.

Prof. Mushroom: Yeah, but they were a little shady. Y'see, a whole bunch of 'em weren't legally licensed, and many of 'em were just defective knockoffs. They were super popular for a while, but I don't think they helped out the industry. Reminds me too much of the crash of '83.

Mr. Why: The crash of '83?

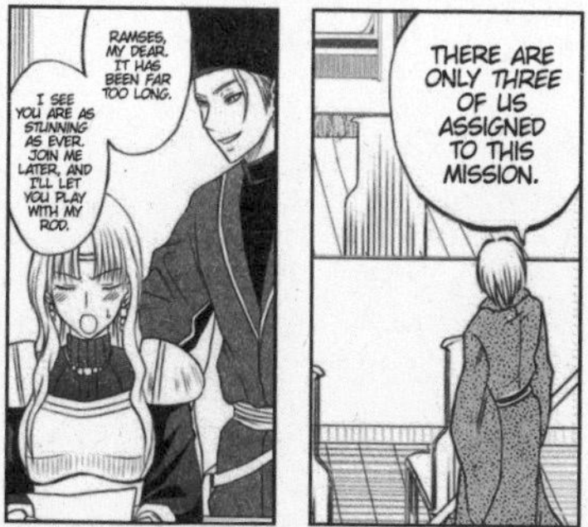
THERE ARE ONLY THREE OF US ASSIGNED TO THIS MISSION.
RAMSES, MY DEAR. IT HAS BEEN FAR TOO LONG.
I SEE YOU ARE AS STUNNING AS EVER. JOIN ME LATER, AND I'LL LET YOU PLAY WITH MY ROD.

Tejirov was senior to Ramses at the Puzzle Academy. To this day, no student there has ever topped his records.

The Great Atarika Empire collapsed under its own enormous size, due in part to its policy of quantity over quality.

WAS THE GREAT ATARIKA EMPIRE.

ITS NAME...

Here you can see a picture of what Tom, Dick, and Harry might have looked like. Is that a rice scoop?

Dr. Onigiri: In America in the early '80's, there was a huge decline in console game sales.

Mr. Why: Huh? Why?

Prof. Mushroom: It's a little complicated, so I'll just give ya an overview, 'kay? Back then, there was a game company called Atari. Its popularity was skyrocketing with games that sold like hotcakes.

Mr. Why: Okay.

Dr. Onigiri: But lots of those games were from third party developers, and Atari had no control over their content. There was no publisher-level quality control or testing involved. The developers knew this, so they just cobbled something together, slapped pretty box art on it, and shoved it out the door. Sometimes, they sold games that were literally unplayable. Greedy for an easy buck, every Tom, Dick, and Harry set out to produce as many games as they could.

Prof. Mushroom: To make things worse, there weren't many gaming magazines around at the time. Nobody knew what they were gettin' until they bought it, took it home, and put it in their machine.

Mr. Why: So people would buy games, only to find out they were terrible, or didn't even work? Ouch!

Dr. Onigiri: Right. It was unsustainable. The bottom dropped out of the market, stores overflowed with unsold games, game makers' stocks plummeted, and many pioneering game companies went out of business. That was the Video Game Crash of '83.

Mr. Why: Yikes!

Prof. Mushroom: After that, publishers learned their lesson. They stopped relying on volume and established quality control and testing, so they could ensure the release of higher quality games.

TO BE CONTINUED IN VOLUME 2...

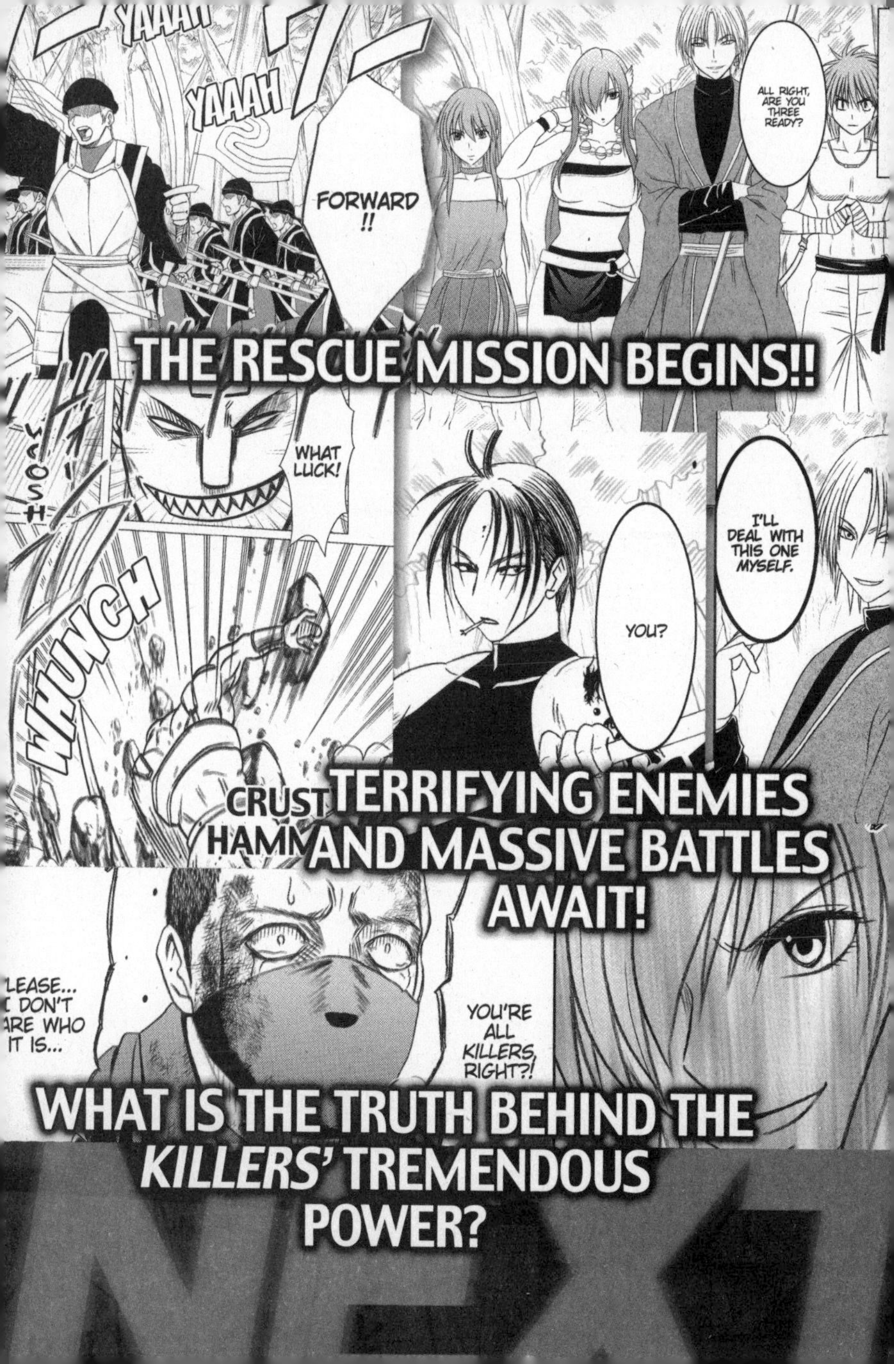
ALL RIGHT, ARE YOU THREE READY?
YAAAH
YAAAH
FORWARD!!
THE RESCUE MISSION BEGINS!!
I'LL DEAL WITH THIS ONE MYSELF.
YOU?
WHAT LUCK!
WHUNCH
CRUST HAMM
TERRIFYING ENEMIES AND MASSIVE BATTLES AWAIT!
YOU'RE ALL KILLERS, RIGHT?!
LEASE... I DON'T ARE WHO IT IS...
WHAT IS THE TRUTH BEHIND THE *KILLERS'* TREMENDOUS POWER?